STARRING BRIAN LINEHAN ☆

STARRING

Brian Linehan

A Life Behind the Scenes

GEORGE ANTHONY

McCLELLAND & STEWART

Library and Archives Canada Cataloguing in Publication

Anthony, George
    Starring Brian Linehan : a life behind the scenes / George Anthony.

ISBN 978-0-7710-0757-6

1. Linehan, Brian, 1944-2004.   2. City Lights (Television program).
3. Celebrities – Interviews.   4. Television talk shows – Canada.   5. Television personalities – Canada – Biography.   6. Radio broadcasters – Canada – Biography.
I. Title.

PN1992.4.L55A58 2007   791.45092   C2007-901294-9

We acknowledge the financial support of the Government of Canada through the Book Publishing Industry Development Program and that of the Government of Ontario through the Ontario Media Development Corporation's Ontario Book Initiative. We further acknowledge the support of the Canada Council for the Arts and the Ontario Arts Council for our publishing program.

Typeset in Garamond by M&S, Toronto
Printed and bound in Canada

Images from the Brian Linehan Collection courtesy of The Film Reference Library / a division of the Toronto International Film Festival Group

Images from the ACCT courtesy of the Academy Photo Archive, Genie Collection, Academy of Canadian Cinema and Television

Lyrics from "Manhattan" on page 78 written by Rodgers/Hart, published by Piedmont Music Company

Every effort has been made to reach the copyright holders of work excerpted in this book.

This book is printed on acid-free paper that is 100% recycled, ancient-forest friendly (100% post-consumer recycled).

McClelland & Stewart Ltd.
75 Sherbourne Street
Toronto, Ontario
M5A 2P9
www.mcclelland.com

2 3 4 5   11 10 09 08 07

for
Team Linehan
with
affection, admiration, and respect

Contents

August 2002

I was still in the shower when my wife walked into the bathroom. "Brian's on the phone," she said quietly. It was hard to hear her with the water streaming over my head.

"Tell him I'll call him back."

"Zane is dead."

"What? What did you say?"

"He killed himself. Overseas."

"Zane is *dead??*"

"And Brian has cancer."

"*What???*"

My heart sank.

I bolted out of the shower. Brian Linehan and I had been close friends for almost thirty years. In the last decade he had been riding an emotional roller coaster, hanging on for dear life. His partner, Zane Wagman, frequently the driver, was sometimes merely a passenger on the ride. Neither one of them had ever been mere bystanders.

I picked up the phone. Brian was in tears, distraught, hysterical. He said that he had been diagnosed months earlier with non-Hodgkin's Lymphoma, and that he and Zane had agreed that he would not go public. Brian wanted to work. He needed to work. And we both knew of instances where potential employers were scared off by symptoms far less threatening than those that came with the C-word. He and Zane had resolved that they would keep it to themselves. Brian would go for treatments, he would rid himself of the cancer, and no one would be any the wiser.

He knew he could do it, he said, as long as Zane was there for him. But now Zane wasn't there for him. Zane had flown off to Finland on one of his eccentric opera odysseys. A few days into the trip, a hotel chambermaid in Helsinki had discovered his body when she went to clean his room. He had killed himself during the night.

Brian was calling from the condo on the outskirts of Toronto where he and Zane had moved less than a year earlier. I told him to stay put, that Gail and I would be over as soon as I got dressed.

After I hung up the phone, I immediately called a mutual friend in New York who was all too familiar with family suicide. She was in the middle of a meeting, and at first her assistant was reluctant to put me through. Perhaps she could convey a message to her?

"Yes," I replied. "Please tell her it's urgent."

In a matter of seconds, she was on the line. "Tell me," she commanded.

I didn't beat around the bush. "Zane Wagman killed himself last night in Helsinki."

I heard a sudden intake of breath. Then she spoke. "Where can I reach Brian?"

Brian was still at home, in tears, poring over the names on his private, justifiably famous contact list, trying to decide who else he needed to call, when the phone rang.

He let it ring three times, and then reached tentatively for it. By now his voice was only a whisper. "Hello? . . ."

"Brian," said Joan Rivers, "I'm calling to tell you that *this is not your fault!*"

Foreword

by Joan Rivers

I n Hollywood and New York in the 1970s and 1980s, everyone in show business knew that there were only two people in Canada on the media Must list: George Anthony and Brian Linehan. In Detroit, it was Shirley Eder. In Houston, it was Maxine Messenger. In Toronto, it was, quite simply, Brian and George. When you look back, a lot of people interviewed you, but hardly anyone was memorable. When you saw George Anthony, you knew you had print press covered; when you saw Brian Linehan, you knew you had both TV and radio sewn up.

Their interviews were the stuff of legend, and all the major studios catered to them. Because of this, for many years actors and entertainers on both coasts simply assumed that George's columns appeared in the newspaper with the largest circulation, and that Brian's daily show was telecast on the country's largest television network. The joke, of course, was that George wrote for what was then Toronto's newest, smallest local newspaper, and Brian sparkled on what was then Toronto's newest, smallest local TV station.

In Hollywood, nobody cared. George Anthony and Brian Linehan had something everyone in Hollywood respected. They had power. Their interviews and reviews caught the attention of the people who actually went to the theatre, put down their hard-earned money for a night at the movies, and saved up to buy the hardcover version of a new book, rather than wait for the paperback edition. George Anthony and Brian Linehan could sell tickets.

Surprisingly, especially in this business, George Anthony and Brian Linehan were also great friends. Both were highly competitive, and both of them worked hard and played hard. But they were as different as night and day, which may have been the key to their long friendship. George was a family man who would often bring one of his three children with him when he travelled to Hollywood, New York, or Las Vegas. Brian was single, sophisticated, and elegant, blessed with an irrepressibly bitchy wit he was more than willing to share with appreciative listeners.

When I was working in Las Vegas, my husband, Edgar Rosenberg, and I would gather backstage with George, usually in my dressing room, to compare notes on other acts playing the strip, while his son Marc and our daughter, Melissa, played tennis with KC of KC & The Sunshine Band on the roof of the hotel. When we were home in Bel-Air, George would bring his daughter Alex to swim with Melissa while he and Edgar and I compared notes on the current state of the industry (which was pretty much always, as it is today, verging on disaster).

During the day, at least, Brian almost always preferred to sit around the pool at whatever luxury hotel he was staying at and read. Like Edgar and me, he was a voracious reader. Like Edgar and me, he was most interested in biographies. He had an insatiable curiosity about how people got to be the people they became, from cocoon to butterfly, from ugly duckling to swan.

No wonder. Little did we realize, at that time or even years later, how he had totally invented himself. He was a creation of his own imagination and determination.

In the years that followed our first meeting – arranged by George, I might add – we became fast and faithful friends. Brian was my confidant, my clown, my almost-constant delight – whoever he perceived that I needed him to be at that moment.

Toronto was a major stop on the comedy circuit, and over the years I played a lot of dates there. But it wasn't until I started coming to Toronto on a bi-monthly basis, to sell my jewellery on The Shopping Channel, that I was invited to Brian's exquisite home in High Park. Only then did I learn that Brian had a handsome partner, Dr. Zane Wagman, whose existence Brian had somehow failed to acknowledge.

To meet Zane Wagman, to spend time with Brian and Zane on their home turf, gave me new insights into Brian. But it also gave rise to many new questions, and, after June 4, 2004, a sad suspicion that he had taken many of the answers with him to the grave.

I loved him. I miss him. I am not alone. This book by my friend George Anthony – his closest friend – is unabashedly personal. It could only have been written by a friend. And yet it emerges as less of a tribute than an inquiry.

Who was Brian Linehan? . . . and how did he get to be him? As you read on, as you discover how he set out to completely invent himself – and succeeded, against all odds, in doing so – I think you, too, will marvel that he survived as long as he did.

Joan Rivers Rosenberg
September 2007

"It was a stormy marriage."

E veryone in Brian Linehan's life went to work with a lunch pail. When he was young, he wasn't sure what he wanted to do with his life, but he was pretty sure he didn't want to wear overalls to do it. But then, some lives seem to be charted even before they begin.

It was September 1943, and the world was at war. Franklin Delano Roosevelt was approaching the end of his twelve-year run as president of the United States, William Lyon Mackenzie King was at the peak of his third lengthy term as Canada's prime minister, and new Ontario premier George Drew and his Progressive Conservatives had just squeaked to victory. The war effort dominated the hearts and minds of most Canadians. Two months earlier, the 1st Canadian Infantry Division had played a major role in the invasion of Sicily, and moviegoers were flocking to see Jennifer Jones in *The Song of Bernadette*, Ingrid Bergman and Gary Cooper in *For Whom the Bell Tolls*, and an all-star morale-boosting U.S. propaganda film called *Stage Door Canteen*.

Brian Richard Linehan was born on the third of that month in the working-class east end of the small but promising industrial city of Hamilton, Ontario. His mother, Sally Kotur, a middle child of ten children, had grown up in Hamilton's east end, around the Dofasco steel plant. Nicknamed Sadie by her Serbian parents, she was full of life and bursting with energy. Extremely attractive and naturally outgoing, Sadie loved being with people, and people loved being with her.

Les Linehan, Brian's father, was just a boy when his family settled in Hamilton. When war broke out in Europe, Canadian soldiers went overseas to fight Hitler's Nazis, and the Stelco and Dofasco steel plants in Hamilton recruited as many workers as possible to produce more steel for the war effort. Les Linehan was one of them. A handsome, roguish young Irishman who knew a good thing when he saw it, Les Linehan proposed to Sadie Kotur soon after they met. She accepted.

Sadie and Les moved into a house on Northcote Street, a few doors away from her family. Northcote was in a blue-collar neighbourhood, a short suburban street of two-bedroom houses all in a row, little boxes with little porch verandas overlooking little front lawns, behind the Dofasco steel plant. Sadie and Les seemed to be content living so close to her family, but it was soon apparent that theirs was not a match made in heaven.

For one thing, Les was not what you'd call a family man. "He was a worm," says Sadie's younger sister Connie bluntly. "He got away with a lot."

Les joked that he planned to keep Sadie barefoot and pregnant, but it wasn't much of a joke: the Linehans ended up having six kids. Connie was still a kid herself when Sadie gave birth to her first son. "She'd say to me, 'Can you babysit Ronnie? I want to go out for a while,'" Connie recalls. "And because I was only nine years old and had to go to school the next morning, my mother would say, 'Don't you be too late!' But I'd still be at Sadie's house at one o'clock in the morning."

Les and Sadie named their first daughter after Connie. A few years later, their third child and second son, Brian, was born. But the arrival of a third child did nothing to cramp Les Linehan's style. And when Les went out on the town, Sadie often went with him – because she got sick of staying home, her sister Connie believes.

"What was hard about it," Connie remembers, "was when they would come home. Because that's when it would start. He shouldn't have drank. My mother would say to me, 'You shouldn't stay there, you should come home.' And I would say, 'I can't leave the kids!'

"He was very jealous of her. Very jealous. Sadie was very attractive, a very good-looking woman," Connie says. "And even though she put weight on because she was having these babies one after another . . . she had a *personality*. She was friendly with everybody. And he resented it. He used to say to her, 'I'll cut you up so nobody will look at you.'"

One time Sadie was boiling water on the stove, and in a drunken rage Les picked up the pot and hurled it at her. She had raised her arms in front of her, trying in vain to protect herself. She was left with scars on her eyebrows and scalding down her arms. Connie also remembers the time she was visiting Sadie – "I was about ten" – and Les came up with an axe from the basement. Sadie pushed her out the door so she wouldn't see any more.

Their family doctor told Sadie that if Les didn't stop drinking he was going to end up in the hospital. "And he did," Connie confirms. "I was just a kid, I thought it was called 'the tank to dry you out.' I went with [Sadie] on the streetcar up to St. Joe's – he was in St. Joseph's hospital – and the first thing he asked her was 'Did you bring me something?' And she did, she had brought him cigarettes and stuff. But he wanted alcohol. He got really angry with her. And then I started to understand what was happening."

Between binges, Les would work twelve-hour shifts at Dofasco, a job he still held only because of Sadie's constant pleas and interventions with the plant's bosses, former classmates who still regarded her fondly.

When their second daughter was born, Sadie named her Carole. The Linehans now had two boys and two girls, and Les had a family of six to support. A third son, Patrick, soon joined the Linehan household. By the time he was three, young Patrick Linehan already had unhappy memories. "I can still remember standing in the hallway of our house," he says, "and my father and mother were beating each other up. I wet my pants. And I got hit for it."

Jimmy Buzash, the man Connie Kotur would later marry, also lived on Northcote. Jimmy got along well with the Linehans, including Les. One summer evening, before taking Connie out on a date, Jimmy stopped by the Linehans' to say hello. Sadie and Les were sitting on the front veranda, and just when Jimmy got to the top step, Les hauled off and slapped Sadie. "On the *front veranda!* . . . With everybody sitting out there on their verandas," Connie says.

Jimmy, who lived right across the street, turned on his heel and left. "And Les had the nerve to go over to Jimmy's house, and say, 'Oh Jim, did you want something?' Like nothing was wrong. Jimmy lost all respect for him after that."

Les was drinking up his pay faster than he earned it, and Sadie knew they couldn't survive. She got a job cooking at a nursing home. She made pin money cooking for church functions. She took part-time jobs when she could have her oldest daughter, Connie, look after the younger children. "When times were not that great," Carole Linehan says, "we used to mix our cereal with tea. To this day, I will not eat puffed wheat."

Eventually, Sadie yanked her first-born out of elementary school. She wrote a note to the principal telling him to send Ronnie Linehan home. "Sadie went right to Dofasco and said, 'He's got to go to work,'" Sadie's sister recalls. "She fought like anything to get Ronnie in there, because his father wouldn't do it." Ronnie was only a boy when they hired him at the steel plant. He would stay there for the next thirty-seven years.

When Connie Linehan was in her second year of high school, Sadie sent another note to the principal, and Connie's formal education came to an abrupt halt. She got a job at Dominion Glass.

Connie started to buy movie magazines, and Brian started to read them. Her kid brother read everything he could get his hands on, from newspapers to library books. The last thing he wanted was to be pulled out of school. Five years younger than Connie, Brian was still in elementary school, but he saw it all. He was the third oldest, and he knew he was next.

When summer came, Connie took Brian and his younger brother Patrick on an excursion to Hutch's, a popular fish-and-chips beach hangout that still exists today. They took the bus, of course; they had no car. And they made sure they got there by ten in the morning to claim their spot on the beach with their blanket, because they knew the beach would be jammed by midday.

Patrick Linehan remembers the excursion with his older siblings vividly. Connie, who was on her day off from Dominion Glass, gave Brian two dollars for the concession stand. "At that time," says Patrick, "you could get three fries and three hamburgers from Hutch's for two dollars. So Brian and I go up to Hutch's and we stand there, with our blond hair and blue eyes – I don't take well to the sun, and neither does Brian – and we finally get to put our order in, and we're in our bare feet, and all around us is hot, hot sand. There are no walkways like there are now."

Brian and Patrick picked up their hamburgers and fries and started to walk back. "Connie is maybe one hundred yards from where we are," he recalls. "And we get within ten or fifteen feet of my sister and our feet are so hot that we drop all the food to hold our feet out of the sand. And my sister has such a look of despair; I'll never forget it, ever. She worked hard for her money, and those two dollars were probably all she had until she got paid. So we picked the French fries up out of the sand and did the best we could to clean them off. We chucked the hamburger buns – they were covered in sand. But we ate the beef patty with the onion on it."

Patrick Linehan's eyes mist over. "We survived. We did all right."

His older brother – the one who would become famous – agreed with him. "We may have been poor," Brian Linehan would later tell the press, "but you don't know that when you're a child."

Sadie couldn't give her children all the things she wanted to give them, but she tried to make sure they still got a chance to be children. And by Sadie's definition that included going to the movies on Saturday afternoons.

"That was her escape, I think," her sister Connie recalls. "She just loved the movies. When I was still a kid, nine years old, ten years old, Sadie used to give me money for myself and her kids, to take them to the Saturday afternoon matinee, and money for a treat. At the Queen's theatre."

Brian's big sister Connie took them to the movies too. "When they were little, I would take my brothers and my sister to the Queen's on Barton Street," she remembers. "One of them would start to cry, and then they would all cry. Back then they had an usher, and the usher would come up with the flashlight: 'I'm sorry, miss, but you're going to have to take them out.' And I'd say to them, 'Shut up, shut up, or *we're going to have to go!*' And they'd just cry."

His younger sister Carole loved going to the movies with Brian. "When we were really young, we used to go to the Avalon, on Ottawa Street," Carole remembers. "And we could save a few pennies by sneaking in the side door, and just crawling under the curtain."

She and Brian were also regulars at the Queen's. Admission was a nickel, and they would collect pop bottles to get enough money together. She still remembers when the price was raised to ten cents. "We just stood there with our mouths open. We didn't have enough."

Dejected and depressed, they were walking down the street when they spotted one of their neighbours. "She had been shopping, and she asked us what was wrong. And of course Brian and I gave our best performances. 'Here,' she said, and gave us each a dime. We ran back to the Queen's and got the double bill. Two movies, the Movietone newsreel, and a cartoon. So we were there for the whole afternoon. Which made Ma happy. At least she knew where we were."

As they got older, she and Brian went to cinemas in downtown Hamilton. "The Capitol, the Palace, the Century, the Roxy, the Tivoli . . . the Tivoli had a very nice balcony. We used to drop things," she confesses with a guilty grin. "We thought it was so funny." They both enjoyed the musicals. Ginger Rogers, Fred Astaire, Judy Garland, Gene Kelly, Jane Powell, all singing and dancing in a world of wealth and glamour far beyond Hamilton's east end.

In time, Brian and Carole found a new way to support their movie-going habit. "We used to call him the Sheeny Man," Carole remembers. "He used to come down our street in a wagon."

To prepare for his visit, Brian and Carole would hop over the train tracks and go to the dump. There she encountered rats. "I'd look at Brian and say, 'Oh no, oh my God, Brian, did you see that one?' And he'd say, 'Just pretend it's Mickey Mouse.' But it *wasn't* Mickey Mouse. '*Brian, please, let's go!*' But before we left we'd find pieces of brass, and we had a wooden basket, with a handle, and we'd collect it all until we thought we had enough."

When the Sheeny Man came, they would go into their act. She was the front man. "Brian would say, 'As you work out how much he's going to give us, I'll just grab what he's putting in the wagon and we'll refill the basket.'" Just like in the movies. "We got this down to an art. Me at the front negotiating our fee, and Brian at the back of the wagon, just picking the stuff back up that the Sheeny Man threw in."

Carole Linehan has few qualms about this childhood larceny. "Hey, we used our heads," she adds with a shrug. "We couldn't ask Ma for the money. Not to go to the show. So it seemed logical."

Carole was Brian's closest confidante. As a child she idolized him, and he did little to discourage her devotion to him. When she was young, she would wait until he got home from school so they could strike out on new adventures. He was the leader. She was the follower. They were soulmates, playmates, and, occasionally, partners-in-crime.

When they lived on Northcote Street, Carole recalls, "We used to have Mammy's Bread delivery. The best oatmeal-raisin cookies going! Brian and I would watch. When the old man got out of the wagon, bless his heart, lovely old gentleman that he was, he had the big wicker basket with stuff in it. And he'd go up and knock on our door to see our mom and Brian would go, 'Okay, it's your turn, climb in and get us some cookies!'

"But we never got into any real trouble. My mother didn't have police coming to the door or anything. Sure, we were a little rambunctious, but nothing that she would be ashamed of. Because you knew damn well that if you got caught doing anything you shouldn't be doing, coming home to Ma would be twice as bad."

Carole Linehan still blames her big brother for almost drowning her one Sunday at Van Wagner's beach. The recreational beach facility featured a full-size swimming pool, which was fenced in for safety reasons. "Rather than go into Lake Ontario, which had all the slime and dead fish, Brian said, 'Let's go over there where they've got it fenced in.' There were a bunch of us and we crawled under the fence.

"Now of course none of us could really swim. And Brian pushed me, and all I remember was just going down and not coming back up. Someone older had seen what had happened, and pulled me out. So I'm lying there and Brian is sitting beside me, crying, 'Don't let her die, don't let her die, my mother's going to kill me!'"

But mostly their fun was harmless. Carole still remembers the house on Northcote Street, a wartime house of six or seven hundred square feet that has since been demolished to accommodate Dofasco expansion. "Before Eric was born," she says, "the five of us slept in one bed, three across there, two across here. And we used to push our feet at each other. We had an old portable radio. And we'd all lie there in bed listening to radio shows like *Our Miss Brooks, The Whistler, The Shadow.*"

It was their big brother Ronnie's job to set the mousetraps. "We'd be lying in bed," Carole remembers, "and all of a sudden we'd hear *snap!* . . . *SNAP!* . . . and I'd get closer to Connie. 'Connie, is that what I think it is?' It was Ronnie's job to pick it up, so he'd get up and go out, and then he'd come back and stand in the doorway of the bedroom, with just this little light on, and he'd go '*Carole . . . oh CAAA-roll . . .*' And I'd pull the sheet over my head and start to cry. This went on every night. Ronnie thought it was funny."

Hamilton cops were no strangers to reports of domestic violence at the Linehan residence. Over the years the doctor who treated Sadie for some of her cuts and wounds had called the police. Neighbours had also called the cops, and Les had been arrested more than once. "Finally, the judge was ready to put him away for a long time," Sadie's sister Connie recalls. "He asked Sadie what she wanted him to do with Les. Sadie said, 'I have five children! He's no good to me in jail. I need him to go to work!'"

Although traditional forms of corporal punishment like whipping were gradually abandoned in Canadian jails in the twentieth century, a flogging was still considered by some to be a more effective deterrent than jail time. The judge sentenced Les Linehan to the lash and ordered him back to work.

A fourth son, Eric, arrived. Another mouth to feed. But not for Les Linehan, and not for long. When he finally walked out on his family, few tears were shed at his departure. Sadie was more relieved than distressed. And Brian Linehan was happy to see the man he would later describe as "a sad Irish father" leave the premises.

"It was a stormy marriage," says Brian's sister Carole. "Very stormy." She was about seven when her father left, and she was sorry her parents' marriage didn't work out. "But better to have them end up that way than to have them end up killing each other."

☆

In the early fifties, the Linehans moved to a new house on Gertrude Street, where Sadie Kotur Linehan soon fell in love with one of their neighbours. His name was Jovo Rodic, and Sadie found the strapping Serbian steelworker irresistible, especially when he invited her, and her six children, to move into his house a few doors away from theirs.

A few months after meeting Jovo, Sadie was singing lullabies again – when she could hear herself over the cacophony of her six children – and soon the Linehan clan welcomed a new brother with a new last name: Jovan (John) Rodic. Jovan was born in the hospital, another first for Sadie; all of her other children, including twelve-year-old Brian, had been born at home. In the time-honoured Serbian tradition, the new baby boy was promptly nicknamed Mico (pronounced MEECH-oh). A new life began.

Life at the Linehan–Rodic residence revolved around Sadie and her kitchen. In that order. "It was a small kitchen, but it did the job. And Ma was an excellent cook," Carole says proudly. "She cooked for all the Serbian weddings. At one point King Peter from Yugoslavia was coming to Hamilton. The Serbian sisters asked my mother if she would be in charge of cooking. And of course she said yes."

Eric, the last of the Linehans, remembers that the kitchen was never empty. "There was always something going on. In addition to the nine of us, there were all the other people, friends, new immigrants that Jovo would bring in. We had two humungous freezers, always full. My mother would make the dinners for the church, so there'd always be ten or fifteen dinners in the freezer, a nice big chicken dinner, a roast beef or whatever it was she was doing for the church at the time. And our fridge was always stocked. It was a European-style home. Food came first."

Brian's baby brother, Mico, agrees. "There was always something on the stove, there was always something in the oven, because my father was a shift worker at Dofasco and three of us brothers were also working there, so we had virtually an around-the-clock kitchen. Plus, my father's friends looked up to him; he was a focal point for the Serbs when they were coming to Hamilton. So my mother, in addition to cooking for the nine of us, also cooked for about a dozen guys. They would come to Hamilton and they would get a room somewhere and they would try to get an 'In.'" That "In," says Mico, was his mother, Sadie, "because she had gone to school with guys who were high up in Dofasco."

Patrick remembers the Rule of the Spoon. "We used to sit down to dinner at our kitchen table, and there would be Brian, myself, Eric, Mico, and Carole, because Connie and Ronnie were already working full-time at Dominion Glass and Dofasco. We would come home from school for lunch, and my mother would put the food on the table, and you ate it whether you liked it or not. You ate it. And you ate *all* of it. And if you pussyfooted around or took too long, well, watch out. If you didn't eat it, you got the wooden spoon. You knew it was coming. *Whack!* Today, they'd probably call it child abuse, really, because she'd just get you with that spoon! I mean, we never had to be taken to the hospital. But it was, quite simply, Shut Up and Eat."

On Gertrude Street, corporal punishment was the rule, not the exception. Sadie Linehan and Jovo Rodic believed that actions spoke louder than words, and that a good hard slap was an efficient way of cautioning their children. Says Patrick, thinking back on it, "Mico never got hit. Because he was Jovo's son, he could blow up a building and he wouldn't get hit. And I don't ever recall Brian getting hit. But me and Eric, wow! We really got it." Ronnie was too old to hit, he adds. "But Mico escaped Mom's wrath, and so did Brian," perhaps, he suggests, "because Brian started contributing to household finances at a very early age."

Sadie's children were still in school, but they had to contribute to the family coffers, just as they had when they lived with Les Linehan. "We all pulled our weight," says Carole. "Ma kept us all together. She got no help from anyone. And my dad certainly didn't pay anything."

When Brian was a student at Delta High School, he got a job at Dingwall Hardware. Carole got a job at Joosten's German Delicatessen, close by on Ottawa Street. When she was finally old enough, she got a summer job at the A&P, and worked days there and nights at the IGA. Patrick's first job was also at Joosten's German Delicatessen. Then he started going to Central High School in shifts, as all the local students did. "There weren't enough schools. I drew the steady morning shift every year, and I worked straight afternoon shifts at the spinning mill. And I still passed. I made $57 a week and my mother took my paycheque and I got $5. I did that for three years of high school. And then I went to Delta, where Brian had gone, and finally I got the afternoon shift."

His younger brother Eric got a job at Appleford's, a waxed paper factory. "My pay was $90 a week," says Eric. "And I paid $50 at home. We all paid our dues."

The kids also had to help out around home. The worst times, says Eric, were canning times. The Linehan kids would form an assembly line to put down fifteen bushels of tomatoes one day, fifteen bushels of peppers the next.

And then there was smelt season. Eric remembers, "On Friday night my stepfather and his buddies would go out smelt fishing. They'd be gone all night long at the docks. You'd wake up Saturday morning to the smell of smelts in the backyard. There'd be fifteen, twenty bushels of them. We'd have to make our own assembly line. We'd have a head cutter, a footer, somebody to clean it, wash it, and bag it. There was a whole procession. And after we bagged them, we froze them. In those two humungous freezers."

Like Eric, Connie always dreaded the annual home-canning ritual. When she left home, she says, one of her goals was to live a life "where you didn't have to do it yourself, where you always were able to afford to buy food in cans." (As it turned out, her younger brother Brian had loftier goals in mind.)

Despite the difficulties of life on Gertrude Street, the Linehan kids continued to keep themselves amused. Carole and Brian loved their house, mainly because it had two staircases, one at the front and one at the back, so they could sneak out. As Ronnie was already out on his own, Sadie's four younger sons shared a room up in the attic. Mico, being the youngest, had his own bed. Brian, Patrick, and Eric shared a king-size bed with a queen-size mattress. "The mattress was six inches short from the headboard," Eric recalls. "So Brian snuck upstairs one night – it must have been nine, ten o'clock – crawled under the bed, reached up through the springs that were holding the mattress on the bed, grabbed my brother Patrick, and started pulling him down through the bed. Brian scared the living hell out of him!"

Patrick plotted his revenge. Brian, the oldest, would be the last one to come home. So the next night, before they were sent to bed, Eric and Patrick loaded the stairs with thumbtacks to set a trap for him. "But Patrick and I got into an argument," Eric recalls, "and I guess it was kind of loud."

Sadie came to the bottom of the stairs: "Be quiet!" she warned, "or I'm going to come up!"

But Patrick and Eric continued arguing. "By now," Eric continues, "she was hollering at us to BE QUIET! And we still didn't stop. So she came charging up those stairs in her stocking feet. And she must have hit every tack on the way up." Eric chuckles softly. "We never did get Brian."

On another night, Carole recalls, "One of those nights when I guess we were all driving Ma crazy, she stood there at the kitchen sink and looked over at all of us, shaking her finger at us, and said, 'I only ever made seven mistakes in my life, and I'm looking at them!' And Brian piped up. 'Well, Ma, have you ever heard of the word *no*?'"

Sadie still ruled the roost, but her chicks were starting to flap their wings. At home the teenaged Linehan siblings constantly argued and competed with each other for attention – and grew their own peculiar sense of humour.

"When we were teenagers," Carole remembers, "we'd come home from school, and I'd say 'Ma, what are we having for dinner tonight?' And she'd say, 'Shit in a basket.' And I'd say, 'Okay, I'll have a double order.' And then Brian would come in. 'What are we having?' I'd look at him and say, 'Shit in a basket, and I'm having a double.' He'd look at Ma and say, 'I think I'd rather have puke and vomit pie.'"

When Brian turned sixteen, he told Carole that she was not welcome at his birthday party.

"But Brian," she protested, "I'm your *sister!*"

"I don't care," he replied. "I don't want you at my party. I'm going to have all my friends here."

So Carole went to Sadie and gave her a sob story, after which Sadie informed Brian, "Your sister lives in this house. Therefore she will be at your party."

"So it's Brian's sixteenth birthday," says Carole, "and of course all his friends come, and while I'm sitting there, he's opening his gifts. And what does his friend Maureen bring him as a birthday gift? It's in a cake box. She's used a pie shell and she's used cottage cheese, and food colouring, and it looks gross! It looks just like you'd imagine puke and vomit pie would look."

If Brian had any happy memories of his childhood, he seldom, if ever, shared them. In later years, he would characterize himself as a lonely kid who spent his time reading books and watching movies while his classmates played sports and dated cheerleaders. "I was the only sickly one of seven children," Brian would tell reporters. "You should see my brothers, they look like they were born to play football."

Brian was not into athletics. "He hated sports with a passion," says Patrick. "Those fingernails were always clean." His siblings liked to box, play baseball, play football. "Brian was always reading. Always. He would keep the light on in the bedroom and Eric and I would be scream-ing at him to turn the light off. Because he'd be reading."

Unlike his siblings, Brian couldn't wait to get to class in the mornings. Delta High School was a joy, because he did well and felt appreciated there. "At school," he said, "I was praised." He was also increasingly visible. He had begun to write stories for his high school paper and also wrote a high school column for the *Hamilton Spectator*, the city's highly respected daily. (His story on the annual Sadie Hawkins dance at Delta was headlined "Money No Object for Fellows Tonight.")

Jovo Rodic – who was clearly a man to be reckoned with – drew mixed reviews from the children he had taken under his roof. Patrick Linehan admits he found Jovo irritating at times, "but my stepfather, bless his heart, he took on a real challenge when he took a woman with a house full of kids."

Carole and Eric, however, were not buying it. Budding teenager Carole was already displaying the irreverence, arrogance, and independ-ence that would later emerge as Linehan family traits. "We used to joke with Jovo because he would call us 'crazy Canadians,'" says Carole. "I'd say, well, we may be crazy, but you paid to become one! And Brian would just sit there, shaking his head, going, 'Carole, Carole, Carole.' And I'd say, 'Oh *crap*, I'm getting tired of hearing about this!'"

Eric was about seventeen when he "got the boot" from Jovo. "But I was pretty well on my way out anyway," he says today. "My stepfather and I weren't always on good terms. But now that I'm older, I really have no complaints about him. He took on a woman with six kids. And we were always fed. And there was always a roof over our heads."

Growing up Linehan was not easy, says Eric. "But there were no easy lives back then. I think my mother had kind of a hard life compared to some of the other mothers in the neighbourhood. My stepfather was very old country European. The man was the boss of the house. But she was able to cope with that and seven kids. And that's a handful."

His younger brother, Mico, agrees. "We didn't have a whole lot, but everyone on our street was in pretty much the same boat. So I thought it was a pretty normal childhood growing up. You don't consider yourself poor, because you have what you have. You don't miss what you don't have."

"He had the drive to get out."

When Brian Linehan was seventeen, his mother set up a summer job for him at Dofasco. His sister Carole believes he stuck it out for three days. His brother Patrick believes he lasted only one eight-hour shift. Regardless of which version you believe, everyone agrees that Brian came home with his work clothes in a paper shopping bag and stunned his entire family when he announced that he wasn't going to work in a steel mill.

Sadie hit the roof. But Brian was adamant.

Yes, he knew they needed the money.

No, he was not expecting a free ride.

Yes, he would get another summer job.

His decision sent shock waves rippling through the family. "After all," says Brian's older sister, Connie, "everybody worked at Dofasco. But Brian always said he would never do it."

He had sent her a note, many years ago, which she had tucked away for safekeeping. It's now yellow with age, but both the handwriting and the message are unmistakably Brian's: *"I swear that I will never be a steelworker."*

Brian Linehan was as good as his word. Like a lot of other teenagers in Hamilton, Ontario, in the 1950s, he continued to attend high school during the day and work afternoons and evenings at the drug store, to help out at home. But unlike most teenagers in Hamilton, he could also read his byline in a major city newspaper. And seeing his name in print in the *Hamilton Spectator*, knowing that thousands of strangers were seeing it too, was an unprecedented thrill, as was the fact that the newspaper's theatre writer, Ed Hocura, had taken him under his wing and encouraged him. According to Brian, Hocura "was one of the first people to say a kind word to me." He would later credit Hocura with getting him a job interview with Odeon Theatres Ltd., a chain of Canadian movie houses with links to the celebrated J. Arthur Rank film company in Great Britain.

At the time, Odeon was engaged in a fairly civilized but none-theless relentless competition with another Canadian exhibition chain, Famous Players Ltd., a company partly owned by Paramount Pictures. Both chains had exclusive housekeeping deals with major studios; Universal and Columbia Pictures movies played only at cinemas owned and operated by Odeon, while Paramount and Warner Bros. movies played only at Famous Players theatres, and so forth, in what had become a fiercely competitive market.

At nineteen, Brian met with Odeon chief Christopher Salmon, who was suitably impressed. Impressed enough, in fact, to offer him a junior-level gofer job as an executive trainee, under the watchful eye of Odeon advertising and publicity honcho Charles Mason. Brian jumped at the chance and gratefully accepted the Odeon offer.

Home from meeting with the Odeon executives, he announced his plans to move to Toronto. Eric Linehan remembers that his mother was "not keen" on the plan. "I think Brian was her favourite son. The rest of us were just regular kids. We wanted to get out and play. We didn't want to hang around the house. He was always a little more attentive to her. He was the one who made her laugh."

Sadie told Brian that if he took the job in Toronto, she would never speak to him again. He ignored her. He understood, probably better than Sadie did, that she was afraid for him, afraid he was throwing his life away, when he could stay in Hamilton and work at Dofasco and *be* somebody.

Eric was only a kid when his big brother took off for Toronto, but he could sense, even then, that Brian had some special energy that none of the others had. "He had the drive," he says simply, "to get out. Most of us were stuck. We weren't going to go any further."

Connie says Brian's siblings felt "a little gypped" by Brian's departure. "Because here's one brother going off to do what he wants, and the rest of us all have to go to work to help out at home." Their aunt Connie thinks that Ronnie, the eldest, "kind of resented it. But with Brian it was a different situation. Because Brian was the only one who didn't work in the steel plant. And at one time I think his mother took Ronnie aside and said, 'Look, it's *his* life.'"

Soon after Brian took the job, Charles Mason sent out a one-sheet "flash bulletin" from the Odeon Tower. The headline was "Meet Mr. Linehan."

> We invite you to meet Mr. Linehan. This young man has just been appointed as a trainee in our department. We have hopes that he will prove to be a valuable "extra pair of hands" once he has learned the essentials of our business. Do not expect to hear from him soon, since his training will be carefully scheduled to ensure he has an opportunity to learn from some of our most experienced showmen, before taking up any advertising and publicity responsibilities.
>
> In order that Brian can come to understand the complete workings of theatre exhibition, and the application of advertising where it counts – at the theatre; he will spend some of the weeks ahead in the hands of a few of our leading showmen. We hope that if your theatre [in Ontario] is selected at his temporary base, you will help us by really "putting him through the mill." Only in this way can he be of real future value to us . . . and to you!
>
> Charles Mason,
> Advertising and Publicity

The visual highlight of the bulletin was a charming photo of a young man, already looking very corporate, with a caption that read: "Brian Richard Linehan is a recent graduate of Delta Secondary School in Hamilton, Ontario, and is a native of that city. He is 19, and during his last two years as a student, was the reporter of High School activities for the *Hamilton Spectator*."

Brian celebrated his twentieth birthday in his rented room on the fourth floor of a boarding house in Yorkville, a bohemian section of downtown Toronto that would later become a playground of the *nouveau riche*. Part of his new job was writing advertising copy for films and screening upcoming movies that would play both the Odeon and Famous Players film circuits. During his five years at Odeon, he would see more than one thousand feature films. "I was in heaven," he would later confess.

He was also shifting into high gear. In his spare time, he studied French for two years at the Toronto French School, took a public relations course at Ryerson Polytechnic Institute, and enrolled in English courses at the University of Toronto. Odeon executives admired and applauded his hunger for self-improvement and cheerfully subsidized his tuition.

Some weekends Brian would go home to Hamilton. "But I wouldn't see him," his aunt Connie remembers, "because he'd be out, visiting friends or something. Sadie would have a box full of stuff on the kitchen floor, and she'd say, 'That's all for Brian, but I don't know how he's going to take it back to Toronto with him, he doesn't drive!'"

Mico still remembers Brian "taking the bus from Toronto to Hamilton, picking up me and Eric, taking us back to Toronto on the bus, taking us for our first subway ride, then bringing us back to Hamilton on the bus, and then taking the bus back to Toronto." Brian did this, Mico suspects, at the strong "request" of their mother. Whether they lived a few minutes away or forty-five miles away in Toronto, Sadie still expected her children to heed her calls and check in with her on a regular basis.

When Brian moved out, his sister Carole was still going to high school, and once in a while she would bump into her father in downtown Hamilton. "He knew which hairdresser I went to. I guess he saw me come out one Saturday. And he would be waiting outside: 'Could you spare a couple of bucks?' So a few times, yes, I did give him the money. But the last time I saw him I said, 'Listen, I will take you to The Chicken Roost, I'll take you wherever you want to go, you pick whatever you want off the menu. But Dad, I'm sorry, I am not going to contribute to the drinking. Because you need help desperately.' It broke my heart to say that."

When she told Brian about it, he said, "Carole, that was the best thing you could have done. But whatever you do," he added, "don't tell Ma, because she'll kill you."

☆

By now Brian had his own tiny basement apartment on Carlton Street, a few steps away from Odeon's Toronto head office.

Occasionally his sister Connie would visit him; she loved the street-cars that clanked up and down Carlton. Whenever Carole came to visit, she would take the bus from Hamilton to Toronto. "We used to go off to Fran's Restaurant and sit there half the night," she remembers. Brian's apartment was basically one room, so Carole would sleep on the floor. "We'd go for breakfast at Fran's, and then he would go with me to the bus terminal. Bless his heart, he would sit there with me until I got on the bus. And then I'd come home and think, what a drag this is – I should have stayed in Toronto!"

By now Brian was also doing so well in Odeon's advertising department that Charles Mason decided to try him out as a talent wrangler, assigning him to meet, greet, and babysit visiting movie stars who would fly in to promote films about to open on Odeon movie screens.

After a somewhat shaky start, Brian acquitted himself admirably. He was only twenty, but he enjoyed being in the company of people whose images filled Toronto movie houses. And he was rarely tongue-tied, even when he was sent to the airport in black stretch limousines to pick up such screen legends as Gregory Peck and Alfred Hitchcock.

He had to arrange two limousines when he went to meet Joan Crawford – "one for her, and one for her luggage and me. She told me to get in the car with the luggage and make sure it got to the hotel. She was a bit frosty," he recalled. "She thought they had sent the office boy to meet her. Which, of course, they had."

When Brian told his younger sister that he had spent the day escorting "one of your dearest friends," Carole Linehan was beside herself.

"Who??"

"Joan Crawford."

"You creep!" she cried. She had been writing fan letters to Crawford for years, and Crawford had reciprocated with personal notes and auto-graphed photos. "Did you get me her autograph?"

Brian burst out laughing. "You don't need her autograph, you *correspond* with her! You have your notes, you have your signed pictures, what more do you want?"

"Did she smoke during the press interviews?" asked Carole. "Did you save any of her cigarette butts?"

Young Eric Linehan was playing on the street with some of his pals one day when Brian pulled up in front of the house in a stretch limou-sine. "My buddies and I are all standing around the limo, trying to look in, trying to see who's in there, and my brother Brian's in the house, talking to my mother," says Eric. "And then he comes out and he says, 'All right, do you want to go for a ride?'

"Oh yeah oh yeah, I say, I want to go. None of the other guys can go, but I want to go. I open the door to jump in. There's a guy sitting in there with a cowboy hat on.

"'Get in,' says the guy with the cowboy hat. 'I'll take you around the block and let you out.' And he did. He just drove down the street, turned the corner, and let me out." It was Eric Linehan's first ride in a limousine.

Years later he found out that the man in the cowboy hat was Clint Eastwood, whom Brian was bringing to the Hamilton premiere of *A Fistful of Dollars*.

Brian Linehan was on his way to becoming the country's youngest movie executive. He would later tell his friend Broadway star Carole Shelley: "I was a sow's ear. I knew nothing. I fought to get a job with Odeon. And then I sort of made up a job for myself. That's how I found out I was good at making up what is needed at the time."

So good, in fact, that five years after joining Odeon, at the young age of twenty-four, Brian Richard Linehan was made general manager of Janus Films, a J. Arthur Rank subsidiary film distributor for elegant foreign films from such directors as Ingmar Bergman, Akira Kurosawa, and François Truffaut. Brian was in his element, meeting with exhibitors, distributors, marketing executives, actors, producers, and directors. Along the way he would discover that he loved the Business of show business almost as much as he loved the Show.

Brian also began participating in acting and writing workshops coached by Eli Rill, who had come home to Toronto after working as a protege of Lee Strasberg at The Actors Studio in New York. Rill's ex-wife, Janine Manatis, had succeeded Edward Albee as moderator of the Playwrights' Unit, was one of the few women in Elia Kazan's Directors' Unit, and counted James Baldwin as one of her mentors. As Rill's workshops became more successful and more numerous, Manatis took over some of her ex-husband's workload, and among the young hopefuls in her classes was a very eager young man from Hamilton.

Did Brian want to be an actor? "No," says Manatis flatly. Half a century has passed, but her voice remains clear, uncluttered, and effortlessly authoritative. "No, he *thought* he wanted to be an actor. In other words, Brian loved the fantasy of being an actor as opposed to the reality of being an actor. And he had come into classes with that fantasy, as so many do."

Linehan and Manatis hit it off right away. "I had great affection for Brian. And great respect. Before he became *BRIAN LINEHAN*."

He talked to her about the business of being an actor, and how you forge your career. "His words, not mine: '*How you forge your career.*'"

She sensed, very early on, that there was a secretive side to him. "And that would have never allowed him to be a really good actor. Because that secretive part would never have allowed him to bring to acting who he really was."

He had enrolled in an acting class, but what he really wanted, she says, was what she was able to give him – a new route, a new road map, to finding and being himself, in public as well as private. What he was doing, really, was searching for the next steps in the creation of Brian Linehan.

Brian's theatrical ambitions were largely inspired by a boyhood friend from Hamilton. Leon Pownall was an accomplished thespian and a highly regarded member of the esteemed company of international actors who dominated the stages of the Stratford Festival. The Welsh-born actor had emigrated to Canada with his family a decade earlier and had settled in Hamilton.

Another friend of Leon's, Charles Dennis, was a talented young hotshot who wanted to do it all: write, produce, direct, star. Charlie, as he was known to his friends, toiled by day as an entertainment writer for the *Toronto Telegram*. He met Brian in the 1960s at the Pownall residence in Stratford. It seemed to Charlie that Brian, who was still working for Odeon, was in Stratford all the time. "Brian," he says, "was besotted by Leon. He idolized him. When he came to Stratford, he stayed with Leon and his wife and their children."

Charles Dennis was as mad about the movies as Linehan was, and it was Charlie who ended up putting Brian Linehan on stage. Dennis had succeeded Henry Tarvainen as the artistic director of the University College Players' Guild and decided to produce Arthur Miller's *Incident at Vichy*, a play that had never been staged in Toronto. Brian was cast as the Prince, while Dennis played Leduc – "the only Jew who escapes, thanks to the Prince's noble sacrifice" – and tried to channel Humphrey Bogart in *Passage to Marseilles*. Brian, he says, modelled his role on Paul

Henreid, "and carried himself with a suitably grand, detached manner, both onstage and off."

Playing a prince wasn't a stretch for Brian, adds Dennis, tongue-in-cheek. "*But*, he was marvellous. *Very* grand as the Prince. I don't know where he got it from."

Carole Linehan was among a handful of Brian boosters who came to cheer him on. After the curtain came down, Brian asked his younger sister what she thought of the performance. Carole told him she was sure he'd improve with a little more practice. "You're a bit stiff," she confided. "But hey, it was your first role!"

Incident at Vichy ran for a week at the Colonnade Theatre in the spring of 1968. Producer Dennis subsequently won the McAndrew Award for contributions to campus drama and left Canada to try his luck in Great Britain. When he returned from London two years later, he met Brian for a drink at the rooftop bar of Toronto's Park Plaza. Now working at Janus Films, Brian was dying to tell Dennis about all the famous people he had met. At first Charlie was amused. He had spent a number of years interviewing famous people for the *Telegram*, and was tickled by Brian's unbridled enthusiasm.

"But getting together to talk turned into a two-hour litany of whom he'd met. Finally, I said okay, okay, enough – Brian, I *don't* care!"

"Oh c'mon, Charlie," said Brian, almost pleadingly – "just a few more!"

Dennis was taken aback. "Brian was so totally hooked on celebrity."

☆

Carole Linehan, still Brian's greatest fan, would soon follow his example. In more ways than one.

When Carole graduated from high school, Sadie had already lined up a job for her at Dofasco. Carole refused to go. "I did not spend all this time in school to be flipping tin!" she railed. Despite her mother's protests, she went to work for a chartered accounting firm in Hamilton, to pay her way for the night classes at McMaster University that would bring her the CA degree she coveted. "It took me eight years, but I did it."

When she married her Hamilton boyfriend Bruce Dingwall, they too decided to move to Toronto. "To get away from *both* mothers," adds Carole with a wry smile. Sadie was not happy. And at times Carole wasn't all that thrilled about it either. For the next eighteen months, to get her degree, she drove back and forth to McMaster from Toronto.

Now in Toronto, newlyweds Carole and Bruce met Brian for dinner. "Well!" he said, embracing his sister. "You finally made the break."

Carole frequently sought the advice of her older brother, now an old hand at big-city living. When CBS was set to telecast a live outdoor concert by Barbra Streisand from Central Park, Carole and Bruce didn't want to miss it. But they didn't have a TV set because they thought they couldn't afford one. "So I called Brian. And Brian said, 'Get down to Bad Boy and get a TV!'" Carole and Bruce drove down to Bad Boy — a justifiably famous discount department store in Toronto — and bought a black-and-white television for ninety-nine dollars.

Carole says she got a lot of her thinking from Brian. "Brian would say, 'Carole, don't go out and buy a bookcase! Just get some bricks and some boards and do the same thing I did.'" She beams. "Which is just what we did."

Brian was busy, and appreciated, and having a ball. He was still in constant touch with his mother and his brothers and sisters in Hamilton. But he was building a new family, a family of friends and co-workers who seemed to think he was someone special, someone unusual. Someone worth knowing.

One of his new friends was sultry honey-voiced actress Marilyn Lightstone. He met her in the summer of 1967, at a party at the Pownalls' in Stratford. Leon and Marilyn were both working at the Festival that summer, and Brian was visiting Pownall. "I remember dancing with him to 'Goodbye Ruby Tuesday,'" says Marilyn with an angelic smile. "Brian was a great dancer, a *wonderful* dancer. And we became friends."

They both came from working-class backgrounds. "And yet, for both of us, being in the arts was what our lives were about. And I think it was much harder for him than for me. Because although my family didn't have much connection with the kind of world I wanted to live in, they were always supportive. Whereas with Brian, it made him a stranger, I think, to the world that he came from."

By then Brian was working at Janus Films, and he was very proud of his efforts to build the company's film library. Marilyn was floored by his knowledge. "It wasn't just a job," she says. "Everything he did, he did with passion."

Neither one of them knew it at the time, but Marilyn Lightstone was destined to play a pivotal role in Brian Linehan's future.

☆

Brian Linehan was in his early twenties when he started to feel very, very good about himself. Sadie Kotur Linehan was in her early forties when she started to feel not quite right. Mico remembers her being sick, on and off, for six or seven years. Eric remembers times when his mother was in and out of hospital. His sister Connie had already moved out of the house, and Carole was still commuting between Hamilton and Toronto.

Sadie was not getting any better, which both worried and puzzled her children. One night, just before Christmas 1969, Sadie asked Carole to call her doctor, to ask him for more morphine. When Carole reached him, the doctor said, "Carole, if I give your mother any more morphine, I am going to lose my licence."

Carole explained that she was concerned because one night Sadie was pretty good, and the next night she wasn't, and that Carole just didn't know what to do for her.

"Carole," the doctor replied, "I've tried talking to your mother and she will not accept this. Your mother is going to die. It's terminal. It's right through her body."

Carole was shocked. So were her brothers and sister. "We all thought Ma was indestructible," says Carole. But, of course, she wasn't.

Sadie Kotur Linehan Rodic died the following spring, on her wedding anniversary: June 18, 1970. She was only forty-nine. The official medical diagnosis was breast cancer.

Sadie's last two teenage sons, Eric Linehan and Jovan "Mico" Rodic, were still living at home. With Sadie gone, Jovo Rodic invited Eric, who was then seventeen, to leave. Eric accepted Jovo's invitation. Mico, fourteen, was now home alone. "Our mother was everything," says Mico. "She was the backbone. When she spoke, you listened. She was the glue that held us all together. When she died is when we kind of started drifting apart."

Years later Brian would tell journalist Philip Marchand that his mother "slaved over a hot stove, making enough to accommodate nine people who were about to sit down and devour everything but the cutlery. None of this occurs to you at the time. It's like, well, big deal. All you can remember is, Eat It, or Else. And so you eat it."

It still troubled him, he said, that he had been unable to make her life easier.

"I did nothing," he told Marchand. "I didn't buy her a washer or a dryer or a four-speed Mixmaster mixer. I did nothing. I mean, I showed up; I was there. But I didn't make her life easier on a material level. I did nothing."

"I blame him for everything."

Canadian broadcaster Phyllis Switzer had already excelled in a number of network posts when she became convinced that Toronto needed a locally oriented television station. Switzer applied to the federal broadcasting regulator, the CRTC, for a licence. The licence was granted in her name, and City TV became a reality, debuting in 1972. Switzer became a key member of City TV's board of directors and senior vice-president of programming and community relations, a fancy title for a gritty job. City TV was very much a seat-of-your-pants experiment, and in its early years she was credited with doing everything but the engineering and the accounting.

The creative thrust for this brave new venture came from an ambitious CBC Television producer and on-camera host who had jumped ship when the Canadian public broadcaster wouldn't support his pitch to remake *Cross-Country Check-Up*, a successful weekly series he had hosted on CBC Radio, into a national television program. His name was Moses Znaimer.

Google "Moses Znaimer" and you'll find more than twenty-five thousand web pages that mention his name. Look him up in Wikipedia, the free Internet encyclopedia, and you'll find "a mercurial, unpredictable, and ego-driven leader" who inspired "equal parts adoration and loathing" in his employees, "many of whom still tell 'Moses stories' which Znaimer does his best to refute, or embellish, as the mood strikes him."

Moses Znaimer co-founded the new station with Switzer, set its maverick standards, and was determined to keep the new station well ahead of the curve. Accordingly, City TV was the only station that was purposely designed without a film department. "In those days," Znaimer explains, "everything outside the studio was shot on film. Even the smallest station had its own cameras and lab to process the film that was shot.

"I had none of that. I knew we were moving into an electronic world. And I loved the immediacy of video. Because no one else was making the equipment, we were the first in the world to struggle with what was then black-and-white portapacks created primarily for security cameras. And we were the first in the world to begin to adapt that to what became known as ENG (Electronic News Gathering). ENG equipment as we know it didn't come along for maybe another ten years. And when it finally did we were already there with the psychology oriented to that experience."

With no VHF licences available, and a frankly modest bankroll, City TV – soon to be marketed as one word, Citytv – began as Canada's first commercial UHF station, Channel 79, with offices on Toronto's Queen Street East. It was scrappy, free-wheeling, and borderline smart-ass, and it didn't look like anything else on the dial. Znaimer even commissioned an original tune by singer-songwriter Tommy Ambrose for the launch, appropriately called "People City."

As fate would have it, Brian's friend Marilyn Lightstone was Moses Znaimer's partner. "I remember telling Moses about this fellow who just knew so much about film," Marilyn recalls. "And I think maybe something happened that way. Because Moses generally listens to me when I'm very impressed by someone, and thinks that he should follow up. It wasn't a formal introduction. Sometimes I just throw something out that Moses picks up on. And that's what happened with Brian. And the next thing I knew, he was working at City."

When City was founded, *Bonanza*, the first Western to be telecast in colour, was winding up a successful fourteen-year stint on NBC. It was an era before cable, before "specialty" channels, a time of *All in the Family* and *Front Page Challenge*, and Canadian viewers were cheerfully addicted to both. But Moses Znaimer had decided that he didn't want to perpetuate the model of conventional series-based television. Citytv would be a different kind of animal.

He chose movies to be the mainstay on air while he got the station up and running, so he needed someone who knew movies. He had met Brian, knew he worked in film distribution, and knew he had a background in exhibition. Znaimer was prepared to gamble that Brian was the right guy for the right time, and Linehan was one of the first people he hired. He brought him to Citytv as producer of film programming, responsible for the buying and scheduling of movies.

The legend of Linehan had begun.

Brian was once again in his element. He bought old movies and created new, themed strands he dubbed "afternoon film festivals." My personal favourite, his *Suffer With Bette* festival, showcased Bette Davis in some of her best roles from the 1940s. Other viewers cheered his collection of vintage Deanna Durbin musicals. And schlock movie lovers applauded his mini-marathon called *Monsters You Know and Love*.

To capture public imagination, Moses Znaimer needed to create media attention for the fledgling station. He succeeded in doing that and more when he devised a weekly late-night series of sexy adult films all but guaranteed to win both young male viewers and headlines. He called it The Baby Blue Movie and gave it to Brian to program. "It was the primary part of his job to find movies that were appropriate for that slot," Moses explains, "but also ones we could play, since the window of what we could get away with without causing my licence to be lifted was a very narrow one. That was his job," he reiterates, gently but firmly. "He was not hired as an on-air personality."

Linehan rose to the challenge, programming soft-core porn flicks every weekend on Citytv, in which luscious blonde stewardesses, almost invariably Swedish, spent inordinate amounts of screen time undressing, taking showers together, and soaping each other up (and, frequently, down). "If this doesn't persuade Torontonians to conserve water and bathe together, I don't know what will!" Brian deadpanned. His favourite acquisition was *Wanda the Sadistic Hypnotist*, not because the film was particularly erotic, but just because he liked saying the title aloud.

Almost instantly notorious, the weekly Baby Blue Movie made Citytv Toronto's most-watched station Fridays at midnight. The naughty weekly series, tame by today's standards, would later be immortalized by a controversial theatre piece, *I Love You Baby Blue*.

For Brian, life at Citytv was lively, exciting, fun, and young. Nobody was making a lot of money, but everybody was having a good time – *and* accumulating a lot of hands-on experience in television. "You flew by the seat of your pants," he would later recall. "Half the staff slept on the floor because you never knew when something was going to break down."

By then Brian and I had known each other for a while. We had a pleasant, nodding acquaintance, greeting each other at industry screenings, especially when films were shown in the Astral office building where the Janus Film Library was housed. At one screening, shortly after Brian started at Citytv, he introduced me to his roommate, one Dr. Zane Wagman. I immediately suggested, teasing, that Brian could save some bucks on medical bills by having a doctor for a roommate.

"Only if he gets a toothache," Dr. Wagman replied with an easy grin. Brian explained that Dr. Wagman was a dentist, and I'm sure I had something silly to say about that too. The lights dimmed, the movie started, and I thought no more of it. At that particular time in the early 1970s, I regarded Brian as a very quiet, very conservative young man (yes, this is Brian Linehan I'm talking about) in whose personal life I had absolutely no interest whatsoever.

Brian went to every screening he could; he was interested in seeing everything. I was attending screenings as a film critic – the direct result of another brave new venture. Led by three newspaper veterans, a small group of us had launched an upstart tabloid newspaper called the *Toronto Sun*, one short year before Citytv transmitted its first signal.

The *Toronto Sun* was the struggling new local paper, determined to bring Toronto readers new perspectives on their own city. Citytv was the struggling new local TV station. Ours was an easy synergy – two bold new media shops fighting large-circulation dailies and long-established TV networks. As feisty, under-resourced Davids, we shared the same battle against the fat-cat Goliaths and looked to each other for comfort and support. As the town's most visible underdogs, both Citytv and the *Sun* were regarded with affection by hundreds of thousands of Toronto media consumers. We just needed more of them to buy us and watch us.

One day I was browsing through a copy of *TV Guide* when I saw an ad for Citytv's afternoon *Suffer With Bette* festival. It was so cheeky, so delightfully camp, that it made me laugh out loud. I saluted the series in my daily entertainment column in the *Sun*. Brian called the next day to thank me. And so it began.

At Citytv, Linehan was one of a talented team of gung-ho mavericks that included aspiring director Ivan Reitman, aspiring actor Dan Aykroyd, and award-winning newspaper columnist Ron Haggart, a veteran of both of Toronto's major dailies, the *Toronto Star* and the *Toronto Telegram*. Haggart was in charge of the station's flagship show, appropriately titled *The City Show*, which ran for two and a half hours every night, and required a lot of news coverage, and lots of feature material too, to fill out the time.

One day Brian got a call from Haggart's office. Apparently, the Citytv reporter scheduled to interview Canadian director Eric Till hadn't shown up for work, and Till, who was promoting his new film *A Fan's Notes*, was already in the studio, being miked for the interview. Would Linehan be a sport, take one for the team, and do the interview?

Haggart's request was only logical. He was asking the one person at Citytv who knew more about movies than anyone else to talk to some guy who made movies, for maybe ten minutes tops.

Brian didn't want to see his colleagues embarrassed. Besides, how hard could it be? True, he'd never been on TV before. "But I'd watched Pierre Berton, Joyce Davidson, and others interviewing people, and it looked pretty easy," he later recalled.

He agreed to do it, and went into the men's room to prepare for the interview. He brushed his teeth and combed his hair, and then went down to the studio.

He was sitting there, having a fairly innocuous chat with Eric Till, when he noticed this guy off to one side of the camera, waving his hands like a madman, trying to get his attention. Brian thought that maybe he had to go to the bathroom, and couldn't understand why the man was asking him for permission. "What do you want?" Brian inquired.

"I want you to take a commercial break!" hissed the exasperated floor director. "And I want you to come back with a film clip."

A few minutes later, the same guy started waving his hands again. He wanted Brian to take another break. As the interview was winding down, Brian saw him wave his hands yet again. "From the signals I'm getting," he told film director Till, "it looks like the interview is over."

So, ostensibly, was Brian Linehan's career as an interviewer.

Director Ron Meraska emerged from the control room. "Linehan," he said, "you are the worst visual I'd ever had to shoot. You do not have a good side. And you don't know what you're doing. The interview is terrible. Unusable." Brian himself wrote about that fateful day years later, in his column in the *Toronto Sun*. "The laughter from the rest of the crew," he said, "made the humiliation complete."

However, he did not retreat to his office. He asked Ron Meraska to let him try again, and Meraska agreed. If Linehan could get Eric Till to come back the next day, he could do it over again.

Brian telephoned Till, who agreed to come back in. The second interview was acceptable. Even air-worthy. *City Show* producer Ron Haggart was relieved, and asked Brian if he would like to take a crack at a few more interviews. Also, he could have a little more time, if he needed it.

And the rest, as they say, is history. Show-business history, granted, but history nonetheless. When Till agreed to come back the next day, Linehan wrote, "he not only gave me my second chance, he gave me a television career."

Almost two decades later, Brian revealed that his original interview with Eric Till was for years a party tape that was played to much acclaim. "I've been told it no longer exists," he wrote in his column in the *Toronto Sun*. "I am grateful. But not as grateful as I am to Eric Till. I blame him for everything."

Enter Michael Levine. A bright young attorney with a decidedly liberal background, Levine had decided to try his hand at one of the country's most under-served fields: entertainment law – a career course that over the years would prove to be phenomenally well-chosen. Levine's first entertainment law client was Astral Films; in 1971, he had worked on the sale of Astral to the Greenberg and Bronfman families. While Linehan programmed the Janus film library, he worked out of Astral Films, and during that time became friends with Laurie Fein, who was then the president of Astral Television Films Limited.

In April 1973, Levine received a call from Laurie Fein, who told him that his young friend Brian Linehan was now at a fledgling television station called Citytv programming the Baby Blue movies. He told Levine that Moses Znaimer had offered Brian a show, that Brian was "absolutely petrified" about having to negotiate with Znaimer, and that Fein thought Levine would be the perfect person to assist him.

"So the two of them, Laurie Fein and Brian Linehan, came trooping into my office, sat down, and we had a conversation," Levine remembers. "I found Brian so funny, so witty, so charming, so outrageous that I took on the assignment. I don't even remember whether he paid me for it," he adds, eyes twinkling. "Of course, that wasn't his long suit."

Brian Linehan became Michael Levine's first Personality client. From then on, Levine negotiated all of Brian's contracts with Citytv.

That initial deal negotiation was memorable, in more ways than one, and led to what Levine describes as "a very profound aspect" of his relationship with Linehan. "I went in to visit Moses," Levine recalls. "And Moses was a rather eccentric, brilliant but not exactly classical television executive. During the course of that first conversation he said to

me, 'I hate lawyers. I should throw you down the stairs. But you fasci-
nate me. What do you want?'

"And I said, 'Half the program.'

"Now Citytv before, during, and after never gave away half of anything. And he basically turned to me and he said, 'On one condition:
you be my lawyer from now on.'"

Znaimer agrees with most of Levine's version. "Brian was *my*
employee," he notes, pointedly. "He was on staff. All the people at City at
that time were staff. There were no independent producers. If you wanted
someone to produce something for you," he explains, "you took them in,
made them a member of your staff. But just as I was about to throw
Michael down the stairs, I thought, this wouldn't be a bad exercise to go
through, because it will acquaint the rest of my staff with dealing in this
world. I had already begun to work in show business and deal with personalities, rights, and all those kind of things. But these were still relatively
new ideas in Canada in general, and in my little world in particular.

"So instead of throwing Michael down the stairs, I paid Brian the
respect of treating him like an entity and carving out a sort of contracted
arrangement, when in fact he was just an employee. With all the benefits
and security of an employee. Which he appreciated, because that certainly wasn't the Canadian way."

Michael Levine had gone into negotiations hoping to secure a generous deal for Brian, and walked out with Brian owning half of his new
daily series. Which meant he would be entitled to half of any profits the
series might earn down the road.

Flushed with victory, Levine called Brian with the good news,
admittedly "very proud of the fact that I had acquired not only 50 per
cent of the program, which at that time looked like it was worth
nothing, but also a new client. Brian was not amused by this. And for
the rest of his life he could never get over the fact that I actually liked
Moses Znaimer."

☆

The year 1973 was a banner year for movies – one of those when celluloid magic strikes again and again and again, when newcomers and
veterans all seem to hit the mark. A scrappy young writer-director named
Martin Scorsese was making a name for himself with a potent little
film called *Mean Streets*. Terrence Malick directed Martin Sheen and

Sissy Spacek in *Badlands*. George Lucas gave us *American Graffiti*. William Friedkin frightened us with *The Exorcist*. Nicolas Roeg made us look now, especially at Donald Sutherland and Julie Christie, in *Don't Look Now*. Sydney Pollack seduced us with *The Way We Were*. New-force-on-the-block Peter Bogdanovich teamed matinee idol Ryan O'Neal with his young daughter Tatum in *Paper Moon*. Federico Fellini delivered *Amarcord*, Ingmar Bergman showed us *Scenes From a Marriage*, and François Truffaut gave us *Day for Night*. If you were going to launch a new television talk show about the arts, hiring a host who was steeped in both classic and current cinema was not such a shabby idea. So when Citytv launched a new daily interview show in 1973, they took a flyer on Brian Linehan. *City Lights* was a thirty-minute show with Linehan, a coffee table, and a celebrity guest.

"I have always chosen people for their idiosyncrasies rather than their smoothness," says Moses Znaimer. "'Smooth' slides off your eyes and blends in with all the other 'professionals.' But Brian was oddball enough for me to realize that he would make a dent on the air for precisely that oddball quality."

Behind the camera was Jane Fairley, who directed several other Citytv shows, including *City Pulse*, *Sweet City Woman*, and *The Money Game*. "You just stayed in the control room. The sets moved," Fairley remembers. "I said to Brian, I'd like to do our push shot here, and move the camera to the opposite angle over there, and I really think that would give your show a better look. And he said, 'I just want one thing, Jane. Would you please keep the coffee table clean?'"

A future vice president of Citytv, Marcia Martin was working on the switchboard when *City Lights* went on the air. After she passed Switchboard 101, she got to work with Brian as a script assistant. Monday through Friday, studio time from two to four was reserved for *City Lights*. "The crews were sometimes very raw, and very unprofessional," says Marcia. "We were all learning on the job. But everyone snapped to attention when it was time for *City Lights*. Brian was demanding, but he never demanded more of you than he did of himself. He was on a first-name basis with everyone on the crew, but on the set he called every grip, every soundman, every cameraman, by their surnames. It was Mr. This and Ms. That. Very cordial, but very professional, and the crew had to rise to meet his standards. We had to be on our toes for him. Because he was on his toes for us."

Jane Fairley agrees. "Sometimes the tapes would snap." She rolls her eyes. "Quite often, in fact. Or the light would pop. And I do mean *the* light. And I would have to go out into the studio to speak to him. He would be sitting with his guest, ready to roll, and I would say, 'Mr. Linehan, we are experiencing a small technical difficulty, and we hope to have it corrected shortly.' And he would turn to his guest and say, 'This is my director, Ms. Jane Fairley,' and introduce you to his guest. And suddenly you weren't just another cog in the wheel. And suddenly you were ready to do anything to make it work."

Jane Fairley was one of the first to sense the impact that Brian's one-on-one interviews were having on Citytv audiences, not to mention potential advertisers. "We had no money and only two black-and-white ENG cameras, and we were running movies and bits and pieces of this and that: How to Exercise and Not Lose Weight," she says. "And suddenly there are movie stars waiting in the lobby, and people are buzzing, and suddenly we're a force to be reckoned with. Because the big guys are coming. And they aren't coming to *The City Show*."

By starting *City Lights*, Moses Znaimer had generated one of the major paradoxes of Citytv, because in his view the show demonstrated what he still regards as a "pandering devotion" to Hollywood. "On one hand I was going to be movie-based, which made me dependent on Hollywood," he admits. "But at the same time I wanted the station's personality to emphasize the local, the Canadian, the original." The irony was not lost on Znaimer, who saw *City Lights* "as an antithesis of what I was trying to do. Which was to build a Canadian star system of some kind."

At that time Canadian media, like the Canadian public, were obsessed with U.S.-manufactured celebrity. Canada, then as now, lacked the media propaganda machinery to adequately support its artists and help make them household names. Star-laden American talk shows designed to promote movies, books, and television shows continued to dominate daytime and late-night Canadian television. *City Lights* was a refreshing and unexpected antidote. On Brian Linehan's show, Canadian artists got the same air time and the same on-camera treatment as any American movie star.

"It also became very clear," says Znaimer, "that Brian's show was a way of getting personalities to the station. At the beginning, of course, we were number one hundred in a field of five or six. So anything that would stimulate people to find Queen Street East – which was also the tenderloin of Toronto at the time – was going to be a good thing."

Linehan's guest list was quickly seen as a video version of *Who's Who in the Arts*. We had all seen one-on-one talk shows before, but we had never seen anything quite like this one. ABC had hired Dick Cavett in 1968 to compete with Merv Griffin, Johnny Carson, and other talk show hosts he had worked for as a writer. Occasionally, Cavett would devote an entire show to a single guest – Katharine Hepburn, Orson Welles, Alfred Hitchcock, Fred Astaire, Woody Allen, Lucille Ball, David Bowie. But his stint at ABC was now over. U.K. pond-hopper David Frost had already won a following for his star-based specials in the United States, but only fared well in the ratings if his interview subject was popular with his viewers. And at NBC's *Today* show Barbara Walters was still a dark horse in the celebrity interview sweepstakes; another four years would pass before she would secure her headline-grabbing sessions with Egyptian president Anwar Sadat and Israeli prime minister Menachem Begin.

In Canada, Carole Taylor had graduated from her interview show to coveted host positions on CTV's *Canada AM* and *W5*, and radio talk show host Larry Solway had taken a fairly aggressive run at a nightly TV talk show. Most successful of all Canadian TV talk show hosts was Pierre Berton, whose elegant one-on-one interviews on CTV enjoyed a spectacularly long run starting in 1962. But Berton wanted to move on to other projects, and in 1973, as *City Lights* made its modest debut, Berton and his indefatigable trail-blazing producer Elsa Franklin signed off. Consequently, the timing for Brian's debut as an Arts interviewer, in a field about to be vacated by some of his key potential competitors, was fortuitous.

No one knew quite what to make of Linehan or *City Lights* when the show started. By the current media standards, this host was hardly an eight-by-ten glossy. Impeccably groomed, he displayed elegant manners and didn't look or sound like anyone else on television. He also looked like he had just won the Irish sweepstakes; had we ever seen anyone on television, *ever*, who looked so thrilled to be there? Viewers who tuned in found themselves strangely attracted to the show, almost mesmerized by the presence of its off-kilter host. He was different, something to see.

Across town at the public broadcaster, legendary entertainer Juliette – still Canada's favourite blonde – was fascinated by CBC alumnus Moses Znaimer's progress with Citytv, and was particularly taken with Linehan. "People were amazed at the way he looked," she says candidly. "He wasn't your normal TV interviewer type. He had a look that was quite different, a look that probably some producers couldn't come to grips with. He didn't have the looks for his times.

"Today, of course, his looks would be completely accepted and not even questioned. I mean, look at Mick Jagger! That ain't no beauty, my dear! But back then Brian looked almost as if he had been in a car accident. His face wasn't a well-chiselled face. He looked like a boxer who had had his face bashed in a couple of times. Looking back, I think maybe he was darn lucky to be doing what he was doing at that time."

Linehan's friend and former acting teacher Janine Manatis was thrilled for her pupil. "I would never have thought that Brian would be a TV 'personality,'" she admits with typical candour. "Absolutely not." As his teacher she saw aspects of his personality that she believed people would not find appealing. "What overcame that, in my opinion, was the brilliance of his ability, which was to me absolutely unique. How he investigated, found out, looked into, and came up with information. *Information.* Not gossip. Gossip is the conversation of cowards. What Brian came up with was *not* gossip!"

What Brian came up with was research. And yes, he really did do his own research. Not just in those early years, but for all the years that followed. "I thought that you went home at night and you had a big folder and you read a book and you did your homework," he said later. "I'd never heard the term *researchers.* This was Citytv! Everybody had three jobs. It never, ever dawned on me that there was anything unusual about it."

If the stars he interviewed were dazzled by him, and they were, it wasn't just because of his research. It was the way he used it to connect the dots to take them places they had never been before in an interview, regardless of what book or film they had come on his show to sell.

"You went into the Navy," he told Peter O'Toole. "You came out of the Navy two years later and applied for a scholarship at RADA. Which you indeed won. You came out of RADA and went straight to the Bristol Old Vic. What was happening to you during the two years in the Navy as a signalman and a decoder in the submarine services?"

O'Toole stared at him, obviously intrigued. "You're a very interesting man," he remarked.

Peggy Lee listened politely as Brian spoke about the rigours of touring. At least, that's what she thought they were going to be talking about.

"Someone asked you," he reminded her, "if there was any place you hadn't been, and you said, 'Paris, unless you count standing at Orly, waiting to get on another plane.'"

Peggy nodded knowingly.

"And yet you wrote a song about Paris . . ."

Peggy's eyes fluttered in surprise. "Why yes, I did! . . ."

". . . after looking at a painting . . ." he continued.

Peggy's eyes lit up. "I'm impressed with you. I really am."

Jane Fairley was constantly impressed by Brian's ease with visiting stars. "He was so captivating to those guests. He enveloped them in a feeling of security and safety. They weren't going to be pounced on. They were actually going to be asked about their craft. Brian was so good with people." Interview subjects were so taken by his manner, and his questions, that they remember it as being the fastest half-hour in show business. "You were on, you were off," Carole Shelley says.

Shooting Linehan's show, Jane Fairley recalls, "was slightly complicated by the fact that we didn't have any money." She still remembers novelist Peter Benchley coming in for his interview and excitedly handing her a tape of exclusive footage from Steven Spielberg's future blockbuster about a monster shark.

"I've got this two-inch tape from the movie version of my book *Jaws* that we can play," he told her, his eyes dancing.

"Sorry," she told him, "we've only got two machines, and they're both playing back commercials."

"So we didn't play the tape," says Fairley, with a rueful chuckle – "the tape that would have captivated the country – because we only had two machines."

For most of his years on camera, Linehan's interviews were live-to-tape. No editing. No sweetening. One time, after Brian and I had become friends, we spotted Barbara Walters in the lobby of the Beverly Wilshire hotel in L.A. "She does very good interviews," said Brian matter-of-factly.

"Yes," I agreed, "she does some very good work. But, you know, she should be good – she's shooting five-to-one."

"Oh, yes," he said, "I suppose you're right."

Later, in my rental car on our way to dinner, he shrugged his shoulders and said, "All right, I give up: What's five-to-one?"

I explained that shooting five-to-one meant you shot five times as much tape as you needed. So if you needed twenty minutes, you would shoot about two hours of interview, and take the best twenty minutes from that.

"*Really?*" He had never done anything that wasn't live-to-tape. "Is that really how Barbara Walters does her interviews?"

"Brian," I told him, "the joke here in Hollywood is that they cry to get her *to leave!*"

☆

At first Brian was too excited not to show his feelings on camera. He was so thrilled with his life, so thrilled with his job, that half the time he couldn't wipe the grin off his face no matter how hard he tried. Not that he tried all that hard. Not that he tried at all. And why would he? By the mid-1970s, he was sitting across from all the people he admired and respected – keeping company on camera with actors, dancers, directors, designers, novelists. He was getting noticed. He was getting praised. He was getting invited.

I was already a seasoned veteran on the Hollywood press circuit when Brian received his first invitation from Tinsel Town. It was something special – a once-in-a-lifetime event. Founded in 1924, Columbia Pictures was throwing a fiftieth birthday party for itself, and a handful of major U.S. press had been invited to attend. Brian was informed that only two invitations were being issued for Canada – "one for George, and one for you." He was delighted.

A few weeks later, we were on the same American Airlines flight to Los Angeles, sipping champagne in first class, courtesy of Columbia Pictures. As an over-privileged child who had grown up to be an over-privileged adult, I was no stranger to first-class travel, but it was exotic and extravagant for Brian. He seemed to be transfixed by the whole experience, and remained elegantly aloof when the stewardess came by, as she did constantly, to refresh our crystal champagne flutes.

That night Columbia sent a car and driver to bring us from the hotel to the studio back lot in Burbank. Set decorators and designers had transformed one of the sound stages into a white-on-white banquet hall with a long head table running down the middle of it. Sitting near the centre of the table were Barbra Streisand and Charles Bronson and a clutch of other stars, flanked by high-powered directors like John Huston and high-powered producers like Ray Stark. Mae West, a vision in a white satin pantsuit, was holding court at one end of the room, while

Groucho Marx, a vision in anyone's vocabulary, held court at the other end. All of them had made pots of money for the studio at one time or another, and all of them were discreetly on display – well, discreetly by Hollywood standards – for the rest of us to gawk at.

Jon Peters was Streisand's escort and as usual looked like he'd rather be anywhere else. I stopped by to say hello and cheered him up briefly when I reported that Mae West had already expressed her disappointment that Chasen's, the legendary Hollywood restaurant, was catering the dinner. Again. ("Don't they know anyone else's phone number?" Mae had grumbled softly to me. "I mean, how much chili con carne can anyone eat?")

I also stopped to chat with Bronson and his wife, Jill Ireland, one of my favourite people. Back at our table Brian was taking it all in. He was holding court too, entertaining the wives of two Columbia publicity chiefs when I returned. I offered to introduce him to Jill.

"If you're going to introduce me to somebody," he said, "introduce me to Mae West."

I brought him over to her table. After getting a reluctant okay from her constant companion-cum-bodyguard Paul Novak, I crouched down so she wouldn't have to look up.

"Miss West," I said, "I'd like you to meet Brian Linehan from Toronto."

Mae nodded languidly and accepted his outstretched hand.

"It's an honour to meet you," said Brian.

Mae smiled, just long enough to acknowledge that she agreed with him. Then she withdrew her hand and resumed the conversation she was having when we first intruded.

The next day, as we waited for our flight back to Toronto, sipping champagne in the Admiral's Club, Brian said he hoped Citytv would keep him on the air.

"I thought you were doing so well!" I said. "Are the ratings down?"

He laughed. "What ratings? The Citytv signal doesn't go as far as Eglinton Avenue. We don't have enough reach to get rated!" He shook his head. He was getting lots of press, and lots of interest, "but they've never heard of me past St. Clair."

Which wasn't true, of course. My family and I lived in the wilds of suburban Scarborough, about sixteen miles from downtown Toronto, and we could tune in to Citytv. And we did.

"Okay, I'm exaggerating," he admitted. "But not by much."

We had another glass of champagne, and he told me he was going back to Hamilton next weekend, for another family function. I asked how his family was reacting to his new and sudden celebrity.

His sister, he said, was so proud of him that she carried a copy of *TV Guide* in her purse, which she would produce at the drop of a hint, happy to show friends and acquaintances ("and probably total strangers") the TV listing that read CITY LIGHTS: Host Brian Linehan.

"That's sweet," I said. "Tell me, what does she think of your show?"

"Oh, she's never seen it," he said with a shrug. "None of them have seen it. Maybe you can get *City Lights* in Scarborough, but you sure can't get it in Hamilton."

The flight from L.A. to Toronto was a breeze. We guzzled champagne all the way home.

Brian Linehan thought about the white-on-white sound stage and the chili from Chasen's and Barbra and Jon and Mae and Groucho, and the line of shiny black limousines that stretched as far as the eye could see. And he smiled. Like Noel Coward, he'd been to a marvellous party.

It would be the first of many.

4

"You know more about me than I do!"

When Brian Linehan first started taping his daily shows in 1973, Citytv was a small UHF station still struggling to reach its target audience. When visiting stars came to town to promote their new movies, Linehan's name was not on their Must lists.

Many of the Toronto-based film studio executives knew Brian from his days at Odeon, and most of them were genuinely rooting for him. But because the station was still an infant in an industry of giants, it was difficult for the branch offices in Toronto to persuade their L.A. bosses that something special was happening at Citytv.

Brian's relationships with local studio publicists were ambivalent. Most of them had met him when he was at Odeon or Janus, so most of them considered him not as arm's-length media but as one of them. Because of that most of them also felt they had to be especially diligent about his constant requests for interviews with visiting stars, because they would inevitably have to justify taking a star to Citytv, a local station with a dubious address and an even more dubious reach, instead of doing three print interviews for suburban or even campus newspapers with a guaranteed readership.

When Kirk Douglas came to town to publicize *Scalawag*, a family movie in which he not only starred but had also perhaps unwisely invested, he agreed to be interviewed by the *Globe and Mail*, the *Toronto Star*, and the *Toronto Sun*, plus a couple of national television types. Studio publicity honchos wanted to make the most of his limited availability by booking him with big-audience media outlets. As usual Brian had petitioned Paramount, the studio releasing *Scalawag*, to bring Douglas to *City Lights*. Bob Yankovitch, director of advertising and publicity for Paramount in Canada, turned him down, for all the right business reasons. Despite Brian's impassioned entreaties, there was no room for Linehan and his fledgling station on the list.

Enter Dianne Schwalm, a young woman who would play a significant role in Brian Linehan's professional life for years to come. Dianne was working as Bob Yankovitch's assistant, taking care of all the intricate, occasionally messy Girl Friday details her boss didn't want to handle. After Yankovitch turned him down, Brian turned to Dianne.

"He came to me," she remembers, "and he said, 'You've got to help me do this. I'm the best person for this. I know *everything* about his life. I can do a great job.' And I was fairly new to the business as well. But you know Brian; he just captured your heart because he was so sincere and sweet, and he made you feel like you were an important person in his life, and an integral part to what he wanted to achieve."

Brian asked Dianne for a favour. "I'm going to write a letter," he informed her. "Will you personally make sure it gets handed to Mr. Douglas?"

"Oh my God, are you kidding me?" said Dianne apprehensively.

"Dianne," Brian persisted, "just slip it to him. No one has to know you gave it to him. Mr. Yankovitch will never know how he got it. It could be the hotel that delivered it. You just say, 'Oh, this came for you.'"

Dianne wanted to help, but she also wanted to keep her job.

When Douglas landed in Toronto, Dianne Schwalm and Bob Yankovitch picked him up at the airport and checked him into the then-Hyatt hotel in Yorkville.

"We were in the big suite on the thirty-second floor," Dianne recalls. "Mr. Yankovitch went into the bedroom to use the phone in there, and I took out the letter that Brian had given me. It had *Mr. Kirk Douglas* written on the envelope in Brian's beautiful penmanship."

She handed it to Douglas. "Oh, this came for you." She smiles softly, remembering. "And of course he's standing there, a big movie star in an empty suite, with two people he doesn't know, and at the moment there is nothing better to do than open the mail. So he opens up the letter."

In a few lines, Brian revealed an uncommon grasp of the actor's humble beginnings, only one of several things they had in common in addition to their Slavic roots. If Kirk Douglas wanted to do the same old interviews and give the same old answers to the same old questions, that was his prerogative. But if Issur Danielovitch Demsky (Douglas's real name) wanted to do a real interview, with questions even he hadn't heard before, with someone who actually knew his body of work, then he should show up at Citytv between two and four, the only time Brian could tape an interview.

Bob Yankovitch came back into the living room and wondered what Douglas was reading. Dianne was busying herself, meticulously underlining names already on the interview schedule, "like I have *no idea* what he's reading."

Douglas wandered into the bedroom, then came back out again. Holding the letter in his hand and looking straight at Dianne, he said, "I want to see this guy."

"Oh, okay," said Dianne, determined to keep playing dumb. "And who might that be?"

Douglas handed her the letter. Bob Yankovitch took it out of her hand and examined it. He saw Brian's signature and frowned at Dianne.

"Beats me!" said Dianne, replying to his frown with an innocent shrug. "So . . . shall I go ahead and set that up?" Her boss, she recalls, "almost had fire coming out of his ears."

She called Brian. "You're in."

At two-thirty that afternoon, Kirk Douglas walked into the lobby of Citytv and said, "I'm here to do an interview with Brian Linehan." The station was buzzing in seconds. Douglas, an old hand at causing excitement, was enjoying every minute of it.

"And there's Brian," Dianne remembers fondly. "Not going to the star, ever; always waiting on set. And, as always, impeccably dressed, impeccably groomed, with that head of hair we'd all die for. And then, stepping down off the riser to greet him. 'Mr. Douglas, thank you, it's so good of you to come.'"

As he was being miked, Douglas reached into his breast pocket, pulled out a folded piece of paper bearing Linehan's ornate, easily identifiable handwriting, and held it up in the air for all to see. "I'm here today," Douglas told the crew, "because this man wrote me a letter."

Nervous but energized, Brian began the interview. Douglas flashed his best movie-star smile, tilting his head so the light would catch the famous cleft in his chin.

Ten minutes later, he seemed to have forgotten all about the camera and was leaning forward, fascinated, wondering where Brian would take him next.

When they took a two-minute, eleven-second break so the director could roll in some commercials, Douglas slumped in his chair. He was more than flattered. He was flabbergasted. "Jesus, Linehan!" he murmured appreciatively. "You know more about me than *I* do!"

Uncommon research would become Brian's trademark. And his party trick. Let Barbara Walters make them cry. He would dazzle the stars with his research, illuminating shadowy moments, long forgotten or repressed, from the past. He would remind them of significant moments in their lives, frequently having to explain to them why those moments were significant. They would be enchanted, entranced, mesmerized. "How did you know that? Who told you that? I've never told *anyone* that." It was music to his ears, and Citytv was humming right along with him.

Broadway legend Carol Channing, in town with her one-woman show, turned to the camera in the middle of her interview and told us, in case we hadn't already figured it out, that "this young man is *amazing!*"

He continued to amaze. He'd seen a lot of movies, and stored the best parts of most of them in his amazing memory bank.

While Brian was honing his act at Citytv, the "Little Paper That Grew" (a.k.a. the *Toronto Sun*) was still having growing pains. At the beginning, I was pretty much a one-man Entertainment department. Bob Blackburn filed a daily TV column, and I did everything else, including a daily column and most of the interviews, movie reviews, and theatre reviews. I only had time (and space) to cover the main events, from the creation of the Canadian company of *A Chorus Line* to the return of the Rolling Stones. Some of our former colleagues from the now-defunct *Toronto Telegram*, whose demise had given birth to the *Sun*, volunteered to help us out with theatre and concert reviews if the show in question held some appeal for them. John Fraser delivered a couple of highbrow dance reviews before going on to carve out a new career for himself at the *Globe and Mail*; former *Telegram* drama critic DuBarry Campau brought us some succinct, well-versed reviews on new Canadian theatre offerings.

It was DuBarry, in her own way every bit as exotic as her name, who tipped me to the fact that Brian Linehan's roommate, Dr. Zane Wagman, was a classical-music aficionado of uncommon taste and knowledge. Perhaps, she suggested, I should ask Dr. Wagman to write something for us.

The next time I saw Brian, I mentioned the matter to him. The next day, Dr. Wagman called to say he'd be delighted to give it a shot. His byline appeared for the first time in the *Sun* the following week: By ZANE WAGMAN.

My secret weapon at the *Sun*, the quietly brilliant Kathy Brooks, who kept our Entertainment pages on track, gently reminded me that lovers of classical music were unlikely to reach for a Toronto tabloid to get their serious music fix. We both knew that serious music was off target for us and that we needed to refocus on the pop music audience whose attention was essential to our future success.

I stopped asking Zane Wagman and John Fraser for classical music reviews.

By now I was getting to know Brian. He had told me at one point how he and his roommate Dr. Wagman planned to buy old houses, live in them while they fixed them up, realize substantial profits, and then buy a bigger old house and do it again. The end goal of this ambitious game plan was to end up, somewhere down the line, living in a wonderful new house that all their other houses had paid for.

"Isn't that a clever idea?" I remarked to my wife, Gail. I think she was pregnant with our third child at the time.

"Very clever," she agreed. "And perfect for two single guys." (She might have said DINKS – i.e., Double Income No Kids – but that acronym had yet to be coined.)

"Oh, by the way," I added, "I don't think they want anyone to know."

"Know what? That they buy and sell houses?" Gail shook her head. "Who cares?"

"I dunno," I said with a shrug. "I just sort of got that feeling. From Brian."

"Well, you can tell them not to worry," replied Gail, with just a soupçon of sarcasm. "Their 'secret' is safe with me!"

And, of course, it was. Mainly because we didn't know they had one.

☆

Brian Linehan wasn't on the A-list yet, but he was getting closer. And then an invitation to his first movie junket arrived.

Brian knew all about junkets, both from his days at Odeon and from his own insatiable research. It was the mid-1970s, and studios were changing the way they did business. In the old days, they would send their stars on the road, for two to three weeks at a time, transporting them from city to city to promote a new movie. It was an expensive proposition, usually involving an entourage composed of hair-and-makeup artists, the star's personal assistants, and his or her travelling companion of choice, plus studio publicity executives and occasional friends whose job it was to keep the star happy during the endless rounds of wardrobe changes and print interviews. Presidential suites were reserved in five-star hotels from coast to coast. Limousines and their drivers were booked months in advance. It was a costly operation, but it got the job done. And, at that time, there seemed to be no reasonable alternative.

Studios saved junkets for special event films, luring the press with on-set interviews in foreign, and sometimes exotic, locations. On one occasion, Warner Bros. had flown a plane full of press to the Bahamas, for a five-day junket in which they unveiled four new films, making the stars of each film available for interviews. On another occasion, they took a bunch of press pals to the screening of a new Warner Bros. flick at the Cannes Film Festival. And in careful consideration of their hefty investment in the screen version of *Man of La Mancha*, United Artists brought two dozen North American press to Spain to interview Peter O'Toole and Sophia Loren. But such upscale events were the exception, not the rule.

Now times had changed, again. Actors were no longer prisoners of the studio system. Although contractually obligated to promote their films, almost all of them balked at the mere suggestion of a cross-country tour. Their agents and managers were acutely aware of the fact that three weeks on the road promoting a movie was three weeks during which their client would not be earning money. Such excursions could benefit only studio coffers – and what was the percentage in that? New clauses and catchphrases started to appear in more and more contracts. The bigger the star, the less time he or she would be willing to surrender for promotion. One star might agree to do ten days of publicity, another might draw the line at five days, and some wouldn't commit at all.

One day, someone in Hollywood figured out that if you brought all the key cities to the star, instead of trying to bring the star to the cities, it might be possible to maximize national press coverage without ever leaving L.A. At first blush, the cost of flying three dozen journalists to Los Angeles, from all parts of the country, was presumed prohibitive. But when the accountants started to crunch the numbers, they realized that importing press, *and* putting them up in a hotel for two nights, *and* feeding them, was not nearly as expensive as they had imagined it would be. Not only was it comparable with sending a star out on the road, but it also suggested unexplored economies of scale. Costs for a one-film junket would be charged to that film's publicity budget; costs for a two-film junket, using the same hotel space and the same airline tickets, could be split between the two films. And sharing a junket with another studio could prove to be even more cost-effective, even if more money was spent to razzle-dazzle the visiting firemen.

By the time the accountants and the studio executives compared notes, the junket had become the new Hollywood art form, and it was considered *de rigueur* to the selling of any major release, from *Rocky* to *Heaven's Gate*.

Some media outlets had a No Junkets policy, which was strictly enforced. Others were less adamant about it. I had previously worked at a newspaper where junkets were regarded as opportunities, not liabilities. The philosophy at the *Toronto Telegram* was based on trust in the integrity of its employees. Publisher John Bassett believed that if a movie studio could buy you for an airline ticket, they could buy you for a free meal. And if you could be bought in the first place, you probably weren't worth the free meal.

We worked according to a similar philosophy at the *Toronto Sun*. As far as I was concerned, the studios were acting as a catalyst between the press, whom they were constantly wooing, and the movies, which they needed to publicize. In most cases, the *Sun* was happy to have the stories but, in truth, didn't need them. If the paper didn't run *my* interview with Meryl Streep, we could run a wire-service interview with her. We paid an annual fee for the service, so it wasn't going to cost us extra. So if the studio wanted to invite me to come to New York to do an exclusive with Meryl, the *Sun* was happy to have the story – happier, in fact – as long as it didn't cost us any more money. And if the studio insisted on picking up the tab, well, so much the better.

Brian and I were both blessed by the circumstances of our particular market. Toronto was a bellwether city for movie studios, a statistical anomaly. Movies in Toronto grossed far more than they did in other cities with similar population bases. It was not uncommon to see a hit film held over again and again; *Annie Hall, 2001: A Space Odyssey, Fiddler on the Roof,* and a handful of other films played for more than a year in the same movie house in Toronto, and even films as specifically American as *Apocalypse Now* and *Yentl* often fared better at the box office in Toronto than they did in New York or Los Angeles. Toronto had and continues to have the best movie audiences in the world – witness its world-renowned film festival, which was born in the 1970s as well. So

Brian and I had an unusual advantage over most of our U.S. colleagues. We were preaching to the converted. And we were grateful to be doing so.

We also had home advantage, because writers from the *Globe and Mail* and the *Toronto Star* and reporters at CBC Television were not allowed to accept studio-subsidized flights and hotel rooms. All three venerable media institutions had a strict No Junkets policy, which they diligently upheld and frequently bragged about.

After former *Toronto Telegram* film critic and veteran Hollywood junket-goer Clyde Gilmour was hired to review movies for the *Toronto Star*, we met in New York for the premiere of *Last Tango in Paris*. Because it was such a controversial film, the *Star* had agreed to fund Clyde's trip to New York. But it was extremely inconvenient for him, because all of the arranged interviews took place in our hotel, where he wasn't allowed to stay, or at a studio-hosted lunch, which he wasn't allowed to attend.

"Can I stay in the same hotel," he asked his boss at the *Star*, "if I promise to not like the movie?" His boss was not amused. So Clyde had to turn down my invitation to join us for lunch. "Because you never know," he added, with a wink, "I might get corrupted just sitting next to you."

If a star was "hot" enough, CBC Television would sometimes send arts reporter David Gilmour (no relation to Clyde) to a junket to get an exclusive one-on-one interview. He would arrive with his own camera crew, either travelling with him from Toronto or hired freelance in New York or Los Angeles. Studio publicists would provide him with a separate room, so his crew had time to set up the lighting and position the cameras.

I remember when he came to the Century Plaza hotel in Los Angeles one time to do a shoot with Sylvester Stallone. As I recall, Stallone had already done about eighteen TV interviews, but had agreed to give Gilmour ten minutes. Two hours earlier, Brian had done a full twenty minutes with Stallone, with a camera crew provided by the studio. He would be taking his interview tapes with him on his flight back to Toronto, flying first class on a ticket provided by the studio, and was almost certain to get his session with Sly on the air before the CBC would get to telecast Gilmour's interview.

On another occasion, the *Globe* and the *Star* both picked up the tabs for their film critics, Jay Scott and Ron Base respectively, to attend the New York junket for *Yentl*, so they could secure interviews with its star, first-time director Barbra Streisand. Informed that Toronto was a highly competitive and extremely valuable movie market, Streisand agreed to see all three of us – together. We walked into her hotel suite, took turns (more or less) asking her questions, then left her suite together. Each of us shaped the information in our own particular style, but considering the fact that we all ended up with pretty much the same interview, did it really matter who was picking up the bill for the hotel room?

Shortly after that Jay and Ron seemed to be turning up on a lot more junkets. Maybe their bosses decided to make exceptions for special occasions. But from a competitive perspective, both Brian and I were absolutely in favour of maintaining a strict No Junket policy, just as long as it didn't apply to us.

I had also observed that certain U.S. writers were always the last to arrive on L.A. junkets, even though some were coming from nearby states like Colorado, Texas, and Oklahoma, and were much closer to California than we were. I got the feeling, more than once, that they couldn't get there sooner because they had to finish their regular workday first; and that in some cases they would just "disappear" on Friday afternoon and reappear Monday morning with new stories for their columns or their editors. Maybe it was a see-no-evil kind of thing. If these writers didn't ask their editors for permission to go, if they went to L.A. on their own time, and, ostensibly, their own dime, perhaps their editors were happy (or at least willing) to look the other way. The stories those writers brought home could spark their entertainment pages for weeks. Still, it was clearly a delicate balance for some.

Brian's first junket invitation came from United Artists, which had been watching his progress with great interest. Encouraged by reports from its Toronto office, UA invited him on its New Orleans junket for a sneak preview of a film called *Thunderbolt & Lightfoot* by a new apparently-Italian director named Michael Cimino.

It was also the first junket for a beautiful blonde entertainment reporter named Sue Lumsden, who had just joined Global Television and was married to Jim Monaco, a publicity executive at A&M Records in Toronto. She and Brian were both excited and nervous when they met me in Air Canada's first-class lounge in the Toronto airport, and Sue kept glancing apprehensively at her watch.

"Relax, relax," I assured them. "We have tons of time."

Brian looked somewhat skeptical but graciously deferred to my expertise. Since this was his first junket, and since I was an old pro at junkets, he and Sue would put themselves entirely in my hands.

We relaxed.

We missed our flight.

Sue was shocked. Brian was crestfallen. I was, frankly, stunned. And feeling more than a little guilty.

"What do we do now?" asked Sue. "Should we call and tell them we're not coming?"

"Hold it!" said Brian. "They're not showing the movie till eight o'clock tonight. And we don't start our interviews till tomorrow morning."

We went back to the lounge. "Oh dear, did you miss your flight, Mr. Anthony?" It was good to have friends in first class. "Well, we'll just have to get you another one. Why don't you and your friends just relax and have a drink, and we'll get on the phone. Don't you worry, we'll get you there!"

And they did. Not only in time for the movie, but also in time to join our fellow junketeers for dinner *before* the movie. When we arrived at the restaurant, Brian immediately made his way to a table dominated by Toronto media, including Janine Manatis, who was now freelancing as a film critic on television, and Canadian film historian Gerald Pratley. I had quite naturally gravitated to a table occupied by some of my U.S. colleagues, including two writers who would become personal favourites of Brian's, local New Orleans writer Al Shea and bubbly San Francisco scribe Barbara Bladen. Unbeknownst to me, Brian had already reserved a chair for me at the Toronto table. Seeing me sit down at a table of strangers, he assumed I thought there was no room left at his table and soon came over to quietly invite me to join them. I thanked him for saving me a seat but assured him I was happy where I was.

"But we're all sitting over there," he said softly, obviously puzzled.

"Brian," I whispered, so he alone could hear me, "I didn't come to New Orleans to sit with Canadians."

He looked at me and blinked. Hard. I could hear the pennies dropping. Years later he would still remind me of that moment. "One of the best travel tips you ever gave me," he would say.

The star of *Thunderbolt & Lightfoot*, by some happy coincidence, was an actor Brian had trotted around Toronto and Hamilton almost a decade earlier: Clint Eastwood, now a bona fide box-office giant. United Artists provided on-camera interviews with Cimino (who had also written the script), Clint (who was responsible for Cimino getting the chance to direct), and Clint's co-star, Jeff Bridges (who would earn an Oscar nomination for Best Supporting Actor for his performance).

In retrospect, some critics saw the emotionally stunted characters of this off-kilter action drama as a precursor to Cimino's seminal film,

The Deer Hunter. But before it opened, *Thunderbolt & Lightfoot* was simply regarded as The New Clint Eastwood Movie. And that was all most moviegoers, and movie-star interviewers, needed to know.

On Saturday morning, we did our print interviews. On Saturday afternoon, Brian gave United Artists executives their first taste of what a Linehan interview looked like. They were unabashedly gobsmacked. On Saturday night, after a spectacular dinner at the Commander's Palace, we joined Eastwood on a Bourbon Street jazz prowl, ending up at Preservation Hall, where Clint, Brian, and I and a few others happily sat cross-legged on the floor, at the feet of some of the greatest blues players in New Orleans.

A sudden spring rain ended almost as soon as it started. It left the French Quarter looking like a movie set under the street lamps. The night was sultry and the air was sweet with the fragrance of fresh blossoms. Bliss.

Brian Linehan was one happy fella. He loved everybody, and everybody loved him. Well, almost everybody. A few TV people had complained that Brian was given more time with Clint than they were.

Carl Ferrazza, the man who ran the crackerjack UA junket unit, feigned surprise. "Oh, did you want more time?" he said to them. "Because when we asked you, you said seven minutes was more than enough." Carl knew that most of the TV people on the junket were taping interviews for three-to-five-minute news spots. They didn't need more time. They just didn't want anyone else to get more time than they did. Especially the Canadian guy with the pages of handwritten notes. What was he doing, a TV interview or a Ph.D.?

"Carl," said Brian *sotto voce*, "I hope I haven't made trouble for you."

Carl Ferrazza laughed out loud and put his arm around Brian's shoulder. "I did *my* job, Brian, and you did yours." He smiled. "I hope we'll be seeing a lot of each other from now on."

When Carl got back to New York, he started to sing Brian's praises. When Brian got back to Toronto, he received a phone call from a publicist from another studio, which was planning an elaborate junket in Chicago and was hoping that Brian might be able to fit it into his busy schedule.

Brian Linehan was now on the Hollywood A-list. He would stay on it — almost always at the top of it — for the next sixteen years.

5

"Pipe down, or I'll kick you in your good leg!"

Ask Dianne Schwalm and she'll tell you that after Brian had scored interviews with Kirk Douglas and Clint Eastwood, "everybody knew that [his] show was the show you had to be on when you came to Toronto. And it was the icing on the cake. It was Talk to George, Talk to Brian, and suddenly you were the star's favourite place, the best city on their tour." From Paramount alone, Dianne delivered Robert Mitchum, Jack Lemmon, Robert Towne, Peter Bogdanovich, Mariel Hemingway, and Cybill Shepherd to Brian at Citytv. Interviews were frequently followed by private, often extravagant lunches and dinners with the stars. "And there would be laughing and drinking all night long. Brian was a master at nurturing relationships."

Toronto Sun film critic Bruce Kirkland believes Linehan's career lasted as long as it did "because he had real, in-depth conversations with people. And it wasn't a one-way street. Every time I would interview Anthony Hopkins, the first thing he would say was 'Have you seen Brian Linehan recently? Oh I just so love that man. Those were the best interviews I ever had.' And this is from someone who's been interviewed thousands of times, and normally hates it. His interviews with Brian Linehan still stand out in his mind to this day, because it's all about engaging with the heart of a person, as opposed to, 'Okay, we've got to get you to say something in fifteen seconds that sounds really cool or exciting or controversial.'"

Stars respected Brian for his knowledge, Dianne agrees. "But he was also the life of the party. He was the court jester."

In the years that followed, Brian Linehan redefined junket protocol. There were rules for junket media, and then there were rules for

Linehan. Other TV interviewers, some with network affiliations, were given between five and ten minutes on camera with the stars they interviewed. When they got home, they produced short three-to-five-minute "items" for their local stations. Brian Linehan was given twenty minutes. When Brian got home, he produced a half-hour television show devoted to a single star. Studios trying to sell a movie knew the difference between a five-minute "hit" and a thirty-minute in-depth conversation. And so did the stars of those movies.

Other TV interviewers balked at doing on-camera sessions with "no-name" producers, screenwriters (gawd forbid!), and even supporting players; they just wanted face time with the stars. Brian welcomed every opportunity, and prepared brilliantly for all of them. On camera he gave every interview subject the same respect he gave to the stars. By doing so he also made the studio publicity executives look good, and oh-so-smart, for inviting him. And when those "no-name" producers became major players, when those "B-list" writers became producers and directors, when those "bottom-feeder" supporting players became stars, they all remembered the Canadian with the mashed-in nose who had treated them with such respect. And all of them, without exception, asked to be interviewed by him again.

Most of the time we were together on the same junkets. On one international jaunt, Carl Ferrazza and his irrepressible United Artists publicity team flew us over to London to interview producer Cubby Broccoli and Roger Moore on the mammoth set of their latest James Bond movie, *The Man with the Golden Gun*. Three days later, they took us to Munich to visit the mammoth set where Norman Jewison was directing James Caan in *Rollerball*.

We loved "roughing it" in Europe, especially when we were billeted at The Savoy in London and at The Four Seasons in Munich. We thought it fair and just compensation for the excruciating boredom we would endure spending hours on a movie set, which on an excitement level was only half a notch above watching paint dry. Happily, Carl Ferrazza and his junket specialists made sure that all our off-set activities, which almost always involved good food and wine, made up for it.

While we were in Munich, director Jewison hosted a dinner for all of us visiting firemen at which Brian was placed next to the diminutive Manhattan-based *Hollywood Reporter* columnist Radie Harris. Radie was already seated when Brian joined the table, which was designed to accommodate ten but had been set for twelve. Brian had to squeeze in between

Radie and the person on the other side of him, and Radie soon found him disarming – especially when he accidentally kicked her.

Brian was in mid-conversation with someone on the other side of the table when Radie tugged at his sleeve. "Brian, you just kicked me!"

"Oh, did I? Sorry," said Brian, returning to his conversation.

Radie was miffed. "Brian, you really kicked me, you know!"

Brian did not appreciate being interrupted for the second time.

"Radie, I said I was sorry. Now pipe down, or I'll kick you in your good leg!"

Radie's chin dropped so far it almost hit the table. She sat there slack-jawed, in shock. So did the rest of us. Brian was the only one at the table who didn't know that Radie had a wooden leg. Which, of course, was not the one he had kicked.

Blissfully oblivious to what had just gone down, Brian started to grill Radie on the Broadway scene she knew and loved so well. Radie's replies were frosty, but he persisted, and she warmed up a little.

As the dinner was winding down, a waiter appeared with a cane.

"Hold it!" said Brian. "Are you gonna sing and dance tonight, Radie? Because if you are, I wanna go get my camera!"

He stopped mid-wisecrack when he saw the waiter hand the cane to Radie. She gave him a withering look. "I'm trying to protect my good leg," she hissed as she made a slow and tentative exit.

The next morning, we clambered onto the luxury motorbus United Artists had arranged to take us to the *Rollerball* set. Brian was already on board with the rest of us when Radie hobbled onto the bus. "Radie, over here!" Brian called out almost contritely. He gestured to the empty aisle seat beside him. "I saved this spot for you."

"No thanks!" Radie replied. "I only have one good leg left!"

But she relented on the ride back to the hotel, and sat with him that night at dinner. She sent him postcards from her beloved "Dorch" – the Dorchester hotel – when she flew to London the next day. "Thanks to you," she wrote, "I now have phlebitis in my good leg, I hope you're pleased with yourself."

Brian mailed her his reply.

> *Dear Radie:*
> *Very.*
> *Regards,*
> *Brian.*

He also added a long, wonderfully funny postscript, which she adored, and they soon became friends for life.

I loved puddle-jumping to Chicago and New York for junkets because both cities were close to Toronto, less than two hours away. I liked Hollywood junkets because I could catch up on my reading: five hours in the air from YYZ to LAX, another five hours coming back, and *no phones.* (Yes, this was the 1970s.) Still, I was picky. I had young children at home, and didn't want to spend too many weekends away from them. Also, I found some junkets too rushed and too tiring. The studio would ask us to fly in on Friday, see the movie Friday night, do our interviews Saturday, and fly home again Saturday night or Sunday morning. We lost our weekends, and we got home tired. What was the point of that?

Luckily for me, studio execs went out of their way to keep me happy. When I said I didn't want to be away from home so much, they invited me to bring one of my children with me. If I complained that a proposed schedule was too tight, they would urge me to fly in one day earlier and/or leave one day later. All as the guest of the studio, of course.

Brian thought this a splendid arrangement. When a studio rep assigned to book his flights called to ask him when he wanted to travel, he would reply, "Oh, just book me on the same flights as George."

They were only too happy to do so. For one thing, they knew they wouldn't have to worry about keeping us amused if we landed twenty-four hours before the rest of the press.

"Brian loved to get all his work done so he could go down to the pool," Dianne Schwalm recalls. "I'd never seen anybody as a guest at a hotel clean up around the pool like he did. He couldn't stand to see used towels or stuff other guests had left. He'd go around and literally collect up all the magazines, *Vogue*s and *Cosmo*s and *Time* or whatever, and then take them back to his room. If people had left unruly newspapers, he would roll them all up and put them in an area where they could be disposed of, and pick up cutlery and glasses just so that the area where he'd be sitting would be neat and tidy. He would have everything he needed for the day, including the sunblock that he would slather on his lips and his nose, and he would just park himself by the pool."

No, no need to worry about Brian and George. We arrived amused. And we stay amused. And we kept a lot of other people very amused. Especially the studio executives and the stars.

Our colleagues, by and large, did not find us quite so amusing.

On one occasion, junketeers were invited to the lavish launch of a

Metro-Goldwyn-Mayer potboiler called *The Wind and the Lion*. MGM had transformed the largest studio on the lot into a veritable oasis, with palm trees, belly dancers, and sand, sand, and more sand, as far as the eye could see. The brightest star of the evening was *Wind and the Lion* leading lady Candice Bergen (her leading man, Sean Connery, had shrewdly taken a pass). Even lovelier in person than on screen, Ms. Bergen adorned the arm of MGM production chief Daniel Melnick, her steady fella at the time, at a flower-strewn head table, while hundreds of invited guests lined up for dinner at elaborate buffet tables.

A thousand stars winked back at us from the painted sky, and waiters in what appeared to be harem pants raced about the vast space offering gold goblets of wine and silver goblets of Perrier water. (Yes, Perrier. We were in Hollywood, after all, where consumption of spirits is still primarily regarded as an East Coast vice.) Impeding the speed of the brightly clad servers was their fancy footwear, curly-toed throwbacks to *Tales of the Arabian Nights*, which kept sinking in the sand. And yet, despite their exotic ensembles, the waiters looked strangely familiar.

The line at the buffet tables seemed endless, and Brian and I weren't inclined to wait in line for anything, including dinner. "At this rate we're never going to get served," Brian observed. "Maybe we should go back to the hotel."

I was about to agree when Brian suddenly recognized one of the waiters. It turned out the whole event was being catered by our favourite Moroccan restaurant in Hollywood, Dar Magribe. "Hello there!" the cheerful Dar Magribe waiter beamed. He feigned snow blindness for a moment, visually distracted by the sheer emptiness of the white damask cloth on our table. "Aren't you guys having anything to eat?"

We whined, gently, about the long lineups at the buffet.

"Aw, c'mon!" he replied with a grin. "*You guys* don't have to wait in line!" And with that, our new favourite waiter vanished, just like Aladdin's genie. Three minutes later he was back, accompanied by two other Canadian-friendly Dar Magribe waiters. While our fellow junketeers glowered from the buffet line, our genie and his pals produced plates of Moroccan delicacies and goblets of wine for everyone at our table. (Good waiters in Hollywood, like good waiters everywhere, remember good tippers and reward them with good service.)

One of them was pouring more wine for us when one of his captains approached him. "YOU," the captain admonished him, "are SUPPOSED to be looking after the HEAD TABLE."

"You mean this ISN'T the HEAD TABLE?" cried Brian, without missing a beat. And then, pretending he was about to burst into tears: "George, we're at the WRONG TABLE!!"

The captain scurried away, leaving our three waiters with us.

Later, Brian stopped by the head table just long enough to say hello to Candy Bergen, whom he had interviewed on more than one occasion and who had become a personal friend. "I'm just sitting over there with George Anthony," he said, gesturing in our direction.

"Oh, we all know where you're sitting, Brian!" Ms. Bergen replied with that sexy, throaty chuckle. "We just watch where the waiters are going."

Brian and I added to our own amusement by finding new and interesting ways to make our journeys more glamorous, more luxurious, and, always, more fun. I had discerned very early on in my showbiz travels that bigger planes were more comfortable than smaller planes, so Brian and I trained travel agents and studio executives to investigate what equipment the airline was using before confirming us on any flight. On American Airlines we preferred the DC-10; our choice of equipment on Air Canada was a Boeing 767. In a pinch, we were willing to fly on Boeing 747s, but in first class they lacked the wide-bodied living room comfort we much preferred.

Both of us were great favourites with airline attendants and airport personnel. Many of them read my column every day, and because of their erratic work hours, many of them were home in the afternoon and caught Brian on TV. My newspaper accounts of his exploits, as well as the press coverage he was starting to accumulate from other media, only worked to our advantage.

When we started commuting to Hollywood, American Airlines had the only direct flight from Toronto to Los Angeles. We always had great service on American, but one particular purser named Cynthia impressed us more than any of the others. Although she was based in California, she seemed to know a lot about us, which puzzled me.

"Half the people on this flight are reading the entertainment pages of the *Toronto Sun*," Brian observed dryly. "That could be a clue."

Whatever. In any case, our first flight with her was a delight. "It's been a pleasure having you on board," she said as we disembarked. "My face hurts from laughing so much. You guys are a riot. I hope I see you again."

"As long as you're on the Toronto–L.A. run, and as long as you don't run out of champagne," Brian responded, "you can count on it!"

Cynthia laughed again.

Ten days later, we were boarding another American Airlines flight to Los Angeles. Waiting for us in first class was Cynthia, who welcomed us with champagne. "I saw your names on the manifest," she confided, "and I've taken the liberty of changing your seats."

Configuration of the first-class section of the DC-10 was six seats across – two seats on either window side of the aircraft and two seats in the centre. For some reason unknown to us, Cynthia had reassigned us to the two middle seats in the last row of the section. Also, something new had been added. What appeared to be a dinky little coffee table was now positioned in front of the middle seats in the last row.

Brian was mildly miffed. He preferred a window seat. He always carried seven to ten pounds of reading material with him on every flight, and if no one occupied the seat next to him, he would use that tray table as a desk. He couldn't very well do that in this set-up.

"This is better," said Cynthia, politely but firmly shutting the door on further debate. She left us to assist another passenger.

"Never mind," I told Brian. "I'm sure the flight isn't full. We can switch to other seats after we take off."

He looked disdainfully at the mini coffee table. "At least I have somewhere to put my book," he said, sipping his glass of champagne.

After we were airborne, Cynthia stopped by to bring us more liquid refreshment. "Here," she said, "let me make you more comfortable." She reached under the dinky coffee table, pulled a lever, and presto! the coffee table was suddenly twelve inches higher, a perfect cocktail table. Brian and I were suitably impressed.

When it was time to serve dinner, Cynthia raised the table another six inches and produced a round tabletop that anchored snugly to the top of the existing cocktail table. She then covered it with a damask cloth, on which she prepared two place settings of American Airlines china, crystal, and silverware. "Now," she inquired, "isn't that better?"

We were dazzled, and exceedingly grateful that she had so thoughtfully reassigned our seats, which also swivelled, much to our delight. "Do all the chairs in first class swivel now?" I asked, amazed.

"No," said Cynthia, with a conspiratorial smile. "Just the chairs next to the coffee table."

Thanks to Cynthia, we had finally discovered the only way to fly.

Cynthia had a special gift for wrangling show-business refugees. And as it turns out, she came by it honestly. Her last name was Hagman. She was the cousin of headline-making *Dallas* star Larry Hagman and the niece of Broadway musical comedy legend Mary Martin.

"You already know we like you," Brian told her. "Now we like you even more."

Our Hollywood days were hardly halcyon, but they were happenin'. We worked hard, and we played hard. When Brian and I travelled together, I was partial to drinking champagne on the rocks for the five-hour haul to L.A.; Brian preferred to start with martinis, then move into the red and white wines with dinner. He would eschew the desserts (I was never so disciplined) for the cheeses, which on Air Canada were always accompanied by an excellent port. And after liqueurs, we always tried to make time for at least one more glass of champagne before we landed. If the flight got in early, of course, we had to improvise. A studio limo was usually sent to greet us at LAX, and our drivers were always happy to make a stop en route for more champagne so we wouldn't arrive at the hotel parched.

Yes, I know what you're thinking. Why we didn't end up in rehab remains a mystery to me too. We knew how to say No; we just had no particular interest in saying it. And, of course, we were young. But we were hardly innocents abroad. Peter Allen had written a song called "Continental American" and when Brian heard the lyrics

> *When rules did not apply*
> *We would drink fountains dry*
> *In a club filled with sound*

he quipped: "Is he writing about us again?"

We were the all-Canadian spoiled brats of Hollywood. And we loved it.

We were also making a science of business travel. My good friend Maria McClay, the wife of legendary Hollywood publicist Booker McClay, was an accomplished and highly successful travel agent. "When you check into a hotel," she taught me, "never take the first room they offer you. Ask to see two or three rooms in the same price range, so you can choose the one that suits you best."

Brian took Maria's philosophy to the next level. When he found a room he liked – almost inevitably a large corner room, with a view – he would make a note of the room number so he could specifically request the same room when he returned to that hotel on another junket.

Hoteliers were impressed by his obvious appreciation of their gestures to make him feel welcome. If a fruit basket or an arrangement of flowers was delivered to his room when he arrived, he immediately sent a personal, handwritten note of thanks to the manager. Unaccustomed to such displays of good manners, hotel managers responded in kind, occasionally moving other guests to another room so that "Mr. Linehan's room" would be available when he checked in.

Sometimes I was given one-bedroom suites at The Plaza in New York, often after Brian called Judi Schwam at Columbia or Linda Goldenberg at 20th Century Fox to let them know that I was bringing Gail with me on a weekend junket because it was also our wedding anniversary. Or that I was bringing one of the kids with me for some quality one-on-one time, and wouldn't it be a nice gesture if the studio paid extra attention to my accommodation? It was indeed a nice gesture, but they did it for Brian as much as they did it for me.

Brian did not take to most children, and his lack of enthusiasm for spending time in their company was more often than not reciprocal. "He likes your kids, and he likes the Levine kids, Michael and Carol's children," Marcia Martin noted one day. "But as far as I know, from everything I've heard him say over the years, that's it. And let's face it, that's a pretty short list!"

He liked Dianne Schwalm's daughter Emily, too, and loved telling her that she was born on the same day as his sister Connie, June 4. "So that makes you a Gemini!" he would tell her. He was always good to my children, Marc, Alex, and Joe, and constantly asked to be updated on their activities. My children doted on him. Perhaps it was because he spoke to the three of them the way my wife and I did. We tried to treat them as small adults, sometimes endearingly childlike, who had ideas, opinions, and concerns worth hearing, which we encouraged them to express. I recall only one time when this philosophy backfired. My daughter, Alex, who was then six or seven, had accompanied me to L.A. on a junket at the Beverly Hilton hotel (before Merv Griffin bought it). As usual we had gathered the troops, and on this one particular evening we were having dinner at Trader Vic's, one of our favourite watering holes, with Brian and one of our all-time favourite people, Claire Olsen. Claire did her weekly *At the Movies* series from a strong-signal station in Barrie, Ontario, and was faithfully watched by insatiable Toronto movie-goers. A successful radio broadcaster before moving to television, Claire was smart, chic, and charming. She was also about half an hour older than the rest of us. Dianne Schwalm promptly dubbed her "Mother," and Linehan & Olsen quickly became the formidable new duo on the film circuit.

As young as she was, my daughter, Alex, had already started to develop the quick wit and sassy humour that has since made her a suc-cessful writer and television producer. So when Brian made a wisecrack, Alex followed through with another. Brian then tried to top her with another *bon mot*, only to find her all too ready to respond. Claire and I were mesmerized by this witty duel between two such disparate competi-tors. Brian was both amused and bemused, torn between his pride in Alex's dazzling display of wit and his own need to command the spot-light. At one point he actually started to get irritated, but quickly checked himself. Despite her young years, Alex sensed the shift and immediately clammed up. Brian was flummoxed by this. What had happened? Why was he doing this? She was only seven years old, and obviously eager to please him. To his credit, he spent the rest of the evening getting her to open up again.

In many ways Joe, our youngest son, was the perfect foil for Brian. He was younger, more impressionable, far more interested in cartoons and video games than show business. He knew Brian was on television, but he had seen me on television, too, so obviously television was no big deal. He loved Brian for who he was, not what he did or who he inter-viewed. Brian sensed this almost immediately, and was devoted to Joe (well, as devoted as Brian could be to a child) and seemed to look forward to spending time with him on junkets, on a plane, in a pool, in a limo.

Even when my children weren't with me on a junket, Brian still made sure they were remembered. I am reminded of this every time I hear the familiar strains of Henry Mancini's addictive *Pink Panther* theme. That film franchise was a gold mine for United Artists, and UA planning wizard Carl Ferrazza always made sure that every *Pink Panther* sequel was launched in style. For one *Panther* film, we were treated to a spa weekend at La Costa, just outside of San Diego. Our dinner music was provided by legendary crooner Johnny Mathis, who sang with a small band of great studio musicians personally conducted by *Pink Panther* composer Henry Mancini. A small stuffed pink panther sat on an elaborate centrepiece on each table, and Brian saw me looking at it longingly.

"You should take that for the kids," he said.

"No, I can't take just one," I replied. My three children were all very young at the time, and I felt I couldn't take only one Pink Panther home.

Brian plucked the pink stuffed animal from the centrepiece. "Hold on to this for me!" he said, thrusting it in my lap. He got up, circled the room once, and returned with two more miniature Pink Panthers. I was delighted, but suspicious.

"Brian, are you sure that the people at those tables don't mind giving these up?"

"Shall we go and ask them?" he inquired, his voice dripping with sarcasm. And then, barely moving his lips: "*Just put them in your bag and shut up.*"

I did as I was told. My children were thrilled.

On another *Panther* occasion, Ferrazza and his team took over most of a resort hotel in Oahu. While we enjoyed the sun and surf, Peter Sellers tried to smoke dope underwater. Sellers's co-star, the seriously sexy Dyan Cannon, had just finished shooting a movie with Warren Beatty and was pretty sure it was a career-ender. "Warren kept shooting my back!" she moaned in a confidential aside. "I don't know why he even wanted me in the picture." Brian and I shared the pleasure of coaxing Jennifer Grant, Dyan's pre-teen daughter by Cary Grant, onto the dance floor at the *Pink Panther* party later that night. On the flight back to L.A. from Hawaii, we were sitting in the same first-class cabin, and at Brian's urging I showed Dyan a huge ad in the Sunday *New York Times* showcasing her rave reviews for *Heaven Can Wait*. She was dumbfounded, but ecstatic, and would later be nominated for an Oscar for her performance in Warren's film.

It was all going splendidly. We were getting great interviews, and great behind-the-scenes gossip to share with our friends. Everyone was having a good time. Except, perhaps, those other people – the other print and television people – who were slowly but surely becoming more and more aware that Brian Linehan was getting Special Treatment. And that they weren't.

6

"He hated to be thrown in with the mob."

Within six months of joining the junket circuit, Brian Linehan was seriously resented by both television and print junketeers who didn't like his, for lack of a better word, Attitude. And the extra privileges his Attitude seemed to bring him.

Brian could be diplomatic, sensitive, tactful. He was all those things when he was talking to his guests on-camera. Off-camera, however, he did not suffer fools gladly. And in his view, there were a lot of fools on junkets: press people who said Yes to a free weekend in New York so they could go Christmas shopping at Bloomingdale's and Macy's; pseudo-journalists who never opened the press kit provided by their hosts; entertainment writers who never asked a question at round-table interviews; TV presenters whose idiotic questions revealed a total lack of respect for the actors and directors they were interviewing, who glanced nervously at their watches during taping to make sure they could still use the two-for-one seats they'd bought at the TKTS booth in Times Square for a Broadway matinee. All fools, in his view. All parasites who fed and lived off everyone else's work. And all so unprofessional.

Brian was also arrogant, which irritated his colleagues and almost always made me laugh. He knew some of the TV junketeers had complained about the special treatment he was getting, and he enjoyed their discomfort when they were told that there were different rules for the well-spoken, well-dressed young man from Canada. To make them even more miserable, he made sure he gave the complainers a consoling, sympathetic look – a Be Kind To Losers smile – whenever they entered the room.

Brian loved language and prided himself on using adverbs and adjectives thoughtfully, concisely, cleverly. He admired the distilled acid wit of Dorothy Parker and other wordsmith pundits who expressed themselves fearlessly and with style, and he was determined to do the same. He succeeded, frequently to the guilty pleasure (a.k.a. amusement) of others, if seldom to his own benefit. He was incisive, bitchy, funny, brilliant. And he knew it.

Hollywood publicity guru Judi Schwam ran many of the junkets that brought us to New York and L.A., and over time she became a life-long friend to both of us. "Brian always thought everyone was out to get him," Judi remembers, laughing, "and they were! All those years when we spent almost every weekend on the road, I think back to his relationships, or lack of relationships, with those people. And they were overtly hostile to Brian. Brian was so good at what he did – he was the best at what he did – that he put them all to shame. He was the consummate professional.

"He was discerning, too," she adds, "about what he would and wouldn't do. He wasn't going to be a pony in the circus. Even though he knew that part of what he did was a dog-and-pony show, he would never overtly acknowledge it."

The "Other Schwalm," Toronto-based publicist Dianne, remembers that when Brian walked onto a set "the crews adored him. Oh, they did. It didn't matter which crew. He'd come in and say, 'Good morning, ladies and gentlemen,' and he'd go around and say, 'Hello, your name is? . . . Nice to meet you.' He'd go to every single person. And of course I'd always sneak in and give him a few more minutes, whether it had been approved or not. The crews just did it. And usually if it was someone new, the star's personal publicist, whether it was Stan Rosenberg or Peggy Siegel or whoever, would come running out afterward going, 'Who the hell was that?' They'd want his card and they'd call him afterward just to get a copy of the show."

Brian wanted the TV people he worked beside on junkets to share his passion for good manners, for dignity, and, especially, integrity. He wanted too much.

Judi Schwam was running a junket at The Plaza when she learned that one of Brian's fellow junketeers, Stu Rosenthal, from Portland, Oregon, had died of a heart attack. "Stu," Judi remembers, "was a nice healthy guy who went to the YMCA in every city and swam." Sure that Stu's demise was now on everyone's mind, as it was on hers, Judi invited the junket press up to the studio hospitality suite in the hotel for a little remembrance. "Brian showed up, and I think two other people showed up. That was it, out of thirty-five television people on the junket. And these were people who saw each other week in and week out, year after year. Kind of sad, really."

Another time, when the star of a movie junket in Washington, D.C., had to leave earlier than anticipated, he insisted on taping his session with Linehan before he left. Brian's interview was quickly moved up earlier to accommodate the actor's new departure time. When Judi Schwam went to retrieve Brian's tape for him, she discovered that studio publicists were making copies of the Linehan interview to share with other junketeers, so they too would have footage of the elusive star.

"Have you asked Brian?" she inquired.

No, they said, they hadn't.

"Then you'd better stop dubbing!"

When Brian asked what the delay was, she told him. "At first he was really, really angry. And then, after he calmed down, he was really flattered." His colleagues resented him, but not enough to turn down a free Linehan interview, with all the painstaking work that he had put into it.

On major TV junkets, studios frequently had as many as six interview rooms, with six crews shooting, going simultaneously. The actors, the producer, the writer, the director, whoever was going to be interviewed, would each be given his or her own hotel suite, to which lighting and camera crews would then be added. Television interviewers from across North America would go from room to room on a tight rotation schedule, usually spending less than five minutes with each interview subject in each room. Based on a six-hour call, it was possible to shoot two hundred to two hundred and fifty interviews, and hit forty separate markets, before the end of the day.

I believe it was Judi Schwam who initiated the first monitor room for junkets. Up to that time she had to assign a studio publicist to each interview room, to audit each interview and report back to her later, so she would know what was being said. Finally, she created a master control centre, one suite with an audiovisual feed from every camera in every room, where trained observers could monitor five or six interviews simultaneously, adjusting volume to sample any conversations that could later prove contentious or problematic. With the monitor control-room system she devised, she could watch content and do a tape check for all rooms at the same time.

Judi remembers both print and TV press sneaking into the monitor room at The Plaza on one of her junkets to "audit" Linehan interviews "so they didn't have to do their homework." She put a stop to it immediately.

In his heyday, Brian would get twenty minutes when everyone else was getting seven. "Today," says Disney's Arlene Ludwig, veteran publicist and long-time Linehan pal, "junkets are not based on the interviewer, they're based on the outlets. *Entertainment Tonight*, *Extra*, *Access Hollywood*, and *E* get the biggest chunk of time – fifteen minutes, which is usually whittled down to twelve. Then it goes down to seven minutes for the A-list interviewers. And then by the end of the afternoon, it's four or three minutes."

Even though many of the junket press attempted to "borrow" from Brian's research, very few of them ever saw his show. Hollywood publicist Ronni Chasen, who worked with him for years, says it was years before she actually saw Brian's show on television. "The strange thing about Brian was that, doing the junkets, you saw him do the interviews, but you never saw the finished product. You never saw the show. So we only knew how smart he was, and how informed he was, and how much homework he would do, because we hung out together."

Many of the stars she brought to Brian "were just waiting for a smart, intelligent, in-depth, informed interview with a point of view. With someone who would have a frame of reference for their work in the theatre and in film. Someone who knew. When they sat with Brian, they knew what was going to happen. And if it was supposed to be five minutes, they'd say, well, give me ten for this one.

"It was a different set of rules for Brian. He knew what he was talking about. He had seen everything. He was kind of like an oasis of intelligent information in a sea of not always the most intelligent interviewers. On junkets, the hardest thing for the actors is that you sit there and you do thirty or forty or fifty interviews a day and it's pretty much the same. With Brian it was always something a little different and fresh. Everyone knew that. And everybody budgeted for that kind of time."

Most studio publicity chiefs carefully planned where Brian's interviews would fit in the taping schedule. Stuart Fink, another veteran Hollywood publicist who became a personal friend to Brian, would purposely place him on interview schedules "in such a way as to keep the interview subject alive. Because I knew that if I put him too early in the schedule, everyone else's interview was going to look dull. And I would use him as the adrenalin rush to get the subject thinking again. And maybe open it up for the next wave, or the last wave. And I would always hear after the interview how good the interview was."

"Brian," says Dianne Schwalm, "was always put in at a time when we thought the star needed to be cheered up."

Still, the grousing continued, from both newspaper and television press.

"If I had his research department," one TV reporter from Baltimore complained to me, "I could be every bit as good as he is."

"If you had his research department," I told her, "you'd be him. He *is* his research department."

The fact that Brian was an incorrigible mischief-maker did little to enhance his popularity.

On one Fox junket, I was assigned a rather sumptuous suite at the Beverly Wilshire. A beautiful arrangement of flowers arrived from Jon Peters and Barbra Streisand. I had recently interviewed Jon, and they had apparently liked my story.

I had invited a dozen or so people, a few of our pals and a few 20th Century Fox executives, for drinks before we left for that night's screening. I put the flowers on display in the hall but put the card on the bureau in my bedroom. Brian was the first to arrive, and immediately admired the imposing floral arrangement. I showed him the card. "No wonder they gave me a suite," I said. "They think I'm tight with Streisand!"

The suite doorbell rang. By the time I returned with my first invited guests, Brian had repositioned the card in a prominent place beside the flowers, so no one could miss it. Much to Brian's delight, jealous tongues were wagging all weekend.

At studio dinners, we cherry-picked the writers and interviewers we wanted to sit with. Like Claire Olsen, Shirley Eder had a lifetime pass; we held a seat for her at every table. "Brian and Shirley together were just a treat," Arlene Ludwig remembers fondly. "And *so* funny." Shirley Eder was a syndicated Hollywood gossip columnist who also dabbled in radio and television, mostly as a much sought-after guest. She had also written a modest bestseller about her adventures in Tinsel Town entitled *Not Tonight, Cary Grant!* and unlike most junketeers was extremely generous, and maternal, in her affection and concern for both Brian and myself.

Radie Harris was somewhat put out by Shirley's long association with certain stars – Ginger Rogers and Barbara Stanwyck both counted Shirley as one of their closest friends – and the fact that Shirley refused to slag anyone. "Shirley Eder, the world's oldest bobby-soxer," Radie would sniff. But Sinatra always took Shirley's calls, and so did most of

Hollywood. Brian and I adored Shirley and made a point of letting studios know that we valued her company and wanted to see her stay on the A-list with us. Brian would tease her mercilessly, frequently introducing her as the last white woman in Detroit. She loved it.

Ronni Chasen still gets sentimental when she thinks about Brian and Shirley. "Shirley would set up her tape recorder, and in about ten minutes she would call Brian. 'Can you help me with this? It's not working.' And Brian would say, 'Why do you even bring it, Shirley? You can never get it to work.' Inevitably, she would call me the next Monday and say, 'My tape didn't come out!' We'd have to get her on the phone with whoever the heck it was, and they would have to do it all over again. I mean, that was the way it always was!"

Ronni remembers how he developed social allergies to certain junketeers. One of them, San Francisco film reviewer Judy Stone, was justifiably proud of the fact that her brother was the legendary investigative journalist I.F. Stone, and was not shy about sharing that sibling information with her tablemates. On one occasion, Ronni recalls, Judy started talking "and talking, and talking," but Brian had heard Judy's tales of her famous brother once too often. "And Brian turned to her and said, 'Judy, would you just put a lid on it?' And everybody got hysterical and fell about laughing. It was just the way he said it. Just the best."

Brian never, ever stopped driving certain junketeers crazy. Tormenting the ones who sneered at him or snubbed him became something of a sport. Or an obsession, depending on your point of view. When someone out of favour with him – and it was a long list – would approach our table, he or she invariably would make the mistake of saying, May I join you? Alas, it was an irresistible cue to which Brian would respond, "Can you check back with us? We have to take a vote."

Beneath all the bravado, of course, he was hurt by their rejection. He wanted to be regarded as a journalist, not a junket dilettante. He wanted to be respected. He wanted to belong. Established U.S. film journalists like Stephen Silverman from New York and Roger Ebert from Chicago always seemed to get a kick out of him; they saw him not as a threat but as a witty and amusing colleague. Canadian journalists were not always so generously inclined.

And yet Brian could be very generous with people on the tour with him. Michael Levine remembers hearing the story of one particular lady "who I gather imbibed a bit too much. And, in a very non-sexual way, Brian put her to bed many times. And made it quite clear that he was never going to tell anybody about it. That was that wonderful sweet side of him."

Oddly enough, if they got into a jam, some of the more hostile junketeers would call Brian. One West Coast writer called him one morning in tears. He had brought a "young man" back to his room the previous night and realized when he woke up that on his way out the hustler had stolen his wallet with all his cash and credit cards in it. Brian put two hundred dollars in an envelope and had it delivered to the writer's room, so he could pay his incidental expenses and check out of the hotel. Two or three days later, Brian received a money order in the mail for two hundred dollars, with a two-word message: Thank You.

The writer in question had been very critical of Brian in the past, and had always been very vocal about it. I was intrigued by the fact that after they had called him to bail them out of one situation or another, these guys were always sorry they had said all those nasty things about him. Yet they called him, not the studio publicist assigned to assist and protect them. For some reason, despite how they might have behaved toward him in the past, they still believed Brian would help them. And in the end he usually did.

"Brian liked to be wanted," says Michael Levine. "And Brian liked to be needed. Brian would never bridle at people asking him for help. He would only bridle when he didn't think he'd got his due – when he thought that he had earned something and people were not prepared to recognize that he should have a better interview because he was the better interviewer."

Which, of course, he was.

Harriet Blacker, who worked in a Manhattan publishing house, was another Brian booster. When he came to New York on junkets, she could see how conflicted he was. He wanted to do the work, but he didn't want to be lumped in with the junket press he held in such low regard. "He hated to be thrown in with the mob," Blacker recalls. "He hated that. And the mob didn't like him too much either. Because he showed them up."

Although Brian and I were always pals, our friendship was tested from time to time. In the early years of the *Toronto Sun* and Citytv, we were technically rivals, because I was doing a weekly movie-star interview show for the fledgling Global network. I say "technically" because neither Brian nor I believed I was a threat to him. I wanted to capture the moment; he wanted to demonstrate how a star's personal history had led to this moment in time.

Most of the stars who appeared on my series, which mercifully evolved into a series of specials, were also set to appear on his show, which was not a problem for either of us. Brian was doing five shows a week. I went from one show a week for thirty-nine weeks to six specials a year. Clearly we were apples and pomegranates. Still, things got a bit dicey when, on one or two rare occasions, stars agreed to appear on my show but not on his.

The most notable case was Raquel Welch, who was coming to Toronto to do a ten-night stint at the still-swank Imperial Room supper club. I was more connected to Raquel's management team, so I got the exclusive, which made Global very, very happy. And which made Brian and Citytv very, very unhappy.

Brian convinced himself that all I needed to do was tell Raquel's people that I didn't mind if Raquel did his show as well, and *presto!*, just like magic, it would happen.

I was not so inclined.

Brian was relentless in his pursuit of Raquel, but to no avail. And the more he lobbied people to lobby me, the more annoyed I became. At one point Claire Olsen, Brian, and I were on a flight from Los Angeles to Chicago. Claire and Brian were sitting together in the row behind me, but Claire had moved up to the empty seat beside me, ostensibly to show me something she had brought with her for the flight: a cylindrical container of Evian water with a spray top, so you could spritz your face mid-flight.

I spritzed, and smiled joyously. Not because of the Evian spray, but because I could see the stewardess coming up the aisle with a cart full of the hot-fudge-and-butterscotch sundaes that had become a coveted specialty on American Airlines.

I ordered a sundae. Claire ordered a black coffee. Brian, as usual, took a pass on dessert. "Georrrrrge," Claire began, in her mellifluous radio voice, "don't you think you should let Brian interview Raquel Welch too? I mean, you know how badly he wants to do it. Don't you think it would be the generous thing to do?"

I sighed wearily. "Tell Brian," I replied, shaking my head in frustration, "that this is not a generous year."

And she did. But until Raquel Welch got back on that plane to L.A., Brian never stopped trying to get her to appear on *City Lights*.

☆

Despite his salad days at Odeon, from time to time Brian displayed some unexpected flashes of naïveté.

One day he called me, thrilled to bits because Paul Anka, whom he had interviewed during the singer's record-setting stint at the Imperial Room, had sent him a personal Christmas gift: an exquisite bowl from mainland China, complete with pedigree papers citing its historical significance, the dynasty from which it was sourced, and the manufacturer's credentials. Brian was figuratively and literally bowled over.

"How wonderful!" I agreed. "By the way, have you told anyone else about this?"

"No," he said, suddenly suspicious. "I wanted to call you first, because you interviewed Anka too . . ." His voice trailed off. "Tell me."

"He sent me one too."

There was an audible gasp on the other end of the line. "He sent YOU one too?" he cried. "But you had that big fight with him! He hated your review! He threatened to bar you from the Imperial Room!"

"Yes, he sent ME one too," I said quietly. "And my guess is, if he sent ME one . . ."

". . . he sent everybody one."

"Uh-huh."

"Thank you for telling me before I told anyone else."

"Uh-huh."

"Do you suppose he owns the factory in China that makes the bowls?"

"Uh-huh."

A few minutes later he called back. "Did I tell you I received a handwritten thank-you note from Carol Channing?" he inquired. "It was inside her Christmas card."

"Very thoughtful of her," I replied.

"Do you think Charles [her husband, Charles Lowe] actually wrote it?"

"Uh-huh."

"Did you get one from her too?"

"Uh-huh."

"From now on," he said, "I'm going to call you every time I receive something."

"Uh-huh."

And mostly he did.

At other times, however, I couldn't be much help to him. After he finished a *City Lights* session with Paul Newman, he was convinced Newman had made a pass at him. I had met and interviewed Newman, and this scenario seemed highly unlikely to me. "Somehow I don't see Paul Newman as a switch-hitter," I told Brian.

"He told me I had great hair," said Brian.

"You *do* have great hair."

"Yes, but how often does another man tell you that? And he admired my blazer, and he asked who the designer was, and did I wear a lot of Valentino!"

"So what you're saying is that he was flirting with you?"

"Exactly!"

"No, not exactly," I persisted. "He was flirting with you because *that's his job*. It's in Movie Star Manual 101: Flatter the Interviewer. Make Him Feel Important. Make him feel that he has a personal connection to you."

"Oh no, George, you're wrong," he insisted. "You weren't there. It was much more than that."

One time when we were in Hollywood, Universal publicity chief Mike Kaplan took us aside and asked if we'd like to spend some time with Alfred Hitchcock on the set of his new film, *Family Plot*. Would we? Absolutely! We arranged to extend our visit, which was not exactly a hardship for either one of us.

The next morning, I drove us onto the back lot at Universal, where a VIP parking pass awaited us. We watched Hitchcock direct a scene. It was a fairly tedious experience, as *Family Plot* co-stars Bruce Dern and Karen Black would later confirm. Hitchcock was a celluloid architect. His storyboard rivalled the most detailed blueprints, and by the time he started shooting his movies he had already filmed them in his head. Which was great for Hitch and his fans, but fairly dreary for the actors he hired to bring his blueprints to life.

When the Great Man retired to his office – a private apartment on the lot – we were invited to join him. "George, you go ahead," said Brian. "I'd better wait for the crew."

"What crew?"

"The crew who are going to shoot my interview with Hitchcock."

"Oh!" I was surprised. "That's great. I didn't know."

Brian looked at me intently. "George, honestly," he said, "do you think Mike Kaplan would invite me to come to meet Hitchcock and NOT have a crew standing by?"

"Brian, honestly," I replied, "yes."

I could see his heart sinking. "C'mon, come with me," I said. "We'll chat with Hitchcock till the crew arrives."

He shook his head. "How will they know where to find me?"

"Because you'll be where you're supposed to be. With Hitchcock."

He had to admit, albeit reluctantly, that my suggestion made sense.

We had a lovely visit with Hitchcock. I got my interview for the *Sun*. The camera crew failed to materialize.

"Why did Mike Kaplan invite me?" Brian asked me, still sulking.

"Because it's his job," I explained, "to bring VIP media on the set whenever Hitchcock is making a movie for Universal. And tomorrow, when his boss asks him who he brought to the set this week —"

"— he'll say, George Anthony and Brian Linehan. I get it, I get it," he said. "It's not about me getting an interview. It's about Mike getting my name on the list." He sighed dejectedly. "I'll never learn, will I!"

But, of course, he did.

7

"You have your father's eyes."

Brian Linehan liked the 1970s. He was enjoying his success, and having a lot of fun. He was working hard, and loving it. And stars in Hollywood and New York were responding to him with the same astonishment that Kirk Douglas and Carol Channing had demonstrated when they first sat with him on *City Lights*.

"You sure know an awful lot about me!" Ann-Margret said to him with a nervous giggle. But after her first interview with Brian, she and her husband, Roger Smith, put him on their personal A-list, and Brian would later hitch a ride from Las Vegas to L.A. with the couple on Paul Anka's private jet.

"Man oh man, I'm starting to sweat with all the information you've got on me!" said Dustin Hoffman, wiping his brow.

"You have been listening down the drainpipe," Bette Midler told him, starting to squirm in her seat. Midler was launching her film career with *The Rose* and expected he would ask her about the prototype for her screen role, Janis Joplin. Instead, of course, he asked her about Bette Midler. "You know an awful lot about me and I'm getting very agitated here. What else are you going to spring on me?"

"God, you're a good interviewer," Burt Reynolds told him in the middle of their first interview. "You just hit nerves. I'd like to come and lie on your couch sometime." From that day forward Reynolds always insisted on booking extra time for his Linehan "sessions," so they wouldn't be rushed.

"How do you know all this stuff?" asked Gene Wilder incredulously. "That's what I'd like to know!"

Jack Lemmon was dazzled when he sat with Brian to promote *The China Syndrome*. "Has anybody ever known as much about what they're doing before they talk as you? You're incredible!" he marvelled. "You've got 'em all nailed."

Brian Linehan met Shirley MacLaine in 1976. She was wary of him at first, but soon found that Brian was able to put pieces of her past together in a way that gave her new perspectives on her present.

As outspoken then as she is now, MacLaine had no patience for fools and rarely took prisoners. A decade later Brian would still be talking about the late supper they shared at Winston's, how he said something amusing about actors who applaud each other with one hand, and how she leaned forward, looked deep into his eyes, and purred, "Brian, that's a stupid, fatuous thing to say."

"We had known each other all of ten minutes," he would later tell *Toronto Sun* readers. "I started, nervously, to smile."

"Why are you so defensive?" she continued.

Before he could respond, she added, "Do you think it's a Canadian thing?"

"There were others present," he recalled, "but Shirley stared into me and began a discussion that left me believing she cared enough to hit me with her very best."

He soon learned that "what seemed like an abrupt, curt manner was in fact a curious mind."

She would constantly challenge him. During one *City Lights* interview (she did at least seven sessions with him over the years), he asked her a question to which she knew he already knew the answer. When she sniped at him for it, he pointed to the camera. Yes, he admitted, he did know the answer – "but *they* don't," he said, referring to the viewers.

"Oh," said Shirley, "you're not being *sincere*, you're asking for the *audience*."

Nailed again.

All of their interviews were memorable, and they became off-camera chums. Shirley invited him to visit her on movie sets. He attended her opening nights, introduced her at book signings, invited her to his home for dinner. And whenever she could, she always made time to see him. He was the reason, she said, why so many Hollywood stars looked forward to going to Toronto – "so Brian could tell us about our lives."

Show people who are in demand rarely get to see prime-time television; they're too busy working. That's especially true of theatre people and saloon singers, who traditionally work at night. What they do watch, however, is daytime television. And since *City Lights* aired five times a week, Monday through Friday, everyone who came to Toronto to perform in a touring show or to play one of the city's two or three nightclubs inevitably ended up watching Brian Linehan in their hotel rooms.

City Lights was hardly racking up major Nielsen numbers. Far from it. With its limited reach, Citytv was lucky if even one of its shows registered a number. Nonetheless, entrepreneurial Toronto publicity king Gino Empry took a shine to the eager young interviewer and gave him access to the stars who played the two top venues in town, Ed Mirvish's lovingly restored Royal Alexandra Theatre, and the Imperial Room, the swank Royal York hotel supper club that Empry had skilfully massaged into a home-away-from-home to such high-powered, high-profile pop stars as Ella Fitzgerald, Peggy Lee, and Tony Bennett. Almost every *City Lights* encounter continued to evoke a breathless "How did you know that?" from whichever actor, singer, writer, director, or producer Brian was grilling that day. Citytv smartly capitalized on that by creating a promo composed solely of slack-jawed stars reacting to Linehan's uncommonly thorough research.

City Lights opened with a shot of Brian walking his guest onto a small shag-carpeted riser with two chairs. When Shelley Winters came to town to publicize her memoirs, she refused to walk onto the set with him. "You can't shoot me from behind, Brian!" she cried. "I'm not wearing a girdle!" A runner was dispatched to Eaton's department store, the required undergarment was purchased, and Shelley walked on with Brian.

Throughout the interview, she was taken aback by Brian's questions – especially when he pointed out that she couldn't have been Marilyn Monroe's roommate in Hollywood during the years she identified in the book, because Monroe had not yet arrived in Hollywood at the time Shelley claimed. "But Brian!" she protested. "It's MY STORY!!"

Always the gentleman, Brian acquiesced and moved on.

When Ginger Rogers came to town, Gino Empry brought her to the studio two hours late. By then *City Lights* had lost the space to *The City Show*. Brian was heartbroken. "I'm so sorry we can't do the interview," he told the song-and-dance legend. "We can't even stay in this studio."

"Aw, don't worry about it," said Rogers, with a toss of her platinum curls. "I've been thrown out of better places."

Glamour girls brought their own set of challenges. Italian screen siren Gina Lollobrigida called a halt to the taping so she could readjust

the lighting to her needs. "Ees difficult to be beautiful, no?" she murmured, refreshing her makeup before they started shooting again.

"I wouldn't know," replied Linehan, deadpan. He had few illusions
about his looks. He knew he was not matinee-idol material. "One of the
secrets to success on television is, if you can't be beautiful, be memorable," he once told writer John Hofsess.

Several years later, Barbra Streisand was very apprehensive about
the first film she directed, and was doing everything she could to bring
public attention to it. So, to promote *Yentl*, she finally agreed to do an
interview with Linehan. One of Brian's champions, veteran studio executive and expatriate Canadian Irv Ivers brought him to Hollywood on a
first-class ticket from MGM. Leo the Lion also picked up the tab for
Brian's suite at Hernando Courtright's Beverly Wilshire hotel.

A film crew arrived the next day, and took four hours to set up
lights and cameras. When Streisand arrived, she exchanged brief pleas-
antries with Linehan, and then spent the next two hours redoing the
lighting. "Okay, I think that's better," she said tentatively – and then sat
down to do one of the best on-camera interview sessions of her career.
Citytv showcased the Streisand interview as a sixty-minute prime-time
special called *Barbra & Brian*, and Brian added a surprised but thoroughly intrigued Barbra to his fan base.

But not every interview guest was a Linehan fan. Oscar-winning
All About Eve anti-heroine Anne Baxter, in town to promote her autobiography, leaned over during a commercial break and snapped, "Enough
of this nostalgia shit! Let's get back to selling my book!" Brian was
thrilled to meet Sophia Loren, and she was thrilled to meet him, but on
camera they had no chemistry whatsoever. And after her session with
Brian, another Oscar-winning screen queen, the luminous Joan Fontaine
of such film classics as *Rebecca*, *Suspicion*, and *Jane Eyre*, reportedly stag-
gered out onto Queen Street, saying what she needed after a trip down
memory lane with Linehan was a stiff drink.

In those early days, Brian told *Toronto Star* columnist Jim Bawden,
"I was meeting Fred Astaire and Janet Leigh and Gloria Swanson and it
was a whole different world. They would write letters of appreciation.
That's how the studios trained them."

Linehan regularly wrote letters of appreciation too, in disciplined,
ornate script. "Do you ever think you were born in the wrong era?" he
would muse. It was a question that would haunt him all his life.

In time he befriended idols from the era he most admired.

George Cukor, the legendary director who had glorified most of the great MGM beauties on the screen, was flattered by Linehan's attention and corresponded with him, constantly teasing Brian about his relentless cheerleading for Canadian-born movie stars. When Cukor went overseas to direct "Kate and Larry" (a.k.a. Katharine Hepburn and Laurence Olivier) in his award-winning *Love Among the Ruins* – at that time the most expensive film ever made for television – he sent Brian an eight by ten black-and-white candid of himself deep in conversation (i.e., direction) with Olivier. On the glossy photo he wrote: *Lord Olivier and me talking things over. Kindest regards Brian and every good wish – George Cukor.*

Brian was giddy with excitement when Cukor first invited him to dinner at his elegantly appointed home on Cordell Drive, which had been the subject of a lavish photo spread in *Architectural Digest*. Seeing it in person was a thrilling experience for Brian. He felt as if he were walking into the pages of a magazine.

On one occasion Cukor hosted a dinner party for a group of visiting Russian directors. Cukor himself had shot a film in Russia, *The Blue Bird*, an unfortunate screen version of a Russian fairy tale. Elizabeth Taylor, Jane Fonda, and Ava Gardner had all participated as a personal favour to Cukor; tellingly, none of them included it in their official bios. Brian was delighted when Cukor invited him to his dinner for the Russians, but he didn't want to mislead him. "I speak some Serbian, George," he warned him, "but I can't speak Russian."

"Neither can I, dear boy, neither can I," Cukor replied. "I've invited a friend who is fluent in Russian. She can interpret for us."

When Brian arrived for dinner, he walked into the house and saw Robert Wagner deep in conversation with a stylish, petite woman who was admiring one of the paintings adorning the living-room walls.

Cukor greeted Brian warmly. "Brian," he said, "may I present our translator, Natalia Nikolaevna Zakharenko."

Natalie Wood turned to face him. "Hello, Brian! How nice to see you again."

They had met before. In a crater. In Flagstaff, Arizona, on a junket for *Meteor*, a disaster movie in which Natalie co-starred with Sean Connery. The movie was pretty hokey. At the screening Brian was sitting directly behind Gail and me, and as the special-effects meteor was about to pulverize Central Park in New York, he leaned forward and serenaded us with his own version of Rodgers and Hart's great lyrics:

"It'll take Manhattan,
the Bronx and Staten
Island too . . ."

Legendary American International Pictures mogul Sam Arkoff arranged for all of us to receive brightly coloured striped vests to wear on our helicopter ride into the crater. Glasses of cold beer and chilled champagne were waiting for us at the bottom. (We always liked Sam.) Natalie Wood, Ronni Chasen remembers, wouldn't fly. "So she got on the train in L.A. with her playwright pal Mart Crowley (of *Boys in the Band* fame) and her publicist." Fortunately, Natalie didn't have to take the train to George Cukor's house; it was only a short drive from hers. And since she spoke Russian fluently, she was only too happy to help out at George's dinner party.

When Cukor was feted with a Lincoln Center retrospective in 1978, five short years after *City Lights* started, he invited Brian to attend the gala as his guest. Two years later, when Cukor donated his personal papers to the Academy of Motion Picture Arts and Sciences, he invited Brian to the ceremony in Hollywood. Brian added both the playbill from the Lincoln Center gala and the invitation to the presentation of Cukor's papers to his personal memorabilia.

Cukor was both a professional mentor and a long-time personal confidant of Katharine Hepburn. He had guided Hepburn and Spencer Tracy through some of their biggest films, and whenever Kate was in Hollywood she occupied the guesthouse on his property, which he kept exclusively for her use. When Hepburn started touring in *Coco*, the Broadway musical created especially for her by Alan Jay Lerner, she brought her portrayal of Coco Chanel to Toronto's O'Keefe Centre, a short taxi ride from Citytv. But even the diplomatic, sensitive pleadings of her pal George Cukor failed to persuade her to be interviewed by Brian. "Eight performances a week is enough, George, without adding a ninth," she told him.

Cukor suspected that Brian's reputation for research intimidated Hepburn more than it intrigued her. He told Brian that Kate would sometimes watch his show at the Windsor Arms hotel, where she was staying, before she left for the theatre. *If* he was talking to someone she wanted to see.

Hepburn was very gracious when Brian went backstage to say hello one evening after her performance. "But oh no, Mr. Linehan," she said, in that fabled New England drawl, "no no no, you're not getting me in that chair!"

Brian was meeting lots of celebrities. Some would become showbiz friends, and some would become friends for life.

Finnish actress Taina Elg was one of the latter. She was dancing with the Sadler's Wells ballet in London when MGM signed her to a long-term contract and stuck her in costume dramas. She shared Brian's affection for George Cukor, who had directed her with Gene Kelly in *Les Girls*, her best movie role at MGM. (At Taina's request George personally directed her screen test for *Ben-Hur*, but director William Wyler's choice, Israeli actress Haya Harareet, got the part.) In time, the leggy Ms. Elg returned to the stage, where she appeared on Broadway with Raul Julia in *Nine* and toured North America in musicals like *Irma La Douce* and *Gigi*. Her long friendship with Brian developed "organically, because I liked the way he interviewed. Brian and I had many mutual friends, so it was easy to have a conversation."

Prima ballerina Karen Kain would also become a lifelong friend. Back when she and her frequent dance partner Frank Augustyn were rising stars at the National Ballet of Canada, Brian interviewed them on *City Lights*. "Brian was very supportive of the National Ballet; he didn't have to be. But he interviewed every principal dancer, every soloist, any time we had a guest artist," Kain says. "He was trying to help people get known, and trying to help the ballet sell tickets, and he did that.

"I wasn't very good at being interviewed; I was very shy. I couldn't put two words together. There were these really long pauses. I was a little mouse." Despite that, Karen liked being interviewed by Brian, "because he made me relax. He got me interested in what we were talking about, and I was . . . *better*.

"We did two or three interviews, and I don't really remember how we started seeing each other socially. We went to fundraisers together, when I was single, and he was the most fun date. I knew that if I was with him I didn't have to work very hard at entertaining everyone around me, because he would just entertain all of us, and we'd all have a good time. Even if you were with a bunch of strangers, it would be fine. He could be naughty and all that, and still it was fine."

One chilly January, Judi Schwam invited Brian to sit with her at the Golden Globes, at a table reserved for Columbia Pictures, where she had become a major marketing executive. The Golden Globes is the least intimidating of all the award shows, because winning one can help you, but losing one can't hurt you. So there's a real what-the-hell spirit of showbiz camaraderie in the air that isn't present at other events where your peers are voting for or against you. Besides, at the Golden Globes, you get to sit at banquet tables, you get to table-hop during commercials, and, best of all, you get to drink. What's not to like?

As usual, the ballroom at the Beverly Hilton that night was packed with television and movie stars. "Brian was like a kid in a candy store," Judi remembers. "The Golden Globes is still the most fun awards night, but it is a long evening. So he would go wandering from time to time, just to see who he could see."

One of the people he saw was Bea Arthur. He introduced himself, just one of many faces she saw in the crowd that night. But three days later, when she boarded an Air Canada plane to shoot some commercials in Toronto, he happened to be sitting next to her. They started talking, and eventually he interviewed her on *City Lights*. "And to this moment," she told me, "I don't know how he knew so much about what I had done. I mean, such *obscure* stuff . . ." They would remain friends for the next twenty-five years.

In 1977, Carole Shelley was working at the Shaw Festival in Niagara-on-the-Lake, Ontario, starring in *Man and Superman* with Ian Richardson. "Brian invited us down to *City Lights*, and we did two separate interviews. I have a photograph that tells the whole story. If you look at the expressions on both our faces you know that something magical has happened." For visiting Brits like Shelley and Richardson, Brian was "a kind wind of welcome to Canada."

Shirley Lord became another Linehan friend. Before she became one of the high-profile editors of *Vogue* magazine, she had started her career as the youngest woman's editor in Fleet Street, at the London *Evening Standard*. When she came to America, she jumped into the magazine business. "The first time I was interviewed by Brian, I had a beauty book on the bestseller list. But he knew much more, much more, and I was stunned when I sat down with him because of his research. We became firm friends, really, from that interview."

Brian aspired to stardom. But coming up the way he did, through Odeon and Janus, he always felt more comfortable in the early years about being in the business than being in the show. He befriended publicists, not stars, and hoped that some of these relationships, besides being mutually advantageous, might last. Almost all of them did.

Most of the names he would rhyme off in any given conversation about show business were the names of publicity executives: Harriet Bernstein, Gail Brounstein, Rhonda Bryant, Barry Carnon, Hilda Cunningham, John Dartigue, Bob Dingillian, Dick Delson, Al Dubin, Eliza Fernandes, Rob Friedman, Charlotte Gee, Stu Gottesman, Dan Hall, Joe Hyams, Andrea Jaffe, Nick Langston, Lloyd Leipzig, Marvin Levy, Janice Luke, Heather MacGillivray, Melinda Mullen, Blaise Noto, Georgia O'Connor, Charles Powell, Ed Russell, Mary Sinclair, Lois Smith, John Springer, Gabe Sumner, Leo Wilder – names that didn't mean a lot to other people, but names that meant everything to him.

Brian met publicist Harriet Blacker because her pal Stuart Fink urged him to call her the next time he was in New York. "We just hit it off. It was wonderful. And I always felt I was the least glamorous of anyone he knew in New York. I simply couldn't understand why he would want to see me. But even when I left publishing, we were still friends."

Brian liked Rita McKay, another seasoned publicist, the first time he met her. When she moved to the Inn on the Park, the famous fore-runner of the Four Seasons hotel chain, he would meet her for private dinners, and sometimes bring a "mystery guest" – a phrase he'd picked up from Toronto film festival co-founder Dusty Cohl. "One night Brian walked in with Peter O'Toole," she remembers, laughing, "and the waiters were beside themselves, competing for a chance to serve us!" When Rita moved to North Carolina, she initiated a Sunday-morning telephone ritual with Brian, and they seldom let more than a few weeks go by without speaking.

He stayed true to old friends, too. In addition to coaching and training actors, Brian's former acting teacher Jeanine Manatis would expand her career base as a stage and screen producer, director, and even TV film critic, occasionally guesting on *City Lights*. They remained friends for decades. "It was a very interesting, unique kind of relation-ship and it was never false," says Manatis. "He was who he was, I was who I am, and that was it."

☆

In the late 1970s, Brian and I were still living it up on the junket circuit. After one MGM screening, Richard Kahn, the studio's elegant marketing chief, invited Brian, Claire Olsen, and me, and a few others to join him for a nightcap at The Saloon, the newest hard-to-get-into hot spot in Hollywood. Like most Hollywood hot spots, The Saloon was more attitude than atmosphere, and despite Dick Kahn's studio-made reservation, the maitre d' was courteous but curt with him when we arrived. He informed Kahn that yes, they did have his reservation, and yes, they did have his booth, but we would have to wait until our table was bussed before we could be seated.

Waiters were flying around the room delivering drinks and food. Busboys trailed after them, trying to keep up. No one was going anywhere near our booth.

After ten minutes of being ignored, Brian and I assessed the situation. Kahn was too much of a gentleman to make a fuss. But enough was enough. We sauntered up to one of the busboys. "May I borrow that?" I asked him, pointing to the cloth hanging from his belt.

The busboy had no idea how to respond, of course, so I just took the cloth, thanked him in Spanish, and then strolled over to our designated booth. While I wiped down the table, Brian worked diligently to clear the dirty glasses.

Clearly amused, Dick Kahn and the rest of our group watched our Virgo uprising from behind the velvet rope. The curt-mannered maitre d' turned to see what they were looking at. He was horrified, and rushed to the table. "Please don't do that!" he protested.

"Oh, it's no trouble," I assured him.

"No, please, please stop!" he cried.

"That's all right, we don't mind," Brian volunteered. "It's not your fault you're understaffed. But we don't want to wait any longer."

"We'll take care of it!" the maitre d' said nervously, signalling to a nearby waiter. "Immediately!"

He was as good as his word. Our party was seated.

Dick Kahn leaned across the table. "I like your style," he said, with a conspiratorial wink.

An hour or so later, when Brian and I went to get a drink at the bar, the same sentiment was expressed, slightly differently, by a cool, silky champagne blonde who was gracefully adorning one of the barstools. She had watched the whole thing, she said, and enjoyed every minute of it. Her name was Judy Lewis, and she was working on one of the daily TV soap operas. Brian took it all in. "I'm sure everyone tells you this," he said, "but you have your father's eyes."

She stared at him for a second, and then gave him a slow, appreciative smile. "Not everyone," she replied quietly. "But, thank you."

We returned to our table. "Who is she?" asked Dick Kahn. "Is she someone you know?"

"Her name is Judy Lewis," said Brian, as quietly as he could manage. "And she is the love child of Loretta Young and Clark Gable."

Years later Judy Lewis wrote a book about her life in Hollywood and came to Toronto to promote it. Naturally her publisher booked her for an interview with Brian Linehan. Brian reminded her of the night we'd met, and asked her if, in addition to the copy she was signing to him, she would sign a book to me.

He brought it to me the next time we met for dinner. The handwritten inscription reads:

> *To George*
> *It's been a long time since The Saloon days*
> *Best Wishes*
> *Judy Lewis*

☆

In 1977, Citytv was eager to broaden its reach, and Brian's. Four years and eight hundred shows after *City Lights* started, Brian was seen once a week on CKSO in Sudbury, CFCN in Calgary, CFPL in London, KVOS in Washington State (his Vancouver outlet), CFRN in Edmonton (where the show was the top-rated program in its time slot), CKND in Winnipeg, CFCF in Montreal, CJCH in Halifax, and CKPR in Thunder Bay. It wasn't worldwide syndication, but it was a start. His fame was spreading, slowly, methodically, step by step, city by city.

Brian was now getting criticized in print for the same technique that had won him all the early kudos when he started in 1973. One writer described Brian's show as "equal parts of ego massage, hero worship, ruthless research and intelligent idolatry." Harsher critics called him sycophantic and claimed the big names lined up to appear on his show only because he flattered and fawned over them.

Writing in *Maclean's* magazine, columnist Hartley Steward expressed the feelings of many Canadian critics when he agreed that much of the early criticism "was bang on. Linehan did tend to smile ingratiatingly like a teenage fan who suddenly found himself at the next table to his favourite movie star." However, Steward also alluded to underlying reasons behind Linehan's early TV persona. "Today, Linehan is enjoying the first flashes of stardom," he wrote, noting that Brian took a certain delight in the fact that his old friends in Hamilton could see him rubbing elbows with movie stars. He quoted Brian directly: "They're all so proud of me now. The girls who wouldn't dance with me and the boys who used to beat me up."

When it came to being criticized, Brian Linehan was not exactly neutral. "Yes, I know I'm not a neurosurgeon," he would snap. "At the same time, I'm not about to let anybody minimize my contribution, because I do it well."

Because Linehan was mannered, he was easy to parody. But Brian was shocked, and hurt, when he first saw young comics Ken Finkleman and Rick Moranis spoof him on their CBC Television series. They were sending him up, using his real name, on national television. He felt elated and humiliated, all at the same time.

When he told me about it, I was thrilled for him. He was confused, and suspicious. Had I turned against him too? But after he thought it through, he realized what a great compliment it was. He had been on the air only five years when the parodies started. And we both knew far more established Canadian TV personalities, household names all, in whom Canadian satirists had shown no interest whatsoever.

True, those trademark Linehan questions were not so much questions as statements of fact, and were all but tailor-made for parody. But clearly that was Brian's style. And his strong suit.

"He's mannered and, in that sense, memorable," Moses Znaimer would say. "His manners are courtly."

According to Znaimer, members of the Sales department at Citytv were the first to become disenchanted with Brian. They felt his tastes were too elitist, too snobbish, too far from the average viewer, and pressured Znaimer to yank the show.

"They're unhappy," said Linehan, "because I would rather spend half an hour talking to Margaret Atwood than to someone like Tony Bennett who might get higher ratings." Besides, he added, in his experience, "pop singers – generally – have nothing much to say." Pop singers who were truly artists – Anne Murray, Ella Fitzgerald, and Peggy Lee were shining examples – were the exceptions that proved the rule. Anne Murray, the biggest international music star Canada had ever produced, was one of the first megastars to give Linehan an exclusive interview; Brian never forgot it, and he let Murray's manager, Leonard Rambeau, know that the singer had *carte blanche* anytime she wanted to come on. In town performing at the Imperial Room, Ella Fitzgerald watched a week of *City Lights* in the afternoon in her suite at the Royal York before asking Gino Empry to see if he could get her on Brian's show. "This one," she told him, "I really want to do." Brian welcomed her with open arms.

Moses Znaimer maintained that any television show that is different or innovative in any way takes a long time to gain public acceptance. Linehan and *City Lights*, said Znaimer, went beyond interviewing. "It's hagiography," he told one writer. "It's a description of the lives of the saints."

☆

While Brian was sitting with stars in Toronto, his siblings in Hamilton were leading decidedly less glamorous lives. Bruce Dingwall's mother, a registered nurse, was in charge of nursing homes in Hamilton. When she learned that her daughter-in-law's estranged father, Les Linehan, was up at St. Joe's, she told Carole, "You really should go see your father."

"Why?" said Carole. "He left us."

Brian's younger brother Eric Linehan had a similar reaction. "I never met my father," he told me. "The biggest joke, I don't even know if it was a joke or not, was that he came home the day I was born, looked in the crib, and said, 'Another one!' – and left.

"I guess I was about twenty-eight or thirty when I got a call from the hospital. 'Leslie Linehan is in the hospital. We need somebody to take charge of him, he's going to die.' And I said, 'Why are you calling me?'"

Eric's wife talked him into going to see Les. "We went to the hospital," Eric recalls, "and there was this man lying in bed, and I looked at him, and I said to my wife, 'If you want to stay, stay. I'll wait for you outside. But I'm going for a smoke.'"

Eric's wife stayed and talked with Les Linehan for a few minutes longer.

"I just left," says Eric with a shrug. "I never knew the man."

When Ronnie Linehan learned his father was up at St. Joe's, he took his rebellious teenage son Paul to see Les, just to scare some sense into him. "If you don't want to end up like that," said Ronnie, pointing to the dying man in the hospital bed, "*smarten up!*"

During her turbulent years with Les Linehan, most of Sadie Kotur's siblings knew she had her hands full trying to protect her children, and herself, when Les went on a rampage. Years later Connie Kotur found out that their brother Paul had made contact with Les Linehan shortly after Sadie died. Close, physical contact.

"Our brother Paul," she told me, "apparently beat the living daylights out of him, for what Les had done to Sadie all those years."

Now Sadie and Les were both gone. One circle was closing, but another was opening. Brian was growing a circle of new admirers, and CTV executive Arthur Weinthal was one of them. Their friendship quickly developed, and less than a year later Brian was one of the gang at Arthur's stag night. Weinthal took a hands-on rooting interest in Brian's career, trying to persuade him to find a broader audience for the material he was gathering, via radio and print, and acted as Brian's ex officio agent to cut a deal with Toronto's top radio station, CFRB. As Weinthal recalls, he made the deal after talking to a couple of radio stations. "CFRB was looking to develop on-air personalities, and they liked the idea of Brian being able to do the big star schmooze. It was meant to be a gossipy thing. On junkets he would either go live to air, which he was very good at, or phone it in. To make his life easier I persuaded them to put a broadcast line into [their house], so he could phone it in directly from home."

Brian was a good talker. His daily quick-hit showbiz news and gossip broadcasts on shows hosted by beloved CFRB morning man Earl Warren and rising station staffer Andy Barrie, as well as his weekly hour-long interview special, only added to his professional lustre, and CFRB management noted that ratings frequently spiked when Linehan came on.

Unlike most professional interviewers, Brian was also a great interviewee. He made it a point to be one. He'd seen enough and read enough to both understand and admire the discipline of Hollywood studio media training. He did the same diligent preparation for an interview when he was the person being interviewed. He always arrived armed with a clutch of funny, glamorous stories that he hadn't told in public before, as well as some sound bite–friendly quotes that would always make it into print sooner or later.

By the time *City Lights* entered its seventh season, Brian Linehan was everywhere. The series, still nationally syndicated, had expanded to include hour-long weekend specials.

By now Brian needed a new production assistant. When the job was posted at Citytv, an attractively confident young lady from On-Air Promotion applied for the job. Lorraine Wilson had produced radio shows back in Australia but had never gone to broadcasting school. She had learned her work on the job, and she had been taught by experts. Brian took to her immediately and gave her the job.

Wilson still remembers her first day. "He just made everything special for you," she recalls with a smile. "By taking pictures . . . so you could capture these memories along the way."

Brian, says Lorraine, had a way of "making people feel special, and not just the movie stars. It would be simple things. He would go to CFRB in the morning and he would do his radio thing there with Earl Warren, and then he'd stop by this bakery and bring these unbelievable cheese Danishes back to the office for us!"

She admired and respected him for the way he treated people around him. "He always tried to give people breaks," she says. "And when he would take me out, he would always be so proud. He would show he was proud of me. 'This is my colleague, Lorraine Wilson.' He treated the guy in shipping at Citytv the same way. Brian had time for everybody. Not just because you were a movie star. You could be the mailman and he would find something special about you."

Lorraine Wilson had only been working with Brian for a couple of weeks when he won the 1980 ACTRA Award for Best Television Interviewer. He stole the show that night at the ACTRA Awards, with a disarming, charming acceptance speech. He gave full points to Citytv by duly reciting the station ID – "Citytv . . . Channel 79 . . . Cable 7," and allowed, "I may, in fact, be the proudest Irish Yugoslav from Hamilton you will ever see up here."

Lorraine Wilson smiles. "I remember him that morning when he got off that old elevator at Citytv, and he was holding his ACTRA Award. It was a proud moment for him."

Brian taught Lorraine how he did his research. "We really got a flow going," she remembers. "It got to the point where he could bring it in and I would know what he was looking for. So I'd be able to help pull that research together. But then he would take it and he would absorb it in the way that he absorbed it. He had envelopes and boxes of stuff on every key movie star that you could think of, so if he ever got to do an interview with them, he already had the material.

"There was no Internet, so he was his own clippings service. I would open up the file, and there were all these newspapers that he'd saved for years."

She would go through them, "and then he'd go home and he'd read it. Then he'd come in the next morning and we'd talk about some of the information before he sat down to tape the interview with whoever it was."

"He had a system," she explains. "A definite process for himself. You would start with the early life, and then at the end of it there were certain things, family, key things that you would find. And then at the end there were the movies. But he taught me how to look for what he was looking for."

What she admired most about his "system" was the integrity of its creator. "He would get books," she recalls, "and before he would interview an author he would definitely go and read that book. He didn't bullshit it. And everybody knew it."

When he wasn't on camera on Citytv, Linehan was quietly raising his public profile with appearances on other networks. He introduced a clutch of Canadian film gems, from *Murder by Decree* to *Outrageous!* on a national series called *CBC Premiere Presentation*. And he flew across the country at least once a month to expose his increasingly bitchy wit, and, occasionally, guest host on Alan Hamel's CTV talk show in Vancouver, a city only a short flight away from Hollywood, where most of Alan's showbiz friends – and his wife, Suzanne Somers – lived.

In 1980, when Hamel decided to move on to other things, CTV chief Arthur Weinthal considered three potential candidates for the chair behind Hamel's desk: Don Harron, Alan Thicke, and his friend Brian Linehan. All three candidates auditioned on camera for the job, guest-hosting for a week or two so the CTV brass could assess public reaction. Weinthal soon discovered, however, that Brian was much better at being a guest on the show than being its host.

Mackenzie Phillips, who was then starring in a hit series called *One Day at a Time*, was one of Brian's guests, and high on the hot list were questions concerning the recent fire that had almost destroyed her home in Los Angeles. As Weinthal tells it, he was in the control room in Vancouver, monitoring the candidates, for the start of the Linehan–Phillips interview.

"I understand you had a fire at your house," Brian began.

"Yes," said Ms. Phillips. "I lost two hundred pairs of sneakers."

Arthur whistled softly. Wow, what an opening line! He leaned forward expectantly, eager to hear what Brian would say to that.

"I understand," Brian continued, "that you also lost a painting in the fire . . ."

Weinthal remembers bolting out of the control room to tell one of the assistant directors to whisper to Brian to ASK ABOUT THE SNEAKERS!!!, but, he says, he knew then and there that it wasn't going to work. "When he was interviewing guests," he says, "Brian was so intent on getting *his* information out that he wasn't listening to theirs."

Besides, Weinthal needed a talk show host who could be goofy, silly, natural, spontaneous, accessible. Which was pretty much the equivalent of saying, Not Brian Linehan. "Brian Linehan," says Weinthal, "was Armani. Alan Thicke was Tip Top Tailors. Alan Thicke was *commercial.*" Alan Thicke got the gig. And kept it, for the next three years, using it as a valuable training ground for his own syndicated late-night U.S. talk venture, *Thicke of the Night.*

Brian had lost some points with CTV, but he was still scoring plenty with viewers. He soon became a popular game show panelist (especially if the game involved quizzing a Mystery Guest). He could barely boil water, but he learned how to prepare curried chicken breasts for host Bruno Gerussi on *Celebrity Cooks*. He made his screen debut as an actor in a CBC-TV suspense melodrama, *The Phoenix Team*, engagingly miscast as a despicable killer. And producer Marlene Smith coaxed him back on the boards for a two-week stint as an onstage narrator for her musical revue, *A Bite of the Big Apple*, at the Teller's Cage, a cabaret room in a downtown Toronto bank complex.

Still, thorns would occasionally appear among the roses. Lorraine Wilson remembers the *Caddyshack* junket with Chevy Chase and Bill Murray as one of them. "There were a couple of interviews that were horrible for him," she says, wincing at the memory. "They weren't very respectful. I think those guys were all just wired at the time. And they were making fun at his expense, and it actually devastated him, the way they treated him. He was very affected by that. They were cruel. They were *very* cruel."

"I think he did go back to see one of them again, for another movie," she recalls. "And I think one of them did apologize. But he was devastated by it."

But he recovered and continued to do what he did best. When Gloria Swanson was in town to promote her autobiography, she turned to the camera in the middle of her interview with Brian and told his Toronto viewers how lucky they were to have an interviewer of his calibre in their fair city. At the end of the interview, she insisted on inscribing a personal message to him in a copy of her book *Swanson on Swanson*. The inscription read:

To Brian
I'm truly indebted to you –
the interview was fun and exciting
joy & love to you –
Gloria Swanson

It could have been her standard inscription, of course, the one she signed to anyone and everyone who interviewed her. But it wasn't.

"I have been interviewed by David Frost, Dick Cavett, Barbara Walters, and many other of the so-called top names," Swanson told Random House exec Patricia Cairns. "I must confess I never have been at an interview that I have enjoyed more than the one Mr. Linehan just did. He is absolutely marvellous and makes those others look pale by comparison. That was the best interview I've had during the entire tour."

Cairns included Swanson's quote in a letter she sent to Brian after the star had left Toronto and returned to her home base of New York. "Brian, you have won this lady's respect – no small feat," Cairns wrote. "Congratulations. Also, congratulations to your crew. She was impressed with the professionalism and thought it was a lovely touch to have them introduced to her individually. If you ever need a publicity rep," added Cairns, "you might consider hiring Gloria Swanson."

As the 1980s rolled in, the Academy of Canadian Cinema and Television took over the administration of Canada's annual film awards – then nicknamed the Etrogs for the sculptor who had designed the award, Sorel Etrog – and transformed them into the Genie Awards. Brian and *City Lights* were now the darlings of the Canadian film industry, and Brian hosted a special Canadian Women in Film segment for the first Genies telecast on CBC Television. He was subsequently tapped to host the next two Genie Awards. In 1981, he walked onstage following a 1950s-style chorus line fanfare reminiscent of the weekly swanning performed by the June Taylor Dancers around Jackie Gleason; in 1982, he made an even more spectacular entrance in a mind-boggling visual illusion choreographed by acclaimed Canadian magician Doug Henning.

There was lots of buzz, inside and outside Citytv, that Linehan and *City Lights* were about to cross the border. Brian and Michael Levine were weighing U.S. interest, talking to American television executives about broadcasting his *City Lights* interviews in U.S. markets. Rumours abounded that the program was on the verge of U.S. syndication, and gossip was swirling that Brian would take up permanent residence in

New York or L.A. – especially L.A. – despite his insistence that he did not want to make his home in the United States.

In 1981, in one of the best pieces written on Brian over the years, journalist Philip Marchand identified Linehan as "one of the best interviewers in the country that has produced superb interviewers, people like Patrick Watson and Barbara Frum."

Marchand appeared to be fascinated by the fact that after eight years on television, Brian was still hypersensitive to criticism. "He seems unable to shrug off meanness or comprehend the meaning of the phrase 'it comes with the territory,'" Marchand observed. "He confronts gossips, for example. 'People tell me terrible things about me,' he says, 'terrible things. And I say, who told you that? Who told you that? I would just like to know.'"

He also included a cautionary note about Brian's way with words. "Linehan didn't survive the streets of downtown Hamilton for nothing," he said. "Others may have developed their fists, but he developed a scathing wit and a wicked tongue. When aroused, Linehan can be a deadly antagonist."

"I know they outnumber me, but they're not going to get me," Brian told him.

That statement alone may have prompted Marchand to conclude perhaps the largest print essay on Brian to that time with an alarmingly perceptive analysis. "Linehan," he wrote, "needs continually to escape, to prove himself, to show beyond a shadow of a doubt that he is loved. And when people are nasty (it happens in the media), the need expands into a sense of grievance unpleasantly close to paranoia."

And Brian was escaping. Most of the time, successfully.

Winston Collins, writing in *Front Row Centre* magazine that same year, reported that Brian still cherished the memory of a Hollywood dinner party given in his honour by George Cukor. "Now his private life includes late-night tête-à-têtes with Maggie Smith and Peter O'Toole at the Courtyard Café, and dinners at Sardi's followed by dancing at Studio 54 with award-winning actress (as he would introduce her) Carole Shelley.

"The celebrator of the stars has become a celebrity. He loves it."

8

"Just tell him Dr. Wagman called."

D r. Zane Wagman embodied every Jewish mother's dream for her daughter. He was young, single, athletic, elegant, well read, almost shamefully handsome. But as soon as those mothers learned that Zane was a dentist in the Toronto public school system, maternal enthusiasm tended to wane. Private practice, maybe. Toronto school system? Uh-uh.

In the late 1960s, young Dr. Wagman patronized a popular Toronto lunch spot called Mary John, a delicatessen located behind the Hospital for Sick Children, which is where he met Brian Linehan. Years later, when Michael Levine learned of this, he was stunned. Levine's maternal grandfather ran Mary John, and in her youth she had lived upstairs, over the deli, with her sisters and her brother until the family moved to Brunswick Avenue.

"Brian told me he came into Mary John, which was crowded, and there was a handsome young man sitting at one of the tables, reading the newspaper," Levine recounts. "Brian said, May I share your table? . . . and never went home."

Home was a key word for Brian and his dentist roommate. Years later, I told Marcia Martin what Brian had told me so very long ago – that he and Zane planned to buy old houses, fix them up beautifully, and buy bigger old houses with the profits. Marcia, or Marci, as she prefers to be called, said that buying and selling houses was strictly Zane's domain. "Zane did that," she said flatly. "The first house they shared was near me. And it was Zane who bought it. It wasn't Brian. It was always Zane's house."

Not that she knew that at the time. Marci, who worked with Brian on *City Lights* before working her way to top management, remembers helping him gather up some interview tapes from his office to take home when Zane pulled up in the car. "I had known Brian maybe ten years," Marci recalls, "and even then, he never said, 'I'd like you to meet my partner,' or anything like that. No, it was 'this is Dr. Wagman.' I said, 'nice to meet you,' and put Brian's stuff in the car, and that was that. Brian never said another word about it."

At that time, Marci says, Brian never went anywhere with Zane. "It was 'Zane would be bored, he doesn't want to be part of this, he doesn't like the Hollywood thing, he doesn't like the phoniness.' So whether that was true," she says, "or whether Brian was just protecting his gay life, or whatever life he had, is another thing. But he just never talked about Zane. I think it was about twenty years before they ever went out together, just the two of them, to dinner."

At the beginning of her relationship with Brian, Shirley Lord also had no idea Zane existed. "There's no question that Brian was, I would say, deliberately secretive. Because if I ever would say, Brian, who is your mate, who is your love?, he would say, 'Oh, no one.' And I think of the years he was living on Grenadier Heights with Zane!"

Although it was only their second real estate investment, Brian and Zane had hit the jackpot when they purchased 5 Grenadier Heights. Its modestly attractive exterior suggested a family home that might have been passed down to generations of inheritors. But the interior revealed the real dimensions of the house, with separate dining room, living room, and kitchen, and a parlour they frequently used as a music room. The two second-floor bedrooms were generously appointed – they used one as a guest room – as was the spacious library, and a self-contained third-floor suite was an added bonus. Best of all, perhaps, was the location of the house itself, perched atop an embankment that sloped gently down to a small lake known as Grenadier Pond. Their front door was situated in an urban suburb, but their back door opened onto natural, idyllic countryside.

Karen Kain also had to wait to meet the enigmatic Dr. Wagman. "I didn't even know about Zane," she admits. "Brian was my escort for things. He would never take Zane, and he never talked about Zane. I remember thinking at one point that it had been at least a decade that I'd known him, that we had sort of hung out together and done things together – I didn't know him intimately – before he confided in me and introduced me to Zane."

Lorraine Wilson agrees. "There was a part of Brian that was very private," she says. "I didn't know about Zane for a long time. Zane would phone and say, 'Just tell him Dr. Wagman called.'"

But eventually Brian did introduce some of his friends to Zane, and when Karen Kain bought a house in Toronto's historic Cabbagetown, he and Brian were the first people she invited to dinner. "I had no furniture. I made lasagna, which was the only recipe I knew how to make. I met Zane, and Zane was even shyer than I was."

Early on, Karen realized that Zane had a serious crush on her. He would subsequently tell close friends that she was his idea of an Ideal Woman. She still remembers hearing about a tango club in Argentina that Brian and Zane had visited. One particular tango dancer with whom they were smitten apparently bore more than a passing resemblance to Karen, which inspired both Zane and Brian to get up and join her in what they facetiously reported as a dazzling display of dance.

Over time, Karen began to see "a darkness" to Zane. She remembers how he struggled to get to sleep each night, the prescription sleeping pills he took, and how he went to a sleep clinic to be tested one night in an attempt to combat his relentless insomnia. At times he could be unshakeably moody, almost brooding.

Brian's long-time confidante Marilyn Lightstone, who by now was also his neighbour in High Park, recalls that his relationship with Zane "was very hidden. At that time when there seemed to be a lot of people 'coming out' all over the place" – especially, perhaps, in the arts community – "Brian and Zane were 'sharing a house.'"

A house, maybe, but not their sleeping quarters. Brian had his bedroom, and Zane had his. Says Michael Levine: "I never had a conversation with Brian, for at least the first twenty years, in which he would ever describe Dr. Zane Wagman as his lover, or his partner, or his spouse, or in any other endearing way. He was simply a friend with whom he lived. And while I totally respected his right to characterize it as he would, he was never comfortable with it. I got the sense of a friend who was dangling at the end of a rope and really didn't want to let anybody inside.

"I was never an intimate of Zane," says Levine, "and I was never quite sure whether it was because I was a threat to Zane, because I was a person to whom Brian listened . . . sometimes . . . or whether he just didn't relate to my personality, that I was too extroverted, or whether it was a sense of privacy, a sense of competition. I liked Zane but I didn't know Zane."

The Zane he glimpsed, he says, was something of a misanthrope. "He was basically a depressive, and he was basically a culture vulture, who would rather watch a beautiful ballet, listen to a wonderful opera, listen to a concert, than actually have to engage in conversation with people."

Zane had a lifelong obsession with opera, and at one point serious interest was shown in his hosting a classical music program on the radio, until the producers hit an unexpected and unusual snag. "They wanted him to use his honorific, his 'Dr.' – like 'Dr. Zane Wagman,'" Marilyn Lightstone recalls. "And Zane said, 'No, because they will think I am a doctor of Music. And I am a dentist.' He felt that would be false representation.

"Zane," she says, "was a very shy kind of man . . . he was very reserved. So the whole thing never went any further. And Brian was very upset with Zane, because he just thought it was such a waste. And it probably would have been great, because Zane really was tremendously knowledgeable."

Zane Wagman had three great passions. Dentistry, alas, was not one of them. But mention anything to do with cooking, gardening, or opera and you quickly gained Zane's undivided attention. Getting him to talk about his own profession, however, could be like – pardon the expression – pulling teeth. "Zane hated dentistry," says a dentist friend, Dr. Allan Harris. "He just couldn't wait to get out of that. It was so painful to watch."

Zane was also very fitness-conscious, proud of his prowess with his kayak on Grenadier Pond, the large mini-lake in the park on which their property bordered, and devoted to weekly workouts at the health club with Brian, when he wasn't out of town on a junket. Marilyn Lightstone says, "At a time when nobody went to the gym, they were at the gym. Swimming and going to the gym and working out were very important to them. And discipline, discipline, discipline." She remembers going to a yoga class with them at Hart House, the sports and recreation wing of Zane's alma mater, the University of Toronto. Zane religiously used the pool there, where he swam nude with other U of T males until the facility went co-ed in 1975. His weekend rituals with Brian included Saturday market shopping for groceries and flowers, and a rigorous Sunday workout at the gym, followed by a reward: a rich Sunday brunch.

Arthur Weinthal, Michael Levine, and Brian never worked out at the gym together, but as friends they frequently went out to dinner. "But it was always Michael, Arthur, and Brian, never Arthur, Michael, Brian, and Zane," says Weinthal. Brian also loved spending weekends with Arthur and his wife, Susie, at their summer retreat in Ontario's Hockley Valley. "Susie would encourage Brian to bring Zane to the country when he would come for the weekend," Weinthal recalls, "but he never did. He kept his Zane life off to the side, across the street. Susie and I never, ever socialized with Zane. I don't think that it was all Brian's doing. I don't think Zane wanted to socialize either. They spent vacation time together and cultural time together, at the ballet, at the opera. Although I always had the impression that that was more Zane than Brian."

Brian and Zane's guest list was very select. Bea Arthur stayed with them. Doris Roberts came to tea. And when Taina Elg was touring in *Gigi*, Brian and Zane invited Gail and me to dinner with Taina and her co-star Betsy Palmer. Taina Elg fondly remembers Zane constantly talking "about the plants and the rosebushes and the pond down below, with the view of the pond from the kitchen, where he liked to spend so much time cooking. And how it was really like being in the country there."

Brian served Taina an extra-special dessert that night. He had been through the archives of film stills in the nostalgia shop of the MGM Grand hotel in Las Vegas, where he had uncovered three or four eight-by-ten black-and-white glossies of Taina's wardrobe tests for *Imitation General*, one of the films she had made years earlier at Metro-Goldwyn-Mayer. She had never seen them before and couldn't wait to show them to her husband, Rocco Caporale, when she returned to New York. The photos are still on display in her Manhattan apartment today.

Ironically, Zane saw those photos more often than Brian did. He was particularly fond of Taina and Rocco and always looked forward to seeing them. "Zane was such an opera lover that he came to New York quite often," says Taina. "And we said, what's the point of staying in a hotel? Come and stay with us. So he had a little guest room here."

Over the years, Zane met only a few of Brian's sisters and brothers, and on one occasion joined Brian in celebrating his brother Patrick's wedding anniversary. When Patrick arrived in Toronto with his wife, Linda, he discovered that their standard Harbour Castle room had been upgraded to a suite. "Jesus Murphy, I didn't pay for something this fancy!" Patrick protested.

"Oh yes, sir, this is your room," the manager assured him.

"There was a big bowl of fruit, a bottle of champagne, and strawberries dipped in chocolate on the table," Patrick remembers.

"Brian's treat," Linda interjects shyly.

It was a memorable evening. Joining Patrick and Linda for their anniversary dinner at a Greek restaurant were Carole Linehan and her husband Bruce Dingwall, and Brian and Zane. Patrick, who looks more like Brian than any of his other siblings, was acutely aware that Brian's face "was plastered all over subways and billboards and everything. So everybody in the restaurant was looking at us. 'Oh that's Brian Linehan.'

"I kinda got Brian and Zane going, because I was saying, 'See, look, they all think they know me.' Brian started to laugh. Zane was laughing too. Zane was a great guy. He had a great sense of humour."

Zane loved to travel the world, with or without Brian. Together they shared many exotic adventures, beautiful beaches, extravagant dinners. Brian, a confessed snapshot addict, took hundreds of colour shots of Zane, who more often than not was wearing a Speedo, looking tanned and happy in one luxurious beach location after another.

Brian was shameless in his pursuit of free upgrades and airline reward miles, coaxing and cajoling them out of as many sources as he could. "Oh Dianne, you know you're never going to use those!" he would tease Warner Bros. Canadian publicity chief Dianne Schwalm. Karen Kain remembers being booked on the same flight to Paris as Zane and Brian: "Suddenly I was upgraded, just because I was with Brian."

If Frieda Creighton wasn't spoiling us in Air Canada's ultra-urbane Maple Leaf lounge, Dorothee Anne McLean and Eleanor Clements were treating us like princes in the American Airlines' cozy Admiral's Club. Brian enjoyed all that pampering, but Zane loved the pampering too. He ate it up with a spoon. He didn't much care for show business, and he didn't much care for show folk, but he loved all the perks – the hotel suites, the seats in first class, the complimentary everything. And he missed them a bit, maybe even more than a bit, when he would board a plane and fly on his own dime to some obscure European destination to see some obscure German opera that hadn't been performed for half a century or more. ("And usually with good reason," Brian would mutter under his breath.)

Brian and Zane had a short list of friends around the world who invited them to stop by whenever they were in the neighbourhood. On one trip to Paris they ended up staying with celebrated broadcaster

Adrienne Clarkson – by then Agent-General for Premier William Davis's Ontario – and her consort John Ralston Saul.

Brian and Zane especially loved travelling together in December, when they could escape the mawkish, insincere sentiments of both Christmas and Chanukah and the inevitable emotional traps set by their respective families, traps that they had no intention of falling into.

Zane seldom talked about his family, but on the rare occasions he did, it was clear that he was anxious to distance himself from them. His father had a ladies' hat store on College Street – it's a restaurant now – and he and his older brother, Stanley, and their parents lived behind the store in a modest but comfortable two-bedroom flat.

According to Zane, his mother and father were horrible parents, and he and his brother no longer had any connection other than the essential maintenance of their elderly, widowed father. According to Stanley, their father was "an *angel*." Born in Poland, he came to Canada as a boy and supported his family of eight by working in a factory. By the time his own sons were born he was the foreman of a factory that made ladies' hats, while his mother ran the hat store. Their mother, Stanley told me, could be "difficult" at times, but not without cause. Asthmatic, she also suffered from a heart condition and spent most of her life in and out of hospital.

Their two sons had clearly chosen different paths. Stanley had been in the restaurant business until he decided to explore his private passion for antiques as a retailer. Today Stanley Wagman & Son is one of the best known antique houses in Toronto. Zane, on the other hand, had pursued a more conventional career, one which he was not remotely passionate about, but that promised him a modicum of financial security. Sadly, the two brothers were never able to resolve their personal differences, and the mere mention of one brother to the other, however innocent, often provoked an angry, unhappy emotional response.

Brian had stopped talking to his family, too. He had gone home to Hamilton to attend yet another family wedding and, perhaps after too many Scotches, his older brother, Ronnie, had called him a queer, and made it very clear how real men felt about queers.

The incident occurred at the Hamilton hotel, where Brian had invited the family to his room for drinks. Patrick and Linda weren't there, because Patrick was working the Saturday shift at the steel mill. Jovan and his wife, Cathy, had left to attend another party. But Connie and Danny were there, and Ronnie's wife, Gerri. And suddenly, Brian was in tears, flushed with the hot shame of humiliation. What was said couldn't be unsaid, and whatever was left of the Linehan family was in pieces.

Patrick Linehan believes he could have stopped it if he had been there. "Ronnie," he says, "didn't agree with Brian's lifestyle. But, you know, Brian's lifestyle was Brian's choice and Brian's prerogative. I loved my brother Ronnie, but he was a redneck."

Patrick's wife, Linda, says the incident with Ronnie "turned Brian off about coming home. And naturally so. But it was a shame. Because then Brian painted the whole family with the same brush. I felt bad about that.

"Brian was included, always, in everything with the families," says Linda. "Whenever there was a wedding, he always received an invitation. At Ronnie's birthday party, the one they had for his sixty-fifth, Brian didn't come, but he did send a case of Scotch. And Ronnie was so happy when he got to that party. 'My brother Brian sent me a case of Scotch!' He just was beaming. And I thought, now there's forgiveness if I've ever seen it."

Brian's youngest brother, Mico, only heard about the altercation between Ronnie and Brian. "Brian was in everybody's wedding party but mine," he notes. He shows me photos of Brian at Ronnie's wedding, at Patrick's wedding. "But by the time we got married he had already had his falling out with Ronnie and said he was never coming back to Hamilton. We sent him an invitation, but he sent the telegram back: *I wish I could be there but business prevents* . . . and it became kind of a joke because the same telegram came all the time. Like when we sent him a thing about our kids being born. *I wish I could be there but business prevents* . . . He wasn't coming back. That was obvious."

When Philip Marchand interviewed Brian for *Chatelaine* in 1981, he noted: "When asked what he has in common with his siblings, Linehan tends to answer, 'One mother and one father.'"

After that Brian and Zane agreed that no family celebration, Serbian or Canadian, Christian or Jewish, would be allowed to interfere with their holiday travel plans. Not ever.

In later years, Zane would sometimes join Brian on junkets, sharing Brian's room in whatever first-class hotel he was staying at, especially if there was an opera or a concert he wanted to attend in the city where we happened to be. The hottest ticket for Zane was always

New York City, where he would go to galleries and museums by day and concerts and operas by night, to the point where we rarely even bumped into each other in the elevators.

One night his plans changed, and Brian and I persuaded him to join us for dinner at Trader Vic's. Everything was fine for the first hour, as we indulged ourselves with silly drinks and sordid gossip, by now a time-honoured junket tradition.

Back then, I was an insatiable chain-smoker. But in Hollywood, smoking was considered an unfortunate addiction, not a vice, so my habit proved no impediment to me. Brian, on the other hand, was a selective smoker, but not really by choice, mostly because Zane was vociferously opposed to it. Brian and I were both smoking that night, but we had cleverly positioned Zane so that the air-conditioning would blow our cigarette smoke away from him. Or so we thought. It turned out that the restaurant air-conditioning was no match for us. Brian and I kept smoking and chattering and smoking and drinking and smoking and eating, until Zane had finally had enough of us. He stormed out of the restaurant, thoroughly disgusted.

"Oh well," said Brian with a shrug. "At least now we can smoke without feeling guilty."

"Are you feeling guilty?"

"Not a bit," he replied. "Zane knows how to order room service. Especially when the studio is paying for it. He'll be just fine."

At home in Toronto, it was a different story. Brian thought Zane had every right to a smoke-free environment, so he respected his wishes. When Zane went away on one of his opera excursions, Brian would sometimes light up furtively in the basement, where he stored his legions of personality files in a series of metal filing cabinets.

One spring, after the L.A. junket for the Taylor Hackford movie *Against All Odds*, Gail and I persuaded Brian to fly to Hawaii with us for a week of R&R in Honolulu. On our first night there, we took him to the original Trader Vic's on Waikiki Beach, and walking home he was recognized at least half a dozen times by visiting Canadian tourists. He loved it, and Hawaii, but what he seemed to enjoy most was being able to light up whenever he wanted. "I can't smoke at home, because it really bothers Zane," he reminded us. "I can't smoke on the way to work, because I use public transportation. And now I can't smoke at work, because Citytv has gone non-smoking."

Brian shrugged his broad, gym-defined shoulders and exhaled languidly. "It's a miracle I smoke at all!"

☆

One day, Brian and Lorraine Wilson were at Citytv, reviewing research for an upcoming interview, when she paused to check messages and learned that Jovo Rodic had died.

"I think it was his sister Connie who had left the message," she says. "And I had to tell him. I said, Are you okay? He was so composed. He just said, 'I need to go for a walk around the block.' He did, and he just kind of kept it together. I don't think he was prepared for what he felt when he heard that news about his stepfather."

Brian's mother, Sadie, hadn't lived long enough to see her son become famous. And if Les Linehan saw Brian on television, he never told him. Brian's stepfather, who had outlived both Sadie and Les, once asked Brian when he was going to stop talking to people on television and get a real job.

"It was so funny," Brian's brother Patrick told me. "When Brian was going to Delta, when he started writing for the *Spectator*, my stepfather Jovo would sit at the kitchen table with his friends and he would say in Serbian, 'Brian is going nowhere, he's going nowhere!'

"And then of course Brian outgrew Delta, he outgrew the paper, and then he went to Toronto, and he got his foot in the door at Odeon, and he got his foot in the door at Citytv, and the next thing you know, a year and a half later, he's all over the place. You know my stepfather; he wouldn't say nothing. But you couldn't, you'd dare not say 'I told you so.' Because you'd get a smack right in the yap!"

Brian took another walk around the block, then came back and closed his office door. He had to prepare for his dinner meeting with Michael Levine that night.

Levine drove him home after dinner. "I remember pulling into the driveway at Grenadier Heights," Levine recalls, "and I said good night, and he turned to me and said, 'My stepfather died today.' I stopped, and I said, 'Oh, I'm really sorry.' And he said, 'I'm not. I had no relationship.' And I said, 'Are you going to the funeral?' 'No.' And I said, 'Do you want to talk about it?' 'No. Good night.' And he walked into the house.

"From my background that was profound, because I could never shut up about my parents. And there was such hurt there. I used to call him the Purple Rose of Cairo," he adds, "after the Woody Allen movie. To me, Brian was the man who walked into the movie screen because that world was more real to him than the world that he had escaped from."

Brian Linehan had come a long way from the steel mills in Hamilton. Zane Wagman had come a long way from living behind a store on College Street. Surely the best was yet to come.

9

"This is going to cost me a fortune!"

By the time *City Lights* was halfway through its eighth season, Brian Linehan was on the verge of becoming a Player. In show business, his was the only Canadian name on the A-list of television interviewers. There was only one thing holding him back: his nationality. In New York and Hollywood, Canada – especially Toronto – was regarded as a great place to open a movie. It was also regarded as a great place to come from. If you couldn't come from the U.S.A., that is.

International stars like Maggie Smith and Rudolf Nureyev – stars who don't "do" television – were starting to beat a path to Brian's door. So were Hollywood's hottest box office names. And then, as now, most of the biggest stars in the world were American. And then, as now, generations of Canadian exports from Mary Pickford to Donald Sutherland, from Anne Murray to Jim Carrey, were immediately adopted by Hollywood as American stars. With the possible exception of Quebec, America had the best star-making machinery on the planet, and was not shy about using it. Images of American movie stars flooded the universe, keeping the American Dream alive for millions of offshore innocents.

Yes, America had it all, including some of the dullest, laziest, most ill-informed interviewers in the world. And American stars put up with them, convinced they had no other choice. That is, until a surprising, odd-looking alternative from the north showed up. And suddenly the standard Q&A went out the window. Doing an interview with Brian Linehan could be hard work for movie stars, but he worked harder than they did, and the result was frequently the best interview work they'd ever done. So the stars and the studios wanted the world to see it.

Well, okay – they wanted America to see it. They wanted all their fans and friends and relatives to see how smart they were, how funny, how clever, how intelligent. And they found the fact that only their fans and friends in Toronto and a few other Canadian outposts could see their work both disappointing and distressing.

He heard it from star after star. "I can't understand why you're not on television in the States!" "You're better than all the others! So what are you doing here in Canada?" "Oh Brian, I wish everyone in America could see your show!"

Brian felt exactly the same way. And so did Michael Levine. Because of Levine's initial conversation with Moses Znaimer, Brian owned half of *City Lights*, and therefore had a say in the distribution of the program.

Enter Bill Miller at King Features. A deep-pocketed distributor of newspaper and television features, King Features was part of the Hearst Corporation, the communications empire founded by William Randolph Hearst, the legendary publisher who inspired Orson Welles's classic *Citizen Kane*. After a series of conversations with Levine, Miller decided that King Features should take on the distribution of *City Lights*. Miller launched a splashy media campaign aimed at selling Linehan and *City Lights* to independent TV stations all across America.

For Brian, the big, bold, brassy ad campaign with his name and face all over it was nothing less than a dream come true. King Features, one of the biggest players in U.S. television, was trumpeting, yes, *trumpeting* his show, his accomplishments, himself. The syndicator was investing tens of thousands of U.S. dollars, buying ads in the trade magazines, producing glossy brochures, all extolling the Linehan mystique.

Brian had been reading the weekly show business bible *Variety* since the first day he showed up for work at Odeon. Now when he opened it, he saw a two-page double-truck ad, the most expensive ad you could buy in that paper, not for a new blockbuster movie, but for him. For Brian Linehan and *City Lights*.

> *Something incredible happens when the most famous people in the world appear on this show . . . No idle conversation. No over-zealous plugging. No same old stories. No nonsense. They really talk . . . they confide, they confess, they laugh, they cry. They become totally human. And Brian Linehan is the reason. Linehan gets facts. Not chatter . . . the series that gets*

guests others can't . . . with a host who asks the questions others don't . . . there is nothing else like it on TV.

It was fabulous while it lasted. It just didn't last long enough to become real. At the end of the day, says Michael Levine, King Features "wined us and dined us and took the programs out and never did a damn thing with them. So again it was one of those profound expectations that didn't get realized."

The King Features deal was the only significant proposal to bring Brian Linehan and *City Lights* to mainstream U.S. audiences. The show was telecast on the USA Network, a cable network, for a period of time before and after the King Features episode. City International also tried to sell *City Lights*, "but their hearts were never in it," adds Levine. "The big problem that Brian had was that in this country he was a celebrity interviewing celebrities. In the other parts of the world they only wanted the celebrity. They had their own interviewers."

At one point Arthur Weinthal tried to get Brian on CBS Cable, but a deal failed to materialize. As Weinthal remembers it, CBS was trying to broaden its base by testing some new faces. But nothing happened with Brian, even though they really liked him.

"Part of what they liked, of course, was that Brian was really enthusiastic about the possibility of being New York–based," Weinthal recalls. "He loved what he did. He loved the action. He loved the attention. He loved the Armani suits. He loved the integrity of it. He needed to feel worthwhile and important. What he did was one of a kind and very important. And aside from the occasional departure into silliness after three martinis," he adds, "Brian conducted himself with great dignity."

Screen siren Arlene Dahl, a dazzling Hollywood redhead, had reinvented herself as a beauty expert and cosmetic manufacturer by the time Brian met her, and he counted Arlene and her husband, Marc Rosen, among his best friends in Manhattan. At one point the former MGM glamour girl arranged an appointment for him in New York at ABC. "But Brian was not the handsomest of men," she notes with regret. "And that's what they look for here."

Consequently *City Lights* was never able to break into major U.S. markets. And after years of praise from interview subjects, media, and distributors, Brian found this impossible to accept. "Brian desperately wanted to be down in the United States," says Judi Schwam. "He didn't get what a Barbara Walters gets, or what a Diane Sawyer gets, and he worked just as hard. He got that level of respect, I think, in Canada. He just never got it here in America."

Shirley Lord also felt that Brian was a very disappointed man. "He came to New York and everyone around him, including myself, said, 'You are so great, you should have a bigger audience.' And I know that someone in California told him he needed to get his nose fixed. And he was very upset about that."

Ah, yes. The Nose. The unsolved mystery. He told early interviewers he had broken his nose four times. Not true, says his big sister Connie. Even as a boy, she says, "he could flatten his nose right on his face."

Patrick Linehan swears it happened when they were kids, at the beach. "Every hundred feet or so they have all these giant rocks; they act as a breakwater. Brian and Eric were playing on the rocks and Brian fell, and when he fell on those rocks he broke his nose."

Brian's youngest brother, Mico, was with Brian one day when he told someone "he was on the deck roof of our porch, untangling my diapers from the line, when he fell off and broke his nose. And I know that's not true." But, he adds, one of his cousins and two of his nieces have the same nose. "So the nose is genetic somewhere along the line."

In 1981, Philip Marchand, who was interviewing Brian for *Chatelaine*, observed that the "obvious damage" to his nose occurred "when, as a child, he dove into the shallow end of a pool and hit bottom."

That same year Brian told writer Winston Collins: "Yes, I've broken my nose. No, I never dove into a swimming pool that held only two feet of water. I ask you, do I seem like the kind of man who would do that? No, certainly not. I'm the kind who would test the water first."

Brian once told *TV Guide* that he had actually made an appointment to reconstruct his nose, because he couldn't breathe through it properly. "But," he said, "I changed my mind. I decided that I would not change my appearance. I didn't want to have to deal with being good-looking. Perhaps if I've made a contribution, it's that I've made it easier for people who are not eight-by-tens."

A decade later Brian had changed the story again, probably for his own amusement. In a 1998 *Lifestyles Magazine* cover story, he told writer Pearl Sheffy Gefen that he had broken his nose several times as a child playing various sports, including floor hockey. "But I don't want to come across as the jock of the year," he quipped, "because that would throw people, that's not their perception of me."

A young Brian Linehan riding his tricycle in Hamilton, Ontario

Sadie Kotur Linehan and
Jovo Rodic in front of their house
on Gertrude Street

(left to right) Mico Rodic,
Carole Linehan, Eric Linehan,
Brian Linehan, and
Patrick Linehan

(left to right) Mico Rodic,
Carole Linehan, Brian Linehan,
Connie Linehan, Eric Linehan,
and Ronnie Linehan (in front)

Zane Wagman and Brian in Europe

Zane cooking at Grenadier Heights

George Anthony, Brian Linehan, and Gail Anthony at the
Toronto International Film Festival

Sylvester Stallone and Brian Linehan

Brian Linehan and John Travolta

Peter O' Toole and Brian Linehan

Legendary director George Cukor and Brian Linehan

Woody Allen and Brian Linehan

Brian on the other side of the desk, being interviewed by
Alan Hamel on his CTV talk show

Brian and Karen Kain

Brian Linehan and Barbra Streisand

Someone also asked him if he was going to do anything about his grey hair. "I have not had my nose fixed, my teeth are still chipped, why would I worry about my hair?" he told Sheffy Gefen. "Did I want to be better looking? Only most of my life. My siblings are good-looking. I am unusual-looking. I get mail that says 'dear pig face, flat face, pug nose.'" Yes, he admitted, he got a lot of other mail, too. "But you never remember the good stuff."

"He was SO vain!" says his publicist pal Harriet Blacker. "So wonderfully vain. Several times we actually talked about why he didn't fix his nose. And it was 'love me as I am, or f——— off.' Which, again, was *so* Brian."

☆

Despite uncommonly generous support from the *Toronto Sun* and Citytv, the struggling Toronto film festival was being soundly ignored by most of the Canadian media. Co-founder Dusty Cohl asked Roger Ebert for his help. The result was three consecutive major media-magnet film festival tributes, to Martin Scorsese in September 1982, Robert Duvall in September 1983, and Warren Beatty in September 1984, that changed the media face of the Toronto festival forever. Robert De Niro showed up to salute Scorsese; Francis Ford Coppola flew in to toast Duvall; and Robert Towne, Jerzy Kosinski, and Jack Nicholson joined Ebert and his co-host Gene Siskel on stage at Beatty's tribute while Diane Keaton and Sandra Bernhardt watched from the audience.

The tributes became huge events for the Toronto festival, and created the buzz that helped it become the biggest and most successful public film festival in the world. But they, too, had their critics. Canadian media carped that Ebert and Siskel were carpetbaggers, high-profile U.S. movie critics "hired" to do a job that Canadian film critics could have done. At that time, Brian was getting a lot of attention for his *City Lights* interviews, and kept waiting for the call from then-festival director Wayne Clarkson. But no call came.

Uncharacteristically discreet, Brian remained publicly supportive of Roger and Gene, but was privately resentful. "I wished they'd asked *me*," he confided, almost wistfully.

On one level, he understood that he hosted a local show in Toronto and that Roger and Gene were currently co-hosting the hottest weekly movie show in the United States, watched by viewers all across North America who actually went to the movies. All studio doors opened to the opportunity to appear before Siskel and Ebert's nationwide television audience. Brian understood the business case, and the reasons for it. But he still resented it.

"None of the Canadian journalists who were pissed off with the tributes understood the structure beneath the creation of the tributes," says Dusty Cohl. "None of them could understand that, especially in Toronto, if you're creating something, you can't have a situation where you ask different people, and if they turn you down, then the word is out that they've turned you down, and so the next person you ask knows that he or she is not your first choice. You have to be pretty sure that the first person you ask is of great enough stature and is going to come. And who better than Siskel and Ebert to do that?

"Could there have been a better format for doing it? Siskel and Ebert were not at their best sharing an interview, because they had never done it before," Cohl admits candidly. "And it was extra tough on them to do it, especially in their own combative styles. Could somebody have done a better job up there? Brian being one of them? Quite likely. I don't know. But could they have pulled off the evening?" He shakes his head slowly. "No. Not for a second. Not a chance."

Brian found this very difficult to accept. He knew he still lacked the American TV profile of, say, Roger Ebert, but his popularity with viewers was growing in what seemed to be leaps and bounds. He was receiving more press attention than ever. Some days it seemed like everybody loved Linehan.

Well, maybe not *everybody*. When he learned that his interview with Brian Linehan was about to be telecast on the USA Network – a cable channel which at that time reached a modest 13 million homes across America – Woody Allen saw red. Or green, depending on your point of view.

Allen's lawyers claimed that Woody and Brian had agreed that the most recent interview they taped would air only in Canada. And definitely not in New York, where Woody liked to live as low-profile a life as possible, for all sorts of reasons (use your imagination). Linehan's lawyers insisted that Woody had said he would *prefer* that his interview with Brian not be broadcast in the States, but that this stated preference was never a condition of his participation.

After it aired on *City Lights*, the Allen interview had been gathering dust in a Citytv storeroom until it got included, by mistake, in a package of shows for the USA Network. The USA Network started plugging *City Lights* like crazy, using clips from Brian's interview with Woody as promos, which seemed to bug Woody even more than the appearance of his interview with Brian.

Woody's lawyers filed a $5.1-million lawsuit – about $6 million in Canadian dollars – in Los Angeles superior court, against Citytv and against Brian Linehan personally for breach of contract. Brian was devastated and angry. Most viewers were stunned to learn that Linehan, an object of adoration for legions of major film stars, had somehow offended Woody Allen. More stunned than anyone, of course, was Brian, who had chalked up previous interviews with Allen without incident.

Michael Levine was called in to represent Brian and Citytv. "And of course we knew nothing about a contract," says Levine. Allen's lawyers claimed the "contract" was an oral agreement between Woody and Brian. (And we all know what Sam Goldwyn said about oral agreements.) They also insisted that Allen did not consent to having his "likeness and image" used in advertising devised to promote the telecast of the interview.

Michael Levine knew "you don't die from a piece of paper" and took it all in stride. Brian was hysterical.

"This is SO wonderful for you," I assured him. "Being sued by Woody Allen may be the best thing that ever happened to you. It's certainly the biggest. Every paper is carrying this story. People who don't go to movies are seeing this story. People who don't watch television are seeing this story. Your name is being spoken all around the world!"

Brian wasn't buying it. "This is going to cost me a fortune!" he wailed.

"Do you have a fortune?" I asked him.

"No," he replied, "I don't."

"Do you have six million dollars?"

"No, I don't."

"Then relax!" I said. "Sit back, put your feet up, and enjoy the ride!"

But he couldn't. Intellectually he understood that this lawsuit may have had more to do with money than integrity. But he didn't respond intellectually. He responded emotionally. And, as always, took it personally. *City Lights* was about to celebrate its tenth anniversary on the air, and Brian Linehan was reasonably sure that his career was over.

Michael Levine hopped an Air Canada flight to L.A. and hired California counsel. The tab for preparing a defence for Brian and Citytv ran about US$100,000. Fortunately, Citytv was backing him, and the insurance companies were behind him.

Brian had almost calmed down.

He and Zane were about to embark on a much-needed holiday in England.

Little did they know what lay ahead.

10

"It was mockery."

While the Woody Allen lawsuit hung over his head like a menacing black cloud from a Looney Tunes cartoon, Brian Linehan continued to make a name for himself as the guy who had all the big stars, Canadian *and* American, on his show. He was also keeping a watchful eye on new talent. Brian had followed fellow Hamiltonian Martin Short's career since first seeing the versatile young actor brighten a Toronto stage in the *Peanuts* musical *You're a Good Man, Charlie Brown*. He cheered as Short and cohorts Andrea Martin, Gilda Radner, Jayne Eastwood, and Eugene Levy graduated from musical revues to wowing audiences nightly in a marathon run of Stephen Schwartz's Broadway musical *Godspell*. When the famed Chicago improv company Second City gave birth to a bold Canadian franchise, Eastwood, Levy, and Radner would go on to become charter members of Canada's first Second City company. Martin Short and Andrea Martin would later join Eugene Levy, John Candy, Catherine O'Hara, Dave Thomas, and Rick Moranis as major players in the unique ensemble that would become the weekly Second City television show called *SCTV*.

By then, he and Short had become personal friends. As Brian's reputation grew, Marty, as he was known to his friends, decided to salute his long-time supporter. "I want to do you on *SCTV*," he told Brian. Brian was thrilled, and immediately sent him a box of video cassettes – tapes of *City Lights* episodes that Marty could study to capture as many of Brian's mannerisms as possible.

The resulting impression was one of Short's best. "Brock Linehan" was an affectionate homage to his friend's success, except Marty's fake Linehan always ended up tripping over his own research. Superlative

SCTV makeup artist Beverly Schectman had even taken the time and trouble to duplicate the mole on "Brock's" cheek.

At first, Brian was somewhat shocked by Marty's exaggerated version of him, but the dawning reality that he was now famous enough to be spoofed on *SCTV* as a recognizable TV icon soon took precedence over that initial reaction.

In July 1983, a story appeared in *Toronto Life* magazine that would forever colour all future references to Martin Short's send-up of Brian. Written by arts chronicler Martin Knelman and illustrated with an unflattering caricature of Brian, it was a slick, frequently clever character assassination that interpreted Short's creation of Brock Linehan as a justified attack on what Knelman perceived to be Linehan's sycophantic fawning over his celebrity interview subjects.

Many months earlier, Knelman had seen the costly media campaign aimed at selling Linehan and *City Lights* in America. Perhaps it was the two-page double-truck ad in *Variety* that jangled Knelman to the point where he felt it was time to say something about it. That, and Woody Allen.

Brian was so shell-shocked by the fact that Woody Allen was suing him – for *money!!* – that he had taken Michael Levine's warnings to heart and doggedly kept his mouth shut, refusing to comment on Allen or the lawsuit to anyone who might even *own* a pen.

"When I saw Linehan at a screening and asked for his phone number," Knelman wrote in *Toronto Life*, "he revealed a side of his personality that is rarely seen by viewers of his TV show. '*If it's about Woody Allen,*' he hissed at me, '*I have nothing to say to you.*'"

Knelman, however, had plenty to say. In a story headlined "Extreme Unction," Knelman led off with a word-by-word description of the ad produced by King Features in the fall of 1982. "*If you think it's just another talk show,*" he quoted the sales pitch, "*you haven't heard the talk.*" He then reproduced some of the "talk" – a series of high-profile raves from Peter O'Toole, Gene Wilder, Jack Lemmon, Bette Midler, and Burt Reynolds, all of whom were featured in the ad. He concluded, later in the article, that it was safe to assume that Woody Allen wouldn't be adding his endorsement to that list.

It was big-time American ballyhoo, and some Canadians found that offensive. Clearly Martin Knelman was one of them. "If you think this sounds suspiciously like one of those fiendishly hilarious fantasies concocted by the gremlins at *SCTV*, it's a good guess," he wrote, "but you're wrong. Not even the wickedly satirical mind of Martin Short – whose periodic appearances as the pious, long-winded, self-important, celebrity-show host named 'Brock' Linehan became a running gag to which *SCTV* aficionados could gleefully look forward – was capable of dreaming up this loony, star-studded grab for new markets."

Subtitled "Except maybe to Woody Allen, Brian Linehan is so very, very nice," Knelman's article likened Linehan to Eve Harrington, the anti-heroine of *All About Eve*. Yes, he allowed, at first Brian's "fannish enthusiasm" and "staggering" research had "a certain sweetness" that set him apart from the standard pack of superficial TV hosts. Linehan, he agreed, wasn't like anyone else on TV. But, in his opinion, Brian had now lost his "charming amateurness." Brian's questions, he maintained, had become more "ostentatiously knowing, the desire to have the flattery reciprocated more naked."

Reporting that King Features had given up trying to sell Linehan in the United States, Knelman observed that U.S. stations didn't have the same incentive for buying it: "They don't need the Canadian content credit."

He also ventured that American viewers must be "baffled" by Martin Short's Brock Linehan routines on *SCTV*, because they'd never seen the Canadian interviewer who inspired the spoof. "It must rub salt in the wound," Knelman continued, "when Linehan notes that *SCTV*, with its mockery of him, has had the success in penetrating the U.S. market that he has craved." And then, in what would prove to be the unkindest cut of all: "After seeing the devastating satirical *SCTV* version, can anyone look at Brian Linehan without chortling?"

Brian was overseas when the July issue of *Toronto Life* hit the news-stands. Michael Levine was on his way to England, and knew Brian and Zane were staying in central London, at the Athenaeum on Piccadilly. "I remember it profoundly," Levine told me. "I remember handing him the magazine and simply saying, somebody's going to give this to you, this is terrible, this is cruel, this is inaccurate, but it's out there and we have to deal with it."

Brian was hurt, humiliated, and genuinely shocked. What, if anything, had he ever done to Martin Knelman?

Well, okay, there *was* that one dinner with Pauline Kael . . .

Brian had done several interviews with Kael, the high priestess of 1960s and 1970s film criticism. Kael's brilliantly literate, frequently clever, and occasionally witty film essays in the *New Yorker* were revered by the cognoscenti; accordingly, she was secretly (and at times not so secretly) despised in Hollywood. A fearless writer, her bright ideas inspired two generations of film critics, including Roger Ebert and current *New York Times* reviewer A.O. Scott. Collections of Pauline Kael essays, most notably *I Lost It at the Movies* and *Kiss Kiss Bang Bang*, frequently won literary awards and dominated non-fiction bestseller lists. And whenever Kael had a book to sell, or a new paperback to push, she almost always came to Toronto to promote it. The top movie town per capita in North America, Toronto was a hotbed of potential Kael book buyers. It was also the home base of Brian Linehan, whose show was always identified on her itinerary as a Publisher's Must.

As usual, Linehan had a private dinner with Kael after they taped her interview. Kael was famous for attracting a following of young film critics who aspired to her stature; she played den mother to them, encouraging and nurturing them as if they were her private prize pupils. It was during dinner that Kael volunteered that Martin Knelman, who had served as a film critic for the *Globe and Mail*, was one of her most devoted acolytes. When Brian pressed her for details, she told him that Knelman would send her certain published reviews for her critique, and she would grade them and return them to him with her notes. Martin Knelman, she said, got very good marks. A passionate gossip, Brian had subsequently and quite gleefully shared this information with just about anyone who would listen.

Nonetheless, Brian was shocked when Knelman's piece was published. Equally shocked was Martin Short, who felt the character he had created out of affection and respect for Brian's accomplishments had now been twisted into something ugly, and was being used as a battering ram to knock Brian off some imaginary media pedestal.

The first Brock Linehan sketch had spoofed Linehan's justifiably famous research, with Brock committing the outrageous gaffe of confusing black blues singer Linda Hopkins with screen veteran Miriam Hopkins. Short followed up with an even more exaggerated skit showing Brock revisiting the small town where he grew up, and where – you guessed it – absolutely no one remembers him. Brian loved that one, especially since he and Short both came from the same small burg. In Hamilton, where reading *Toronto Life* was not considered *de rigueur*, the Short spoof was regarded as an affectionate tease acknowledging the success of a hometown boy who made good. Over at Dofasco, Patrick

Linehan's co-workers started calling him "Brock." Patrick, who most resembles Brian physically, adopted a grin-and-bear-it stance. The nickname stuck, and guys at the plant would call him Brock for years to come.

How did Brian Linehan, who was notoriously thin-skinned, really feel about the spoof? A bit sensitive, at the beginning: "Is that really me?" he asked, somewhat anxiously. But Brian, Short assured me, was never as sensitive about the parody as he was about the media reaction to it, and attributed the resulting media "hostility" to Knelman's "hatchet-job."

Short said he refused to speak to Knelman after the story appeared because none of his quotes explaining his friendship with Brian were used. When Knelman later called him to get quotes for a story on *SCTV*, Short said he "ended up doing an interview on why I wouldn't talk to him. He told me that it wasn't his fault, that his editors had deleted my quotes. Oh sure," he scoffed, "we all believe that."

Knelman confirms that Short was indeed reluctant to talk to him for the *Toronto Life* cover story on *SCTV* because of what he wrote about Brian, and that Marty had insisted that his Brock Linehan send-up was done almost as a tribute to Brian, in honour of their long-standing friendship. Knelman maintains that he had not only included Short's quotes in his original piece, but had also commented on them, challenging their validity, and seriously questioning Short's true motives.

Knelman also maintains that at the end of the day the article was judged to be too long, and that his editor felt that both Short's quotes, and Knelman's subsequent comments on them, were somewhat redundant. They were also easy to lose without weakening the overall story.

After he reached Short by phone at his summer retreat, Knelman reported what his editor had said. Short then not only did the interview but also did a photo shoot with Andrea Martin for the cover. Soon after that, according to Knelman, Martin Short started telling interviewers how he would never speak to Martin Knelman again.

Short stopped doing Brock Linehan on *SCTV*. "I just retired the character," he would later tell *Toronto Star* writer and long-time Linehan booster Jim Bawden. "Brian never asked me to."

In the years that followed, Brian was suspicious of any and all interview requests; he was sure that there were jealous media types waiting to ambush him. (Occasionally he was right. More often than not, they just wanted to meet him in person.) He also made a point of avoiding contact with Martin Knelman.

In all the flurry, heat, and gossip spawned by Knelman's article, the real heart of the story had been detoured. In Brian's more recent interviews, Knelman had observed what he perceived to be Brian's searing need, his "naked" desire "to have the flattery reciprocated."

It was a keen observation. Brian wanted desperately to be accepted by his famous interview subjects. He longed for their recognition and respect, and he worked hard to earn it. He wasn't content to simply meet and interview stars. He yearned for personal invitations to their homes, invitations that had nothing to do with *City Lights* or his stellar research. He wanted invitations that signalled that they thought of him not as press, not as media, but as one of them. He wanted to be one of them.

He also longed to be accepted by his so-called peers. He wanted them to regard him not as a studio pawn, as almost all junket press were regarded by non-junket press, but as a professional. He had quickly become a medium-sized fish in the fairly shallow pond that was Canadian media. He didn't have a national show on CBC, but he was still getting the big names. And he remained naive enough to be puzzled by what he perceived to be unprovoked media resentment.

One season he devoted an entire week to Canadian talk show hosts, doing in-depth sessions with Pierre Berton, Larry Solway, Joyce Davidson, and Carole Taylor, among others. He waited eagerly for reciprocal invitations, invitations to appear on their talk shows. But they never materialized. "You'd think one of them would ask me to come on!" he grumbled. He was starting to realize he was the odd man out, and that the club he was so eager to join wasn't interested in having him as a member.

Toronto Star columnist Sid Adilman was not always a Brian booster. On one occasion, Sylvester Stallone flew in to Toronto to be interviewed by Linehan and then flew right out again, without any special regard for the rest of the working press. When Gene Wilder and Gilda Radner came to town on a private visit, their publicists turned down all requests for interviews, but they spent an hour on camera with Linehan. Perhaps at the behest of his bosses at the *Toronto Star*, Adilman subsequently wrote a column chastising film studios for playing favourites. But Sid had no personal axe to grind.

In 1996, former Sutton Place movie star magnet Hans Gerhardt arranged a cozy dinner at the Old Mill, one of the city's oldest and most revered restaurant inns, to mark the twentieth anniversary of the Toronto film festival. At the dinner, a number of media types were presented with commemorative twentieth-anniversary leather jackets, designed and created by Roots founders Michael Budman and Don Green, to acknowledge their contribution to the phenomenal success of the festival. Among the recipients were Martin Knelman, Sid Adilman, and Brian Linehan. It was Sid who made a point of telling both Linehan and Knelman that it was time to bury the hatchet.

A few weeks later, Brian told me that Knelman was working on a book about John Candy, and that Knelman had called him, and asked to screen his John Candy interviews for possible inclusion in the book.

"I hope you told him to go fuck himself!" I said flatly.

"No, I didn't," Brian said wearily. "I mean, really, what's the use?" We changed the subject.

Years later, Martin Knelman told me that after their initial rapprochement at the Old Mill, Brian surprised him with tapes and notes on John Candy, "shopping bags full of stuff, because he knew I was writing a book about John." Brian was still yearning for Knelman's respect.

Knelman said he thanked Brian for the gesture, but explained that the timing was unfortunate, since the book was virtually finished. He doubted if any of the Linehan material could be used.

Laughing on the Outside: The Life of John Candy was published in 1998 by St. Martin's Press. Knelman included Brian in his acknowledgements and gave him four mentions, including one in which Candy told Brian that when he crossed the American border without a visa, "the U.S. immigration guy thought I was a draft dodger sneaking back after moving to Canada."

At Sid Adilman's continued urging, Knelman and Linehan agreed to meet for lunch, to see if they could resolve their differences. The lunch eventually happened, at Pangaea, a chic restaurant on Bay at Bloor – Knelman picked up the tab – and Brian learned for the first time what had motivated Knelman to write the article. Knelman had revealed two motives in the article itself: the Woody Allen incident in the screening room, and Brian's negative response, and the fact that Michael Levine had gone on record saying that Brian was about to crack the U.S. market. What Knelman hadn't revealed in the article, however, was his personal belief that Brian had treated their mutual friend DuBarry Campau very shabbily.

DuBarry Campau was an original, a frankly fabulous dame and formidable journalist who was a writer and drama critic for the *Toronto Telegram* in the mid to late 1960s. Known for her theatrical appearance, she wore wigs that seldom disguised the fact that she was completely bald. She did not suffer any particular pangs of regret about this. Although it was rumoured that her hair had fallen out after a bout with scarlet fever as a child, she denied it. Her hair had simply refused to grow in, she said. So she had no traumatic memories of waking up bald one morning, because she had never seen hair on her head.

DuBarry also had a whisky voice so deep that she made Lauren Bacall sound like a soprano. Her brilliant wit and serious social graces were legend, and constantly prepared the way for the success of her husband, Serrell Hillman, who was *Time* magazine's Toronto-based chief correspondent for Canada. As transplanted Americans working in Canada, DuBarry made sure they were quickly embraced by the Canadian arts community by presiding over weekly Sunday salons in which ambitious young talents such as Brian Linehan could mix and mingle with established stage stars, famous authors, provocative playwrights, and American and Canadian politicians of almost every stripe, all in the privacy and comfort of the modest Hillman home in downtown Toronto.

The Campau–Hillman salons would run from two to five, and for the first hour DuBarry would stand, casually regal, in the foyer off the front door, greeting her guests. Sometimes a complete stranger would walk through the door and offer DuBarry a letter of introduction from a mutual friend who had told them that if they ever happened to be in Toronto, she was the woman they needed to know. We observed this first-hand when the actress Rosemary Murphy, in Toronto performing in a play at the Royal Alexandra Theatre, showed up one Sunday, un-announced but not uninvited. "I'm so happy you came!" DuBarry would purr. She would then appoint someone, often someone famous, to introduce the newcomer to the key players in the throng. After 3 p.m., DuBarry would join us in the living room, where the formally attired bartender was serving and refreshing our highballs. Serrell stayed close to the bar most of the afternoon, chatting up key journalists and political EAS who were both acquaintances and contacts. At 4 p.m., mildly inebriated and delightfully sanguine, DuBarry would waft back to her post in the foyer to bid her personal farewells to each departing guest.

Serrell Hillman left Toronto, and DuBarry, in the mid-1970s to take a university post in Hawaii, where he was holding his own salons, with a new and younger hostess. DuBarry, never a stranger to spirits, was drinking heavily and would make late-night phone calls in her loneliness. She told Martin Knelman that one night she had called Brian at 11:30 p.m.

and he was very rude to her. "I told you never to call me after eleven o'clock at night!" he allegedly railed at her. DuBarry was hurt and upset. Knelman was hurt and upset for her. ("You didn't know her," Brian would later insist over lunch. "She was a monster.")

True, Brian had not always felt that way about DuBarry. She had been one of his early champions, and he had admired and, when occasion demanded it, defended her. They had seemed so simpatico, in fact, that they had gone on an adventure together, a trip to Ireland and Dubrovnik. We'll never know what really happened on that trip; clearly there was some consumption of alcohol involved. But after they returned to shore, the closeness that Brian and DuBarry had once enjoyed was replaced, on his part at least, with a more cautious, decidedly arm's-length relationship.

Although he had at one time experienced the dubious delight of receiving telephone calls in the wee hours from famed female illusionist Craig Russell, Knelman himself had never been on the receiving end of late-night entreaties from DuBarry Campau. Still, he knew how hurt she was. Pissed off by Linehan's abrupt screening-room response, offended by the hype for Linehan's potential U.S. syndication, and upset by Dubarry's account of Linehan's cavalier treatment of her, Martin Knelman had decided that the boy from Hamilton had gotten just a little too big for his britches. He needed to be taken down a peg or three. And Martin Knelman was just the man to do it.

In retrospect, Knelman's negative reaction to the flood of positive media building around Brian Linehan was hardly unique. Most Canadian media suffered then, as they suffer now, from crab-barrel mentality. Ask anyone from the Maritimes and they'll tell you that when you catch crabs, you can put them in an open barrel. You don't even need to put a lid on it, because as soon as one of the crabs starts to climb out, the others will pull him back down.

Knelman's crab-barrel attack on Linehan was greeted with covert glee by much of the Canadian press. Not that they wanted to be Brian Linehan; gawd knows, they didn't. But they didn't want Brian Linehan to be Brian Linehan, either. And Knelman's article gave them permission to come out of the tall grass, where they'd been lying in wait. For years to come, whenever Brian was interviewed, the spectre of Brock Linehan would inevitably raise its shadowy head.

A year after the *Toronto Life* piece broke, Brian told *TV Guide* writer Paul Budra that the first time he saw Short spoof him, "I laughed a lot, but I was thrown. Who wouldn't be? I talked to Marty and asked him, do I really act like that? I'm going to have to watch it."

Decades later he was still answering questions about the sketch. Few media remembered the Knelman article that had sparked the firestorm. But all of them knew it was a sore point for Linehan. He told *Toronto Star* writer Greg Quill that Knelman had used Martin Short's parody "to construct something mean. It was mockery." And when he went to Vancouver to guest on her CTV talk show, he confided to Vicki Gabereau that when it came to Brock Linehan, "I accept it, I deal with it, but I've had enough of it."

"You sent for me?"

After a year of frayed nerves and sleepless nights, a court date is finally set. Like it or not, Brian now has a firm date on his calendar.

When the lawsuit finally comes to trial, it features a cast of characters worthy of a Woody Allen comedy. For one thing, when Levine goes to New York to cross-examine Woody Allen for eight hours in the Plaza Hotel, he does so in front of Allen's personal counsel, Irwin J. Tenenbaum, whom Levine recognizes from Tenenbaum's cameo role as a Thanksgiving guest in Allen's classic *Hannah and Her Sisters*.

Levine opens: "Tell me, Mr. Allen, why are you so upset about an interview being shown in New York? You are one of the most famous people in New York."

Mr. Allen: "It's not my fault!"

Ironically, the punch line dénouement of the lawsuit takes place not in Manhattan, which Allen had so frequently rhapsodized in his films, but where the legal writ was filed, in Los Angeles, which Allen had so frequently belittled in his films.

"They have a procedure, Discovery before Trial, in which you go to a judge who is not the judge who is going to hear the case," Levine explains. "You go into chambers, the judge has read the file, he asks a few questions, and he tells you what he thinks is going to happen in trial, to try to encourage settlement."

There are nine lawyers present, representing Woody Allen, Brian Linehan, the broadcaster, the distributor. The first eight lawyers introduce themselves by twos; they're all California lawyers. Michael Levine stands up.

"Your Honour," he says, "I really have no standing in the California court. I am a Canadian. I am the attorney for Mr. Linehan."

The judge's curiosity is piqued: "Tell me," he asks, 'do you say *abowt* or *aboot*?" And then: "Do you know Norman Jewison?'

"Well, actually, I'm involved with the creation of the Canadian Film Centre," Levine replies, "and yes, Mr. Jewison has been a neighbour for many years . . ."

"Counsel leave chambers," says the judge. "The Canadian and I will solve this case."

The judge dismisses the eight other lawyers. The minute the door is closed, he turns back to Levine. "Do you have any contacts with the London theatre?"

"Of course, your honour."

"Do you think you could get me four tickets to *Phantom of the Opera*? I'd be delighted to pay for them."

"Consider it done, your honour."

"You know," he tells Levine, "Woody Allen doesn't have a case here. Do you think you could convince your insurer to pay for the costs? I'm going to tell them to settle the case."

"Your honour," says Levine, "consider it done."

The judge calls the California contingent back into chambers. "In they troop," Levine recalls, "and the judge says, 'The Canadian and I have decided you don't have a case. You're more than welcome to fight it, but I'm telling you, you're going to get killed. I think you'd better get on the phone. And I think you'd better settle it."

"Well, the eight lawyers are around a pay phone, and Irwin Tenenbaum is on the phone to Woody saying, 'Well, Woody, it's not so good, Woody . . . well, you know, we'll get our costs back, Woody . . . no, they said they'd take the episode off the air in New York.

"That was the end of the case. And that is the absolute accurate truth."

Brian was relieved. Not happy. But happy to be off the hook. He had been spared financially, but he was spent emotionally.

Still, he had survived Woody Allen and Martin Knelman. Now he wanted to have some fun. Coincidentally, so did I.

I had left the *Toronto Sun* in 1980 to try my hand at film development. My hand was, at best, shaky. Two years later, I was invited by publisher Doug Creighton and his new associate editor, the bright, brainy, and bewitching Barbara Amiel, to return to my old job. I jumped at the chance.

Like gold dust twins, Brian and I immediately picked up where we had left off. We were back on the road again, and in the immortal words of Patrick Dennis's favourite aunt, it was high time for a high time.

In 1983, Judi Schwam summoned us to Miami, where she was launching a new romantic comedy from director Blake Edwards, one of the greatest talents in Tinsel Town. *The Man Who Loved Women* featured Burt Reynolds as a man inextricably tangled with Kim Basinger, Marilu Henner, and even his psychiatrist, who was played by Blake's wife, Julie Andrews. After seeing the movie, our first priority was, as always, to secure the best table in the hotel ballroom where the post-screening bash was being held. Naturally, we asked Judi Schwam to join our handpicked gang. She declined, because she had to be on hand to greet Julie Andrews when she arrived.

"Okay," I said. "We'll save you a seat."

"And when Julie arrives," added Brian, "if she's looking for the FUN table, just send her over!"

Judi cracked up. "Okay, honey!" she said, grinning, "I'll be sure to do that."

About twenty minutes later, a vision of loveliness stood before us. A very famous vision of loveliness. "You sent for me?" inquired Julie Andrews cheerfully.

Brian leapt to his feet and pulled out the chair we'd been saving for Judi. Julie Andrews slipped into it effortlessly, and for the next forty minutes grilled us on our responses to the movie, positive and negative. "Blake's still in California," she explained, "so I have to report all the details to him later tonight."

After the premiere, she was planning to fly back to Los Angeles, pick up Blake, and jet overseas so they could spend some downtime at their home in Switzerland. When one of us showed her the attractive sweatshirt Columbia Pictures had produced to promote the film, she nodded appreciatively. "I must ask them for one of those," she said, making a mental note. "Do they come in extra-large?"

The idea of the diminutive Julie wearing an extra-large sweatshirt evoked memories of classic Blake Edwards sight gags. "Does Blake prefer extra-large?" I inquired, assuming she wanted the sweatshirt for him.

"Oh no," she replied, "the extra-large is for me." And then, with a helpless shrug: "My housekeeper in Switzerland shrinks *everything*."

We had a good time at our table that night. But then, we always did. Julie Andrews's first choice of tablemates did not go unnoticed by other junketeers, which, of course, pleased Brian. Once he realized that the junket press, with a few notable exceptions, were not his biggest fans, he took great delight in finding new ways to irritate them.

When Paramount Pictures hosted a mini-junket for *Terms of Endearment*, Brian and I flew down to L.A. to do interviews with its stars. Unfortunately, Shirley MacLaine was "unavailable" – trekking, I assumed, through some exotic land on top of a mountain, as Shirley MacLaine the Author was wont to do when she was researching and working out the rhythms of her next bestseller.

Shirley's absence was a disappointment to both of us, as we had both become comrades-in-showbiz with her over the years. Professionally, the trip was doubly disappointing for Brian, as Jack Nicholson had agreed to do some print interviews but still refused to do television. At that time in Hollywood, the handful of superstars whose names could actually make the box office jump shared a series of unwritten rules. And one of the rules was, No Television. For Streisand, Redford, Newman, and Nicholson and their advisers, it was simple economics. Why would moviegoers pay to see you on the big screen if they could see you on the small screen for free? And how could you maintain a movie-star mystique if you kept showing up in their living rooms on TV interviews and talk shows? Such devices were judged to be useful for launching careers, but could be detrimental to maintaining them. Thus, aside from telecasts of his earlier movies, the only time you could see Jack Nicholson on television was on Oscar night, when he was usually a nominee. It was a Superstar rule back then, and it remains a Superstar rule for Nicholson even today.

Consequently, with Shirley out of the picture, and with Jack diligently following his Rule, Brian was left with only Debra Winger and Jeff Daniels, neither of whom were exactly marquee giants at that time. All in all, a major letdown.

After attending the screening in the theatre on the studio lot, we were invited to a Paramount dinner at the Beverly Wilshire, where we were staying. I immediately called our Disney pal Arlene Ludwig, who agreed to meet us at one of our favourite Beverly Hills haunts, The Mandarin restaurant on Camden Drive. I was sure a great dinner at

The Mandarin would cheer Brian up. It usually did. "C'mon, we can walk over, it's only a couple of blocks," I urged him. "The walk will do you good. And they'll never miss us at dinner."

"No, I don't think so," he said glumly. "I think I'll just stay here and go to bed early."

I went to dinner with Arlene.

In the morning, I arrived a few minutes late for the interviews and received an unusually chilly reception from my colleagues in the press. Some of them were glaring at me. Others seemed to be avoiding eye contact altogether.

I checked my fly. I was all zipped up. I checked my watch. I was only five minutes late, for gawd's sake. It wasn't as if they had actually waited for me.

When there was a break in the interviews, I walked over to the buffet to get a cup of coffee. "Did you have a glamorous dinner last night?" one of the younger Paramount publicity executives inquired, with a bit of an edge in his voice.

"Oh, well, I wouldn't say 'glamorous,' exactly," I said. "But we had a lot of fun." I handed him some milk for his coffee. "And how was your dinner?"

"Not as much fun as yours, I'll bet," he said, and walked away.

Brian strolled in a few seconds later. "Good morning!" he said, in a booming voice I wasn't used to hearing. "Did you have a wonderful time last night?"

I took him aside and lowered my voice. "Did something happen at the Paramount dinner? Because everyone here this morning is acting positively weird!"

"Really?" He pursed his lips. "*Comme c'est curieux . . .*"

I was starting to get suspicious. "Brian, did you say something at dinner last night?"

"*Moi??*" he replied, feigning innocence.

"Brian, did you tell them I was down the street having dinner with Arlene Ludwig?"

"Of course not!" he replied, *sotto voce*. (Beat.) "I told them you were in Malibu having a private dinner with Shirley MacLaine."

"Oh BRY-an!" I groaned. "WHY?"

He shrugged. "I got bored."

His face lit up like a kid at a birthday party. "I only told one person, and then I just sat there and watched it spread around the room like wildfire. And suddenly," he added, beaming, "I wasn't bored any more!"

I rolled my eyes. It was time for me to go back to the interview session, and "meet the press," as it were. Brian took a croissant from the buffet and wrapped it in a napkin. "I'm going back to my room to study my notes," he announced. "And if someone gets up the nerve to ask you if you had dinner with Shirley last night, make sure you deny it. That way they'll know it's true."

As I headed back to the interview session, one of the press junketeers was standing in the doorway. "Well!" he said. "I hear you had quite the dinner last night!"

I looked back at Brian, who was sporting an angelic smile. "Yes," I said weakly, "just . . . delicious . . ."

In December 1985, Brian and I were in New York, doing a junket for *The Color Purple*, Alice Walker's bestselling novel, which Steven Spielberg had now brought to the screen. Due partly to the casting of Whoopi Goldberg and Oprah Winfrey, there was an overwhelming number of requests for TV interviews.

Brian had originally been slated to do his time-honoured twenty-minute exclusive sessions with the stars, but as the afternoon wore on, tapings started running late, and the time allotted to him was cut from twenty minutes to fifteen minutes to twelve minutes. Nobody, including Warner Bros. brass, was happy about it; that's just the way it was. Finally, when he was about to get his interview with Steven Spielberg, a Warner Bros. publicist took him aside. "Brian," he murmured softly, "we're so far behind, we're just so jammed up, that we can only give you five minutes."

"I understand," said Brian, with a resigned shrug. "I'll take a pass." He then walked out of the suite.

He caught me in the lobby. I had finished all my print interviews for the *Sun* and was about to grab a cab to the airport. "Wait for me," he said, "I'm coming with you!"

Off we went to LaGuardia. We checked in at American Airlines, and were in the Admiral's Club, having a drink, when the phone rang at the skipper's front desk. It was Rob Friedman, Warner Bros. publicity chief and a huge Linehan fan. "Brian," he said, "Steven wants to talk to you."

Steven Spielberg came on the line. "Brian," he said, "I know it's only five minutes, but please come back. I want to do the interview!"

"I don't think so, Steven, but thanks very much for calling. I appreciate it."

"Oh Brian, please come back," Spielberg persisted. "Five minutes with you will be better than twenty minutes with anybody else. It will be a *great* five minutes."

"Steven," said Brian, "my first *question* is five minutes!"

We boarded the American Airlines jet to Toronto and flew home.

That story made the rounds in Hollywood the next day. The day after that, it was repeated everywhere.

It wasn't all fun and games. In 1984, Judi Schwam invited Brian to L.A. to interview Melanie Griffith and director Brian De Palma after the premiere of De Palma's new thriller, *Body Double*. Linehan had meticulously prepared his notes, but he wasn't prepared for what he saw. Ostensibly an homage to Hitchcock, the film left Brian deeply disturbed.

"Brian went to the afternoon screening," Judi recalls, "and after it was over he came to me and said, 'I can't do the interview. I grew up with that kind of violence and I cannot do this interview.'" He thought he had buried the past. He just hadn't buried it deep enough.

Jane Hawtin, a rising radio star on Q107, was on the same junket. She remembers the incident, "because it was so unlike him. He was really distressed by it. He could not do the interviews."

Hawtin knew who Brian was, of course. "But it was quite a long time before he talked to me. I don't know whether he had a magic number in his head, that if he saw you on five junkets or seven or ten – I don't know what the magic number was, but all of a sudden you existed and you were a friend. I was on a Warner Bros. junket when all of a sudden it's like 'Jane, hi, how are you?' And I literally looked over my shoulder, thinking that there had to be another Jane, because he'd never really spoken to me before. But I'd obviously crossed over. And I was now one of the gang. You always wanted to be at his table for dinner because of that wicked wit of his. We started sharing limos from airports, me and Claire Olsen and Brian. And it was always fun." In the years to come, like Marilyn Lightstone before her, Jane Hawtin would play a key role in Brian's professional life.

Another important figure in Brian's professional life, Lorraine Wilson, met her second husband around that time. He worked in sales and marketing at Citytv and coached the Citytv baseball team; she met him when she tried out for the team. When she told Brian she had fallen in love and was going to get married, he said, "You shouldn't be doing that, that's not going to last."

She laughs, remembering. "I said to him, well, I'm getting married, and I need someone to give me away. Will you? And he said, 'I'd be honoured, Lorraine.' After I got married, I stayed with Brian and *City Lights*, and then I got pregnant, and he was so amazing, looking out for me." After Lorraine had the baby, her new husband was offered a great job in Vancouver, so she had to leave Citytv.

The day she left, Brian took everybody out for lunch. "We got back from the lunch and the two of us just had this total meltdown together. It was like severing the umbilical cord. I had been with him only five or six years, but we had gone through these amazing journeys together," Lorraine says.

☆

A few years after Martin Knelman's scathing profile of Brian appeared in *Toronto Life*, the spectre of DuBarry Campau returned to haunt Linehan once more, this time courtesy of journalist John Fraser. Fraser was a celebrated Toronto newspaper dance critic who made headlines when he assisted in the cloak and dagger defection of Mikhail Baryshnikov from the Soviet Union. He would go on to reinvent himself as an award-winning *Globe and Mail* correspondent in China before becoming the newspaper's Ottawa bureau chief, national columnist, national editor, and then London correspondent.

After producing a major bestseller on his exploits in China, Fraser turned his attention to his real passion – gossip – and produced some two hundred pages of it in a book called *Telling Tales*. Among the tales he told was one on Brian, in which he noted DuBarry's professional generosity to young and eager aspiring talents, including "and especially" Brian Linehan.

"Mr. Linehan," he wrote, "was neither down nor out during this period in the early Seventies, but he was certainly far from having arrived although all the ingredients for his later success were well in place. The watery eyes and soulful concern, the intense stare that seemed to plumb the very extremities of the tip of your soul, the encyclopedic knowledge of the stars of stage, screen and television."

The crux of his complaint about Brian, shimmering in Fraser's sleek, well-worded prose, was that one day DuBarry realized she had not heard from Brian for more than a year, "and it was to be nearly a decade before she would do so again." By that time DuBarry was in her decline, personally and professionally. When she did hear from Linehan, Fraser reported, it was only because he had lost his private telephone book, which Fraser claimed was "studded with the nuggets of DuBarry Campau." According to Fraser, Brian had called solely to ask if she, DuBarry, "could please give his secretary the phone numbers for all their mutual friends and acquaintances?" – a request Fraser clearly regarded as an astonishing act of insensitivity.

"How could he write this without at least talking to me!" Brian wailed. Over the years, he said, he had provided DuBarry with all sorts of introductions to actors and directors and producers. "I didn't want to copy ALL the phone numbers in her book. I only wanted to copy THE ONES I HAD GIVEN HER!"

Michael Levine remembers how upset Brian was by Fraser's digs at him. "The irony," Levine points out, "is that the very characteristic that he sought in others was the thing that he was most insulted by. He loved being the 'fuckor' but not the 'fuckee.' He loved the whole gossip side of these things."

In *Telling Tales*, says Levine, Fraser "got one version. He should have gone to Brian. But knowing Brian, Brian might not have co-operated with him, and John Fraser would still have written what he wrote."

Brian talked about suing Fraser, but never followed through. When I urged him to insist that the pages referring to him not appear in any subsequent editions, as another of Fraser's subjects had done, he agreed that taking such action was definitely the way to go. Once again, he did nothing. Given a choice between being slagged by John Fraser in his new book and/or not being mentioned at all, he would willingly take the slagging.

Around this time, Martin Short, Brian, and I ended up at the same Arizona spa, on a junket for *Three Amigos*, a delightful, gag-laden send-up of U.S. westerns featuring Steve Martin, Chevy Chase, and Martin Short. Although we were booked to interview all three stars, Brian and I were both especially looking forward to our sessions with Short. We were not disappointed.

When the cameras started to roll for Brian's interview, Marty got right to the point. "Brian, I've known you for many, many years," he began, "and to me it was always Gilda doing Baba Wawa, me doing Brock Linehan. There was never any attempt to hide or disguise it; hence the use of the name Linehan. To me it was a total compliment to you. The joke was your research, because you were so researched.

"What bothered me about doing Brock Linehan, the reason I stopped doing Brock Linehan, was because the Canadian press took what was done in good intentions with great affection and tried to imply that it was done as an attack. And I'm specifically talking about Martin Knelman right now. That statement was not in his article, that it wasn't being done as an attack, or if it was, that I was doing it wrong. And I resented it. And I just stopped doing it. Because it was wrong. It was not the intention. And that was a shame."

By the time we sat down to do my print interview, Marty was genuinely dismayed. All the American TV interviewers, he said, had directed their questions "to all three of us – Steve, Chevy, and me. All the Canadian interviewers asked me the same question – Brock Linehan – and then directed all the rest of their questions to Chevy and Steve. It was embarrassing." He slumped in his chair. "These people make me feel like I'm doing a vicious satire on Brian. Don't they know that Brian and I are friends?" he asked incredulously. "If Brian had been doing this show in the U.S., we would have been parodying him on *Saturday Night Live* the next week," he said with a shrug. "Barbara Walters was thrilled when Gilda did Baba Wawa, because when people parody you, it means you're famous enough to be parodied. When they parody you in the U.S., people say, *hey, good for you!* When they parody you in Canada, people say, *good! . . . They got him.*" He sighed. "There's always a certain amount of jealousy in this business. I just had no idea," he added with a sad smile, "how much the Canadian media resented Brian's success."

By the end of the year, Canadian media had even more reason to resent him. Taina Elg was walking past a display of new television sets in a downtown Helsinki department store when on every screen she suddenly saw Brian Linehan interviewing Peggy Lee. Writer Shirley Eskapa kicked off her shoes in her London flat and switched on the television, only to find Brian Linehan interviewing Whoopi Goldberg. *New Music* alumni John Martin and J.D. Roberts were shooting in Zurich when they saw Brian Linehan interviewing Matthew Broderick.

Citytv had sold a celebrity package – *City Lights*, *The New Music*, and a weekly *MuchMusic* special – to Rupert Murdoch's Sky Channel. In addition to existing deals in Australia, New Zealand, South Africa, and the United States, Brian Linehan and *City Lights* were now reaching viewers in Austria, Belgium, Denmark, England, Finland, France,

Holland, Iceland, Ireland, Luxembourg, the Netherlands, Norway, Portugal, Spain, Switzerland, Wales, and West Germany. Sky Channel executives had bought *City Lights* for a six-month trial run, five days a week, with an option for six more months. But viewer response was so favourable that they exercised their six-month renewal clause four weeks after the Linehan series premiered. According to statistics buffs, it was more than probable that Brian Linehan was now the most viewed Canadian broadcaster on the planet.

On Oscar night 1987, Brian was in California on a junket, watching the Academy Awards on television in his hotel room in Burbank, California. He was happy to watch the show on TV and file a radio report on the evening and the outcome, just as long as he didn't have to be stuck in the press room. The idea of being pushed and shoved by other on-camera interviewers while holding a hot microphone in an attempt to capture non-essential quotes from nervous nominees was distasteful enough to make him shudder. Nor could he see himself wedged between other cele-brated reporters, some of them more famous than he was, sitting at one of the narrow desks provided by the Academy, trying to get a line out to reach CFRB while the TV broadcast blared from the three video screens in the room. When Brian Linehan imagined himself at the Academy Awards, he saw himself in orchestra seats, close to the stage, surrounded by movie stars whose secrets he'd kept. It wasn't merely the world's most glamorous mutual admiration society; it was where he belonged.

Years earlier, his pal Dianne Schwalm had invited him to escort her to the Oscars. "That year with Brian," she remembers fondly, "he must have told everybody in the world that he was going to the Academy Awards. When we walked up the red carpet, having done it a bit, I told him to get on the inside by the press line and go real slow. And they're yelling *get moving, move forward, come on, move up*, and I said, ignore them, just keep tucking in behind the crowd. And of course there's Jodie Foster, and there's Candice Bergen, and there's Barbra Streisand. He was in his element."

After the awards, an over-eager female watchdog refused to let them into the Miramax party, despite Brian's personal invitation from Miramax chief Harvey Weinstein. "She didn't care who he was," Dianne recalls with a wry smile. "And you know where she is today? She's nowhere. She slept with one of his clients once, a major leading man, we all knew him, and that was the death of her. After that no one would give her the time of day.

"But it was a good night. We had a great time. And all he kept doing was saying, 'Thank you, thank you for having me, thank you for including me. This is my dream.' What he was living that night wasn't that moment. He was living the history of the Academy Awards and the Oscars, the days when Joan Crawford would be there, and Humphrey Bogart. That's what he was living, that tradition."

At that time, Joan Rivers was actively engaged in a very stormy relationship with the Fox television network. She was still doing her daily trail-blazing late-night talk show, "live" to the East Coast, but it was a very tough slog, and not only for her. The pressure of dealing with the start-up growing pains of the new network and its mercurial chief executive Barry Diller was clearly taking a physical and emotional toll on her husband, Edgar Rosenberg, who was also her producer. Joan and Edgar were planning an early evening that night – just do the show and have a quiet dinner at home.

Meanwhile, I was working in the press room, as usual, at the Dorothy Chandler Pavilion in downtown L.A., filing Oscar coverage back to the *Toronto Sun*. I had called Joan and Edgar that morning to say that a friend of mine was in town and I wanted them to meet him; could we stop by the house after the Oscars if I promised to bring all the gossip as well as my friend? They were both intrigued. Yes of course, they said, please come.

Because he didn't drive, I had to navigate Oscar traffic successfully enough to pick up Brian at the Sheraton Universal and bring him to Joan and Edgar in Bel-Air. They were sitting in the kitchen of their exquisitely appointed home, doing their nightly postmortem on the show, when we arrived. I had briefed Brian en route – unnecessarily, as it turned out – that Joan and Edgar's home was one of the most raved-about in the industry. The attractive pool and grounds were pure California; the automated eight-foot iron gates and the attack dogs were pure Hollywood. But, like Dorothy landing in Oz, once you stepped through the threshold you found yourself in another world. Within the walls of their lush estate, the Rosenbergs had created an East Coast oasis, a sumptuous mix of rich dark woods, plush carpets, fine china and crystal, with a spacious master bedroom and a book-lined library where they kept Joan's scripts, which Edgar had had bound in embossed leather. If they had added a second-storey window with a view of the

Empire State Building, you would be convinced that you had somehow been beamed back to Manhattan.

"I've told Brian what a wonderful house you have," I announced, creating the perfect cue for a guided tour. But we never got out of the kitchen. Their houseman, Jacob, and his wife, Inger, quickly assembled an array of cheeses and pâtés and opened a bottle of wine. Joan and Edgar were both immediately taken with Brian. He was smart, erudite, urbane, and full of funny things to say. And it didn't hurt when they learned that some of his personal friends, some of the people he most admired, like Roddy McDowall and Nancy Walker and David Craig, Walker's husband and a vocal coach of international renoun, were also personal friends of theirs whom they held in the same high esteem.

First, we did the gossip. Brian gave his impressions, outrageously funny as usual, of the evening's on-camera fashion disasters; I gave a play-by-play of the press-room action with Rona Barrett, Marilyn Beck, Roger Ebert, and the hundreds of other print and television journalists. So Joan and Edgar got all the Oscar highlights – and the really good gossip – without having to sit through the show.

When the subject switched to books, they immediately found a kindred spirit in Brian. Brian and I had both interviewed Debbie Reynolds's daughter Carrie Fisher when she made her unexpectedly auspicious screen debut in *Star Wars*. I asked Brian if he had received a copy of Carrie's first novel.

"Yes, I gave it to one of the girls at the station," he said, with a sniff that suggested a bad smell.

"You *gave it to one of the girls at the station?*" I repeated, in disbelief.

Brian shrugged. "I only read non-fiction," he said flatly.

"A man after our own hearts," said Edgar, beaming.

Publishers flooded Joan's talk show offices with books, hoping for an interview with an author or at the very least a mention, and Joan and Edgar, both voracious readers, kept a stack of review copies in their bedroom upstairs. As Brian and I were leaving, Edgar insisted that we take some books with us. Brian was familiar with most of the titles in the stack.

"Here, George," said Edgar, eyes twinkling as he handed me a book. "You're shallow, you'll like this." The book was *Postcards From the Edge* by Carrie Fisher. I cracked up. I loved Edgar's cynical wit, which played brilliantly against his polished Savile Row manners.

Joan phoned me at my hotel the following morning. "Edgar and I like Brian," she announced. "You can bring him around any time."

Joan and Brian were starting down a road that would lead to an extraordinary friendship. But there were going to be an awful lot of bumps along the way.

☆

By the mid-1980s, to feed the gaping and at times insatiable jaws of multiplex cinemas, Hollywood was producing more films than it had since the 1940s, and the number of junkets had doubled and tripled. I assigned more than half to other members of my staff, but still maintained a high profile on the circuit. One junket Brian and I both enjoyed was the 1987 launch of *Ishtar*, a film that would become legend for all the wrong reasons.

Director Elaine May and co-stars Warren Beatty and Dustin Hoffman were all at the peak of their popularity (i.e., sizzling "hot" in Hollywood) when they joined forces to make a novel, off-the-wall comedy spoof, slyly inspired by the Bob Hope–Bing Crosby *Road* movies of the 1940s, about living your dreams in show business.

I had rented a car, as usual, so we wouldn't have to go on the bus with the rest of the junketeers. After I parked nearby, we strolled into the cinema, greeting our chums from Paramount along the way. The theatre was packed, but our studio reps had saved two seats in the very back row of the main floor for us, which we gratefully accepted.

"Isn't this great?" I murmured to Brian. "I love sitting in the back, in the last row. These are my favourite seats."

"I know," he whispered back, "but try to look unhappy. They think they're punishing us for being so late by making us sit in the last row!"

Although we hadn't seen a frame of footage, we were already predisposed to dislike *Ishtar*. A writer from the revitalized *New York* magazine, which was now out-selling the *New Yorker* as the newest Must Read magazine for the chattering classes, had been given exceptional access to the production during its long and arduous shooting schedule. The resulting story depicted a vanity-cursed runaway film disaster, over budget by millions due to the idiosyncratic whims of May, Beatty, and Hoffman, all of whom came off as self-indulgent cinema dilettantes.

The movie started. We braced ourselves.

What a relief. It was *funny*. Three minutes into it, Brian and I were both chortling. We continued to be amused, and frequently delighted, and sometimes laughed out loud. And as we did, we became acutely aware of the fact that there didn't seem to be a lot of people laughing with us. From time to time we were also aware of a couple of guys who were pacing back and forth behind the half-wall behind our seats in the last row. "They must be checking the sound," I whispered to Brian. "Maybe that side of the house can't hear the punchlines."

"Or maybe they can," he replied.

Finally, the pacing stopped. The "sound-checkers" stood behind the half-wall for the next half hour or more, and then quietly disappeared. We got back to enjoying *Ishtar*.

After the screening, we slipped away from the crowd and went to Spago, the Wolfgang Puck dining oasis on Sunset Boulevard that had permanently raised the bar for Hollywood cuisine, for a post-show nightcap with Joan and Edgar. Less than a year after it had launched the new Fox network, *The Late Show with Joan Rivers* was television history. Word on Sunset Boulevard was that Barry Diller had pulled the plug after Joan refused to dump Edgar as her producer. So Joan and Edgar were ready and more than willing to embrace amusing distractions, and Brian and I qualified. Naturally, they also wanted to hear all about *Ishtar*.

"How's the movie?" asked Joan.

"Fantastic!" I told her. "Very funny, and *so* clever. Very 'In,' but really, really funny."

"How was the audience response?" asked Edgar.

"Like a still-life painting," said Brian.

"That explains it," said Edgar. Joan nodded in agreement.

"Explains what?" asked Brian.

"Why Warren and Dustin look like they just came back from a funeral," said Edgar. He tilted his head gently but pointedly toward the Hollywood Hills. We followed his glance. Warren Beatty and Dustin Hoffman were dining with two attractive young women less than six tables away from us.

"You should go and tell them you like the film," said Joan. "They can probably use some cheering up right about now."

"Oh, we'll be seeing them tomorrow," I said, "at the press interviews. Besides, they're obviously having a private dinner."

"Oh, don't be so *Canadian!*" Edgar teased us.

We got up from our table, walked over to theirs, and interrupted their dinner. Warren, ever the gentleman, sprang to his feet.

"No, no, please sit down," I protested politely. "We just wanted to tell you how much we liked *Ishtar*."

They seemed to be genuinely pleased we'd stopped by. When Dustin asked if there were any scenes in particular that stood out for us, I described my favourite, in which he and Warren are crawling across the burning desert, caked with sand, while vultures circle overhead. I then recited verbatim the punchline Dustin delivered – no, I'm not going to give it away here – and Dustin and Warren both laughed out loud.

"Well, we knew you were enjoying it," Warren admitted, somewhat shyly.

"We were standing behind you," said Dustin. "We were standing on the other side of the theatre for a while, but it was awfully quiet over there. So I said to Warren, 'Let's go stand behind the two guys who are laughing!'"

The next day, we did print and television interviews with them. The studio hospitality suite was full of press who normally eschewed junkets. Roger Ebert and Gene Siskel had even flown in to tape a segment with the controversial tag team, and Brian had to wait longer than usual for his television time. "But not because of Roger and Gene," he told me. "The TV schedule fell apart because they shot all the interviews on film instead of videotape. So they had to load and unload new film magazines for every interview, and test each one first. Which ate up a lot of time." (Almost all junket interviews were shot on film before videotape became both sophisticated and accessible. But it had been years since a studio had used film on a junket.)

"I don't understand," I told Brian. "Why would Paramount use film for the TV interviews?" Brian said he had posed that very question to several studio reps, all of whom came back with the same answer: Warren wanted to be interviewed on film, not videotape – partly because he felt that the visual contrast going from TV interview to film clip was too extreme, but mainly because, in his interviews, he wanted to look like Warren Beatty. And the Warren Beatty he wanted to look like was the Warren Beatty we saw on film, not videotape.

Brian couldn't have cared less. He did his thing. As usual, Dustin and Warren were appropriately spellbound.

"How long have you been doing this?" Warren asked Brian, hoping to turn the tables on him.

"Fourteen seasons," said Brian, trying to hide a smile.

"But you're a Canadian citizen, right?" Warren turned to Dustin. "So we can rule him out of the CIA or the FBI. But this guy, wow! He's *good!*"

Some time after that, I met Shirley MacLaine for afternoon tea at the Four Seasons. She'd already heard (from Brian, probably) about her brother's quirky request to shoot his *Ishtar* junket interviews on film. "Film is much softer, much kinder, to actors than videotape," she noted. "But you don't have to shoot film. As you get older, you just lower the key light, to give you more of a wash."

"Maybe next time," I said, "he'll ask you first."

"Oh sure!" she replied, rolling her eyes. "When was the last time in recorded history that a brother asked a sister for advice?"

She laughed, and so did I. We ordered a fresh pot of tea.

☆

On August 14, 1987, unable to shake off the constant and crippling depression that had been dogging him for months, Edgar Rosenberg took his own life in a hotel room in Philadelphia. Joan was in California when Edgar committed suicide. After she and their daughter, Melissa, struggled through the first few weeks, Joan fled Los Angeles and moved into the Westbury hotel in New York.

Brian went to see her there when she was still deep in shock and mourning. "We were walking down Madison Avenue at night and it was fall," she recalls. "And Brian started saying something and making me laugh and I remember saying to him, 'This is not right, my husband is dead six weeks,' and he was the first one that really, really, really made me have a good time. It was the first time I went out, and I totally had a great time.

"It was all about gossip and fun and stories, and he had just come from some junket and it was all silly and dishy. I was living at Madison Avenue and 60th and by the time we got to 57th I was doubled up with laughter. I always loved Brian because he made me laugh again. And that gave me hope."

Brian made a point of calling Joan whenever he made one of his frequent visits to Manhattan. He flew to New York to attend Shirley Lord's wedding to *New York Times* editor Abe Rosenthal. The couple exchanged vows in the Kluge apartment, with bridesmaids Barbara Walters and Beverly Sills, who had introduced them. ("We don't have many pictures from the wedding because the photographer got drunk," says Shirley Lord with an ironic smile.) Brian, of course, loved it. He didn't go to a lot of weddings, but he liked glamorous ones. And when Canadian hockey legend Wayne Gretzky married dancer Janet Jones the following year, Brian Linehan's name was on the VIP guest list.

After one trip to New York, he told me about a documentary someone was making about press junkets, and how the filmmaker (no, not Michael Moore) had waited in the shadows at a junket screening, hoping to ambush some unsuspecting junketeers. Most of them, he reported, saw it coming and went the other way. Brian himself had simply brushed by them. Brian was sensitive to the fact that many of the biggest stars who appeared on his show, from Meryl Streep to Mel Gibson, had been taped at studio-paid junkets. It was no secret in the industry, but it wasn't widely held public knowledge, and he didn't want *his* public to start looking at him, and *City Lights*, with anything but an open mind.

In November 1987, to warm up potential holiday box office, Carl Ferrazza and his crackerjack junket team, who were now working with Orion, hosted a press conclave in Palm Springs for a clever black comedy directed by Danny DeVito called *Throw Momma From the Train*, with Billy Crystal and DeVito in attendance. Taking advantage of the captive-press situation, Walt Disney Studios hitched a ride on the Orion junket and brought director Leonard Nimoy down to Palm Springs with stars Tom Selleck and Ted Danson to launch its U.S. remake of the French hit *Three Men and a Baby*.

Los Angeles Times columnist Jack Matthews was handicapping holiday movies that year, and it was quite a horse race, with new films by James L. Brooks, John Hughes, Steven Spielberg, and Oliver Stone set to open before Christmas. After chatting up numerous movie theatre owners who had seen *Throw Momma From the Train*, Matthews ranked it twelfth – in a field of thirteen. Upset to read such a negative box office "prediction" before their film had even opened, Orion executives jumped on the *L.A. Times* and Matthews. Perhaps Matthews should talk to some of the press who were on the junket in Palm Springs?

Shirley Eder took the high road. "I saw *Three Men* with a regular audience and they howled," she told him. "I saw *Throw Momma* with the press at nine-thirty in the morning and they screamed too."

Brian took the No road. "No comment," he told Matthews. He hung up, sighed with relief, and dialled my number to warn me that Matthews might be calling. But he couldn't reach me, because I was already on the phone with Jack Matthews. "*Throw Momma* is a much better film," I told him. "I can see *Throw Momma* opening well and having a long run."

Rod Lurie, the New York film writer who would later graduate to a major film career of his own, disagreed. "I was very disappointed with *Throw Momma* . . . it is not going to do well," he told Matthews.

Jack Matthews led off his press reaction quotes with mine, on the front page of the *L.A. Times*'s best-read Calendar section.

Orion was thrilled. Disney was not. Our pal Arlene Ludwig was instructed to "contact" me. (Translation: Read me the riot act.) She reminded me of one of Hollywood's unwritten laws (which in fact was probably written somewhere): Never Compare Movies With Other Movies. Disney had no problem with the fact that I liked *Throw Momma From the Train*. The Disney execs were unhappy because I had casually, perhaps even thoughtlessly, compared *Throw Momma From the Train* to *Three Men and a Baby*, a film I'd also enjoyed.

I conceded. I'd goofed. Darn that Jack Matthews anyway. He'd reported every one of my direct quotes with appalling accuracy.

Brian couldn't believe I had agreed to talk to Matthews in the first place.

"Why wouldn't I?" I said.

Brian was unusually quiet. We changed the subject.

I didn't need junkets. For one thing, I had a life. For another, I had limited but finite funds to spend in the pursuit of Hollywood stories. When I covered the Oscars and the Cannes Film Festival for my paper, as I did almost every year, it was the *Toronto Sun*, not the studios, that picked up the tab. Brian did not attend the Cannes Film Festival, ever, and attended the Academy Awards only when someone else invited him.

When I went off to New York or L.A. for a junket, my taxis, my airport limos, my rental cars, and much of my entertaining, were all financed by my departmental budget at the *Sun*. Brian had no such budget. He was very diligent about getting receipts for cab fares, and would urge me to do so as well. What I didn't realize at the time was that while I was turning in my receipts for my *Toronto Sun* expense account, he was turning in his receipts to the studio executives who had invited him to Hollywood in the first place.

Citytv never picked up the tab. "We knew nothing of those expenses," CHUM vice president Marcia Martin confirmed. "Brian would leave on a Thursday or a Friday and return home on a Monday or a Tuesday with taped interviews with the stars. We simply never questioned it. But obviously it was a great arrangement for us."

Brian Linehan was on television five days a week, interviewing the biggest stars in show business, mostly due to the kindness of studio strangers he had shrewdly befriended. That's why he was afraid to talk to Jack Matthews and the *Los Angeles Times*: he was afraid of repercussions. Afraid a Disney or Orion executive might take offence at something he said. Afraid a studio like Disney or Orion might take him off the A-list. And then where would he be?

12

"He never said Thank You."

C*ity Lights* celebrated its fifteenth anniversary with next to no fanfare. Brian Linehan was still a household name, but the households were changing. So was television. Late-night and morning talk shows had "cured" long-form interviews into snappy five-minute quick-hit segments. Once Linehan's champion, Citytv chief Moses Znaimer had grown weary of defending him.

"The style of the station was youthful, energetic, fast-moving," says Znaimer. "And there he was, doing a 1940s talk show. It was the kind of TV I would have done a parody of. Which of course the *SCTV* people did. And that only became more and more apparent as the station flourished. And there was this eccentric oddball who contradicted everything we stood for.

"And yet," he admits, "for conventional servers, conventional critics, Brian was the thing they could get their heads around, the thing they could laud. And *City Lights* did have the desired impact. Which was that, over time, as Brian's reputation grew, anybody who had a personality profile in this world came to the station. And of course the station was very chuffed by that, and every once in a while even I would be, because some of those people were exceptional and were great artists.

"I just hated the slavishness of it," he says. "I'm not inclined to fall down and kiss anybody's toes, let alone their ass, let alone turn me or the station inside out to have access to them."

Industry gossips whispered that Moses was jealous of Brian. There was an endless parade of stars showing up at Citytv, but they were all asking for Brian, not Moses.

Znaimer maintains that the major thorn in his relationship with Brian Linehan was Brian Linehan. "Brian," he says, "was so star-focused that he could only see the stars out there. He was never interested in the stars in here, and that was always my point. And I made it forcefully, because I was the boss. That we were a star maker. That the station had the makings of a star. That our personalities were stars. And that Moses Znaimer was a star. But Brian couldn't see it."

Znaimer says Brian thought of himself as a star "almost from the very beginning. In his mind it was The Brian Linehan Show, and I was the carrier. And because of that he never settled into City. Because at every point in what turned out to be a very long history with City he was waiting for the call from NBC. In his mind, he was better than Citytv, and he was constantly being told by the people around him, you should have a network program, you should be in the United States, Brian."

He leans forward. "Everything I'm saying in the course of this interview," says Znaimer, "needs to be grounded on this basic fact, which rubbed his ass no end: I'm the guy who put him on television, and I'm the guy who kept him on television. But he wasn't there for Citytv, and never really supported or promoted City, or spoke well of City, let alone me, because at every stage he had his bags packed."

For Brian, he says, "the real confirmation that you had 'arrived' was that you would leave. So Brian wasn't interested in our approach, or our style, or our position in the community. His 'community' was in Los Angeles."

Meanwhile, back in the spotlight, Brian's questions had become so information-loaded, and so lengthy, that some of his subjects found the prospect of a Linehan interview quite daunting.

"Near the end of City Lights," his Hollywood publicist pal Stuart Fink remembers, "Brian's questions started to get too long and people couldn't always remember what the question was. Brian was courting them, and he was introducing himself, and he was setting them up for the Big Moment when he planned to amaze them with some question, some information from their past, something known only to them and maybe their mother. But some of them had a hard time following him."

It had started to show up on camera, too. Gene Wilder and Gilda Radner loved Brian, but when they sat with him on City Lights even Gene was stymied by Brian's complex set-ups.

"So," Brian began, "the principals are always in danger, but there's always time for a kiss. And while it heightens the danger, you never lose track of the romance. I suppose, in all of that, Mr. Wilder, the question is —"

Wilder laughed out loud, with obvious relief. Brian was actually going to get to the question.

"I was trying to figure out," Wilder exclaimed, "WHAT THE HELL IS THE QUESTION!?!"

Peter Allen, another Linehan fan, did his cheeky impression of Brian before a packed cabaret crowd at the Imperial Room in the Royal York hotel. "I'm thinking of that time, back in Australia," he began, imitating Brian's deadpan delivery, "when you were seven, and so very curious, and you went into the bathroom, and you closed the door, and then you *locked* the door . . ."

Joan Rivers told me that when Roddy McDowall travelled he would send his friends minutely detailed itineraries outlining where he would be and when he would be there. "Roddy would write, 'Tuesday, I'll be in Spain in the morning and in the afternoon I'll be having lunch with the Duchess of So-and-So and I'll be having dinner with so-and-so. Wednesday I'll be going to Holland.' So we used to have a running joke: 'It's four-thirty, Roddy is now in Amsterdam, taking a piss.' That was our joke about Roddy. Everybody's joke about Brian was 'When you and I met in 1972, do you know what you said to me?' 'Oh my God! Oh my God! I don't remember. I *don't remember!* I'm a *bad person!*' . . . because of course he had that memory that was like a steel trap."

Brian knew the set-ups to his questions were long, and frequently too involved, for his interview subjects to cope with. But his questions were now as much of a trademark as the astonished looks they would almost always produce on the faces of his interviewees. Yes, sure, he was showing off a little. And why not? It was his party trick; he'd created it, and he owned it.

But not for much longer. In 1989, Moses Znaimer decreed that there would be no more "talking heads" on Citytv. And no more *City Lights*.

Znaimer announced that Brian Linehan would co-host a new weekly series, *Movie Television*, that would play to his strengths. A new photo layout featuring Linehan, elegant in pinstripe shirt and suspenders, and his chic co-host, *New Music* veteran Jeanne Beker, was soon picked up by all the major dailies and weekly TV magazines across the country.

According to Znaimer, *City Lights* really came to an end "when I moved out of Queen East and moved into Queen West, and did away with the one and only studio we ever had, and built for him a participating functional office, and actually got him to come from behind the desk, and perch his ass on the end of it. But he hated it. He was totally uncomfortable."

Movie Television, the antithesis of *City Lights*, was a hyper-magazine show where the shortest sound bite ruled. Brian watched in horror as his nine-minute interview with Meryl Streep was reduced to a series of fast-paced (albeit undeniably entertaining) interview clips.

Says Marcia Martin: "The half-hour interviews were just not what people wanted to see. The Dick Cavett days were over. We wanted to do something a little bit snappier, so we went from *City Lights* to *Movie Television*.

"It was a hard transition," she admits. "And Brian gave it a shot. But it just never worked for him. Sharing the limelight, number one, but also sharing it with someone like Jeanne . . . it was so different for him. Jeanne was more commercial. She knew that she could handle it. But Brian didn't want to share that limelight."

"By that time," Znaimer says, "Brian had run through everybody in the station and people wouldn't put up with him. I kept him on the air for many years when people were saying, get him the fuck out of here, I can't work with him, I can't stand him. Really, that was the heart of the relationship issue.

"The irony for him was that the call from Hollywood never came. He ended up putting in all those years at a place that he thought was beneath him."

Moses Znaimer, says Michael Levine, "is probably the most complex figure in my life. Complex because I truly respect his originality. I truly dislike his dark side, because his dark side, whether it comes from insecurity or whatever, is cruel."

Quite apart from Znaimer's misgivings about what he perceived to be Linehan's attitude, Levine says that Znaimer also "liked to blame Brian for his frustrations around both Marilyn Lightstone and himself in relation to the Hollywood scene."

In the 1980s, Znaimer had produced successful runs of the hit play *Tamara* in Toronto, New York (with Cynthia Dale and Sara Botsford), and Hollywood (with Helen Shaver and Marilyn Lightstone), brilliantly showcasing it as a "Living Movie." At that time Brian already had an enviable collection of Hollywood connections, and was building on them. But he also kept them to himself, and guarded them jealously.

"Moses said to me on more than one occasion that Brian could have made a difference but wouldn't," says Levine. "My view was, Moses, you have a home in California, you have relationships, you have television networks, you have money, and you have power. Brian? . . . he's an interviewer."

But Marilyn Lightstone, he notes, "never broke with Brian. Any estrangement was because there had been such an estrangement with Moses. And when I confronted her with Moses' accusation that Brian hadn't co-operated, or hadn't done this, or hadn't done that, she denied it. She simply said it wasn't true. I think it was in Moses' head. It was sad."

Workers at Citytv say that at times they saw a vindictive side of Moses. "There's a little bit of a bully in him," one alumnus told me. "When he cancelled *City Lights*, it was 'either Linehan gets with it or there's no place for him here,' that kind of thing."

Znaimer bristles at the suggestion that he was "unnecessarily cruel" to Linehan. "I'm sure all those little nattering nabobs run around saying that," he retorts dismissively. "*Unnecessarily cruel?* It was an act of supreme kindness and enormous patience. Because anyone else would have fired his ass fifteen years earlier!"

Brian, he says, "had no real appreciation for the station that created him, harboured him, and gave him his livelihood. He never would have lasted at CBC, let alone NBC or CBS or other places that he considered real broadcasters. But the fact is, *I* put him on the air, *I* kept him on the air, *I* begged him to change. I begged him to advance, I begged him to learn, I begged him to be part of the station. And he didn't move an inch. He did not care about City. He did not see the stardom in City. He was stuck in the old cliché where he made his little living. And that's all he was capable of.

"And, by the way, since you're collecting little tidbits and toting them up: he never said Thank You."

Despite Moses' displays of animosity, Michael Levine believes he could have kept Brian at City forever, "because at the end of the day I could beat it out of Moses. But there came a moment when Moses insulted Brian for the thirty-seventh time, and Brian's sense of dignity got the better of him, and he wouldn't let me. And he lost.

"So it's the best of Moses and the worst of Moses. The best of Moses was the insight into the talent, into the love, into the affection, giving him the support, giving him the platform. The worst of Moses was the cruelty. Unnecessary, demeaning, for no particular reason."

Not surprisingly, Moses Znaimer doesn't see it that way.

Znaimer maintains that what he was attempting to do with Canadian television was the same thing Garth Drabinsky was attempting to do with Canadian theatre and Robert Lantos was attempting to do with Canadian film. "We were trying to build personalities. It was very early days. We were trying to create private Canadian show business.

"Brian was caught in his world. He would sit in his office and make these meticulous, long, tremendous lists, and constantly tell people things they had forgotten about. So on one level, you have to say, that's kind of interesting, curious . . . but it ain't the cure for cancer.

"Deep down," he says, "I knew that *City Lights* was inconsistent with the philosophy of the station. And I tried for many years to bring Brian along. Brian, take a camera, and go out into the world. Brian, not everything can carry a thirty-minute quality interview. Citytv had a drive, a look, a feel – and then there was *City Lights*."

This was the new world order, and Brian saw no place for himself in it. A year after he'd started on *Movie Television*, he and Citytv parted company.

Now, suddenly, Brian Linehan was just another page in television history.

☆

Those close to Brian knew his world was falling apart. For the first time in his life, Brian Linehan was unemployed.

"He had nothing," Dianne Schwalm remembers. "And you could just see this little boy crumbling in front of you. He had this beautiful home, and he had no place to go every day. Brian needed routine. He needed a place where people said hello and welcomed him. He wanted to work hard, and he wanted to be seen working hard, and he wanted to see results at the end of the day."

Brian started coming down to Dianne's office at Warner Bros. at Church and Carlton. They gave him a desk – "where we kept all our supplies; it wasn't fancy" – and he would sit there and do clippings. "And read the papers, and catch up on what he needed to research, and make his notes, and do his highlighting, and make his files. And talk to people. He was a permanent fixture at our office."

Brian and Zane also were not getting along, and the strain had started to show. I knew Brian had been struggling in his relationship with Zane. Years earlier, we had gone to L.A. on a junket for a film about a legendary Australian racehorse named Phar Lap. I had brought my youngest son with me. Joe was eleven, and Brian introduced him to smoked salmon on our flight to L.A. and to grilled swordfish that night when the three of us had dinner in the dining room of the Mondrian hotel in Beverly Hills, where we were staying. The swordfish steak was the undisputed highlight of Joe's trip, and he finished every bite of it. After dinner, he excused himself to go to our room and watch TV, leaving Brian and I to liqueurs and gossip. We were talking about everything and nothing when Brian turned to me earnestly and lowered his voice. "I don't know what I'm going to do about me and Zane," he said, his voice slightly tremulous.

I was taken aback. We rarely discussed his personal life. "What do you mean?" I said.

"Zane doesn't believe in oral sex," he said quietly. "Zane doesn't believe in anal sex. Zane doesn't believe in mutual masturbation."

He stopped short to allow the waiter to bring us another round. Two Grand Marniers, gently warmed, in two large snifters. The waiter took our empty glasses and departed. What *did* Zane believe in?

Dr. Wagman, he said, believed in affectionate hugging and separate bedrooms. "I am going out of my mind," he said, quietly and calmly, but his fists were clenched so tight they were turning white, the blood draining out of them. "I don't know what I'm going to do."

Seeing the stunned expression on my face, he sat back in his chair. "But I do know what I'm going to do now," he said.

"What?" I asked, somewhat apprehensively.

"I'm going up to my room, I'm going to work on my notes for tomorrow's interviews, and go to bed."

We finished our Grand Marniers and got up from the table. "I think Joan is hosting the Carson show tonight," I said, making a lame attempt to respond.

"I'm sure Joe and I will both be sound asleep by then," he replied, pushing the elevator button for his floor. We were alone in the elevator, standing in silence, and when the doors slid open he gave me a hug. "Good night." He smiled. "See you in the morning."

So some of us knew that the trouble in the relationship had started long ago. But now, just as Brian's professional life was unravelling, his personal life was also in disarray. Karen Kain and her husband, actor-producer Ross Petty, inadvertently witnessed the seeds of the big split. Brian and Zane were entertaining at one of their Sunday salons when Zane suddenly announced that he was planning to move to the South of France.

"It was 'I'm going to live in the South of France,' not 'we,'" Kain remembers. "Brian and Zane had talked for some time about spending winters in San Miguel and summers in Toronto. And there had been some discussion about buying property in the South of France. But this came completely out of the blue, and Brian was clearly stunned. The rest of us were just looking at each other thinking, 'Do I pretend I didn't hear that? Do I go now?' It was extremely awkward."

Zane put their house on the market, and it was snapped up in no time. After the purchaser produced a sizable non-refundable deposit, Zane and Brian struck out on their own. Separately.

Zane, who loved swimming, bought a house with a black swimming pool in Mississauga, a suburban city far away from Toronto's vibrant downtown theatre district. Being black, he explained, this swimming pool held the sun's heat much better and much longer than a pastel-coloured swimming pool would. And, he said, the reflection of the sky produced a stunning contrast with the blue, blue water.

Brian, as usual, had gone the opposite way from Zane, and bought a townhouse in the heart of Toronto's gay village, on Monteith Street off Church Street. "His townhouse looked fabulous," says Marcia Martin. "He really did it in his style, and he really tried to make it work. But he wanted to be with Zane. He wanted to be with somebody."

While Michael Levine was in Turkey on a romantic vacation with a lady friend, he bought Brian a small prayer rug for his new home. When he brought it to Brian, he took one look around and wondered what Brian was doing there. "Except he was so frightened that I don't think he ever left the place," he recalls. "And after all the warmth of Grenadier Heights and all that nineteenth-century wood, to go into this kind of little marble palace – I was thinking, oh my God, he doesn't belong here. And of course he didn't."

Dr. Allan Harris had met fellow dentist Zane Wagman at a party in Yorkville. But he was still surprised when he picked up the phone in his office one day to hear Zane Wagman's voice on the other end of the line. "Would you mind seeing my partner, Brian Linehan, as a patient?"

Zane inquired. He and Brian had separated but were still in touch with each other.

Zane was still working in the school clinic, "so he couldn't treat Brian," Harris explains. "And I said, of course, I'd be thrilled. So Brian came in and we had a wonderful conversation, and he met my partner, Isaac. And then he and I would frequently meet in the morning, and we'd go to a coffee shop on Church Street, because Brian really just needed to unload at that point. He was going through a lot of emotional baggage with the whole separation."

Brian, says Harris, "was trying to figure out what he was going to do with his life. I think he knew he had made a mistake leaving Zane at that point. Or letting the relationship dissolve. He saw us as people outside the showbiz community. People with roots, you know, real people."

After he moved to Monteith Street, Brian told me he'd had a close encounter with a couple of guys who he suspected were gay bashers. Two men had followed him, taunting him, as he walked the three or four blocks home from the Wellesley subway station. "Aren't you the guy on TV? You live around here? Then you must be a fag too!" He had barely escaped into his house.

"I hate this goddam area," Brian told Allan Harris and Isaac Van Lange. "It just drives me crazy."

Harris remembers that when Bea Arthur came to town, "she and Brian used to have their martinis at his apartment and then go up to Centro for dinner. And one afternoon he invited us over, and we were bowled over to walk in and see Bea Arthur on Monteith Street."

A number of times, Allan and Isaac went to visit Brian and were surprised to find Zane waiting for them as well. The four of them started to spend a lot of time together. Says Harris: "I remember Zane and Brian telling us that basically we were the only gay couple they had as friends." More significant to their new friendship, Harris suspects, was the fact that he was one of the few people who actually knew Brian Linehan through Zane Wagman. "That was very interesting, because they took us in on a very different level. I don't think anybody else ever met Zane first and then became friends."

A friend of Allan and Isaac, Toronto real estate wizard Daryl Kent owned a beautiful home in Port Hope, Ontario, which Isaac was able to secure for a weekend for the four of them – "just a wonderful weekend sitting around." Isaac also brought his children's dog, a little Schnauzer. "Isaac was playing the piano," Harris remembers, "*Crazy*, the Patsy Cline song. And Brian was there, holding the Schnauzer in his arms, singing to the dog. It was just one of those delightful relaxed times, when he wasn't on show and when Zane got to be an equal partner. Which was something that we would not see that frequently if you were in a showbiz or public crowd, because Zane would step back and be in the shadows and really not want to be there."

Karen Kain remembers that during the split she and Ross didn't spend a lot of time with Brian. "We were actually babysitting Zane more. We had rented a cottage for a couple of weeks and Zane came up and stayed with us. And he was just moping around, depressed." About six months later, Brian invited Karen, Ross, and Zane to dinner at Monteith Street, "and it was kind of uncomfortable, because they were just starting to talk again. But Brian was still really angry with Zane."

Zane, she says, "was still contrite. 'How could I be so selfish? What was I thinking?'"

As Brian and Zane started to try to patch things up, a funny thing happened on the way to their haltingly awkward reconciliation. The once-eager buyer of the High Park home they had loved so much, the wonderful big house overlooking Grenadier Pond, defaulted on the purchase. Surely this was a sign that they were meant to be together, in the home they had created for each other, in the house they treasured.

Brian and Zane had both spent small fortunes on their new homes, partly in anticipation of the revenue they expected to receive from the sale of 5 Grenadier Heights. Suddenly they owned three homes – Brian's, Zane's, and Grenadier Heights – and a considerable amount of debt.

Brian sold the townhouse on Monteith Street, and took a loss financially. Zane sold the house in Mississauga with the black swimming pool, and took a loss financially.

Still, it was only money. And if they could make their personal partnership work, they knew they had everything to gain.

13

"He was the wife, and Brian was the star."

Shortly after Brian and Zane reclaimed their status as the residents and rightful owners of 5 Grenadier Heights, they invited Gail and me to dinner. It was all very laid-back, and instead of broiling a duck – our favourite of his several specialties – Zane took some packages of President's Choice Peking Duck out of the freezer and served them up, allowing him to spend much more time with us than he usually did.

At one point Brian and Gail were upstairs in the library – I think she was trying to teach him how to set their VCR, a challenge Zane had abandoned long ago – while Zane was pouring me a glass of wine in the kitchen. "The whole thing, all of last year, was a big mistake," he volunteered somewhat sheepishly. "We've made such a mess of things, and we've lost a lot of money. But I love Brian, and he loves me, so, y'know . . ."

"So here you are!"

He grinned. "Yes. So here we are."

He made no secret of how happy he was to be back home at Grenadier Heights. Later that evening, Zane repeated the sentiment, almost word for word, to Gail, making us wonder if this unexpected personal candour was a new mantra for them, perhaps a result of some sort of couples counselling.

Brian was as vocal as ever that evening; business as usual, you might say. Except that he too found a way to make a personal declaration by the end of the evening. Zane was engrossed in a conversation with Gail and had failed to notice that my liqueur glass and Brian's were empty. "I love Zane," Brian proclaimed, rising to his feet, "but since he's not going to offer us another round of liqueurs, I will!"

We all laughed – even Zane, who seemed to be more at peace with himself, more connected to Brian, than we'd ever seen before. They'd come a long way, baby.

Gail and I assumed that they were declaring themselves to all their friends, perhaps even as part of prescribed therapy to correct the omissions of the past. Years later when I shared this conversation with two of Zane and Brian's closest confidantes, Karen Kain and Marcia Martin, both of them stared at me in disbelief.

"He said *what?*" said Karen, obviously stunned.

"I never *ever* heard Zane say anything remotely intimate or affectionate!" said Marci, who was equally amazed.

Apparently Gail and I were wrong.

Canadian passports usually include a half-page form on which the passport holder is supposed to provide the name of someone who should be called "in case of accident or death." Brian was twenty-three when he picked up his first passport in 1966. He identified the person to call as Mrs. S. Linehan of Hamilton, Ont. Under the "Relationship" section he wrote "Mother." When he applied for his second passport in 1971, he listed Dr. Z. Robert Wagman, and identified him as "Guardian." When he applied for his third passport in 1976, he listed Dr. Z.R. Wagman as a "Family Friend." By the time the 1990s rolled around, Brian was identifying Zane as his "Companion."

Zane, on the other hand, was still identifying Brian as his "Friend." But clearly they were making some progress.

Both of them were blissfully free of any family ties. Who needed family when you had friends? Doris Roberts came for dinner. Bea Arthur came for the weekend. Carole Shelley looked forward to snuggling down in her bed in the guest room after dinner. "It would be divine as I arrived," she says. "There would be little soaps and shampoos and facecloths. The perfect hosts."

The best moments for her were cooking with Zane in the wonderful new kitchen at Grenadier Heights. "Brian would just sit there with a big silly grin on his face, watching two people he loved cooking for him."

Karen Kain recalls the Sunday afternoon gatherings that Brian initiated, the cocktail parties where she met artists Tony Scherman and Margaret Priest, and newspaper columnist Liz Braun and her doctor husband, Vince DeMarco. "And often Carole Shelley would be there, or interesting people who were in town, whom he knew and would invite. And then there were the dinners."

When Harriet Blacker flew in from New York to attend her nephew's wedding, Brian and Zane invited her and her partner, Henry Spector, to dinner at Grenadier Heights, "and then we stayed until midnight. It was fabulous. Brian clearly had the interviewer's knack of bringing things out of you, if he wasn't talking about himself. Mostly, he was talking about himself," she adds, grinning. "Zane sort of acted as the housewife. I mean, he did the cooking and the preparing, and things were set up exactly how he wanted them."

Myrna and Jack Daniels had the opposite experience. "We were invited to lunch at their home," Myrna recalls, "and Brian had always raved about how well Zane cooked. We arrived for lunch and Zane made a point of telling us that everything that we had for lunch he had purchased. He did not want to be cast in that role."

According to Allan Harris, when Brian and Zane moved back to Grenadier Heights, "they invited us over for dinner and they were wonderful hosts and friends. They were always inviting us over for our birthdays, and Zane would make a wonderful meal. And we had an Airedale at that time which Brian loved. Apparently Ginger was the only dog Zane would ever allow in the house or in the garden. She got to go in his prize-winning flower garden. That was quite an honour. My God! Zane wouldn't even let *people* walk down the pathway. 'Don't go down there. That's my prize-winning iris.'"

Zane was so at ease with them, Harris says, because they "were a safe harbour, in as much as we had something in common with Zane. We'd go over there and we would talk about his music – I had a music background – and we'd talk about his records." Zane had a unique record collection that included multiple recordings of the same pieces. ("Zane didn't buy just one Don Giovanni," Brian would later comment. "He would buy four. He'd sit down and tell his friends, 'Listen, this is why this variation is different.'")

Dinners at Grenadier Heights, however, were not always what Allan and Isaac expected them to be. "I'm vegetarian and always have been," Harris explains. "And Zane knew it, and usually went out of his way, which I don't expect anybody to do. You don't have to make a special meal for me. Well, of course, whenever Zane would cook, it was a production. The whole evening was a production, from the martinis to that wonderful hummus he made. We would always start with that and a few martinis and our dog Ginger would be sitting by the fire, and the fire would be blazing, and Brian would have a few little treats for her, and then we would go into the dining room."

He remembers one particular dinner when Zane brought out a very lovely and elaborate chicken. When Isaac gently reminded them that Allan was a vegetarian, Brian replied, "Oh that's okay, our friends in California are vegetarian too, and they eat chicken." Another time, he recalls, they served veal. "And every time the two of them would go to the kitchen, Isaac would reach across and take a little bit more off my plate!"

Despite the occasional display of culinary eccentricities, Harris and Van Lange loved going to Grenadier Heights with their Airedale for dinner. Ginger was not so keen. "Isaac has always said that dogs sense everything," says Harris. "Ginger would go to that home and there was always some altercation during dinner. There was always something. Maybe the knife wasn't turned properly, I don't know. But Ginger would be at the front door. She couldn't wait to leave. Because there was always just that level of tension."

Today, he says, they feel privileged that they were allowed to see "a more personal, deeply troubling side of both of their lives. When you get close to any couple and they allow you into their lives, you see the bickering that goes on. That's great, because that's human."

Harris remembers Brian bringing them presents – "everything he got off the latest junket. Caps and ponchos and the whole bit. He used to bring over these bags. And one time he brought all these porn magazines he had. And he said, 'Don't tell Zane, Zane doesn't know about them.' And I thought, oh my God, you're fifty-something years old!

"He was so innocent. He told us about this other actor in Toronto 'ordering in' through *Xtra*, the weekly gay and lesbian tabloid newspaper, and he wondered if he should do that. We told him he couldn't risk it here in Toronto. He could do that easily in L.A. or somewhere where he wasn't known. But he was just bursting. He so wanted to."

Brian was very open about the sexual frustration in his relationship with Zane. "Brian would come and have dinner and invariably the conversation would turn to sexual frustration as such," says Harris. "And he knew very little of the outlets in Toronto, such as the bathhouses and that kind of stuff. I remember telling him one night, and he sat there agog. Almost like, how did I miss this? He said that night he was very tempted."

Harris has a unique claim to fame in their relationship. "I am the only person who ever got Zane Wagman to go to a gay bar," he reports, eyes twinkling. Brian and Isaac had gone off somewhere, he recalls, so he and Zane went out for dinner. After dinner, Harris suggested stopping at Woody's, a famous gay watering hole on Church Street, for a nightcap.

"I've never been to a place like that," Zane told him.

"Then we must go," said Harris.

Zane reacted as though he had entered an alien world. "We just did a walk-through and left," says Harris. "But it was something Zane had obviously never experienced in his life, to be in one of those hyper-gay environments. As a man he had always suppressed it so much his entire life, and didn't want to discuss anything even remotely sexual, and found even the word to be in bad taste. And I honestly don't know how it occurred. But afterwards, we were just astounded that it had. And of course Brian just about fell over when we told him."

Over the years Brian had a number of on-the-job experiences with gay men. Newspaper columnist Jim Bawden, who filed Linehan interviews at the *Hamilton Spectator* before moving to the *Toronto Star*, remembered Brian telling him that when he met Noel Coward, the celebrated playwright greeted him by sticking his tongue down his throat. I myself remembered when Sir Ralph Richardson and Sir John Gielgud were in town performing their hit play, David Storey's *Home*. After his *City Lights* session, Sir Ralph invited Brian to join him and Sir John for lunch at the Three Small Rooms, the elegant dining room at the Windsor Arms hotel. Gielgud was waiting for them at the table when they arrived.

"John," said Sir Ralph enthusiastically, putting his arm around Brian, "I've just done a truly marvellous interview!"

"Really!" Sir John responded, casting a lascivious eye on Brian. "And was this young man the prize?"

George Cukor, of course, Brian's Hollywood hero and patron, was also gay, and reportedly had a long and closeted "friendship" with actor Lon McCallister. But despite occasional protests to the contrary, neither Zane nor Brian seemed to be fans of the gay culture suddenly exploding around us. Dianne Schwalm still remembers a night in Los Angeles when she and fellow Canadian film publicist Jill DeWolfe took Brian to Studio One, at that time the hottest gay disco in Hollywood. Brian loved to dance, and Studio One was as trendy-chic as you could get, with buff, bare-chested young men in satin shorts serving drinks to straight designer-suited studio executives and their wives and girlfriends.

"The dancing was wild!" Dianne remembers. "And we lasted, I'm betting, maybe half an hour, and Brian said, 'We've got to get out of here.' He was so uncomfortable in that environment. He never liked that part of the culture. He liked the upscale classy traditional, the Polo Lounge, the garden, breakfast at the Four Seasons downstairs early in the morning. The power breakfasts."

Filmmaker Barry Avrich remembers inviting Brian and Zane to dinner, adding that he and his wife, Melissa Manley, were thinking of inviting another couple, Joe and Danny, to make a setting for six. "And Brian goes, 'Why?'" Avrich recalls. "I said, 'Because they're wonderful.' And he said, 'Why do you feel you have to have this other gay couple there?' And it was the first time I even thought of him and Zane in those terms. It was a weird awkwardness on the phone. I said, 'I won't invite them, then.' And Brian said, 'Fine, don't.' And . . . we didn't."

On weekends in the summer, Allan Harris and Isaac Van Lange would invite Brian and Zane to join them at a cottage they owned on a small lake. "The cottage was very rustic," says Harris. "In fact, it was on a rocky island so there was no sewage system; it was basically an out-house. Zane is the only man I've ever known who went to the outhouse to have a pee. I mean, Zane, loosen up!"

A lot of the tension between Brian and Zane, Allan Harris believes, was due to Zane's background and his lack of self-acceptance. "It was very sad to see. I think that Zane had huge psychological problems with being Jewish, with being a dentist, doing a day-to-day job that he loathed with the kids in the school system. He was a very erudite, schol-arly man; he appreciated the finer things of life, and yet he never really kicked back enough to just love life.

"Brian cherished Zane. And he cherished all of that complexity that Zane was. I think if Zane had just been able to loosen up and have sex it would have changed their whole relationship."

Joan Rivers met Zane Wagman in 1998, two years after she started making bi-monthly pilgrimages to Toronto to promote her line of costume jewellery on The Shopping Channel.

"I liked Zane," she says. "Although Brian never called Zane Zane. He always called him Zane Wagman. 'Zane Wagman and I are here.' 'You remember Zane Wagman?' Always Zane Wagman."

Brian and Zane, she says, "were both snobs. I think that's why they worked so well together. Both snobs. Both loved the finer things; both loved that they had been here, they had been there, they had been invited to this or went to that. I don't think Brian in any way represented the proletariat to Zane."

What Brian was constantly seeking, she believes, was full-fledged membership in that group of people he regarded as elite. "That was certainly what Brian was striving for. And certainly where Zane wanted to be." Zane, she observed, "dressed like the term 'a gent.' Yes. Landed gentry. As did Brian. Brian never came by in a jogging outfit."

Rivers was romantically involved with producer and philanthropist Orin Lehman at the time, "and I think Zane liked me because of Orin. Because Orin was so to the manner born and represented that whole kind of family that was right out of our crowd. And Lehman Bros. And the education. And he owned polo ponies as a youth. And Zane and Orin got along very, very well. It was very easy to go out to dinner because Zane would sit next to Orin and have a wonderful time."

Rivers says she can easily relate to what was perceived as Zane's reluctance to acknowledge his Judaic roots. "Zane was very typical of second-generation Jews," she says. "They don't fit in anywhere. *I* don't fit in anywhere. I mean, I worship in a temple, but these are not my people."

Zane, she adds, was also an "extraordinarily handsome" man. "I liked having Zane on my arm. Once we went to the theatre, the three of us, and it was wonderful walking in with Zane, because he was a great-looking escort."

When Rivers came to Toronto for one of her whirlwind weekends she spent most of her hours at The Shopping Network in Mississauga, a city-sized suburb miles away from downtown Toronto. Since she had less than two hours between on-camera stints, she couldn't invite Brian and Zane to an elegant dinner. So she would try to find other ways to amuse them.

One time, just for fun, she took them to a Denny's in Mississauga, and ordered hors d'oeuvres and red and white wine. "We only had an hour and I just thought, how hilarious if we went to Denny's," she remembers, laughing. "They were such elegant men. And I just thought it was a hoot and a howl. Let's go to Denny's and order off menus that have been washed. And Brian thought it was very funny too. But Zane couldn't handle it.

"It really kind of ruined the hour for us. Zane didn't get the camp; he didn't think it was funny saying to the girl at Denny's, who has her name 'Miriam' stamped on her shirt, 'What do you have in the way of hors d'oeuvres?' Miriam thought it was funny. Zane didn't."

Zane found stories of our escapades in Hollywood both frivolous and shallow – which, by and large, they were. Sadly, he took no pleasure in them, and would wait patiently for Brian to finish gossiping so he could bring the conversation back to a higher level.

If friction between Zane and Brian was exacerbated by Brian's love of show business, Joan Rivers believes it was probably inevitable. Even in later years, she noted, Brian "still enjoyed all that opening night stuff, wearing a beautiful dinner jacket, seeing a movie first or seeing a play, and going to a party afterwards. Brian always thought that Zane may have looked down his nose at it, but I think Zane never saw things like that in his life. Zane may have gone to the opera but he wasn't invited to a first night at the opera unless Brian was invited. Because Brian was the celebrity."

Rivers believes that Zane's often-declared disdain for show business gave him his strength in their relationship.

"Otherwise," she says, "it was Brian, Brian, Brian, Brian, Brian, Brian, kissy Brian, hello Zane, Brian, Brian, Brian, kissy kissy, hello Zane. He was the wife and Brian was the star."

☆

Jane Hawtin had moved from Q107 to a brief stint at CKFM when her boss Gary Slaight asked her to see if her pal Brian Linehan wanted to do radio again. Brian said yes. Nearly a year later, movie fans were listening to Hawtin and Linehan on *Hollywood North*, a weekly radio program that aired across Canada, syndicated through Sound Source. "That's when I first realized the yin and yang of Brian," says Hawtin. "That it's wonderful and then it's horrible. The more confident he got, the bossier he got. So it went from being I-love-Jane-because-Jane-brought-me-back-to-radio to being 'well, you do that.' You know, with that imperious wave of the hand. 'I'm Brian Linehan and I don't do that.'"

In Canadian radio, in fact, Hawtin was the "hot" name. Linehan was an added attraction. "But I would just roll my eyes, and off we'd go," she says with a shrug. "Because I also loved the magic that he would get."

One season of *Hollywood North* was enough to persuade both Brian and Slaight that Brian should come home and do his own thing on CFRB. Hawtin wasn't unhappy about the idea. "Because, to be honest, I was exhausted. It was too much, too much. And the unfortunate thing is that once Brian got confident – and I really think that's what it was – once he sort of got back into his stride, then all of a sudden all these rules came about. He wouldn't talk to this person and he wouldn't talk to that person and he wouldn't talk to them unless he got this many minutes. And it always had to be special."

Brian was back at CFRB doing daily stints as an entertainment commentator cum culture specialist when publicist Martha Watson first called him. She was working at TVOntario, "and I was pitching him on something." About a year later, he called her. She was now in the book business and had Mary Higgins Clark and Gloria Steinem coming in to promote their new books. Watson and Linehan became very good friends very quickly, over the phone. "Brian had that ability, to become close to people quickly. If he wanted to. I used to invite him out for lunch, and he'd say, 'I don't eat lunch. But I DO eat dinner, and I LOVE martinis.' And I just fell in love with him."

As a young woman, Watson had watched Brian on *City Lights* – "He was a legend, really" – and she was admittedly a little intimidated by him. "And then you'd talk to him, and there was nothing intimidating. Unless he wanted to be. He was just charming and funny and bright. Everyone I brought to him unanimously walked out raving about him," she remembers. "Reeve Lindbergh, Charles Lindbergh's daughter, told me, 'That's the best interview I've ever done. Who is this guy?' It was always that way."

She, too, witnessed some of the "yin and yang" of Linehan. Before his interview with Charlton Heston, she recalls, "he said terrible things about him. But he was very nice to him when he interviewed him."

By now Martha knew that Brian interviewed Shirley MacLaine in New York, L.A., Toronto, wherever and whenever he could. In Toronto, he and Shirley would go out and play, sometimes in pursuit of the Perfect Carrot Cake (one of her several passions and few weaknesses).

Over the years, several friends and acquaintances were puzzled by their relationship. I wasn't. Shirley and Brian shared the same demanding, admirable work ethic. Whether he was interviewing or she was giving interviews, the work always came first. Both had a very strong sense of responsibility to their employers and an even greater sense of responsibility to themselves. No *City Lights* interviews were rescheduled because Brian wanted to go out and play with Shirley. No studio or publishing meetings were postponed because Shirley wanted to go out and play with Brian.

From everything Brian told her about Shirley, Jane Hawtin thought MacLaine must be similar to Brian. "She seemed to blow hot and cold too. And apparently would get in these moods. Which sounded very Linehan to me."

One Thanksgiving weekend, Brian and Zane hosted a dinner party at Grenadier Heights in MacLaine's honour. Shirley had returned to dancing with the same single-minded determination that had made and kept her a star, and a best-selling author, for decades. She looked sleek, svelte and glamorous in what I remember as an elegantly trim purple pantsuit that set off her vibrant red hair.

Zane was preparing something wonderful for supper, and we had all gathered in the kitchen, where Brian was making martinis and offering wine to the less adventurous among us. I seem to remember Shirley nursing a glass of white wine, which probably lasted her most of the night; she was living proof of the beneficial results of self-discipline.

Zane and Brian had spent a small fortune renovating their kitchen, which was now more welcoming than ever. A spectacular kitchen island with a countertop of Italian marble had been added. Zane had personally chosen the marble, and was apoplectic when it arrived in Canada with a major crack in it. He and Brian had already waited months for the marble to arrive, and Zane was so frustrated by what he perceived to be the importer's lackadaisical (i.e., Italian) attitude that he refused to accept the shipment, causing further frustration and delay. But that was all behind them now. They had a beautiful kitchen, and a beautiful island, and they were about to sit down to a wonderful dinner with good friends, one of whom happened to be a bona fide movie star. What could possibly ruin this perfect evening?

Zane was preparing to serve us some sumptuous foie gras. Brian was mixing up a fresh batch of martinis and had lined up the martini glasses on the island, close to the fridge. Shirley was sitting on a stool beside the island, chatting with Brian and Gail. While they talked and gossiped, she was stretching – that limbering-up stretch that dancers often do, especially on a day off from touring. Heels up, heels down. Knee up, knee down. Leg up, leg down. They do it on the subway, at the movies, anywhere at all, wherever they think you can't see them doing it. So Shirley was stretching, and making no attempt to disguise it. She was, after all, among friends.

At one point, she thrust her left leg out in front of her but couldn't extend it far enough to get a really good stretch. So she got to her feet, nimbly raised her leg, rested her foot on the island countertop, and gracefully leaned forward, getting the good stretch she was seeking.

Zane's jaw dropped. He was horror-struck. "SHIRLEY!!" he barked. "PLEASE take your foot OFF the ISLAND!!" He was furious. "THIS is where I prepare FOOD!!"

Now Shirley's jaw dropped. "Zane, I'm sorry!" she said, obviously stunned by his response. She was still frozen in her stretch. We all stared at her foot, which was still resting on the countertop.

"*PLEASE!!*" Zane barked, still fuming.

Shirley quickly raised her leg and removed her foot. "Zane," she began, "I'm sorry, I didn't know –"

"WHAT did you THINK it was FOR??" Zane asked irately.

"Zane, I *said* I was sorry!" she responded defensively.

Brian quickly intervened. "Shirley, I have something to show you," he said, taking her by the hand. "In the living room."

After he whisked her out of the room, Gail gave Zane an affectionate pat on the back. Shirley, she gently reminded him, was justifiably famous for her acting, for her dancing, for her writing, and for being a world-class entertainer. "For what it's worth," Gail added, "I don't think Shirley has spent an inordinate amount of time in the kitchen."

"I'd say that's fairly OBVIOUS, wouldn't you?" Zane grumbled under his breath. He was still sulking, but he pulled himself together, and served us a Thanksgiving dinner to be thankful for. He even let Shirley sit at the table.

Years later, Martha Watson found herself wrangling Shirley on her latest book tour. Martha set up a media interview dinner with Shirley, her long-time publicist Dale Olson, Brian, and herself. The night they had dinner, Watson says, Shirley focused all her attention on Brian, and pretty much ignored her.

"Brian, who loved to boast about his friends, took the time to tell Shirley that 'Ms. Watson is a VERY important publishing executive.' Which was absolute crap, since I was a lowly publicist," adds Watson with a sardonic shrug. "Shirley's like, yeah, big deal. And Brian said, 'Actually, she's even escorted . . .' and started rhyming off names. And one of them was Henry Kissinger."

Ms. MacLaine was suddenly interested. Said Shirley, without missing a beat: "Didja fuck him?"

Ms. Watson's jaw dropped. "*NO!!*" she replied indignantly.

Brian phoned Martha from home about two hours later. "I am SO disappointed in you!" he teased.

"BRY-an!!"

"Couldn't you just have said you slept with him?" he persisted. "Because clearly SHE has!"

All in all, another memorable evening.

In his personal papers now housed in the TIFFG Film Reference Library is a copy of one of the Shirley MacLaine books Brian liked best: *Dancing in the Light*.

Inside the flyleaf the inscription reads:

> *To Darling Brian*
> *A dancer of time and memory*
> *while you can . . .*
> *continue . . .*
>
> *Much love, Shirley*

☆

Brian was working, but not as much as he wanted, and not doing what he wanted to do. He loved radio, but it wasn't television, and it wasn't *City Lights*. He distracted himself with theatre-going. When Shirley Lord and Abe Rosenthal came to Toronto, he took them to see a new production of Athol Fugard's play *The Island*, and Brian, with his usual flourish, introduced them to Garth Drabinsky, who was producing the show.

Zane would fly to New York to see an opera, but Brian attended as many Broadway shows as he could wangle comps for. Joan Rivers, whose first love was the stage, found Brian's devotion to legitimate theatre refreshing. "He put his money where his mouth was. He loved theatre. When he came to New York, he saw theatre. All my friends who say they LOVE the theatre come in for a week and see two plays. Brian would come in for two nights and see four plays."

To take Brian's mind off the fact that he wasn't working, Barry Avrich would arrange to get him the best theatre tickets and go to New York "just to hang out with him, because he was fun." Barry invited Brian to the opening of a new production of *42nd Street*. "The curtain goes up just a little bit so you see the dancers' feet," he reminds me, "one hundred and forty of them, and for some reason there's a woman behind us who starts singing, 'Come and meet / Those dancing feet . . .' and Brian is annoyed. And she continues with the singing. Finally, he turns around and says, 'Madam, did you write this show?' And she says, 'No.'

And he says, 'Okay, for God's sake, shut up. I want to hear it and I don't want to hear you singing, for Christ's sake!' And that was the end of her."

"He was always a very generous theatregoer," says Carole Shelley. "He always looked for gorgeous. If it wasn't, he would almost apologize. 'I'm sorry I have to say it, but it wasn't as wonderful as I hoped it would be.' Or else he would say, 'It was brilliant. I loved it. It was breathtaking.' He didn't want it to be bad. Unlike some other people and a few critics we know."

Brian and Zane still loved to travel. "They went down to Cuba a number of times," Allan Harris recalls, "to the point where I remember Brian saying that one time when they arrived, the Cuban authorities took each of them separately to try to figure out what was going on, why they were coming to Cuba so frequently."

Myrna Daniels frequently invited Brian and Zane to Palm Beach. Zane, she says, "wasn't happy travelling with Brian all the time. The reason he came down to Palm Beach again was that he loved swimming in the ocean. That was the lure that Brian used to hold out to him." At breakfast, she says, "Brian would entertain. And mention names and dates as he always did, which was impressive, and then a little redundant after a while. But that was just his act."

Years earlier, he had confided to Myrna that he felt he was invited places to be the unbilled, unpaid entertainment, and complained about hostesses making him "sing for his supper." "And in the back of my mind I was always aware of that, hoping he didn't feel he had to do that."

The best times, she says, were the times when he came down to visit her alone, without Zane. "A lot of our friends down there invited him out. They just adored him. He was just so wonderful and the perfect guest during the dinner party and the perfect raconteur afterward, because he would skewer *everyone*. He was wonderful, wonderful."

Inspired and informed by her term as a board member of the Toronto film festival, Myrna Daniels was one of a group of devoted cineastes who wanted to start a film festival in Palm Beach. "We were desperately trying to get it going. And there was no response in Palm Beach. They couldn't have cared less. So I invited Brian to come down and interview Anthony Quinn."

The evening at the Rinker Playhouse, a small venue in the Kravis Center, was sold out. Brian spent the entire day writing out all the information he needed for the interview. Anthony Quinn had said, "I don't care what you do but I don't want to hear a word about *Zorba the Greek*."

The young man who had put together the clips of Quinn's film career, Myrna recalls, had used the theme from *Zorba the Greek* as a soundtrack. "And Tony loved it. He was as happy as could be when they played that. Or at least he pretended to be."

Brian sat up on the stage with Anthony Quinn, "and the questions were getting better and better – Brian was really getting in there –" when Quinn's third wife, sitting in the front row with his four-year-old daughter, pushed the girl off her lap, which prompted her to run up on the stage and crawl up onto her father's knee.

"She had a sash that kept opening," Myrna remembers, "and Tony kept trying to tie it, and of course he was distracted, so the whole thing was broken and it limped to an end. It accomplished what it set out to do, it was great PR and everything else. But it was really a horrible ending for the interview."

Brian, of course, had done hours and hours of preparation. "And this little girl had just ruined everything." She shakes her head, laughing. "I'll never forget Brian's remark after it was all over. He said, 'If I had had a stake, I would have plunged it through her heart.' I cracked up. I thought that was so wonderful."

Not long after that, Anthony Quinn came to Toronto with his art show, and Brian did another interview with him. "He used the questions he never got to ask in Palm Beach," says Myrna. "And Tony actually cried during the interview. Brian had brought up the fact that Tony had carried his mother into church on his back, or something like that. Great stuff. I don't know where he got this information. Neither did anyone else."

☆

The fact that Brian enjoyed rubbing elbows with the wealthy was not lost on his friends. Including Michael Levine. "What is that line? *I never met a rich person I didn't like.* To a certain extent, that was Brian," he says. "Brian liked creature comforts. I think it's really, really simple. This was not someone who had family heirlooms, who had a sense of history. I think he was profoundly charmed by people who had enormous wealth and were able to live that lifestyle. But after a while, unless they had something more to them, he was considerably less charmed by them. Most of the wealthy people he spent time with were self-made. They were not that obnoxious brand of inheritor who, as the saying goes, think they've hit a triple when they were actually born on third base. I think he liked interesting people.

I think that while he succumbed to the creature comforts, he tried to do it with people who actually were stimulating. Although when he was on, he didn't need anybody. All he needed was an audience."

"Brian loved all the perks," says Marcia Martin. "*City Lights* was the best thing ever for him. He travelled first-class, he had the best wardrobe – Valentino suits, the works! – limos everywhere. So he left a lot behind when he left Citytv. Because *City Lights* bought a lot of first-class living for them."

When Brian left Citytv, Marci and Brian had a falling out. "Leaving was very hard for him," she allows, "and I represented Citytv, because I was still there. We were friends for eighteen years when this happened. And so when he finally did leave, and his personal life wasn't going very well, it affected our relationship. There was nothing gracious about his leaving; no one made any gestures to make it easier, I must say.

"I remember calling the house, and Zane would answer the phone, and I know many times when Zane said that Brian wasn't there, that he was there. So six, seven months into this – and Brian was very hurt, and bitter, and stubborn, and held a grudge, and still took everything person-ally – I called Zane and I said, Put him on the phone, I want to talk to him. I said, Brian, I can't believe you're prepared to throw away eighteen years of friendship. And slowly we started getting back together again. I had to inch my way back in. But I had to make all the overtures. I had to make all the calls. It was me. He wouldn't have done it. And I really had to work at it.

"I laugh when I think about it now. With all the grief he could give you – you'd invite him to dinner and he'd insult your guests, you'd never know what he's going to say about whom – and still he was worth it."

Marcia Martin's experience of being on the outs with Brian was not unique. Two of his biggest boosters and show-business lifelines, Judi Schwam and Dianne Schwalm, had both found themselves in similar positions.

"Brian was so considerate," says Judi. "He remembered everybody's birthday. I remember nobody's. He would send handwritten notes. Years ago, I decided to follow Brian's example and start writing personal notes, but it was so hard to get that flow. I must have used up half a box of sta-tionery to get one note finished."

A habitual snapshot-shooter, Brian loved to capture candid moments in our junket revelries and then send the most relevant photos to each of us, sometimes slipping them into plastic cubes, sometimes into wallet-sized photo albums. One time Brian got angry with Judi, she recalls, because he had sent her "one of the marvellous books of photographs he would put together for us. And I phoned him and left a message because he wasn't there. But I *didn't* send him a note. And that was one of those 'I don't think he's talking to me' times.

"One year he was really angry with the Toronto film festival," she recalls, "so he decided not to show up for one of the interviews he was supposed to do for me at the festival. I was really angry, because he was misdirecting his anger. Which we know he did, often. And I called him on it. I thought he might not be talking to me again, but that's just the way it was: when you were a friend of Brian's, you had to say what you needed to say."

"We watched him grow up and go through hissy fits and go through withdrawal, and then come back and shine, and then come back and be bitter, and then come back and not talk to you," says Dianne Schwalm, shaking her head. "And letters back and forth. *Why would you think this? And I always thought this and you were my friend and I would never do anything* yadda yadda yadda. And then I'd pick up the phone and I'd say, Brian, I've never hated you, you have to understand I've got a job to do. I have bosses to answer to. If I lose my job tomorrow, are you going to really love me and pay the rent? No. 'Well, I've got integrity.' And I'd say, you know I love you to pieces and this is not personal. 'Well, all right then, if it's not personal.' And then we'd have lunch and we'd drink all afternoon and then bond again like we were sisters and everything would be great for another few years.

"You never wanted to be on Brian's bad side. He would literally shut you out and pretend that you'd never had a relationship. We had sessions where we had to mend fences, and he'd come in and he'd have that pout. And I'd hug him, and I'd whisper in his ear, *you know I love you*. And you could just feel the whole body melt."

Dianne had a special arrangement with Zane Wagman, who gave her his private number. "I said to him, I'll never bother you. But if I really need Brian, may I call you? And I will never abuse that. So you know that if I'm calling, I really need him. And he said, 'Absolutely.'

"Sometimes I would leave a message and I'd say, Zane, if you can hear this, can you call me and let me know if it's okay to talk. Because sometimes Brian wouldn't call for a long time. And you didn't know what was going on, whether he was in a slump, or a depression, or had gone off on his own."

Citytv sent out invitations to station alumni to participate in publicity-generating celebrations marking the twenty-fifth anniversary of the maverick, trail-blazing station. Brian, by then infamous for never letting bygones be bygones, surprised everyone when he graciously accepted the invitation, and showed up at the Queen Street studios, elegantly dressed as always.

"Brian Linehan and *City Lights* could not have happened anywhere else in the English-speaking world," he told the camera crew who interviewed him. "Nobody, NOBODY would have hired anyone who looked and sounded like me. I mean, I was constantly made fun of. The first thing I ever got was caricatures of me. And you know what it was. It was the hair, and the pug nose, and large teeth. And the mole was never forgotten. But no, I could not have happened anywhere but Citytv. I am a product and a creation of Citytv."

Moses Znaimer told me he had never seen the interview Brian had taped. When I told him what Brian had said, he dismissed his remarks as banal. "That's what everybody says at those things," he scoffed. More to the point, he added, "He never said it while he was here."

At the end of that interview, Brian noted that from 1973 to 1989 he had done more than two thousand interviews on *City Lights*. "And only now," he added, "do I know that they were the best years of my life."

It was a rare moment of unguarded, on-camera introspection. It was, I believe, Brian Linehan's way of saying Thank You.

For Moses Znaimer, however, it was much too little, and far too late.

14

"He can be had."

After he left Citytv, Dianne Schwalm kept trying to come up with ways to keep Brian busy and making money. She persuaded the publisher of *Tribute* magazine, an in-theatre movie fan guide and a major beneficiary of her corporate largesse, to hire him as a freelance writer. "So it got him a little extra money. People would say hey, you don't need a tag day for Brian. But every penny was hard work for him. No money fell in his lap just because he was Brian."

Dianne was also struggling with new studio restrictions on the number of interviews she could set up for stars who were contractually obliged to promote their films. "The stars don't want to do 120 interviews. And then it occurred to me: Why don't we get Brian to do one interview? Off-camera, open end. And they can all use it. And he can bank it and save it for specials. So, I proposed the idea to L.A. and they all said, absolutely, sounds great."

Brian was thrilled. He could make some money doing what he did best. But – a big "but" – could he still go first-class? The new studio rule for all junket press was E.O.N.E. – Economy Only No Exceptions. Dianne called her boss, Rob Friedman. Yes, Brian could travel first-class. And yes, he'd get his twenty minutes with the star.

Dianne and Warner Bros. absorbed all his travel expenses, even putting him up for extra days if he wanted to go down early or stay later, and paid him a fee of $3,000–$4,000 per film assignment. At the beginning he was doing about fifteen Warner Bros. films a year. "But of course his art form was something that he took as a gift to us," Dianne says, rolling her eyes. "There was no value you could put on that. So the fact that you paid him was just a token stipend. An honorarium. Not real payment for the true work." She shrugs. "And then of course I'd be on the other side saying, 'Godammit, Brian, I know what you're trying to accomplish but I've got these people chewing my ass off here, and I'm trying to pay you, so I'm trying to find that middle ground.'"

Other studios, including Disney, explored similar ventures with him, but ultimately they didn't take. Despite all good intentions, in some ways the trouble was a case of classic miscasting. Brian Linehan, who lived to be praised on camera, was not on camera and not being praised on camera. He sat out of camera range, asked his questions, took a beat after each response to allow for easier editing, and watched Warners ship the footage of the star's answers to TV outlets all over America, where their interviewers could replace Brian on camera.

It was not an easy fit. Often when Dianne did not accompany Brian on his forays to New York and Los Angeles for Warner Bros., she would get calls. "'He did not behave.' 'Oh Diane, he was so demanding.' *'I'm here and I've been sitting here for four hours. What do you think I am?'*

"He really became chopped liver," says Dianne. "He'd sit in hallways for hours just making those meticulous notes, looking like he was the star, waiting to be called for his close-up. Meanwhile he was getting pissed off because he would get bumped because he was open-ended. He wasn't NBC, he wasn't CBS. The stars would decide to go to lunch, and Brian would say, 'But I've been waiting here two hours!' 'Well, you'll have to wait.' And it just crushed him."

Changes in Warner Bros. hierarchy reduced Brian's interview time to fifteen minutes. "And then it was ten minutes, and then it was seven. And somebody high up wanted specific questions, and it had to be bullet answers, and Brian said, 'I can't do this job. It's ruining my personal ethical belief of what I do. I feel like I'm bastardizing and prostituting myself. Maybe I shouldn't do them.' And I said, you know what, maybe you shouldn't. Let's just save you for ones that matter."

Brian had been travelling to New York or L.A. on Warner Bros. first-class tickets at least once a month, but now the studio started to import him only on Dianne's recommendation. Eventually they just stopped bringing him in altogether.

I wanted to test the water with Brian at the *Toronto Sun* and brought him on board as a weekly columnist for our big Friday Entertainment section. At the time he seemed more interested in having an office to go to than in writing a weekly column. After he took one look at the computer word processors we used, he announced that he would type his column at home on a typewriter, bring it in to our Entertainment department super-secretary Melinda Mantel, and have her input it for him.

"No, Brian, we won't be doing that," I said firmly, with a warm but threatening smile. I sat him down and gave him his first lesson on a computer. He was too intimidated to touch the keyboard at first; I think he had visions of being responsible for blowing up the Sun building on King Street because he had accidentally pressed SEND instead of SAVE. To his delight and my gratitude, he was soon adopted by columnist Jim Slotek and writer and editor John Sakamoto, who helped cure him of his computer complex.

His weekly column, Linehan, ran for more than a year and took many forms. His new mentors helped Brian fashion his prose style to suit our tabloid readers, and by and large his column received spectacular play in the *Sun*, frequently occupying a full page, including huge, eye-riveting photos. He also turned in some startlingly good pieces for the Showcase section of the Sunday *Sun*, including an unforgettable gloves-off report of a close encounter with Charlie Sheen, who was deep into substance abuse at the time. Jim Slotek would later write that Brian, on unfamiliar turf, agonized over each column. "Sitting next to him, I became his de facto editor as he ran every one by me, each written passionately, loaded with anecdotes and dropped names. He had a flair for leads too. 'Movies, like raccoons, should not be seen in daylight,' began one." John Sakamoto remembers his surprise when he discovered how insecure Brian was about his writing, "because he had already accomplished so much. He was one of the people we had watched on TV. He was one of the people we wrote about."

Brian was still at the *Sun* when Toronto film festival co-founder Dusty Cohl launched his first Floating Film Festival in February 1991. Dusty and his festival director, Hannah Fisher, already had their contingent of on-board film critics and presenters booked – Roger Ebert, Kathleen Carroll (Roger's co-critic at the New York *Daily News*), Richard Corliss (*Time* magazine), Mary Corliss (film curator, Museum of Modern Art), Jay Scott (*Globe and Mail*), and myself – when I suggested that Brian might be an asset to the fledgling festival.

Dusty enjoyed Brian's company and was amused by his quick wit and mercurial moods. He'd also seen Brian show considerable grace under fire when he hosted all-star Variety Club luncheons, a popular Toronto film festival event that was almost sabotaged every year, without fail, by the shenanigans of bickering luncheon organizers Al Dubin and Gino Empry. Partly for Brian's potential, and partly to please me, Dusty invited Brian to join us.

Dusty had designed the "floater" (as it soon became known) as a bi-annual event, and launched it in high style. At Roger Ebert's invitation, Martin Scorsese came aboard to toast our maiden voyage at a giddy opening cocktail party. Our pal Arlene Ludwig flew in from L.A. to join the inaugural cruise and brought us the premiere-at-sea of the much-anticipated teaming of Woody Allen and Bette Midler in Paul Mazursky's *Scenes From a Mall.* Kathleen Carroll persuaded up-and-coming director Jonathan Demme to give us the world premiere screening of a new thriller with Jodie Foster and Anthony Hopkins called *Silence of the Lambs.* Brian, again at Dusty's invitation, hosted a tribute evening to legendary stage and screen stalwart Lou Jacobi, the Broadway funnyman who had earned a sterling reputation in Hollywood as a dramatic actor. We were blessed with glorious weather in the Bahamas, the Virgin Islands, Jamaica, whenever and wherever we docked on our first seven-day excursion at sea. All in all, it was a highly auspicious beginning for Cohl's newest project.

I left the *Toronto Sun* before the first floating film festival sailed, to pursue new challenges at the Canadian Broadcasting Corporation. A few months later, my successor, Bob Thompson, called, as a courtesy, to inform me that the Entertainment department budget had been cut back and that the Linehan column was among the casualties.

I was grateful for the courtesy call, and saddened by it, but not entirely surprised. After Brian joined the department, there were staff grumblings that he was being given some plum assignments, specifically interviews, that some writers believed should have been theirs. The *Sun's* Entertainment department was a major destination for good writers; they had to work hard to get into it, and they had to work hard to stay in it. Some felt that I had parachuted Brian into the department, without real credentials, and they resented it. Add the fact that several *Sun* senior editors had reputations for being notoriously homophobic, and the resulting climate was too chilly to accelerate Brian's burgeoning career as a columnist.

John Sakamoto remembers the day Brian was summoned to Bob Thompson's office for a meeting. "His column had really taken off, and he was more confident about his writing, and people on the street were telling him that they liked his column. Not his show; his *column.* He walked into Bob Thompson's office, convinced he was going to get a promotion. And when he came out of the office he was in a state of shock, because his column had just been killed."

The *Sun*'s senior film critic, Bruce Kirkland, had known Linehan for years, in different incarnations. "Brian never fit at the *Sun*," says Kirkland. "It's not that he lacked talent. But anytime that you're engaging with a newspaper and writing about the arts, you have to be given the freedom to have your own voice. And I believe the *Sun* never gave Brian the freedom to have his own voice. There was a lack of understanding of what he could bring to the table. He demanded respect because he earned respect. And he didn't get respect at the *Toronto Sun* in the proper way, it was lackadaisical. That's what I remember about his tenure there. It was a waste for him and it was a waste for the *Toronto Sun* because the newspaper didn't utilize a valuable resource."

"Brian always liked to be employed," says Michael Levine. "He was one of the hardest-working people that I knew and therefore I think having the gig at the *Sun* was profoundly important to him. He liked structure and order. He had to get up in the morning and go somewhere.

"Did the exercise have the same kind of joy that his interviewing and researching did? I tend not to think so."

☆

Enthusiasm was so high after the first floating film festival that Dusty Cohl created an instant sequel for February 1992. Guests included Brigitte Berman, who not only brought her Oscar-winning documentary on Artie Shaw, *Time Is All You've Got*, but also one of Shaw's celebrated wives, film veteran Evelyn Keyes. One of our black-tie evenings, Brian's on-stage interview with the effervescent seventy-four-year-old Keyes was one of many festival highlights.

Once he got on the Floating Film Festival (or the Good Ship Triple-F, as it was sometimes called), Brian was as buoyant as the Holland-America luxury ships that cruised us to a series of sun-washed ports in and around the Caribbean. Brian, Zane, Gail and I usually found the best beach club in every port, sunning and swimming to our hearts' content. And Brian and Zane had no shortage of invitations to dinner; no one could sing for his supper like Brian Linehan.

The guest list for the floater was limited to two hundred premium-paying passengers who had access to all of the facilities regular cruise passengers enjoyed. But the movie theatre was reserved exclusively for our use three times daily, and every night we met for dinner in a reserved roped-off area of the first-class dining room. Dusty had asked all of his programmers to try to sit with different festival-goers every night, so he was disappointed when he saw Brian repeatedly sitting with the same groups.

But Dusty was cheered when Brian told him he would like to do more for the next floater, scheduled for 1994. "What about an evening with Mitzi Gaynor and Donald O'Connor?" Brian proposed. The two movie hoofers had co-starred in a number of hits together, and Gaynor and her manager husband, Jack Bean, had befriended Brian after he interviewed her for the *Toronto Sun* when she was touring North America in a revival of *Anything Goes*.

"Sounds great!" said Dusty, beaming. "Go get her!"

That was a stumbling block for Brian. And for Dusty. Brian believed that it was his job to sparkle on stage, to get The Star to talk. He believed it was someone else's job to get The Star. Dusty Cohl had learned, from orchestrating Toronto film festival tributes more than a decade earlier, that a personal appeal always carried more weight.

Dusty didn't know of Brian's growing resentment of Roger Ebert until a number of passengers mentioned it to him after one of the floating film festivals. At that time, he says, he informed Brian that he had no reason to complain, "because he had no concept of how little he actually gave of himself to the festival and how much Roger did." Roger secured major films for the floater, but even more significant to Dusty, Roger would offer up creative and unusual ideas for guests, such as Pulitzer Prize–winning writer Studs Terkel, whom Roger would then personally invite and personally deliver, and whom he and his wife, Chaz, would then personally shepherd throughout the run of the floating film festival.

Brian was another story. "We got him to do the Lou Jacobi tribute," Dusty recalls. "I don't know if he did anything else on the first floater. He was different from all the other programmers in that he generally did what you found for him to do. He never did go out there and say, 'I've found this picture, I've got this idea' or 'I'll do that.' But when you found something for him, he did it like he did his TV show, overly diligently. I remember the afternoon before the Evelyn Keyes interview, while everybody else went off the boat, he went and reread her autobiography."

Dusty encouraged Brian to spend the day at the beach and let the evening interview evolve naturally. "But he wouldn't do that. He had to do the other."

As the 1990s continued, Brian was still living the high life on OPM (Other People's Money) but was constantly encountering corporate resistance to hiring him. He wanted to do what he did best, long-form interviews with celebrated artists. But the decision-makers who determined television content in the 1990s had no appetite for it, or him.

In 1992, veteran CBC television producer Ray McConnell and I were looking for a way to celebrate the thirty-fifth anniversary of *Front Page Challenge*, the weekly current affairs quiz show for news junkies that was at one time, according to the *Guinness Book of World Records*, the longest-running game show in television history. Its legendary panellists – Pierre Berton, Betty Kennedy, Allan Fotheringham, and Jack Webster – were all acclaimed interviewers in their own right. Brian had appeared on the show as a guest panellist some ten years earlier, and knew all the principal players. He agreed to interview all four of them, plus moderator Fred Davis.

Ray McConnell wanted Linehan-calibre questions but didn't want to see Brian on screen or hear his voice. The sixty-minute *Front Page Confidential* special had to celebrate the panellists, without any other distractions to pull the focus away from them. So Brian remained off-camera. He did a great job, the panellists loved being interviewed by him, and at the end of the day he had managed to put some money in his pocket. But although he was happy when he was interviewing them, he paid no attention when I urged him to consider reinventing himself for television, as an interview gun for hire, as a producer, or even as a much-needed mentor. Brian Linehan didn't want to mentor other people who were going to be on camera. He wanted to be on camera himself.

He soon got his wish. Legendary CBC songbird Juliette had left Toronto years earlier to return to Vancouver, the city where she was raised, started her career and married her musician husband, Tony Cavazzi. Ray McConnell liked the way Linehan worked, and so did his production team, so Ray called Juliette and asked her if she would consider doing a sixty-minute one-on-one with Brian. We shot *Linehan & Juliette* at CBC Vancouver, and it was telecast on January 3, 1993.

Two years later, McConnell initiated a second Linehan special, this time marking the publication of Karen Kain's autobiographical book, *Movement Never Lies*, a collaboration between Karen, *Globe and Mail* dance critic Stephen Godfrey, and Penelope Reed Doob. *Linehan & Kain* was telecast on September 25, 1995. Ironically, both specials were among a mere handful of occasions when a Linehan interview was actually telecast to a national Canadian audience from coast to coast to coast. Brian's interview with Karen, one of many he had done with her over the years, would be his last, and would unwittingly test their friendship.

Before they started shooting, Brian agreed that he would restrict his questions to the contents of the book, the reason for their on-camera reunion. When the camera started to roll, Karen found Brian's questions unexpected and disturbing. He was probing far too deeply into what she considered to be personal and private matters, and halfway through the taping of *Linehan & Kain* there was a tension that neither one of them had anticipated.

At the end of the show, Brian thanked Karen for her time and wished her well. When the cameras stopped rolling, he could feel the sudden coolness between them. Brian was mystified. "Something's not right," he told me when I asked how the shoot had gone. He became increasingly distressed as Karen became more distant over the next few days. He begged her to tell him what was wrong.

Finally, she told him, and he called me right away. He was very upset. "Karen said, 'You betrayed me.' *You betrayed me!*" he cried, repeating her phrase. Brian was shocked. He was sure he had done everything he was supposed to do. And he was sure he hadn't raised one single issue, one single incident, that she herself had not raised in her book.

He called her again, a few days later, and again, and pleaded his case with Ross, and with her, and begged her forgiveness for any pain that he might have caused her, however innocently, however mistakenly. It took a while for both of them to put it behind them.

Looking back on the incident today, Kain says it was her mistake, not his. "I trusted him as my friend," she says simply, "and naturally I thought he would be easy on me. And I thought he asked questions he shouldn't have asked. I felt a little surprised, a little shocked. But of course he needed to be seen as a journalist, especially in the eyes of his peers. And in fact he wasn't all that hard on me. It was my own naïveté. Because he should have asked those questions. I felt a sort of betrayal on some part, but I forgave him. Because it was totally my fault."

Aside from freelance writing gigs in which he could recycle snippets of his classic interviews for magazines like *Canadian Living*, Brian was more and more running into resistance to hiring him. A stint as a *Toronto Star* entertainment columnist disintegrated into a decidedly brief assignment. A Linehan-hosted preview of the upcoming Genie Awards was seen by more viewers than the Awards telecast itself, but CBC showed no interest in developing a new showcase for him. CTV chairman Doug Bassett saw major sponsorship potential in Brian's ability to attract stars, but his effort to bring him to Canada's most-watched private network was voted off the table by other network executives.

In the years since leaving Citytv, Brian had eaten a lot of crow and swallowed a lot of pride. His sense of dignity, however, remained intact. Accordingly, so did his indignation when potential employers asked him to audition to be, well, Brian Linehan. Certain requests, and jobs they might have led to, were turned down with a flat No. When I asked him about an endorsement offer he had rejected, he said, "It has no dignity." There was no need for further discussion. That door was closed forever.

Among those who felt frustrated by this was Michael Levine. "At times," he recalls, "I thought if he said 'dignity' just once more I was going to shove it down his throat. Because I felt that he sometimes was his own worst enemy, by taking offence too easily, from people who frankly were not all that interested in giving him space. There were so many people over the years that he got outraged about, sometimes to his own detriment. I value integrity but I think there are moments, particularly in a situation where people are in positions to employ you or give you an opportunity . . ."

He shrugs. "Brian was enormously intelligent," says Levine, "but his strategic sense was not profound. He could not make himself play the game. Once the City thing had fallen apart, the cornerstone was gone. I tried everywhere. I went from network to network to network."

Levine says he was "downright boring" in his support of Linehan. "I tried to get people to pay attention. He had his brief forays, but nothing seemed to take, either because the independent producers didn't have the money or the broadcasters didn't want him. I know at least one broadcaster who was homophobic; I was deeply disappointed, and in fact confronted him on the issue. Plus there was a cultural change. The cultural change was the dumbing down of television."

Networks had abandoned smart talk for fast talk, which was then replaced by loud talk. Linehan did not fit the bill. "And," adds Levine, "there was a sense that he'd been created by Citytv and he would always be Citytv, and that anybody picking him up would be as if Colgate suddenly decided to hire the Crest marketing guy."

In addition, he says, the library of shows Brian had worked so long and hard to create was now an unexpected liability. As long as Citytv held the rights to two thousand Brian Linehan interviews, which the station could telecast at whim or will, no other network could truly claim "exclusive" rights to Brian Linehan.

So there were a lot of reasons why The Big Comeback didn't happen – not the least being Brian's growing notoriety for his caustic wit. Filmmaker Barry Avrich remembers that in his bachelor days he brought a beautiful blonde named Laurie up to Joan and Dusty Cohl's summer retreat, a rambling log villa hidden away in the Ontario countryside. Dixie and Norman Jewison were there, and so were Brian and Zane. "I'm having a great time with Brian, and I tell him about a new film I'm working on called *Glitter Palace*, and how I want him to be involved.

"I am, by the way, pitching this project on my hands and knees to a man who's not working. And Laurie is standing in the doorway, looking a bit like Kim Basinger in *L.A. Confidential*, and Brian is distracted by her, and annoyed for some reason, and finally he turns to her and says, 'Laurie, for God's sake, you're standing there like Jessica Lange in *The Postman Always Rings Twice*. Either come and sit with us or leave.' And she's completely horrified. Then we sit down for dinner, and Dixie looks at Laurie, leans over to Brian, and says, loud enough for us to hear, 'Who's that girl with Barry?' And Brian says, 'She's a silent screen actress. She doesn't speak.' At which point Laurie gets up, packs her bag, and wants to go home. Drove back in the middle of the night, thank you very much Brian Linehan. I don't remember her last name. After Brian traumatized her, I never saw her again."

"He could be very cutting with what he had to say," Marcia Martin agrees. "He could be a bad boy. He could be as witty as Brian was . . ."

". . . or he could be a pain in the ass," adds Citytv alumnus Jane Fairley. "It all depended on the mood he was in."

According to Marci, who frequently entertained at home, organizing a dinner party where Brian was a guest took special care and planning. "You always had to be sure that you had somebody that, if Brian did offend – because he would! – wouldn't take it personally. So it always had to be right mix." Why did he do it? "He always wanted the upper hand," says Marci with a shrug. "In ANY conversation."

Adds his fan and friend Martha Watson: "He could be brutal at times. Every time he saw me he said, 'Get your hair cut! You're far too old to wear your hair so long!' It was almost an unspoken dance between us." But she also saw another side of him – the side that prompted the caustic wit that could make both friends and acquaintances wince. "He was so bitter. And so angry. It was awful. . . . He was hurt by the industry."

One major bridge he burned was his relationship with the glamorous Floating Film Festival. Brian, with Zane as his guest, had sailed on the fifth floating film festival without us; I had too many television shows on the go in early 1998, so Gail and I had to reluctantly beg off. Midway through the cruise, festival ringleader Dusty Cohl was informed that his mother had passed away. Joan and Dusty, their daughter Karen Cohl, and their son-in-law Mel Crystal disembarked at the next island and flew back to Toronto. As soon as the Holland-America cruise ship returned to Florida, the stories about Brian misbehaving on board started to spread.

There were stories of friction between Brian and Zane, but those weren't surprising to friends who had spent time with them. Brian once told Myrna Daniels that he'd only come back to Zane because he was very lonely. "He also found it difficult to make friends outside of Zane," she recalls. "I think he thought it would be so easy." More troubling were the stories alleging that Brian, in his resentment of Roger Ebert, had been bad-mouthing him in front of other programmers and passengers. Roger Ebert knew that Brian resented him, and occasionally found it irritating. But this was not his first experience with peer jealousy, nor would it be his last. So he was determined to wait it out.

Dusty Cohl was not happy about the situation. "Brian," says Dusty, "thought of himself as a star, but he would not ever really allow himself to think about what the guy he was dealing with was feeling. He was bitching about Roger, there were rumours that he was having his troubles with Zane, and then without ever discussing it with me, he was basically telling people he was unhappy and he was not coming back."

Barry Avrich watched it happen, powerless. "Maybe I was too young and naive and enamoured with Brian," he admits, "but I thought that he should have had a much larger role. But he was difficult, and he resented the favourite sons there, specifically Roger. And I think if Brian committed any sin, it was the fact that in Dusty's eyes he expected it."

A personal friend of Dusty, Brian, *and* Roger, Myrna Daniels still regrets that the floating film festival situation with Brian was never really resolved. "Brian was very hurt," she remembers, "because he felt he was playing second fiddle to Roger. And there was a lot of hurt and a lot of anger that came out of that." Angry at his situation, angry about his frustrating relationship with Zane, angry with a life that was only occasionally dealing him the lavish cards he coveted, Brian would lash out at whoever happened to inadvertently invade his space. He would eventually pay a price for it.

Karen Kain believed his anger ran deeper than it appeared on the surface. "Brian was an angry man. And not just about his career and his work. About everything. After a few drinks, the anger would really come up. I think he had a lot of brainpower, and I think he was probably very frustrated not being able to use it. . . . He took enormous pride in his professionalism, and then it was all taken away from him."

Brian was not unaware of his behaviour. At times his anger threatened to consume him, and at times the unbridled force of it frightened him. "Zane wants me to see someone," he told me one day – "to get help with my anger. I think he's right. Because it's not getting any better."

Joan Rivers believed it couldn't get any better. "It's a hideous business. I don't know anybody who has reached a high point and then had to move aside that isn't angry. Show me one person who isn't. And then the invitations stop. And if you're not Brian Linehan with a show on the air you really find out – just sift through your Christmas card list – who your friends are. I don't blame him for being angry."

Joan Rivers was never surprised by his anger. But after knowing him for years, she was genuinely shocked by how naive he could be. A case in point, she says, was his friendship with Nancy Walker and David Craig. Craig was a celebrated vocal coach to Broadway-bound actors; Walker, his wife, had enjoyed a career as a musical comedy star, on stage and screen, and had graduated to directing before becoming a household face as Rosie the waitress in those relentless "quicker picker upper" TV commercials for Bounty paper towels. The Craigs had befriended Brian over the years, and they were genuinely fond of him, often inviting him to spend a few days with them at their lush garden home overlooking the San Fernando Valley.

When Nancy died of lung cancer in 1992, Brian hopped on a plane, flew to Los Angeles, and took a taxi directly to the Craig residence. David was touched by the gesture and insisted that Brian stay at the house with him.

"Then David died," Joan recalls, "and Brian flew in from Toronto. He got to the house and their daughter Miranda was thrilled to see him. She gave him a big hug and then said to him, 'Where are you staying?' He told me he wanted to say 'well, here, of course!' – but he didn't. He was so shocked he said nothing. She got the car and drove him to a hotel. The next day he went home; he didn't even call.

"When he told me the story, he was very upset, and very indignant, and I wanted to say, 'It wasn't a slight. It wasn't a slap. It never occurred to her that you'd be staying there. She didn't even know the times you *did* stay there.' But that was one of the major slights of his life."

Joan also found him surprisingly naive about celebrity. "He was very thin-skinned, *very* thin-skinned. There was an incident where somebody didn't recognize him, and he was in high dudgeon over it." She shrugs. "I figure I've done a thousand one-person interviews in my lifetime . . . You don't remember. You *can't* remember. And when people say, of course they remember you, they are lying to you."

She mimes reaching for her Rolodex, making press calls. *Now, let me call this one up and say, Hello, Louise! How are you and the two boys? . . . I mean, girls?* And then, in a quick imaginary aside to her assistant: *We have to change her index card, Jocelyn. She has two girls, not two boys!*

"I am surprised that he didn't get it more. I think that was one of his big flaws. That he always bought into the shallowness of celebrity. He didn't know the games celebrities play."

Over the years, Joan tried to get Brian to see modern celebrity not only for what it was but also for what it had become – a global business rooted in the marketing of manufactured dreams. On one occasion, she invited him to join her for dinner with her manager, Tommy Corcoran. Brian later reported that at dinner Tommy had mentioned that it might be unwise for Joan to do an interview with a well-known Manhattan newspaper columnist who had a reputation for being tough on his subjects. Despite Tommy's reservations, Joan appeared to have no qualms about meeting with the columnist. "He can be had," she told Corcoran.

Her remark unnerved Brian, to the point where he repeated the story to me several times. Was he, Brian Linehan, someone who had been "had" by Joan Rivers? Was their friendship merely an exercise in showbiz public relations?

"Do you have a newspaper column at the moment?" I asked him.

He frowned. "You know I don't. No."

"A TV series?"

"No."

"A radio show?"

"No . . ." He was starting to get annoyed. But he was still curious.

"Welllll then," I drawled, "just what is it that you can do for Joan Rivers at the moment?"

It only took him a second to come up with the answer. "Nothing," he replied. "Absolutely nothing."

"Is she still inviting you to dinner?"

He blinked, then beamed, and then grinned like a little boy. Their friendship was real. It was perhaps the first time he had ever questioned it. But it would not be the last.

In the late nineties, Brian's legend as a celebrity interviewer was still strong enough to tempt Canadian comedy wunderkind Rick Mercer and his partner Gerald Lunz to create a role for him in their dark, award-winning comedy series *Made In Canada*. The series, which was seen in the United States and Europe as *The Industry*, was a wickedly funny inside-showbiz send-up of an independent television production company. In the episode they'd written for Brian, Mercer and his chief writing accomplice Mark Farrell created a situation in which Margot Kidder would portray a vain, empty-headed Hollywood actress and Linehan would portray himself as a vain, over-prepared star interviewer. Delighted with the concept and anticipating a similar reaction from the two performers, Mercer sent them their "sides" – script pages with only their scenes on them – to show them the direction he wanted to take with their episode.

Margot loved hers. Brian hated his. And took it personally. And was still steamed when he called me to tell me so. "I told him, this may be just a joke to you, but this is my career, this is my *profession*, this is my *reputation!*"

"You told 'him'?" I said, taken aback. "Who's 'him'?"

"I told him, I've worked very hard to gain respect for what I do! AND maintain my dignity!" he continued, ranting. "And it's no laughing matter *to me!*"

"You told who? Who did you tell?"

"Rick Mercer," he replied, as if I hadn't been listening. "He called me to ask what I thought of the sides. So I told him."

"But Brian," I said, groaning, "it's *comedy*. It's not supposed to be you. It's an exaggerated version of people's perception of you. That's the whole point of it. If you don't like the lines, Rick can change them. He's just trying to give you an idea of what –"

"NO." He was adamant.

I called Rick Mercer and Gerald Lunz. "Apparently your friend Brian doesn't share your particular sense of humour," Mercer noted dryly, paraphrasing the viewer warning CBC Television used on some of its comedy shows. Mercer and Farrell dropped the interviewer character from the show and instead created a cameo role for legendary show business publicist Gino Empry. Gino, who had never met a camera he didn't like, adored every minute of it. "I can't believe that Brian turned down *Made In Canada*," Empry remarked after his scenes were wrapped. "But I'm glad at least one of us got to do it!"

A year or so later, Brian was looking for a misplaced document and came across the original sides that Mercer had sent him. He read them, reread them, and then phoned me. "I made a mistake, didn't I," he said, sounding a bit wistful on the phone. "Not doing *Made In Canada*, I mean."

"Well," I began, "as I recall, you were very busy at the time, and –"

"Thank you," he said, gently but firmly cutting me off. "But I wasn't at all busy at the time. No, I made a mistake. I should have done it."

"Brian was angry for a long, long time," says Karen Kain. "It's so funny, he was angry at Michael Levine until the day he died, and Michael Levine was still his lawyer, doing the most important things for him. It was so weird. I would go, 'So why do you stay with him?' And he would say, 'I have to.' And he would complain endlessly about that whole conflict of interest thing, with Michael representing both Moses and Brian. But he would never do anything about it. I guess he was scared." She shakes her head, mystified. "I never could understand it."

Few people could. And no one is more aware of this than Michael Levine, who still regards his long relationship with Linehan, like his relationship with Moses Znaimer, as one of the most complex of his life. "As I watched him over the years," he says today, "I had a lot of enormously conflicting opinions. I mean, my affection for him was profound, my respect for his intelligence was profound. I was his best audience for his wit and humour. In fact, many people, over the years when we were spending a lot of time together, alluded to the fact that I sometimes got caustic and outrageous, almost like a reaction to having spent time with Brian, who could and would say anything about anybody."

Brian, he notes, "was a very proud guy. And if he felt that I couldn't manage to get him a job, he would try to punish me. It was Brian who helped get me used to talent blaming me. That's why I say he changed my life," he adds with an ironic grin. "It was Brian who blindsided me in this kind of blame game, which had to do with 'I'm having a very bad day so it has to be your fault,' 'I didn't get the job so it has to be your fault.' Until finally I got to the point where I just turned the other cheek."

While Brian was looking for a U.S. network, Arlene Dahl arranged for him to meet with an ABC Television executive in New York. When I ask Levine how much he knew about the meeting, he just smiles. "I'll tell you the problem," he says. "Brian had a profound number of American friends, Arlene Dahl being one of them, who were no longer players. And New York and Los Angeles are towns where, once you cease to be a player, you cease to be a player. So there were a lot of forays into marketplaces that never went anywhere. The difficulty was Brian's pride." Brian wanted to be the one to bring home the offer. "And this is why I say he lacked a strategic sense. I have clients who will come to me and say, 'I've got an opportunity to speak to the *New York Times*. (A) Do you know anybody there? (B) What do you think the hot buttons are?' etc. etc. . . . but, not Brian. So I never knew officially who he saw, or what occurred.

"I think Brian's problem is that he didn't go through the normal system. In other words, I was agent, manager, and lawyer all in one. And in a way I was also a father, even though we were the same age. And you want to prove to your father that you're good. And he didn't completely recognize that it was only his talent that would get me in the room talking to somebody, and that my job was to be able to say nice things about him that he couldn't really say about himself. So sometimes he got it and sometimes he didn't. Sometimes he was the very dependent, vulnerable guy. And sometimes he was the petulant little boy who was going to prove to Daddy that he was smart, so that Daddy would love him."

Michael Levine was better acquainted than most with Brian's mercurial moods. In the mid-1980s, he and producer Robert Cooper were shooting a TV movie in Toronto with Elizabeth Taylor and Carol Burnett. Michael shared his on-set stories with Brian, who was thrilled to get all the gossip first-hand, despite the fact that Taylor, who religiously kept her TV appearances to a minimum, had turned down his heartfelt request for a *City Lights* interview.

As it happened, Taylor's birthday coincided with one of the film's shooting days. "So we decided to give Elizabeth her birthday party at the Four Seasons hotel," Levine remembers. "I invited Brian to the birthday party, and for some reason he was mad at somebody – I don't even think it was me, I think he was just mad – and he didn't go. And for years after that, he must have said to me, kicking himself, at least thirty-five times: 'And *I* DIDN'T GO to Elizabeth Taylor's birthday party!'"

When Marlon Brando came to Toronto to shoot *The Freshman* with Matthew Broderick, Brando inflicted verbal damage on the film as it was shooting. To make his peace with the producers, he agreed to do a Linehan interview. Brian, appalled by Brando's unprofessional behaviour, "declined" the opportunity.

"I know now I was wrong," he would later confess. "It was arrogant of me."

His arrogance, however unbridled it might be at times, did not extend to the world of TVO.

TVOntario, known to its subscribers and fans as TVO, is an Ontario public television channel that is licensed first and foremost to educate. It has many facets, from its celebrated children's programming to its imported Britcoms, to the quiet phenomenon that has given TVO its greatest resonance with the viewing public: *Saturday Night at the Movies*, which started in 1974, less than a year after the birth of *City Lights*. By some stroke of genius or, perhaps, blind but kind good luck, the producers of S.N.A.M. chose a host as "different-looking" as Brian Linehan – a cherubic-looking, balding middle-aged film buff with a truly unusual name: Elwy (pronounced Ell-wee) Yost (rhymes with toast).

The format for S.N.A.M. was deceptively simple. Since TVO was commercial-free, Elwy would introduce a film classic, sometimes American, sometimes with subtitles, usually old enough so that it would not seriously wound the show's modest budget (the first film was Ingmar Bergman's *Through a Glass Darkly*). Sometimes it was a film that Elwy and senior producer Risa Shuman felt had been overlooked. Sometimes it was a film that the producers had secured at bargain rates. But whatever the film, TVO viewers knew they would be seeing it uncut, or at the very least, uninterrupted; there would be none of those pesky commercials that dominated all other Canadian TV channels at that time. And

after the film, in what would later become a celebrated series of relent-
lessly cheerful professional encounters, Elwy would interview someone
connected with the film – a producer, a director, a writer, a cameraman,
occasionally a supporting player, but rarely, if ever, a star.

In the early years, most of these interviews were shot on location in
Los Angeles, at the homes of the interviewees. Most often they were
modest one-camera ventures, and Elwy would almost always chat up his
guests outdoors, around a pool or in lush California foliage, to save the
cost of lighting interiors. The lack of visual distractions only served to
enhance Elwy's interviews, which bubbled with his irrepressibly genuine
enthusiasm. Film fans adopted him like an eccentric uncle who told
wonderful stories when he came to visit on weekends, and *Saturday
Night at the Movies* was on its way.

As it turned out, Elwy was something of a ringer. Before he arrived
at TVO, he had been a high school teacher; a writer, producer, director,
and actor, on stage, screen, and radio; a human relations counsellor; an
experienced hand at promotion and publicity; and the executive director
for the Metropolitan Educational Television Association of Toronto. His
"hosting" duties at *Saturday Night at the Movies* and TVO, where he was
named Executive Producer of the network, ran for an unprecedented
twenty-five years. Yost, whose writer son Graham made a major name for
himself with a big box-office 1994 thriller called *Speed*, took his final
bows and retired to the Canadian tropics (a.k.a. British Columbia).

Now that *Front Page Challenge* had finally folded its tent, *Saturday
Night at the Movies* was the longest still-running series in Canadian television history. It was also TVO's most popular adult program. So when
Elwy left in 1999, the obvious question was, who could possibly follow
in his footsteps?

One candidate stood out above all the others: Brian Linehan.

Friends and fans rallied round. Good words were whispered in the
right ears. Brian himself was on his best behaviour. Even *Toronto Star*
entertainment columnist Jim Bawden, who had written his first piece on
Brian in the *Hamilton Spectator* in 1972, quietly lobbied for him.

Then Shelagh Rogers, the popular, sunny-voiced broadcaster who
had been dividing her time between *Take Five* on CBC Radio and *Imprint*
on TVO, tossed her hat into the ring as well.

She got the gig.

"We all knew it should be Brian," she told me. "We all assumed it
would be Brian. When they asked me, I was surprised. I thought, well,

I guess Brian's turned them down; it probably just wasn't enough money for him."

Shelagh Rogers hosted the 1999–2000 season of *Saturday Night at the Movies* and then returned to CBC Radio as the rightful inheritor of legendary broadcaster Peter Gzowski's morning real estate.

From that day forward, until the autumn following Brian Linehan's death, *Saturday Night at the Movies* was presented in a documentary format, without a host.

Of all the letdowns Brian would have to deal with, says Michael Levine, "his greatest disappointment, I think, was not getting the TVO job when Elwy Yost stepped down."

"He doesn't like to be touched."

Brian Linehan had befriended radio commentator Jane Hawtin on the junket circuit. He admired her intelligence, and her wit, and the fact that she seemed to be uncommonly comfortable in her own skin. During her ten-year stint at Q107, Jane Hawtin had become Canada's first female news director and first female talk show host. She seemed to enjoy being Jane Hawtin, and Brian liked that about her, and perhaps felt a certain kinship. Plus, she was on Toronto radio, and he was on Toronto radio. She didn't covet his spot on CFRB, and he didn't covet hers on Q107. In 1985, when Allan Slaight bought Standard Broadcasting from Conrad Black, CRTC ownership regulations required Slaight to divest himself of Q107 in order to acquire CFRB. Slaight's son and heir apparent Gary Slaight was already a key player in the burgeoning family broadcast empire, and wasted no time in wooing Hawtin away from Q107 to CFRB. Gary Slaight knew what he was doing; *The Jane Hawtin Show* on CFRB was soon the number-one noon-hour program in the country.

Hawtin loved CFRB. But she wanted to spread her wings. And she wanted a piece of the action.

She'd had other opportunities over the years, she says, but she believes most of her suitors were scared away, "so that the princess couldn't leave the tower." When she left CFRB in 1995 to start her own production company, "Gary was very shocked. Very, very upset."

When Brian got sacked a few days later, she suspected that Slaight had fired him in retaliation. "Not true," Slaight reassured her. "I let him go because he became a pain in the ass . . . and would not do any of the things we asked."

She believes the rift between Slaight and Linehan – "their person-alities were quite similar," she notes with a wry smile – started because Brian wouldn't have lunch with Gary. "Brian wouldn't do it. And Gary owned CFRB. It was his station."

Hawtin left CFRB to launch a flagship TV series called *Jane Hawtin Live*, giving her fans a daily sixty-minute helping of what they liked most – the burning issues of their lives, their input, and their feedback, all skil-fully juggled by their friend and advocate Jane. She and Paul Osborn were partners in Electric Entertainment, the company they formed to produce her daily series and a number of other shows. And as soon as *Jane Hawtin Live* became successful she determined that the next thing she wanted to do was to bring Brian Linehan back to television. Yes, he could be difficult. Yes, he could be a pain in the ass. But she still wanted to produce a new series for him. "He was so good at what he did, and people loved to watch him, they loved to hear him, and he would get things that nobody else got, because he honestly had a relationship with these stars.

"There are lots of people who would talk about stars being their friends. But they weren't. They were just professional interviewers and interviewees. That wasn't the case with Brian. I don't think he over-played that, but I think a lot of these stars actually felt he was their friend. Their honest-to-goodness *friend*. They would want to see him, aside from the interview thing, and he was always very careful not to betray their secrets."

Western International Communications (WIC), which had bought *Jane Hawtin Live*, put a string of stations together to secure the series. She was in a meeting with her new bosses when they asked her what else she wanted to do. "And I said, well, if this is successful, then we want to bring Brian Linehan back. And they said, 'Yes, we'd be interested in that, talk to us when you're ready.'"

During the first season of *Jane Hawtin Live*, she had a bout of stomach flu. "I have a real sensitivity to drugs, and my sister gave me a ten mg Gravol instead of a two mg Gravol. So I couldn't wake up the next morning. And I was supposed to interview Mickey Rooney, so I said, bring in Linehan."

Hawtin started bringing Linehan on her show once a month, to discuss film and entertainment news. It was an ideal showcase for Brian, something Hawtin could show the top brass at WIC. "That's what clinched the deal to get him onto WIC with his own show." *Linehan* would be a weekly interview show, similar to *City Lights*. When the new series launched, he would guest on Hawtin's show to promote it. "It was a much bigger budget for his show," she adds. "Much bigger. *Huge.* Mine was a daily show, as cheap as it could possibly be."

Her husband, Chris Allicock, brought in photographer Rob Waymen to do a spectacular photo shoot with Brian, perhaps the best ever done with him. Brian was happy again, and his pleasure at being back on camera, his pure delight in getting a second chance to be Brian Linehan again, seeped through Waymen's lens onto the digital images.

They taped the *Linehan* series, she remembers, "in a beautiful old studio where I think they used to do *The Red Green Show*. In Hamilton." Brian was shooting his big comeback series in the steeltown where he'd been born and raised, and where most of his family still lived. As far as I know, no invitations to visit him on set were ever issued. At least, not to his family.

When Brian started the new series, his confidence was shaky, because he hadn't been on television with any regularity for almost a decade. He hadn't been working for about a year and a half: no studio jobs, no radio jobs, no newspaper jobs. "So we brought him in and got him his great contract," Jane Hawtin remembers, "and then he started becoming a monster again. I would deal with him for about two months, until I would feel so insulted, and then Paul would take over, and after two months Paul would be ready to literally kill him. And then we'd switch back, because by then I'd had a break, and I was ready to tackle him again."

Chrissy LeBlanc was the production assistant assigned to wrangle Brian when he appeared on *Jane Hawtin Live*, "because she had the patience of a saint," Jane says. As Jane remembers it, another PA, Kathleen Monk, was sitting at a nearby desk when she overheard Brian speaking to Chrissy, "who was the sweetest thing you could ever meet in your life," and his tone made Kathleen gasp. She stared at him, and Brian wheeled around. "When you have been in the business as long as I have," he told her, "*then* you can gasp!"

"Who do you think you're talking to?" an irate Kathleen demanded.

Brian went up the stairs. Kathleen followed him, yelling, "You can't speak to me like that! Why do you think you can speak like that to Chrissy?"

"Kathleen was fairly new to *JHL*," says Jane, "and we were all stunned just watching her, because she trailed him all the way up to his office until he shut the door behind him. And then he came to me and demanded that I fire her. And I said, 'Absolutely not, she's terrific. You should apologize to her.'" Jane Hawtin shrugs. "It was always that kind of thing. Then it would all kind of get fixed, and you'd go out and have drinks, and it would be fine until it happened again."

At times, she would chastise him for his rudeness. "I would say, 'Brian, you cannot speak to people like that!' And he'd blow it off. Or sometimes he'd listen and, occasionally, he would apologize. It was never a real apology; it was kind of a half apology. But everybody just put up with it. I'm not sure why."

Brian got increasingly upset, she recalls, when he started to realize the impact of the Internet on his work. Hawtin did entertainment topics every Friday on *Jane Hawtin Live*, which meant they would both sometimes do the same interview. In one case the same interview was LeVar Burton, who played Geordi on *Star Trek: The Next Generation*. "Brian had done so much research, and done so much work," Jane remembers, "and he saw my interview and went almost into a rage. He wanted to know how I'd gotten the information about the illegitimate son that Burton had reconciled with. He was *so* upset. '*What's going on, where did you get it? How did you know that? Did you get that from Virginia?*'" (Virginia Morra was Brian's new assistant and an associate producer on *Linehan*.)

No, she told him, she got it from the Internet.

"No!" he said. "No, that's impossible."

Jane showed him where she had found it. "He had spent hours and hours and hours and hours prepping for this and I'd basically done a search on the Internet and found it within a half hour. It was in an article on Burton. Brian had the same information, but he'd found it, I don't know how, by going to the library or whatever. And he was upset because he thought this was going to be his big 'Brian moment.'

"I think he recognized that this was the end of an era, because he said, 'Well then, *anybody* can have that information.'"

At first, he tried to adapt. Hawtin got him a computer, and he tried to learn. "Eventually Virginia Morra did it for him. And then she would show him what she'd found. But he was very unhappy. Very unhappy."

Virginia Morra, Brian's new assistant, was new to television. Paul Osborn took one look at her cv, saw that she had a degree in social work, and decided she would be perfect for Linehan. And, by all accounts, she was. They became fast friends, and Brian grew to depend on her more and more.

One day, Virginia invited her old high school chum Peter Husar to visit her on the set of *Linehan*.

"I stopped by and they happened to be on a break," Husar recalls. "I remember Brian coming up to me – I was standing at the back of the room – and saying, 'Hello, I'm Brian Linehan, and who might you be?' *Who might you be?* In other words, *why are you here? I don't know you and you weren't invited.* I told him who I was, and that I was friends with Virginia. Virginia told me later on that there was sort of hell to pay after that, for not informing him that someone was coming by."

About a year later, Peter and his partner Ken Lindsay invited Virginia and her fiancé, David, to their waterfront condo in west Toronto for an informal Saturday-night dinner. As it turned out, David was out of town.

"Can I bring a date?" asked Virginia.

"Of course!"

"Can I bring Brian?" That question, says Peter, "just put Ken into a tailspin."

"Virginia called that Saturday morning," Ken Lindsay remembers. "It was supposed to be very casual. We were going to have homemade soup and some crusty bread and a glass of hooch. Instead, we got flowers, we got champagne, we did foie gras with salad, which we melted, we were so nervous. *Oh-we're-having-a-celebrity-to-our-house!!*"

In 1995, Ken Lindsay had written an article in *Toronto Life* about his starry experiences working as a concierge at the Sutton Place hotel, which major-domo Hans Gerhardt had tenaciously transformed into a chic watering hole and celebrity comfort zone for visiting movie stars. Brian was a regular at Sutton Place, and enjoyed all the privileges that noun implies. "Brian walked in that night," Ken remembers, "very elegant, and so tall, and when he was introduced to me, he said, 'Mr. Lindsay, I read your article in *Toronto Life* and I loved it. It was wonderful.'"

That night, he says, "we drank our faces off. Imagine that, he liked martinis and so did we!" he adds, eyes twinkling. "He didn't know us very well, but partway through dinner he was telling us the inside story of a few things."

"And we were prompting him," adds Peter. "*So what's Lucy really like? And who's gay that we don't know is gay?* And he told us two names. And we go, are you *sure?* Because we kinda suspected. And he said, oh yes, I've got a very reliable source. So we loved that. And we blabbed that all over town. And Brian talked about that night for a long time."

A few months after Virginia introduced him to Peter and Ken, Brian invited them to dinner at Grenadier Heights. "We met Zane," Peter recalls, "and it was very much a more formal experience."

"Zane brought out his Kaye Ballard LPS," says Ken. "We listened to the Kaye Ballard record and heard some Kaye Ballard stories about when she was at their house. '*And she sat right where you're sitting, Mr. Lindsay!*'"

"I don't think there were too many other celebrity connections that Zane was very pleased about," he adds.

When Virginia Morra got married, she invited Brian and Zane to her wedding in Italy. She also invited Peter Husar and Ken Lindsay, who were delighted to have a chance to get to know Zane a little better.

Ken told Peter, "When we see them at the wedding, don't touch Zane."

"Why?" asked Peter, mystified.

"He doesn't like to be touched," Ken explained. "Can't you see? He recoils. He recoiled when you went to hug him."

"Did he?"

"And when you went to kiss him, his whole body went 'no, don't do that.' So it's better to just shake hands with him. Because he doesn't want that connection."

Years earlier, Karen Kain had received the same message. Brian said to her, "Zane doesn't like to be touched," she recalls. "And I said, 'Well, all these years, whenever I see him, I give him a big hug and a kiss, right on the lips.' And Brian said, 'Yes, I know, he lets you do that. But he doesn't let anyone else do that.'" She sighs. "I never really got a handle on their relationship."

☆

In 1998, WTN – the Women's Television Network – became the principal electronic residence of both *Jane Hawtin Live* and *Linehan*, but not for long.

"Brian blew off WTN," says Hawtin. "He felt that they weren't promoting his show well enough; that they weren't giving him enough promos. He'd go into a rage if he saw promos for anything on their network that wasn't his show. And he did the same thing again that he did with Gary Slaight. They wanted to have lunch with him, to talk about the show, and he literally went over to their offices, called them a bunch of cunts, and said he wouldn't have lunch with them.

"A few months later, he came to me and said 'So, is WTN talking renewal?' And I said, 'Brian, they're not going to renew you. You called them "cunts." It's not going to happen.'

"But he would just do these things, things that just imploded on him, because he wanted it so much. It was so important to him. And I was like, why would you do that? I mean, this network loves you, lets you do what you want. And because you feel they're not promoting you enough, you're going to call them names and end it?"

She and Paul Osborn managed to get him a smaller renewal on WIC to keep *Linehan* going, but not for long. Like all private Canadian broadcasters, WIC was subject to rules and regulations established by the government's media watchdog, the Canadian Radio-television and Telecommunications Commission, and had to telecast a certain amount of Canadian programming, in a number of categories, to keep its broadcast license. WIC had classified *Linehan* as Variety, which gave them a certain number of points. But the CRTC disagreed and ruled that *Linehan* was not Variety programming. On the contrary, it was Spoken Word programming, which placed it in a News category.

"WIC already had tons and tons of News," Hawtin explains. "So why would they spend money on this? The message was, 'Sorry, we love the show, but it's cancelled.' And Brian was devastated."

On Monday, May 4, 1998, Brian was in Los Angeles, about to have a reunion with Warren Beatty and begin a series of interviews with the cast of *Bulworth*, when he received an urgent message from Paul Osborn: WIC was about to go public with news of the cancellation. A proposal had been submitted to CBC Television but there was no news on any decision there. Paul asked Brian how he wanted to handle the calls coming in from the media, and Brian said to return the calls and tell them the truth – that due to the CRTC ruling, WIC was no longer interested in carrying the show.

By the time he returned from L.A., Brian's answering machines, at home and at the office, were jammed with calls from friends and media. His frustration came through when he returned the call from *Toronto Sun* TV columnist Claire Bickley. "I think what's got me down about the whole thing," he told her, "is that I really believed that the work would count. I really did."

Since Virginia Morra had been let go before he left for L.A., Brian replied to as many other calls as he could, then decided to spend the rest of his time preparing for his taping session that coming weekend in

Hollywood, where he was scheduled to interview Sandra Bullock for a New Movies episode of *Jane Hawtin Live*. But he was distracted, and depressed, and couldn't concentrate.

He decided to get out of the office. Perhaps a workout at his health club would take his mind off his troubles. He took the subway to Yonge and St. Clair. On the subway, a woman approached him to tell him how sorry she was about his program being cancelled. "It just doesn't seem right," she said sympathetically. He thanked her and walked from the subway to the corner convenience store to buy the *New York Times*.

En route he was stopped by a young man who told him how terrible he thought it was that *Linehan* had been cancelled. As he purchased his copy of the *New York Times*, the woman beside him touched his arm and said how sorry she was about the news. He thanked her. The young lady behind the counter asked if he needed a bag. He said no, he would put the *Times* into the bag he already had, with the *Toronto Star* and *Toronto Sun*.

Entering the shopping mall where his health club was located, he was stopped by another woman who expressed dismay over the show being cancelled and hoped he would return to television soon. He thanked her and entered the Pharma Plus store. "Within seconds of entering," Brian would later report, "I was stopped again by a woman and what had been happening for two days happened again."

He picked up a copy of *Time* magazine after he noticed an article on the Warren Beatty movie. He also observed that *In Style* magazine featured a story on summer movies, and decided to purchase both. While looking at *In Style*, a man approached him to say he was sorry that the *Linehan* show had been cancelled. "I thanked him and turned away," he later recalled. "I was holding both magazines in my hand along with a plastic bag containing the newspapers and the black leather gym bag."

By now he was so distracted that he couldn't remember what he had come to Pharma Plus to purchase. Then he remembered: he needed to ask the pharmacist for the correct name of a specific herbal foot ointment. "Turning to walk to the front of the store, I absentmindedly put both *Time* magazine and *In Style* magazine into the bag with the newspapers."

He walked the several yards between the entrance to Pharma Plus and the adjacent door leading to the pharmacy. When yet another man approached him, he assumed it was another viewer, about to offer him condolences on losing his show. "I'm store security," said the man. "May I see what you have in that bag?"

A bad day had just gotten exponentially worse.

Brian explained that he was not leaving the store, he was just making a stop in the pharmacy section, and had no intention of leaving without paying for the two magazines. The security officer told Brian he had seen him put the magazines into the bag, and that he had left the store, and that he was in fact shoplifting. He insisted that Brian accompany him to the manager's office. Brian insisted that he was telling the truth, and if the security officer would speak to a member of the store staff, most of whom knew Brian, he would realize that was the case.

"I know who you are, and I saw you take those magazines and leave the store," the security officer said doggedly. His manner and tone rattled Brian, who started to explain how stressed he was, how distracted he was, and how his television show had just been cancelled.

Maybe the security officer would have been more sympathetic if Brian had told him that he'd just lost his job at the steel mill. Or the factory. Or even another chain store. I'm sure it never even occurred to Brian, who was feeling particularly dejected that day, that losing your television show is not really the same as, say, losing a real job – i.e., a working man's job. So there he was, famous and vulnerable, pouring his heart out to a chain store security officer, who, upon hearing this personal information, became even more stubborn in his resolve.

The store security officer called the police.

"It's the guy from TV, yeah," Brian heard him say to the voice on the other end of the line.

The security officer turned to him. "What's your name?" Brian sat staring at him.

He went back to the phone. "He won't speak now."

"My name," said Brian, "is Brian Linehan."

"It's him, Brian Linehan from TV."

Within twenty to thirty minutes, a female police constable arrived in the Pharma Plus manager's office. Brian stood, introduced himself, and said he had an explanation for what had happened. The security guard told him to sit down, and gave the constable his version of what had transpired. Brian then assured the constable that he was not a thief or shoplifter, and that he was experiencing one of the worst days of his life.

"If everybody just let themselves go when they had a bad day," replied the constable, "what kind of world do you think we'd have? When I have a bad day, I don't go out and blow someone's head off." Brian stared at her.

A few interminable moments later he told her he didn't accept the analogy and insisted once again that he was telling the truth.

She said the truth wasn't for her to determine, that the security guard had made the accusation and Brian would have to tell his story to a judge. After making a brief phone call, she informed Brian that he would have to appear at a downtown police division for fingerprinting. The facility was open twenty-four hours, so he could arrive whenever he chose. On Thursday, June 4, he might have to appear at College Park courts and tell it to the judge. Would he promise to honour those dates? Or would she have to take him in, right now, and book him?

Brian said he would honour those dates.

The store security man asked Brian if he understood that, according to trespass laws, if he ever again entered a Pharma Plus store he could be arrested on the spot. He then remembered that he hadn't done a thorough search of Brian, and asked the police constable if he should. She didn't think it would be necessary, so she asked Brian if he wanted her or the security man to escort him from the store.

"Him, I guess," said Brian, now completely numb.

The security man walked back to the entrance with Brian and stood while he walked toward the door leading to Yonge Street. A woman coming from the other direction stopped him to say how sorry she was to hear that his show had been cancelled. But she was sure something good would come of it, she added, and that he would soon be back on television.

"I think I thanked her," he would later report. "I couldn't breathe. I felt like I was going to fall down, explode, or die at the front door. I walked out toward Yonge Street and leaned against the wall window of Pharma Plus."

He pulled himself together, hailed a taxi, and went home, where he unburdened himself of the whole sordid story. Zane was sympathetic and urged him to call Michael Levine. Michael was in Bermuda, but his personal assistant, Maxine Quigley, sensed something was wrong and got hold of him. Maxine called back, saying that Michael would phone Brian in Los Angeles. He had considered cancelling his L.A. trip but felt it would be unprofessional to do so.

The next morning Claire Bickley's story in the *Toronto Sun* was headlined LINEHAN SIGNS OFF – BUT WHY? Every second person on the Air Canada flight to L.A. that morning seemed to be reading it, and Brian regretted his decision to go to California. He called home from the plane, just to hear a caring voice, but Zane had gone on an errand, so he left a message on their answering machine instead. After he checked into his hotel, he called home again. This time Zane answered. He told Zane that he was having misgivings about making the trip. He was not feeling well. He was having trouble breathing. Zane was sure that he would feel better after he spoke to Michael Levine.

Brian told Michael the whole story when he called, and Michael promised to speak to criminal attorney Earl Levy and to meet with Brian in ten days when he returned from business in England.

Brian felt a great sense of relief. Michael was not merely his lawyer, but his friend and supporter. But he still couldn't sleep that night, and gave up even trying to. In the morning, he explained that he wasn't feeling well and would do only half the interviews originally scheduled.

The following day, one of his junket colleagues, Patrick Stoner from PBS in Philadelphia, discovered Claire Bickley's story on the Internet. Cancellation of Brian's series was soon the talk of the junket.

Back home again on Monday night, Brian still felt ill and was once again having trouble breathing. He wasn't sure he could wait for Michael's return, so at Zane's suggestion he called their friends and neighbours Julie and Derwyn Shea for advice. An ordained minister, Derwyn was also a former member of Ontario's provincial parliament and a skilled politician. The couple was vacationing in Florida when Brian called. Derwyn advised Brian to get a lawyer.

On Wednesday, Brian went to break the news to Jane Hawtin and Paul Osborn at Electric Entertainment. He saw Jane first, and when she saw the state he was in she assumed that the impact of the cancellation was finally sinking in. "There's something else you need to know," he began. He started the Pharma Plus story, and then broke down. Jane, shocked, reached out and embraced him.

"At that moment," he would later recall, "in front of a friend and professional ally, I lost total control." He apologized, and said he was sorry to have imposed this on her. He also told her that although he was supposed to go to New York on Friday to tape interviews for her summer movies special, he didn't know if he was up to it.

"Jane," he said later, "suggested I do what I thought was best, when I felt I could do it. Her concern was for me and my mental health and career."

Unbeknownst to Brian, Jane Hawtin and Paul Osborn then tracked down Norm Puhl, the president of Pharma Plus, and at his request Jane sent him a personal letter, briefly detailing the incident and pleading for his compassion and intervention. "Please understand," she wrote, "that Brian is a man who takes great pride in his work." For him, she said, newspaper reports of the cancellation of his series "has been akin to being fired in front of the whole world." Both the police officer and the security officer were aware of Brian's celebrity, she noted, "and seem to take particular glee in having him arrested." Brian, she said, "is not a shoplifter. He is a fifty-three-year-old man who was having one of the worst days of his life."

Were he to appear for fingerprinting or in court, she pointed out, "it will make news headlines and Brian's career will be over.

"Last Thursday was a day when Brian needed some compassion and understanding. He didn't get it. I'm pleading with you to understand what really happened that day and to have the charges dropped before any further damage is done."

Jane closed by urging the president to give her request "your utmost consideration," and to treat it with "the highest degree of confidentiality."

In his written notes chronicling the incident, Brian made special mention of how supportive Jane had been. "It is almost 5 p.m. on Thursday, May 14, and Jane has a live show to do at 6 p.m. tonight. I have put a terrible pressure on her and I'm remorseful and saddened. She has been incredible. She said she will leave a message if she hears from the president of Pharma Plus."

The next morning, Brian flew to New York to tape his scheduled interviews for the special summer movies episode of *Jane Hawtin Live*.

On May 28, 1998, exactly three weeks after his close encounter at Pharma Plus, Brian received a copy of a letter sent to Pharma Plus president Norm Puhl by barrister Earl J. Levy, Q.C.

Dear Mr. Puhl:
I represent Mr. Linehan who has consulted me regarding his arrest for theft from one of your stores. I have been advised by the Crown Attorney, Mr. Jim Atkinson, that after receiving your letter agreeing to the withdrawal of the charge and speaking to the officer in charge of the case that the charge against Mr. Linehan will be withdrawn. Mr. Linehan wished me to thank you for your understanding in appreciating that he had no intention to steal from your store. He has instructed me to undertake to you

on his behalf that he has no intention to take proceedings whatsoever against Pharma Plus regarding the incident in question and regards the matter at an end.

Yours very truly,

Earl J. Levy, Q.C.

"And the next day," Hawtin remembers, "Brian sent me the biggest bunch of flowers I had ever seen in my life – it was gigantic – along with a beautiful and very touching note."

The cancellation of the Linehan series marked not only the end of Brian's weekly appearances on television but also the end of an era. The days of studio-financed twenty-minute Linehan interviews were over.

"Brian believed that as soon as he got back on TV that he'd be able to do it the way he did it before," says Hawtin with a sad little smile. "And occasionally he'd be able to get twenty minutes instead of the usual seven or whatever it is that junketeers got. But the negotiations that had to go on to get that were pretty horrendous."

"There was no more I could do for Brian," Dianne Schwalm says plainly. "Hollywood didn't give a rat's ass how good he was. They only cared about the new regime, the sound bites. They didn't care about the quality of the interviews, they didn't care if the stars wanted them or not. So that was a hard thing to swallow. And yet when people came to town we'd still bring him in, but then the hardest part was that the new stars didn't know who he was. So he was regarded as some sort of freak.

"You could still sit him with Clint Eastwood. It was psychotherapy for those stars. After an hour with Brian they went, *I'm cleansed. I feel alive.* And they'd have a great time." But the new breed of stars, she says, "did not appreciate what Brian knew about them. That was the problem. The new guard didn't understand that what he knew was a compliment to the work they had done. They just perceived it as somebody being awfully nosey and prying into their private life."

Ronni Chasen had also seen signs that the Linehan era was coming to an end. "I think Brian was bored with some of the younger, more shallow filmmakers and actors," she says. "He felt they had nothing to say. He wasn't interested in talking to them. He was interested in talking to Lauren Bacall and to people with a body of work, the Marty Scorseses and so on." As Arlene Dahl's husband, Mark Rosen, says, "Given a choice between interviewing Arlene or interviewing Gwyneth Paltrow, Brian would have been much happier to talk to Arlene."

Meanwhile, things were going from bad to worse for Jane Hawtin and Paul Osborn and Electric Entertainment. "WTN was in the process of becoming W and wanted us to adjust the format of *Jane Hawtin Live* to suit their new mission statement. They wanted me to do a show for women, which I've never done. I wasn't keen on that," says Hawtin. "I said, let's just say that we're moving in a different direction and go our separate ways."

WTN countered by announcing that the network had cancelled *Jane Hawtin Live* due to poor ratings, a tactic which still makes her bristle. "We were getting like seventy-five thousand viewers, which for a specialty channel were great numbers!"

That winter, unbeknownst to Jane, the folks at WTN asked Brian if he would like to do an Oscar special for them. Brian accepted and telephoned Rob Waymen, the photographer responsible for his dazzling Electric Entertainment photo portfolio. He told Waymen he was doing "a thing for *TV Guide*" and could he use the photos Rob had shot?

"Rob agreed," says Jane, "He said, 'I'm glad he's getting some writing work.' Except that wasn't what it was for. It was for an ad for the show he was doing on WTN, and they used all the pictures. And when he finally came to talk to me, he knew he'd been a bad boy, but this was like the *ultimate* bad boy. It just felt like such a betrayal."

She was fed up with him. "Okay, we're done," she told him.

"What do you mean?" said Brian.

"We're *done*," said Jane flatly. "I've covered for you so many times, but this? You know what they did to me, and still you went for it!"

"I needed the money," he said plaintively.

"I understand needing money, Brian," Hawtin told him. "I understand needing to work. But you were so dishonest. To not even tell me, to let me open *TV Guide* and see this huge ad. It's enough. We're done."

He wished he could tell her that she didn't understand, that he had no choice. This creature he had invented, this amazing Linehan figure, came fully alive only on camera. If the lights burned out, if the tape stopped rolling, if the stars stopped asking for him, he would cease to exist. Everything he had worked so long and hard for, this complex persona it had taken him years to create and polish, could all vanish in an instant, just disappear into thin air.

16

"Anyone but Linehan."

Brian Linehan had lost his second television series, but not himself. And he had no intention of becoming invisible.

As a much sought-after guest, he soon became a talk show favourite again. As diligent as ever, he never accepted a talk show invitation if he didn't have proper time to prepare for it. He arrived on time, witty stories and clever ad-libs thoroughly and professionally rehearsed. He also arrived knowing more about the interviewer than the interviewer knew about him, a trick he had learned from *Globe and Mail* film critic Jay Scott. After Brian appeared with Citytv alumnus Dini Petty on her daily CTV show and Marilyn Denis on her daily Citytv show, both women invited him to return on a regular basis. And after his first guest stint with Mike Bullard, the producers of the late-night CTV talk show asked Brian to consider a recurring contract, by which he would appear with Bullard every few weeks. He didn't want to do it, but he loved being asked.

Academy of Canadian Cinema and Television president Maria Topalovich had hired two young producers, Susan Edwards and Steve Sloan of High SeaSS! Entertainment, to produce the 2000 Genie Awards, and she liked the way they worked. When she asked them to produce the 2001 awards show, they told her they wanted Brian Linehan to host. They had grown up in the business watching him on television, and to them Brian Linehan *was* the movies. Maria Topalovich was fine with it but reminded them they would need CBC approval before they could ask Brian to host the telecast.

Getting an audience to watch Canadian film awards is a huge and daunting challenge. Canadian films get very little screen time in Canadian cinemas, so no matter how many stars you parachute into that night's awards show, the audience has little if any interest in the show, not because they don't care about Canadian films, but because most of them haven't seen the films. CBC entertainment chief Phyllis Platt was well aware of this and thought Brian was not only a logical choice but also a highly credible one. He was approved, and brought wonderful insider energy to the evening. Edwards and Sloan used Brian as the bait to secure major names as presenters and make the event more of an all-star family gathering than a standard awards show, resulting in happy feedback from an enthusiastic but predictably small viewing audience.

"Those award shows," Dianne Schwalm remembers, "were important to him. I'd say OK, we're going to get a limo, and I'm going to pick you up, and then I'll drop you off. So he became a star again. He wasn't just going by TTC and showing up at the gate or the stage door. He was a star and he wanted to be seen as a star."

Dianne was also involved in another starry venture: she was a board member of Canada's Walk of Fame. In 1998, in addition to giving Canadian talent their own sidewalk stars, à la Hollywood's Walk of Fame, Toronto entrepreneur Peter Soumalias and his crack team of arts commandos – the original group that worked on the first event included professional Canadian showbiz boosters Bill Ballard, Dusty Cohl, Dianne Schwalm, and Gary Slaight – staged a lavish gala at which celebrities saluted the stars being honoured.

By 2001, Soumalias's dedicated disciples had definitely gotten the hang of it. A few weeks after Brian hosted the 2001 Genie Awards, media were alerted that the co-hosts for the 2001 Walk of Fame gala, to induct thirteen more Canadians into the Canada Walk of Fame, would be Canadian funnyman Colin Mochrie, Canadian singer Jann Arden, and Canadian interviewer Brian Linehan. Linehan was a late-breaking addition – a "suggestion" from board member Dianne Schwalm, who was still looking for opportunities to get cash-flow gigs for Brian. Brian knew she had engineered it, and was grateful. Or at least he seemed to be when he phoned to tell me about it.

But then things started to fall apart. Brian had received his schedule, he told me, and in his view the time set aside for rehearsal was inadequate. And to make matters worse, he had to wait so long for the car to bring him to Roy Thomson Hall that he was *late* for the read-through!

For Dianne Schwalm, it was the same old story. "Once he had the gig, he had to be Brian, he had to be the perfectionist. But he also saw himself as a star instead of a hired hand. And according to everybody

CBC publicity photo for the 1981 Genie Awards

Brian hosting the 1982 Genie Awards

Sophia Loren and Brian Linehan

Martin Short and Brian Linehan in Arizona

Brian with publicist Dianne Schwalm and Michael J. Fox on Brian's CFRB radio show

Brian and Joan Rivers

Clint Eastwood and Brian Linehan

Brian Linehan and Shirley MacLaine

Brian Linehan on location in Vancouver for the Genie Awards

Backstage in Bea Arthur's dressing room with (left to right) Julia Shea, Brian, Bea Arthur, Marcia Martin, Peter Husar, Norma Rea, producer Jeffrey Latimer, Ken Lindsay, and Bea's musical director, composer Billy Goldenberg

Some of the motley crew behind the 1994 Floating Film Festival

Brian's friend and attorney Michael Levine at the gala tribute
to Brian Linehan in Toronto on September 17, 2004

Gail Anthony, George Anthony, Chaz Ebert, Roger Ebert, and
film festivals founder Dusty Cohl backstage at Celebrating Brian Linehan

John Narvali, Kodak Entertainment Imaging (courtesy Academy of Canadian Cinema and Television)

Brian Linehan

working on the show he was a royal pain, to the point where I was apologizing, because I had pushed them to hire him."

She knew Brian needed to make some money. She didn't expect him to be grateful, but she thought he might be a little more circumspect. "But he'd call and complain, and then they would call and complain, and I thought, oh my God, this isn't worth the aggravation. I mean, this isn't the Oscars. Everything is being done on a shoestring budget."

To add insult to injury, especially for Mr. Preparation, when Brian finally got on stage the teleprompter crashed and he had to wing it. Adds Schwalm: "He did an amazing job under the difficult circumstances that existed."

Gail and I regrouped with Brian at the cocktail reception after the show, and we were comparing notes when Walk of Fame board member Bill Ballard sauntered up to us. A long-time partner of music promoter Michael Cohl, Bill was a friendly acquaintance and a major player in the floating film festival created by Michael's cousin, Dusty Cohl.

"So, Linehan," said Bill, "I hear you were generally a pain in the ass." My jaw dropped, but Brian was ready for him.

"Hold it!" he barked back. "If being a professional and expecting professional behaviour from my peers is being a pain in the ass, then yes, I was a pain in the ass."

Dusty Cohl, also a Walk of Fame board member, says he doesn't recall the specifics. "But when Brian was on stage he was absolutely, as usual, the perfect professional."

Meanwhile, filmmaker Barry Avrich was still intrigued by the idea of doing *Glitter Palace*, a documentary about retirement homes for stage and screen veterans – the same one Brian had earlier declined to work on. In 1986, a group of Canadian show folk created Performing Arts Lodges of Canada (PAL), a national, non-profit, registered charitable organization, to meet the special needs of its people, with particular emphasis on affordable housing for elderly members of the community. In 1993, the organization opened its first lodge, PAL Place Toronto, with the assistance of the Government of Ontario, providing a rent-controlled apartment complex for more than two hundred arts workers. In 2006, retired artists began moving into PAL Vancouver, an eight-storey building with ninety-nine one-bedroom rental units.

Avrich and Linehan were also aware that a similar but much older venerable institution, the Motion Picture and Television Country House and Hospital, still existed in Hollywood. In 1940, then president of the

Motion Picture Relief Fund Jean Hersholt found forty-eight acres of walnut and orange groves in the southwest end of the San Fernando Valley that were selling for $850 an acre. The Relief Fund board of directors purchased the property for the Motion Picture Country House. To offset the costs for the first buildings, seven acres were sold. Mary Pickford and Jean Hersholt broke the first ground on September 27, 1942. Six years later, the Motion Picture Hospital was dedicated on the grounds of the Country House, with Ronald Reagan, Shirley Temple, and Robert Young, among other stars, in attendance.

Who better than Brian Linehan to do the interviews for Avrich's nostalgic documentary? A devoted Linehan fan, Avrich spent months coaxing Brian into participating in *Glitter Palace*. It took Brian a while to accept that he would be off-camera. "He had to be on," Avrich says simply. "And when we agreed on a deal, and what it was going to be, he could not grasp the off-camera thing. My producers kept saying to me, he doesn't know he's off camera. And I said, but I've explained this to him. And they said, no, you don't understand, we're having conversations with him and he's asking about camera angles."

Barry decided to host a production meeting at his home. "Brian sat in the dining room and said, 'How many costume changes am I going to need? How many suits should I bring?' My heart sank. All right, how am I going to tell him this? He saw it in my face and he said, 'I'm not on camera. Is that what you're going to say?'"

Avrich did some quick thinking. "Nooooo," he replied, "not for the interviews. But you're opening the show."

Whew!

Avrich admits that originally he had no intention of having Brian open the film. He shot him walking out toward camera, making a Linehan entrance. And that was the extent of his on-screen presence in *Glitter Palace*.

"It was basically a no-budget shoot," says Avrich. "We're going to shoot in L.A. and Toronto. So we come out to L.A. to the Motion Picture Country House, where we're going to shoot fifteen interviews a day. And we said okay, we're going to have fun. I flew him out business class and I put him up in a suite at the Sunset Marquis and I had a driver for him every day. Because if I'm going to ask him to do this, then it's going to be star treatment for him."

Even though Brian knew he wasn't going to be on camera for his interviews, "he brought the suits anyway. He got dressed up for every interview. When the other people were being made up with makeup, he was moving in. Maybe he could use just a little blush. But he was pure pro, whether it was going to be on camera or off. Which was admirable. And sad. He was a pro, he came out there, and at the end of each day he'd be so fucking exhausted. We'd want to go out and do these great dinners, and he'd say, 'Barry, I have to go back to my room.' He was zapped. Drained."

Avrich also got to see first-hand what people meant when they said Linehan was difficult to work with. "I liked seeing some of the piss and vinegar," he says. "But he would get crazy with the crew. Suddenly it's 'You're in my fucking eye line!' and 'Why is it taking so long to set up?' 'Where is the monitor. I can't see . . . move that over, for Chrissake!' And this was an L.A. crew, these guys were hardly amateurs. But he was tough."

Avrich was asking Brian to do something new to him: to interview people who weren't famous – "people who were part of famous things but weren't famous themselves."

One of the subjects had died prior to Brian and Barry's arrival – a noted cinematographer famous for his work with director Otto Preminger. The Motion Picture Country House called Avrich. Would he mind filming the widow? She wants to go on camera.

Barry agreed but didn't tell Brian until they were in the car, on their way to the Motion Picture Country House. Brian balked at first, but Barry told him that the people at the home had assured him that the cinematographer's widow had also been in the movie business, and would have wonderful stories to tell. She knew all the films her husband had worked on. "Brian, she even worked for Max Factor!"

"All right," said Brian, grumbling, "I'll do it. But I'm telling you right now I'm not happy about it and it's going to be a short interview."

After they set up, Avrich recalls, they asked a nurse to fetch the cinematographer's widow. "So, this lady comes in, and she's had her makeup and her hair done and she comes and sits down. Brian says, 'Are we ready to go?' She says, 'Yes, yes I'm ready.'

"He goes, 'My God, what a life your husband had.'

"She goes, 'Uh-huh.'

"Brian starts to go through Preminger's credits, from *Exodus* to *Anatomy of a Murder*, and he says, 'What was it like when your husband would come home after shooting movies like *The Man with the Golden Arm*, with these amazing casts? What would you discuss at the dinner table?'

"She turns to him and says, with this Russian Jewish accent: 'He never talked about his work.'

"Brian gives me a look that could slay an entire army. He turns around, and he reaches over and he touches her, and he says, 'You worked at Max Factor. The makeup tests then, Rita Hayworth, Carole Lombard, the famous Mr. Factor with his makeup trunk and his brushes. Fabulous. What was it like, in the halcyon days of Hollywood, with these people coming in?'

"She says, 'I worked in payroll.'

"He says, 'It's been a pleasure. This interview is over.' And he turns to the nurse and says, 'Take her out of here!'"

But most of the Linehan sessions at the Motion Picture Country House produced gold. Interviewing off-camera people was not Brian Linehan's stock in trade, but he prepared as he would for any other interview. "He'd have those fantastic moments with these people, like the prop guy on *The Thing*. Brian would go, 'What was it like when the machine went crazy in the movie *The Thing*?' And the guy would say, 'I didn't work on *The Thing*.' And Brian would go, 'Yes, you did.' He'd take him through it, and then the guy would remember that he worked on the film."

Brian really hit his stride, he says, when they started shooting the interviews at the Performing Arts Lodge in Toronto. At PAL the film and theatre people regarded the opportunity to talk to Brian as a privilege. "They had spent an hour and a half with him, being interviewed by the great Brian Linehan, and at the end of each interview they'd lean over and thank him, because they'd had their moment with him. It was okay now. What a gift!"

When Avrich finally finished *Glitter Palace*, he hosted a private screening of the film at a Toronto movie house. "Frances Hyland came, and Paul Soles, and Jack Duffy, and the lady from *The Pig 'n' Whistle*. And for many of these people this was their last chance to see themselves on a large screen, ever again. He was able to transport them back to a world that they were no longer a part of."

When Avrich sold the film to a U.S. distributor, the only condition of sale was that he remove the opening sequence with Brian Linehan. "Not because they didn't know who he was," he hastens to add, "but because it was . . . strange. It's a very awkward section of the film."

Brian told Juliette and others, during frequent telephone visits, that he was just happy to be working. "Times were changing, as they always do," says Juliette. "And he was so ahead of his time. He had been there and done it. And then you get a new generation who think they're the first ones being there and doing it." And although he tried to rise above it, he was still angry.

Some of Brian's other friends sensed that his anger was intruding on his relationship with Zane. "He tried hard to balance his life, especially after he and Zane got back together. . . . And it really was a struggle for him. He understood Zane's feelings, but he still had a need to be up there," says Judi Schwam.

Harriet Blacker was aware of the fact that as far as Brian's career was concerned, "the last eight to ten years were extremely difficult. It was, you know, 'all those fuckers, they're not going to get me.' He was very defensive about it. But you couldn't give him advice he didn't want to take. He wanted it his way."

Most of us were stunned when Brian announced that he and Zane were going to sell Grenadier Heights and move to a condo. He had already figured out what to do with the rows of filing cabinets in the basement that held all his research from his television and radio interviews. He was going to donate the whole lot to the Toronto film festival, for its burgeoning reference library. But the idea that they would willingly give up the dream house they'd worked so hard for baffled most of their friends. Had Grenadier Heights become too rich for them? How could Zane ever leave his garden?

Brian told me Zane was now finding that his beloved garden was just too much work. "And Zane is retired, and I'm really not working that much, and this will allow us to travel whenever we want." They told their friend Allan Harris that they were going to cash in, put some money away, be able to travel, have a condo close to the airport, so they could just fly in and come downtown and have dinners, enjoy the theatre and friends in Toronto, and then fly off again. It sounded like a great idea. It just didn't sound like a great idea for Brian and Zane.

"We thought it was a horrible idea," says Harris. "Zane loved that garden so much. Brian loved to sit out there and read the papers in the morning and sit and look at the birds. Too much work? We said, hire somebody! But oh no, Zane couldn't do that, he couldn't have someone come in and touch his precious garden." The declared rationale behind it, he says, was hard to argue with. "But there was a lot going on in their relationship, and their own personal unhappiness, that very few people knew about."

Joan Rivers was also puzzled by their decision to move. "I kept saying, why are you selling? There was the garden they loved. There was that wonderful kitchen. I didn't understand. If they were both sad to leave the house, why were they leaving the house? I would stay in my house and rent out closets. My aunt did that when she was down and out. Never left Park Avenue but you'd open a closet and see a Russian cooking eggs."

Five Grenadier Heights was sold to a publishing executive named Kevin Hanson. Within a month or two, Hanson became the new vice president of HarperCollins, which also made him Martha Watson's new boss. "So there was Kevin ensconced in Brian's house, and Zane and Brian in their new condo, and Kevin and I working together," says Martha. "It was quite a circle." A circle that in time would prove to be profound.

Karen Kain still remembers her last supper at 5 Grenadier Heights. "They had a small dinner party before they moved to the condo. They had seemed quite happy and ready to go. Brian was trying to make it very special and he spoke about what the house had meant to them, and how they were entering a new phase of their lives."

For most of their friends, where Brian and Zane chose to live was the shocker. The high-rise condo on Islington Avenue, on the western edge of Toronto, was well appointed, with two modest but attractive terraces. Zane had striking California shutters installed to stream the light from their wall of windows. But the only thing their new home was close to was the airport. Most of their friends lived downtown, and to get anywhere on his own, let alone to the theatre district, Brian would have to take a bus or hail a cab just to get to the subway.

"In Toronto," Brian would later remark, sulking, "you have so many great choices. You can live in Little Italy, Chinatown, Little Portugal . . . We live in Little Somalia."

They moved on Zane's birthday, on November 28, 2001. It was unclear whose idea the move really was. Allan Harris believes it was Zane's. Joan Rivers was sure it "was all Zane's way." But Taina Elg got the distinct impression from Zane that it was Brian who had wanted to move, not Zane. "Zane hated the apartment," she says flatly. "He really missed the house."

Allan Harris remembers "all those planes almost on top of them. And the fights we heard about Zane deciding to change the bookshelves, and how they had to get somebody back in to redesign all those. And the deliveries. Everything had to be a drama."

"I think it was a big jolt for both of them," says Joan Rivers.

In December, shortly before Christmas, Brian invited Allan Harris to lunch at the Studio Café in the Four Seasons hotel. "He said he was very close to leaving Zane again. He was so mad at Zane. 'I made the biggest mistake going back,' he said.

"I told him everyone goes through difficulties in their relationship. And we all think about things like that. We talked about it, and we talked about the miserable time he had had when he was living on Monteith Street, where he thought he was going to come out, and either meet somebody or live a glamorous and sexy life. Which didn't happen. And I said to him, 'Brian, you know, being a single person at any age is not easy, but being a single gay man in your later years is, I'm sure, even more difficult. And you have a name, and people assume you have money because you have a name, and you will be taken advantage of.' And we sat talking about this through the whole lunch, and drank far too much wine, and talked and talked. . . . By the end he said, 'I know, you're right, I should stay with Zane. We'll work it out.'

"I don't know what went on in the relationship after that," adds Harris. "They were going through a very complex, very difficult time."

☆

As the months rolled by, Academy of Canadian Cinema and Television chief Maria Topalovich and producers Steve Sloan and Susan Edwards decided to ask Linehan to host the Genies again. Brian was such an industry hit with his 2001 hosting stint that Sloan and Edwards wanted to pitch the network on doing a teaser stand-alone special, *Countdown to the Genies*, which Linehan would also host. But CBC network program director Slawko Klymkiw and Telefilm chief Richard Stursberg, whose agency invested in the annual Genies, were less than enthralled by the low Nielsen ratings for the 2001 awards. Stursberg told Maria Topalovich that he would feel better about her Nielsen chances (and, consequently, Telefilm's investment) if she pursued a more current, higher-profile host such as Canuck expatriate Pamela Anderson. Klymkiw, who had praised Brian's hosting of the 2001 Genies, said he would leave the choice to the Academy, with only one caveat: "Anyone but Linehan."

Maria Topalovich, a skilled veteran at managing network "input," took it in stride. Her young producers, however, were devastated; they didn't understand how Slawko Klymkiw could *not* want Brian to host.

Susan Edwards and Steve Sloan made an appointment with Slawko, who received them warmly. He explained that it was his job to bring viewers to CBC Television and the Genies, and that based on hard numbers he was pretty sure Brian Linehan couldn't do that. Susan and Steve listened patiently. And then it was their turn. They told Slawko how professional Brian was. They told him how people were constantly coming up to Brian on the street, to compliment him, even thank him, for one show or another. They told him how stars who turned them down suddenly became available when they learned Brian would be hosting. They told him how tirelessly Brian worked to promote the CBC telecast. They told him, with the same passion that they had told him everything else, that Brian Linehan should be hosting the 2002 Genie Awards.

Maria Topalovich called me later that day. "Susan and Steve met with Slawko this morning," she said. "And we now have a host for the 2002 Genie Awards."

"We do?" I was surprised that a new candidate had been approved so quickly.

"Who is it?" I asked.

"Brian Linehan," she replied triumphantly, and I could hear the smile in her voice.

Brian hosted the 2002 Genie Awards. He also hosted the first-ever *Countdown to the Genies*, conducting mini-interviews with David Cronenberg, Thom Fitzgerald, Don McKellar, Mort Ransen and Clement Virgo to promote their nominated films, and he did it with style, and grace, and wit.

On the night of the telecast, the Academy arranged for Brian to walk the red carpet so he could be "ambushed" by Mary Walsh, who starred in one of his favourite comedy shows, *This Hour Has 22 Minutes*.

"The gods of Irony are running roughshod over Toronto!" Walsh shrieked. "The dean of interviewers is being interviewed!" Walsh continued in Linehan-ese. "1969. April. Delta Secondary School in Hamilton. You're at your locker, eyes shift to the left. You see Barbara Amiel. Brian. My question to you: Were her breasts smaller than they are today?"

"There are no indiscreet questions, only indiscreet answers," Brian replied with what columnist Jim Slotek would describe as "that pursed, devilishly secretive smile."

After the camera was turned off, Walsh touched Linehan's arm and said, "We miss you, Brian. When will we see you on TV again?"

"When you're running a network," said Brian, giving what had become his standard reply.

That night, when he walked out on stage at the John Bassett Theatre at the Metro Toronto Convention Centre, he received a warm and welcoming ovation from the star-studded audience. It was a nice moment and, as it turned out, a lovely send-off. It would be his final hosting stint on live television.

☆

When February rolled around, so did the seventh annual floating film festival. The screenings at sea on the MS *Statendam* were better than ever, and Barry Avrich scored a personal hit with *Glitter Palace*, which he premiered on board a week before it made its debut on the pay-TV Moviepix movie channel. But the big buzz was all about the sly sleeper Avrich had created with his cohort Brian Linehan. Cunningly called *City Lights*, it was a twelve-minute short in which Brian seemed to be very comfortable poking fun at his now larger-than-life image. Barry cut his famous, intricate questions about the movie business with candid and unscripted responses from a clutch of five-year-old children. The result was funny, sweet-natured, and charming.

"Brian had a tremendous sense of humour," says Avrich. In Canada, their spoof homage to Brian's long-running series became a staple of the pay-TV Movie Network, "and Brian loved that people stopped him on the street and told him how great he was in the film."

With *Glitter Palace* and, especially, *City Lights* receiving such a warm reception on the floating film festival, there was only one thing missing: Brian Linehan.

Brian had made a point of telling shipmates on the fifth floating festival that he was fed up with the floater and was seriously considering "jumping ship." He just never mentioned that to Dusty Cohl. Dusty was not amused.

Brian had used up a lot of his markers with Cohl, who had tried to help him on more than one occasion. "I remember when he was let go at the *Sun*," Dusty says. "I got Eddie Greenspan to help him, look at his corporate books and all sorts of things. I don't think he ever appreciated the thought of people like me, and Eddie, and a few other people spending a lot of time trying to do this. And I phoned people at the *Sun*, and he would act as though it was basically expected I would do that."

The ship sailed without Brian Linehan in 2000. And he was missed.

A year or so after the sixth floating film festival, Brian realized that no one had called to check his availability for the next cruise. He also realized that he really missed being on the festival's VIP list.

To remedy this, he called Dusty. They agreed to meet for breakfast, to thrash things out over morning coffee. Dusty told Brian some of the stories he'd heard about his less-than-becoming behaviour on board the fifth floating film festival. Brian disputed a few of the reports, but only a few.

"I don't know what else I can do," Brian told me later when he reported on their breakfast meeting. "I apologized over coffee. I said I regretted it. I told Dusty, okay, I'm jealous. I'm just plain jealous. I want to be up on that stage, doing those interviews, instead of watching anyone else do them. Including Roger."

Months later I asked Dusty how he felt about Brian's apology. He looked blank. "What apology?"

"When you had breakfast with him," I explained. "When he admitted how jealous he was of Roger."

Dusty almost did a double-take. "I did have breakfast with Brian," he assured me. "But he never said he was jealous of Roger.

"And," he added with a rueful grin, "he certainly never apologized." Ah yes. Another non-verbal fault-free apology, in the time-honoured Linehan tradition.

After that, as Dusty would later say, "Brian was sorry that he wasn't back. And we just never happened to get him back."

So the ship sailed without him again, this time from San Diego. Gail and I were sitting in Toronto Pearson's Maple Leaf Lounge, waiting for our Air Canada flight to San Diego with our friend Lynne St. David, when Jennifer Pierpoint stopped by. Jennifer was one of Air Canada's much-valued concierges, a crackerjack team who specialized in making everyday miracles for the benefit of harassed business travellers. We were happy to see her, as always, until she shared some news with us. Frieda Creighton, the Air Canada concierge who had made my life and Brian's so much easier in our whirlwind Hollywood years, was now in Sunnybrook Hospital. She had been diagnosed with cancer some time ago, and was now in her declining days.

I phoned Brian from the Maple Leaf Lounge. He was at home, poring through some old books, trying to keep his mind off the floating film festival. He and Zane, he said, might go off to Cuba for a week, just to get some sun. "I have some sad news," I said, and filled him in on Frieda's situation. He grew very quiet, very quickly.

I heard them calling our flight. "I'm sorry to tell you this as I'm getting on a plane," I added.

"No problem," he said. "I'll take care of it."

And he did. By the time we returned two weeks later, he had visited Frieda on two separate occasions, spoken to her over the phone on at least two other occasions, and advised Joan Rivers that Frieda, that wonderful woman from Air Canada who always took such good care of her, was losing her battle with cancer.

Joan was concerned. Was Frieda getting enough attention? Was she just one of many patients in a palliative care cancer ward? Was she getting lost in the day-to-day hospital shuffle?

Joan immediately sent a huge orchid plant – "more like an orchid *tree*," as Brian later described it – to Frieda at Sunnybrook Hospital. The delivery was executed by a big-voiced, well-rehearsed courier who got off the elevator carrying the plant, proclaiming, "*Special Delivery for Ms. Frieda Creighton from Ms. Joan Rivers! Special Delivery for Ms. Frieda Creighton from Ms. Joan Rivers!*" until one of the nurses finally brought him to Frieda's room. When the courier pulled the ribbon and lifted the protective cellophane to reveal the spectacular orchids, Frieda and the nurse both gasped with delight.

"Oh Mr. Linehan!" a giddy Frieda reported the following day, "I was the hit of the entire ward!"

Brian was so happy. Well, as happy as he could be, under the circumstances. He was having some health challenges of his own – and waiting for some tests to come back from the lab.

In March 2002, the tests came back, and Brian was diagnosed with non-Hodgkin's Lymphoma.

"I'm really struggling . . ."

In March 2002, Brian and Zane's good friends Anne and Larry Heisey
wanted to do something to celebrate Karen Kain's birthday, so they
invited Karen and Ross and Brian and Zane to spend a long weekend
with them on Key Biscayne, Florida. Brian was about to embark on his
first round of chemotherapy, and had sworn Zane to secrecy. Zane had
also had a bit of a cancer scare in recent months, and had just had a
malignant mole removed. That was a nagging worry, but at least it wasn't
a secret. Still, the thought of spending time with their friends was a tonic
to them both.

In addition to being friends, Larry and Anne were major supporters of the National Ballet of Canada, and were bona fide film buffs too,
who always enjoyed spending time with Brian and Zane on Dusty Cohl's
floating film festival. Karen had introduced them years earlier at a dinner
party she hosted. "I was sure they would get along." She shudders. "They
didn't get along *at all*. Annie and Brian were just at each other's throats
– both vying to be the centre of attention. I was really nervous, because
Brian was getting really aggressive and hostile. And he was drinking
heavily, and it wasn't pretty when he decided he didn't like somebody. I
was thinking, 'Oh my God, what have I done?' But Annie was actually
really enjoying it. She was *loving* it. Somehow they came to some kind of
truce, and by the end of the evening they had decided that they really
liked each other. And then they became best buds."

Buoyed by the Heiseys' invitation, the high-profile quartet packed
their bags for Florida, with Brian getting them upgraded to business
class at the airport. The Heiseys' house was an oasis for them. "They
had this lovely, comfortable house, with a swimming pool, and you

could walk to the beach," Karen says. "And we just spent a lot of time together. Because the mole was malignant, Zane had been told that he wasn't to be in the sun any more. But Zane was still himself, the way I knew him to be."

One night, while they were having cocktails, the subject of anti-depressants came up. A robust and vital man, Larry Heisey had been diagnosed with Parkinson's disease and was starting to suffer its side effects. "Anne and Larry," says Karen, "talked about the fact that they were taking antidepressants, and that these antidepressants had really helped them, and that they were now both much happier." Karen shared with them the fact that she herself had gone through a depression in the previous twelve months, coping with her new administrative role at the National Ballet. "And I told them that antidepressants had really helped me, too."

In retrospect, she says, she could see that Brian was watching to see how Zane was reacting to the conversation. "Obviously the depression thing had come up many times before. And later I found out that Brian had bought all those books for Zane and tried to convince him to get help."

They had a wonderful time with the Heiseys, and Brian and Zane kept his diagnosis secret the entire weekend. After they got back, Karen didn't hear from them for a while, which was unusual. But she was busy, and she assumed they were busy too, or travelling.

She and Ross were packing their bags for a summer cruise when she got a call from Zane. "He acted like he was calling me just to tell me about this friend of theirs who was going to be on the same cruise. . . . But that's not really why he called. Finally he brought it up, and I could tell that it was difficult for him. 'I'm really struggling,' he told me.

"Zane loved me. Brian used to tell me that if Zane were straight he would have wanted to marry me. But this was the most of himself, the most vulnerable, that he ever shared with me. And I was really, really worried for him. I could hear something in his voice, and I was scared. Because for a moment I heard Stephen Godfrey's voice. I had been through this. I had seen this before."

Stephen Godfrey was a gifted *Globe and Mail* dance critic, one of many arts reporters who were unabashedly devoted to Kain. Godfrey, who helped Kain shape her autobiography *Movement Never Lies*, suffered severe bouts of depression and had shocked his friends and family by taking his own life.

What had she heard in Stephen's voice? What did she hear in Zane's? "They go very flat," she says simply. "There is a flatness – I can't describe it any other way – and with Stephen, I didn't know." When she heard it in Zane, "my alarm bells went off, my antenna went up, I heard this flatness in his voice that was scary. So I encouraged him to get help, and he wanted to know what particular antidepressants I took that seemed to help me, and obviously wanted to do his research. He promised me he was going to get help."

She and Ross left for the cruise. "I told Ross how nervous I was, what I'd heard in Zane's voice and how he had scared me. And at every port of call we would send postcards home. I didn't know what else to do."

In June, Zane and Brian went to visit Ken Lindsay and Peter Husar in their new house overlooking the Islington Golf Club. Now that Zane and Brian were living on Islington, they were practically neighbours, and Zane couldn't wait to get out into their new backyard.

"So we took him out," Ken remembers, "and he was just talking about all the plants and everything that was there . . . And he told us what we should be doing and what we shouldn't be doing with what we had planted. 'I'll come over again,' he said, 'and I'll give you advice on your perennials.'"

About two weeks later, they heard from Zane again, on a Sunday afternoon. "He called us out of the blue," Ken remembers, "which was very out of character. Usually Brian would make the connections. But this one day Zane called us up and said, 'We happen to have bought too much salmon, can you guys come over for dinner?' We had something on that night, so we couldn't. And I remember Zane saying, 'Well, some other time.' That was the last thing that he ever said to me."

Soon after, Zane telephoned Taina Elg at her home in New York. "He was very, very tired. I think he was worried about Brian. He had done most of the work, taking care of him, and cooking, and I think he was just simply overtired. And he told us that he needed to go away, and that he had spoken with Brian, and Brian had said yes, go, go by all means."

Zane told Taina that he had been listening to a particular Finnish opera over and over and over again, and it was going to be performed at the Savonlinna Opera Festival, the annual month-long opera extravaganza in Finland. "Do you think I'll be able to get tickets?" he asked her.

Taina knew the festival was probably already sold out. But she gave him a phone number where he could book tickets and she recommended a modest but cozy hotel, The Anna, where she herself had stayed many times. She also gave him the telephone number of her stepbrother, who is also an opera lover, as well as the phone numbers of two actor friends. He told her he was planning to go to Estonia, which you can get to by hovercraft from Finland.

The minute Karen Kain and Ross Petty got home from the cruise, they called Brian and Zane and invited them over for dinner. "It was a horrible dinner," Karen recalls with a shudder. "A *horrible* dinner. In all the years I had known him, thirty-something years, I had never seen Zane that angry and aggressive and accusatory. To Brian. And Brian just kept looking at us, looking like 'what have I done??'

"Now, we *know* Brian. We know how difficult he could be. But the kind of accusations that were coming up were about selling the house, and ruining their lives, and how they were supposed to be travelling, and how they were not. And I said, 'Zane, we were part of the conversation before you sold the house, and you both agreed.' And he said, 'No, I was forced into it, it's always what Brian wants.' It was really difficult. The *anger!* . . . I knew it wasn't a well person. I think I asked him if he got help after we had talked that day, and he said no, that he was coping 'just fine.'

"Brian was bewildered. They'd obviously been having these discussions, and he wasn't able to get anywhere with Zane. Zane hated the new condo. Zane was saying 'my life is ruined,' and talking like that.

"Brian still didn't tell us what was happening, the diagnosis, the chemotherapy. Later he regretted that. He thought maybe it was too hard for Zane to be the only one with that information, not knowing where to put it, not knowing what to do with it. And Zane used to go to the library and google everything. I'm sure he went and looked up what was wrong with Brian, and when you are diagnosed with non-Hodgkin's Lymphoma you only have a 50 per cent chance of survival. Zane would have read this."

Even a glance at Google would have told him that treatment options for non-Hodgkin's lymphoma, a cancer with a high mortality rate, ran the gamut from "watchful waiting" in the earliest stage of the disease to high-dose chemotherapy with stem cell transplantation for patients who fail to respond to standard treatment.

☆

Gail and I had been trying to get together with Brian and Zane for dinner, just the four of us, before Zane left for Helsinki. But as usual my calendar was the culprit. So I had left a message a few days earlier for them, saying we'd get together as soon as Zane returned from Finland.

Neither Gail nor I were home when Zane returned my call, so he left a voicemail message, saying goodbye. At the time we thought, well, wasn't it nice of Zane to call, because usually Brian and I would make the arrangements for dinner, or sometimes Brian and Gail would. But seldom if ever did Zane contact us directly, unless he was calling to thank us for a personal gift.

We didn't realize he was really and truly calling to say goodbye.

As Brian most frequently accompanied Zane on European sojourns, I wondered why he had taken a pass on Helsinki. I didn't know, of course, that he was about to start his second round of chemotherapy treatments. The first round had been blissfully uneventful. He would return home in the late afternoon from St. Michael's hospital and fall into bed exhausted, too spent to even get up for dinner. He would sleep through the entire night, and awake rested, if not refreshed, the following morning. He experienced no hair loss, no major loss of appetite, no major physical discomfort. His physician, Dr. Rashida Haq, was so pleased with his progress that she teased him – he was now her Poster Boy for Chemo, she told him. So as much as Brian wanted to travel to Finland with Zane – especially after Taina pulled a few strings to secure sold-out concert tickets – he had to put first things first. And his priority, above all others, was to rid himself of this insidious cancer.

Brian told Allan Harris that he and Zane had "a little tiff" the night before Zane left. The next day, as Zane was on his way out the door, Brian stopped him. "Come back here!" he commanded. "I want to give you something before you go." And he gave Zane a big hug before he walked out. Later Brian told Harris, "I'll be forever grateful that I did that."

Zane flew to Helsinki. He was sixty-seven years old, just four months shy of his sixty-eighth birthday. He managed to get a ticket for the opera he had been longing to see, and with the same cast as the recording he loved so much. He didn't stay at The Anna. The hotel he chose was quite different. Not homey. Not cozy. Expensive. He never called Taina Elg's stepbrother. He did call her actor friends. Oh yes, they said, Taina told us that you were coming, we must meet for drinks, or maybe lunch. Zane was gracious, and appreciative, and expressed interest in meeting them, and never called them back.

On Monday morning, July 29, 2002, a chambermaid found Zane in a chair, sitting lifelessly at a desk in his hotel room. He'd consumed a

fair amount of Scotch, taken some pills that he had conveniently prescribed for himself, and put a plastic bag over his head, securing it firmly
at the neck.

He had left a note on the desk for the management of the hotel, in
which he apologized for tarnishing "your beautiful city" with his inhos-
pitable act. He asked that his personal effects, still in his suitcase, be
shipped to a Brian Linehan in Toronto, Canada, and provided the appropriate mailing address. He also asked to be cremated, and that his ashes be
disposed of. There need be no concern, he noted, that he would be missed.

"Nobody knows me," he wrote, and quietly, without any fuss or
fanfare, ended his life.

18

"You think you've got troubles?"

It was the long weekend in August, and Martha Watson was on the phone, chatting with her boss Kevin Hanson, the new owner of 5 Grenadier Heights. "Funny thing," said Hanson. "Interpol came by last night, looking for Brian."

Suddenly Watson put it together. "I knew Zane was in Helsinki. And I knew he'd done something to himself. I don't know why I did, because I wasn't that close to him. But Brian and I had been talking a lot about their fractious relationship. So I phoned Brian. Immediately. And he said, 'Zane has killed himself in Finland.'"

While Zane had been lying in the morgue in Helsinki, Brian had been getting on with his life. More bloodwork at St. Michael's hospital. Dinner with Julia and the Rev. Derwyn Shea. Back to St. Michael's, where his revered oncologist Dr. Haq had ordered a CT scan. And then came the calls from Interpol and the Department of Foreign Affairs.

Brian was in shock. So were his friends, who rallied around him with astonishing speed. Karen Kain and Ross Petty were among the first to arrive at the Islington condo. Then came Norma Rea (Brian's diminutive neighbour from Grenadier Heights), the Sheas, Marcia Martin, Ken Lindsay and Peter Husar, Gail and me, all of us trying to make some sense of it.

Michael Levine was on his way to London when he got the news, and he diverted his airport limousine to Islington so he could stop by to personally offer his sympathy and support. Less than an hour after he departed, Norman and Dixie Jewison, long-time Linehan fans, called to offer their condolences. A short time later, Jewison called again, this time from the home of our mutual friend Lynne St. David, who wanted to voice her concern for Brian as well.

Brian was touched by Norman's calls, but he was unhappy that word was getting out so quickly, and started to sulk. "How many people could Michael call before he got on the plane?" he sniffed. "Fifty? . . . Sixty?"

Martha Watson remembers driving out to the condo on Islington. "That's when he told us: 'I have non-Hodgkin's Lymphoma.' I didn't know what it was. And he said, 'I think that's part of the reason Zane did this. He didn't want to watch me die.'"

Taina Elg was immediately pressed into long-distance service to extract information from tight-lipped Finnish authorities. "The police wouldn't give any information over the telephone, of course," she remembers. "At the beginning we couldn't even find out what hotel Zane had stayed at!" Norma Rea was already manning the phones in the condo, telling anyone who asked that Zane died of heart failure, because Brian didn't want anyone to know. When Harriet Blacker asked what caused it, Norma Rea advised her that an autopsy was in the works.

But those friends who knew the truth were mostly stunned by the news. Carole Shelley was sympathetic to Zane's condition, because she herself had gone through a bout of chemical depression that turned into clinical depression. "It *is* terrible, and it *is* overwhelming," the actress told me later. But, she said, "if you have someone who says I love you, I'll help you get through this, that's got to be a bonus."

"Zane I always thought would be more . . . *chivalrous*," said Marilyn Lightstone softly. "It was just so out of character. And such a cruel way, too, not leaving any Goodbyes. But at that point I guess your own psychological needs override everything else."

"For Zane to have ended his life the way he did was shocking to me," Judi Schwam admits. "And obviously it was very well planned. But what was it? Was it selling the house? Was it Brian being ill and Zane not wanting to deal with it? Zane never struck me as being that weak. And, of course, we'll never, ever know."

Everyone speculated about what had pushed Zane to do it. "The combination of losing the house he loved and the garden he loved, along with Brian being diagnosed with an incurable and terrifying disease, and being an insomniac – all of those conditions just plunged Zane into a black hole," said Karen Kain. Sharon Gless said that Zane "was never part of Brian's and my relationship. Brian used to tell me how Zane was never quite the same after they moved because there wasn't any garden. And he told me that Zane was depressed and that he never liked the place where they moved. But still, even with that information, I was stunned when I heard what had happened to him. It was so shocking, so horrible. And of course we were all going around hating Zane. Hating him."

To Brian's friends, it was the ultimate betrayal. Brian had been keeping his cancer a secret. Zane had been keeping a secret too, but not the one Brian thought he was keeping. "To leave Brian like that was not an act of love," Carole Shelley said pointedly. "When you love someone, you put your own problems aside for a little while."

In the weeks to come, Brian would discover books from the Hemlock Society, the world's leading advocates of assisted suicide, in Zane's bedroom. He would also discover that over the preceding months Zane had quietly but efficiently transferred bank accounts and other financial holdings to his name. News of this dashed any gently harboured hopes that Zane's suicide could even remotely be construed as impulsive.

"Zane cared," says Joan Rivers simply. "Zane left everything in very good shape. And Zane left everything as if it was planned for a year."

"I don't think he was 100 per cent sure," says Karen Kain. "He had made some appointments over there. He had given himself options. So who knows? I said to Brian, how did he know how to do this? How did he know to put the bag over his head? But of course he had done his research."

Brian, she says, wondered at one point if there was more to the malignant mole than Zane had told him. "So he asked Zane's doctor, and Zane's doctor told him that there was no medical reason for Zane to take his own life." No medical reason, indeed. It seemed reason, or at least Zane's senses, had somehow gone AWOL.

Shirley Lord believes that Zane must have felt "somewhat overshadowed" by Brian. "As I understand it, the reason for his tragic end was because he couldn't face Brian's illness. That's what I was told. And Brian more or less confirmed that.

"It was a terrible thing for Zane to do to him," adds Shirley. "Do you think it was sort of getting his own back after years of feeling neglected?"

After Zane's death, Ken Lindsay and Peter Husar found themselves spending hour after hour at the Islington condo. Ken still suspects that Zane was trying to connect with people before he left "to make sure that we connected with Brian more."

"It was like Zane's blessing," says Peter. "It was as if he was saying to Brian, Spend some time with these guys because I'm not going to be here. Somebody to look after him, in the west end, because we lived close, only a ten-minute drive away. And we were also gay."

Derwyn and Julia Shea were constantly at Brian's side during those days. Finnish authorities were insisting that an autopsy be conducted in Helsinki before Zane's remains or personal belongings could be returned to Brian, and Derwyn was doing whatever he could to help cut through the red tape and bring Zane back to Canada. More than a week after Zane had killed himself, the police report arrived. Not a pretty picture. It would take more weeks to untie the red tape to bring Zane back to Brian.

Joan Rivers was calling every day. When she flew in to Toronto to spend the weekend pitching her jewellery and her cosmetics on The Shopping Channel, she urged Brian, "Come back to New York with me!"

"I can't, I can't!" he wept. "I can't leave now."

On Tuesday, August 20, the body of Zane Robert Wagman was released from the morgue in Helsinki and, as per his wishes, cremated in the city where he had ended his life. On Friday, August 23, the Rev. Derwyn Shea brought his ashes to the condo in Little Somalia. Derwyn offered a prayer. Brian stayed alone in the condo that night, and made a note in his ledger: *Home with Zane.*

On Sunday, he flew to New York, into the waiting arms of Joan Rivers. She installed him in the guest apartment she keeps for visits from her daughter, Melissa, and instructed her live-in couple, Kevin and Debbie, to see to his every need. Joan was glad he had accepted her invitation, but she was taken aback by his reaction to his situation. "We're all going to get a death sentence," she says philosophically. "But Brian couldn't even say it. In my kitchen that morning, he was so upset. His eyes filled up with tears: 'I've got cancer.' And you know me, right away it's yeah, so, who are you seeing? What are we doing? How many doctors are you going to go to? Because it doesn't mean you don't have at least another chance. Maybe you've got ten more years.

"Then it changed, then he went into the flip side: 'Hey, this is fine, I'm licking it, no problem.' But this was his first telling, and he couldn't talk about it without crying.

"I'd be just the opposite. I'd be making seventeen jokes. But the fact that he couldn't deal with the mortality issue upset me terribly. Because I always thought of him as very smart, as very in control of a situation, very on top of everything. Mr. Smooth. And to see him become so vulnerable about that was a shock. A total shock. Because when he said he had cancer, he had cancer the Emotion, not just cancer the Disease."

In New York, Brian had lunch with Taina and Rocco, and dinner with Arlene and Mark, and even saw a couple of shows – a revival of *The Boys from Syracuse* and a new production of *All Over* with Rosemary Harris and Michael Learned. But even Broadway failed to buoy his spirits. "From now on," he told me, "I only want to see *happy* plays. Comedies, and musicals."

He flew home four days later, hoping to find Zane's effects waiting for him, hoping he would find a message, a personal note of some kind, tucked away in a shirt cuff or a blazer pocket. But Zane's belongings had still not arrived.

On September 3, 2002 – Brian's fifty-ninth birthday – he received a call from Rev. Derwyn Shea. Zane's suitcase had just been delivered from the airport. In the suitcase, Brian found familiar pieces of clothing, toiletries, and an expensive book he had given Zane as a bon voyage gift. There was no personal note. There were no hidden messages. There were no messages at all.

Two days later, Brian made a note of the fact that he was spending a rather significant anniversary alone. With the exception of their one ill-conceived separation, Brian Linehan and Zane Wagman had been "roommates" for thirty-five years.

"It had been so wonderful when people started being able to share their life with them, the two of them," says Lorraine Wilson wistfully. "Zane was a really beautiful man, and I think he was the balance for Brian. They were just two souls that supported each other through this journey of life. I think that was probably the most important connection they had."

Brian was experiencing a terrible and shocking loss. Friends formed a tight inner circle, a ring of protection, around him. They brought him food and drink, and made sure his larder was spectacularly well stocked with salmon and vodka and all manner of prepared delicacies from Pusateri's and other high-end grocers. Long-time neighbours from Grenadier Heights like Norma Rea and the Sheas; old friends like Brian's retired doctor Michel Kady and his wife, Elizabeth, Michael Levine's ex-wife, Carol Cowan Levine; new friends like Ken Lindsay and Peter Husar; we were all at his beck and call.

Having survived some serious health issues herself, Julia Shea was a constant source of comfort to him. She filled his fridge with easy-to-heat pasta dishes and easy-to-eat salads, and stayed with him for hours to talk him through his pain. Karen Kain and Ross Petty would coax him out of the condo for dinner. Marcia Martin, by now a vice president at Citytv, would bring dinner and Citytv alumni Jane Fairley, Sue Gravelle, and Barb Murchie to his condo. Jane Fairley promised Brian some homemade food – just not made in *her* home. "Brian," she adds, eyes twinkling, "*loved* having 'staff'!" After the others left, Marcia Martin would sometimes stay overnight in Zane's room so Brian would not be alone in the morning when he woke up. Shirley Lord was on the phone constantly to him. "He was just a wreck."

Brian loved it, and appreciated it. It was not the first time in his life he had enjoyed being the centre of attention, but it was, perhaps, the first time in his life when so much sympathetic attention was being lavished on him by people he respected and admired and who clearly sought nothing from him in return.

He still didn't drive a car, of course. And there he was, stuck in Little Somalia. So whenever we could, the inner circle arranged to pick him up and drive him wherever he needed to go. Myrna and Jack Daniels arranged for a taxi to pick him up and deliver him to St. Michael's hospital for his appointment with Dr. Haq and his subsequent chemotherapy treatments.

Martha Watson also arrived to support him. When she first saw the nondescript apartment-tower exterior of the condo on Islington, she shuddered. "No wonder Zane got low," she told me. "To go from Grenadier Heights to *that* . . ." When she knocked on the door, Brian opened it himself. "And I thought, *my God, you're in your pajamas*! . . . and my God, aren't they *nice!!*" He was emotionally strung out, but he hadn't lost his sense of style.

It was during one of those visits that she realized he "sort of" wanted to teach himself how to cook. He asked her what broiling was, and how to do very basic things. "Zane was the caregiver in their house," Martha says.

Brian had many visitors in those early days. Some had their chauffeurs cool their heels in the lobby while they spent time *en suite* with Brian. Rita McKay, one of several publicists who had become personal friends, came in from Windsor, Ontario, by train to spend a few days with him. Posey Chisholm Flick, in from New York for a visit, stopped by and tried to persuade him to avoid the oncoming winter. Wouldn't he prefer to visit with her in Acapulco instead?

Brian loved the notion, but was afraid to be so far away from St. Michael's hospital and Dr. Haq. He was trying to be cautious. He was also being practical. To him, Acapulco was a Mexican synonym for basking in the sun, which he was no longer allowed to do. He was touched by Posey's invitation, he told me, but he thought that it would be harder to go to Mexico and not go in the sun than to simply stay home.

The rest of us would come and go, but three women in particular – "my three angels," as he called them, recycling an old movie title – were constant and faithful and determined to see him through his darkest hours. Norma Rea showed up every day like clockwork, adroitly fielding phone calls from New York and L.A. when she realized he was in no condition to speak with anyone. So she apologized to Bea Arthur, and made excuses to Doris Roberts, and promised she would have Brian return their calls as soon as he was up to it.

Brian loved introducing Norma Rea to his friends, because most of them were familiar with Sally Field's Oscar-winning turn in the movie *Norma Rae*. Consequently, he always referred to Norma, in private and in public, by both her first and last name. The devoted Mrs. Rea was aware of this, and amused by it. Brian and Zane, she said, had been extremely supportive when her husband died, constantly inviting her to their home and bringing gifts to hers. As Norma saw it, it was now her turn to return their kindness. A woman with grown children who were married and living away from home, Norma was able to free most of her days to drive Brian on errands downtown and help him sort the paperwork necessary to complete Zane's taxes. Brian didn't know how to manage a household budget, or even pay bills; Zane had always seen to that. But in her earlier life, Norma had also been a bookkeeper, so Brian was relieved, and grateful, when she stepped in to assist him with her organizational skills.

Two more angels were constantly at his shoulder – his financial adviser Pauline Gurden and his long-time friend Maxine Quigley. Maxine was Michael Levine's trusted personal assistant at Goodman's, the Toronto law firm that was home base for Levine's stellar roster of entertainment clients. Pauline was there to hold (and guide) Brian's hand through a torturously difficult time, and Maxine was there to support him as a friend. They, too, kept him supplied with dinners, which he duly noted in his daily ledger (*Dinner: Pauline's Chicken Casserole*).

In September, the Toronto film festival rolled in like thunder, but Brian was in no condition emotionally to roll with it. He even took a pass on attending George Christy's annual star-sprinkled Saturday sit-down luncheon at the Four Seasons.

The previous year Ronni Chasen had chaperoned Kevin Kline for his film *My Life As a House*. She invited Brian to the premiere, "and Kevin Kline came up to him and said, 'Why aren't you on my junket schedule?' Brian said, 'Because I'm semi-retired and I don't do this any more.' And Kevin said, 'Brian, you were the only intelligent person I ever talked to on these junkets!' And I think Brian was pretty happy about that."

Ronni had returned to the festival with a new movie, a taut thriller with Colin Farrell and Kiefer Sutherland called *Phone Booth*. She knew Zane had died, and she was confident she could persuade Brian to join her for a quiet dinner. "But I couldn't get him to come out of the house," she recalls, her voice tinged with sadness. "I called every single day and I called and I called and I called. I just couldn't get hold of him."

In the weeks and months that followed, Brian showed little inclination to keep a "stiff upper lip." If anything, he found himself more inclined to tears than ever before. He was aware of it, too, and often wondered aloud how he had any tears left after such copious weeping. But he was beyond embarrassment. As much as these emotional outpourings disturbed him, he was frankly fascinated by this new phenomenon in his life.

"I just CAN'T STOP CRYING!" he wailed over the telephone one day. "And I simply DON'T UNDERSTAND it. Where are these tears coming from? Where is all the water coming from? I should be completely dehydrated by the end of the day. But I'm NOT!"

He would often get up in the middle of the night, having given up on getting any sleep, and do laundry. Soon he found he was running out of laundry to do, and resorted to rewashing dishtowels and garments of Zane's.

Joan Rivers had given him some sage advice: Don't take down all the pictures of Zane, don't try to erase him. She herself had placed a picture of Edgar in a prominent position, so she could see him every time she entered the room and tell him what a bastard he was for abandoning her and Melissa. So Brian took her advice, and soon he was having nightly conversations with Zane, often weepy, frequently angry, mostly unforgiving.

"After Zane died," Ken Lindsay recalls, "our whole relationship with Brian changed. When he was at Islington, we started really connecting with him. We would just drop by and bring dinner. Or we would cook it at his house."

"He would get the bar all set up," Peter Husar remembers, "so when we arrived he'd go 'Mr. Husar, you can do the honours.' And then he'd add, 'I can only have one.' It changed at the end. But it still became a ritual even when he couldn't drink. He got out the pâté, and the almonds of course. And the cashews. And the Balderson cheese. And he set out the glasses and the accoutrements for the bar. The lemon zester and the lemons and the napkins.

"When we started making those dinners, we would just do pasta and rapini and cheese and that would be it. We wouldn't stay for long. He wouldn't come to our place so much, because it was easier for us to come to him, because we drove."

"If he came to our place," adds Ken, "it was a big deal. And he dressed up, always. Soon after Zane died, he came to our house with Virginia, and that was a very upsetting time, because he was very sad and he cried at the table."

Sharon Gless was in Florida, on hiatus from shooting *Queer As Folk* in Toronto, when she learned that Zane had killed himself. She called Brian as soon as she got back and invited him over to her condo at the Colonnade. "We went to dinner, and he told me the story. Brian wept very easily about what happened. And I'm thinking, it's very amazing and very healthy, 'cause most men won't do it."

Two months later, Gless invited Brian to meet her producer husband Barney Rosenzweig (of *Cagney & Lacey* fame). "We invited him for cocktails, and he was so pleased to meet Barney, and he knew all about him, of course! And he sat and told me and Barney the story again, and wept very freely." Once again she was moved by his openness. "Maybe I'm naive," she says, looking back on those evenings they spent together. "Or maybe he was just at a time in his life where he would tell anyone, and weep freely, with anyone who would listen."

Shirley MacLaine interrupted one of his crying jags by telephoning to see if she could connect Brian with Zane. "Shirley wasn't planning to attempt it herself," Brian later reported. "She had a spiritualist on the line with her, this person who specialized in communicating with the recently deceased." He thanked her for her call but tearfully informed her that he was not interested in communicating with Zane through a medium. (When Shirley told me about this later, I suggested, gently, that Brian was probably under too much emotional duress at that time to consider it. To which Shirley suggested, gently, that perhaps the Widow Linehan was enjoying his grief too much to consider it. "Face it, George," she added with a throaty chuckle, "your friend was quite the drama queen.")

Brian whined and complained about Shirley's call to him for the next three weeks.

"But," adds Martha Watson, who had a unique history with both of them, "I think in a way he was touched that she made any gesture at all."

He answered the phone only when he felt like it. When he didn't, calls would ring through to the answering machine, and a warm if slightly formal request to please leave a message. Still, the message frequently caught unsuspecting callers off guard, because the deep masculine voice delivering it was Zane's.

"It may be time to do something about that," I told Brian.

"I know, I know," he would say with a sigh. "I keep meaning to do a new recording. But it's the only thing I have left of him. And every time I go to erase it . . ." And the floodgates would open again.

The unfamiliar medication he was taking wasn't helping his daily routine. On top of his chemo sessions he was now taking Ativan and Xanax for panic attacks, Zoloft for his depression, Ambien to help him sleep. For years he had chastised Zane for taking too many pills; now he was the one who was popping them, even if it was on doctor's orders, and that troubled him.

He was also upset by the fact that the side effects of the medications he was taking made it impossible for him to get an erection. "I've had a terrible sex life," he complained somewhat tearfully one night. We were sitting in his elegant living room, having drinks and appetizers. Julia Shea reached over and patted his hand consolingly. "*Everyone* has a terrible sex life, Brian," she assured him. "Everything else is fiction."

A number of people I'd met over the years claimed to have had romantic liaisons with Brian Linehan. One man, the handsome lover of a New York film director, had a few too many beers one night and confessed that he had had a "thing" with Brian in his youth. Another mutual friend, a discreetly gay Hollywood publicist, told me that he and Brian had enjoyed a mild "flirtation." Brian, he said, was eager to take it to the next level, but the publicist begged off, explaining that having a sexual fling, however brief, could put them both in a compromising position. "It's an old Hollywood rule," the publicist added with a shrug: "You don't shit where you eat."

If Brian had been involved in any extra-curricular kissing, he certainly hadn't been telling. Zane's death seemed to free him of any real or imagined restraints. It was as if someone had turned off his sensors, or his censors, or both. That night, as we sat in the living room of his condo, he claimed that his most memorable sexual encounters had in fact taken place in Hollywood, with a pool boy at the Beverly Hilton hotel and with one of the muscular masseurs at the Beverly Wilshire hotel.

The incident at the Beverly Hilton hotel, he said, occurred when we were both there on a junket. Naturally, we had both requested Lanai rooms by the pool; naturally, we both got them. According to Brian, he had just left the pool area after a serene day of sunning and was back in his room when he heard a gentle knock at the sliding glass door that opened onto the pool deck. There was the handsome pool boy, looking like he'd just walked out of the pages of *GQ*, smiling back at him.

"Is there anything I can do for you, Mr. Linehan?" the pool boy inquired seductively.

"What did you have in mind?" replied Mr. Linehan, with a teasing Mae West delivery.

What the pool boy had in mind, apparently, was to kneel at Mr. Linehan's feet – a stress-relieving gesture Mr. Linehan gratefully accepted. On two consecutive afternoons.

"Don't you remember him?" Brian asked me. "You were wearing that Adidas wristwatch, you were wearing it in the water, even when you were diving, and he admired it." Brian could remember a watch I was wearing, and I couldn't even remember the pool boy. Then again, all he had offered me was a towel.

The other sexual incident, he said, occurred when he was enjoying a massage at the Beverly Wilshire hotel – enjoying it a bit more than he intended to, because when it was time to roll over onto his back, he realized the handsome, muscular hotel masseur had obviously rubbed him the right way. At which point another mouth organ concert ensued.

Listening to him tell of these misadventures in Hollywood made me suspect that at the time they were probably more traumatic for him than he was letting on. We both knew certain producers who took great pains to keep their private lives away from public scrutiny; I also knew that more than one of them had set their sexual sights on Brian. What I didn't know was if any of them had been successful. Then again, what I didn't know was never my business in the first place. So I didn't ask. And Brian didn't tell.

I knew that Brian had been very frustrated by the lack of a physical relationship with Zane. But Zane was gone now, and Brian was suddenly Gay. Not flamboyantly gay, not overtly gay, but openly gay, which was nonetheless a persona new to most of us. In the presence of his inner circle, he frequently referred to himself as the Widow Linehan. When we met Toronto film festival VIP wrangler David Vella for lunch to discuss the possibility of doing an on-stage one-on-one interview with Brian to celebrate the gift of his archives, Brian made at least two passes at the young executive before we ordered coffee. When he started flirting with Vella, I was sure he was just kidding around. By the end of lunch, I knew better. He was declaring himself.

That he had waited until Zane was no longer in the picture should not have been as much of a surprise to me as it was. In public, Zane was always very reluctant to display any kind of affection that could be considered homoerotic. It was years before he felt comfortable enough with me to respond to the gentle bear hugs I gave him – the same hugs I reserved for Brian, my two sons, and a few buddies.

One of our long-time L.A. pals, publicist Stuart Fink, also noticed the change in Brian after Zane's death. "He was very secretive," says Stuart. "Until Zane's suicide. And until he started getting ill. And then he let his guard down. I think at that point he was so needy that he'd stopped thinking about being protective, and that one thing overruled the other."

Ken Lindsay and Peter Husar were acutely sensitive to the fact that although Zane had seemed to be genuinely fond of them, he had not wished to discuss the fact that they were gay. "Zane didn't like to talk about that. Or recognize it. Or . . . anything," says Peter Husar. "Zane had this kind of homophobia . . . about being a gay man," adds Ken Lindsay, "but they still had tons and tons of gay books. Books on gays in film. Books on gays, period. There was one amazing, amazing book. It was very broad-based – about coming out, about being accepted, about how to live your life as a gay person. Lots of how-to. A self-help kind of book for gay men."

Peter Husar remembers another book called *Sexual Deviancy*. "I kept thinking that that one probably was Zane's. Like he felt that he was a deviant or something. Brian said Zane felt very bad about himself in that way and he could never discuss it."

"Brian was having conversations with us," Peter recalls, "very frank discussions with us, up at Islington. One friend of his, an actor, supplied him with a bunch of porn. Eventually he got quite a collection."

One day, Brian told Ken he had run out of gay porn videos and wanted to get some new ones. He was reluctant, however, to actually purchase any himself. "He said, 'Mr. Lindsay, people know me. I can't just go in and buy porn.'

"Peter and I had never bought porn," Ken adds, with a helpless shrug. "I phoned Peter and I said, all right, I'm going to the store on Church Street. And so I went and I got some, but I didn't know what I should get for him, so I bought kind of cheap stuff. It was VHS, and we put it in a gift bag and gave it to him."

Brian loved it. "'Why, thank you, Mr. Lindsay. Just perfect. I'll watch it this evening.' God, we laughed our heads off at that! And that's what he needed. He needed to have some laughs."

"And he would give us stuff. Like magazines," says Ken, rolling his eyes. "I remember we had that whole big briefcase of magazines. I gave them to another friend.

"We wouldn't tell Brian," he adds with a grin. "We'd go, oh thanks, Brian!"

"He loved to give things," adds Peter, nodding. "Whenever we left his house, we always left with a big bag, but often it was gay-related. Like we were collectors or something. 'Well if it's gay, give it to Ken and Peter and they'll take it.' But we always found a home for it anyway.

"Every time we came to visit, somehow he'd screwed up his VCR and the connections, or the electricity had gone off, and he wasn't able to watch his porn for about three weeks. And so that would be the first thing he would ask us to do, while we were having cocktails."

"He had this one friend," says Ken, "an actor, who said, whenever I'm in Toronto, I always call this one hooker, a guy, like a call boy. And Brian, you can do the same thing. It's discreet. It costs a little money but he'll come and give you a massage or whatever and he'll have sex with you. And it's wonderful. And so Brian would say, well, it kind of interests me but I would never do that. Never, ever, ever do it. And so we were convinced he never did."

Ken also suspects Brian would resist the idea of paying someone to have sex with him. "I think he thought, 'Well, I'm not going to spend money for that. I certainly can get it for free somewhere.' But it was also that he was scared," he adds. "Because these people can be real freaks too."

☆

That winter, Carole Shelley was starring in a new Broadway production of *Cabaret*, restaged at one of our old haunts, Studio 54. She would only have one day off for Christmas, but she was determined to make the most of it. "Brian, you're coming for Christmas," she announced. "And we're not going to have turkey, we're going to have English roast leg of lamb, and it's just going to be yummy."

Brian protested. He wasn't sure he was up to it, physically or emotionally.

"You're not going to stay in Toronto for Christmas; you're coming to New York," she insisted. "And make some other dates to see people, because I'm in the show every night."

He booked a flight, reserved a modest hotel room, and celebrated Christmas in New York with Carole Shelley. It was, if she does say so herself, "an absolutely gorgeous dinner. We practically ate an entire leg of lamb by ourselves. And drank. He said, 'I can't believe this is your one night off and you're cooking for me.' And I said, well, I can't think of who I'd rather do it for more."

Carole had just learned that she had won her much-coveted role in *Wicked*. "So I bought him the book and put a card in it: *Will you be my date for opening night in New York?* And he was so delighted by that!"

What was most significant about the evening they spent together, she says, was what they talked about. "Which was, *everything*. We had stopped fretting about certain things and just decided that life is for living to the fullest that you could, at any given time, without any excuses. And you didn't have to put up with anything. It was so wonderful, so cathartic. We talked about cancer. I had been through cancer. I had breast cancer. Brian was going through cancer. And it was good for us to talk and share and say we were afraid out loud to each other.

"We talked about how it was important to have fun, too. He told me how he came out of the hospital after some bad news and walked down one of the big streets in Toronto, Yonge Street, and saw a coat in the window that cost half a year's rent, and went in and bought it.

"'Good for you!' I said.

"'But I don't really need it,' he said.

"'We don't need to worry about that,' I said. 'You wanted it, you look wonderful in it, so it was worth it.'

"He got very worried after Zane died. He got cautious. And I'd never known him to be cautious. Certainly not that cautious.

"He said to me as we parted, 'I am so glad you made me do this!' And later, when he got back to Toronto he called me and told me, again, how thankful he was."

He spent Christmas Day in New York with friends. On Boxing Day, he went to the theatre again, this time to see *Imaginary Friends* at the Barrymore. Barry Avrich was in town, and had called him earlier in the day to tell him that Phil Kosoy wanted to take them to dinner. A charismatic, high-rolling Canadian real estate entrepreneur, Phil Kosoy had met Brian on a number of occasions, and they had spent more than one enjoyable evening together in Hollywood. When Brian and Barry were in L.A. shooting *Glitter Palace*, Avrich recalls, "Phil called from Singapore, then showed up the next day in L.A. He took Brian and me to dinner at The Palm and we drank all night. It was outrageous."

Phil Kosoy, adds Avrich, is not an easy man to impress. "But he adored Brian. He just loved his talent.

"So now we're in New York, and we're going to have a late dinner," Barry recalls. "Brian had gone to the theatre first. And Phil gets the Côte Basque to stay open past 10:00 p.m., so that we can have the restaurant to ourselves, because Brian is still a bit shaky.

"So we go to Côte Basque and we start to get into the wine. And the one thing with Brian, no matter what particular hell he is going through, no matter how depressed he might be, his appetite remains insatiable. Unbelievable. He eats and eats and eats.

"And Phil says to him, 'So what's going on?'

"And Brian says, 'Oh, Phil, it's awful. I've lost Zane and I can't seem to figure my way out of this hell.' And he starts to cry. It's this awful, horrible moment.

"And Phil says, 'You think *you've* got troubles? That's nothing! Yesterday, I went to order a new Bentley and they can't get the colour I want!'

"Brian is stunned. He stares at Kosoy. 'What?' he says, in total shock and disbelief. 'What did you say?'

"And of course Phil doesn't stop there.

"'So now I'm going to spend $250,000 on a fucking car and I can't get Midnight Blue!' says Phil. 'And *you're* fucking complaining??'

"Brian stares at him again, wide-eyed. He can't believe his ears. 'What?'

"And Phil pounds the table with his fist.

"'GET ON WITH YOUR LIFE!' he tells Brian. 'You're a GENIUS, for Christ's sake! Stop being a fucking IDIOT! The guy is

DEAD. He's DEAD, he's DEAD, he's DEAD, he's DEAD!' – all the while banging the table like a maniac. And Brian just burst out laughing. Maybe for the first time in months."

Brian Linehan flew home from New York, turned on his answering machine, and erased Zane's message. It was time to start living again.

"Some people are born to listen."

t was a new year, and a chance for new beginnings. At the end of January 2003, Brian Linehan was in studio at CBC, taping his host/interviewer bits for a late-night movie series to promote the Genie Awards. Brian was back in his element, barely perspiring under the lights and the make-up – and interviewing some of his favourite people, including Genie nominees Sheila McCarthy and Mark McKinney. Yes, things were looking up. He wasn't hosting the Genies this year but, thanks to his still-loyal fans at the Academy – Maria Topalovich and producers Steve Sloan and Susan Edwards – he would get to walk out on stage, as elegant as ever, to present the biggest award of the night, Best Motion Picture, to Denys Arcand's *Les invasions barbares*. It was a welcome diversion.

After spending six months dwelling on Zane's death, Brian now wanted to find a way to celebrate Zane's life. He found it by arranging to donate Zane's eccentrically eclectic collection of classical music recordings to Hart House, the arts and recreation refuge of the University of Toronto where Zane had maintained his membership until the day he died. The collection consisted primarily of recordings of traditional classical repertoire, stopping more or less at Schoenberg, with lots of Deutsche Grammophon recordings – Wagner, Mozart, Berlioz, Tchaikovsky, Debussy, Prokofiev, Mussorgsky. Brian had to have meetings, and review Zane's collection, and make sure that Hart House would reciprocate by installing a plaque in Zane's honour. He now had something to think about besides himself.

His Hart House connection was facilities manager Chris Lea, a bright young man enlisted to take charge of the Linehan donation ("primarily because I had a car," says Lea with an easy grin). His self-deprecating sense of humour endeared him to Brian immediately, and Lea made several treks out to Islington to meet with him and discuss plans for showcasing Zane's collection. One day, while driving Brian downtown, Lea shyly confided that he was the nephew of one of CBC Television's top singing stars in the 1950s, Shirley Harmer.

"You mean to tell me that Shirley Harmer is your aunt?!" Brian exclaimed. "Is that really true?"

"Yes," Lea admitted, "it's true."

"Well, Chris," said Brian, beaming, "I liked you well enough before, but I like you *much more* now!"

Working on the gift of Zane's record collection was not as good as a paying job, but it was an assignment Brian was happy to take on. And Zane's friends and admirers were touched and delighted when they heard what Brian was doing. "I was so pleased that he gave Zane's record collection to Hart House," Taina Elg told me. "I don't think that Zane had any such idea. It was entirely Brian!"

Meanwhile, Brian was still looking for paying gigs, and Barry Avrich kept trying to come up with things they could do together. The larkish short he had created with Brian and a cluster of five-year-olds played again and again on the pay-TV Movie Network, and Brian told Barry that people still stopped him on the street to compliment him on it. When Avrich was hired to do a very expensive birthday video for a wealthy couple in Palm Beach, he was torn. Should he call Brian? He knew the gig was beneath him. And so did Brian.

"I felt awful calling him," Avrich admitted. "But he was just so hungry for work that we ended up doing it.

"I had this idea where I would use the opening of *60 Minutes* and it would be like a *60 Minutes* special . . . 'I'm Mike Wallace,' 'I'm Diane Sawyer,' 'I'm Harry Reasoner,' and then it would cut to Brian with the *60 Minutes* clock behind him going, 'And I'm Brian Linehan. Tonight: Mary Smith. Who is she? And how did she get here?' . . . He would narrate the piece. And we sat there in the studio and he said, 'What am I doing here?'" He needed to make money. He just didn't want to make it this way.

Avrich said, "Brian, here's the cheque." Brian put it in his pocket and did the narration.

Avrich had several other projects, all of them more appropriate, that he wanted to do with Brian. One was a profile of writer Dominick

Dunne, a personal friend of Brian's. When Brian was sidelined by chemotherapy treatments, Avrich ended up conducting the interview himself. As something of a consolation prize, Avrich decided to fly Brian to New York for the first screening of his film on Dunne, *Guilty Pleasure: The Extraordinary World of Dominick Dunne*. Avrich booked a room at the Royalton for Brian, but after he checked in, Brian returned to the lobby looking somewhat preoccupied.

"Is everything okay?" inquired Avrich.

"Wellllll," said Brian, "I broke a window putting the key in the door. It's a small room."

"All right," said Avrich, "what can we do to fix that?"

A gentleman walked by in a nice suit and Brian said, "And your name is . . . ?"

"My name is *Jesus*," the young man replied with a Spanish accent. Turns out that *Jesus* was the assistant manager of the hotel.

"Well, *Jesus*," said Brian, "I can't get out of bed without hitting my head."

"Well, of course," Avrich recalls, "they moved him to a suite bigger than any of our suites. And of course they billed me for that giant suite. And what was I going to say?"

Brian had a wonderful evening, he says, "and we had a wonderful screening. His buddy Nick Dunne was there, and Shirley Lord was there, and we had a wonderful dinner with Pamela Wallin at Joe Allen's after the screening. It was just a great night."

Brian seemed to be getting some of his energy back. He started making plans. He wanted to move out of Little Somalia, but he didn't want to go back to High Park. He wanted to live downtown, at some location where he could walk to a grocery store, a drug store, the subway, and, ideally, St. Michael's hospital, where he was now a frequent visitor. His cancer was taking up far more of his life than he had originally anticipated. It was, quite naturally, the item highest on his priority list, and he would not rest, figuratively nor literally, until he had rid himself of it.

Our mutual friend Ronni Chasen felt he was typical of many cancer victims. "Once you get a life-threatening, devastating illness like cancer," she says, "then your whole life becomes about cancer, and about surviving the cancer, and getting rid of the cancer, and dealing with the cancer. . . . It's an awful situation."

Brian's former assistant, Lorraine Wilson, knew all about dealing with cancer. Her husband, Mark, had unwillingly left her a young widow, with young children to raise, when his colon cancer metastasized to his brain. She had stayed around the clock in his hospital room, to comfort him and calm him. "I left one night for an hour or so, to go home and check on the children, and my girlfriend stayed in the room with Mark. She left, just for a few minutes, to get a newspaper, and he chose to die at that point."

Lorraine was devastated. But she carried on. Quitting was never an option. Brian called her every now and then, to check up on her. And after Zane died, her friendship with Brian grew even stronger. "After Zane died, he would ask me, how do you get through this time? When is the grief going to end? When is the pain going to stop? We would talk on the phone probably every Sunday. There were times when he had to get through the dark night of the soul, *many* times, as a result of losing Zane. But at the same time he was going through his cancer.

"Brian was so mad that he couldn't be with Zane in the final time of his life, before he left. And he *knew* how pissed off I was that I couldn't be with Mark when he died. He and I would always say, 'Selfish bastards! . . . how *dare* they do that!'"

☆

Sylvia Frank and her crack team at the Toronto International Film Festival Group reference library finally completed cataloguing the archive Brian had donated to them just before he and Zane moved to the Islington condo. His archive was huge, and included more than 2,000 celebrity files, more than 600 books, almost 1,000 videotape cassettes, 350 audio recordings, and more than 10,000 photographs. Festival chiefs Piers Handling and Michele Maheux wanted to publicly acknowledge Brian's gift by staging an evening in his honour, for friends and festival gold patrons, where for a change he would be the one being interviewed.

Brian liked the idea, providing he could choose his interrogator. "We could have a lot of fun," he told me, "if you would do it."

"Yes," I agreed, "we absolutely could." We celebrated by letting Piers and Michele treat us to an extravagant March dinner at Bymark, Mark McEwan's blatantly upscale subterranean oasis in the Toronto-Dominion Centre. It was a wonderful evening, and we had a wonderful time. (Simone Signoret was wrong. Nostalgia *is* what it used to be.)

Brian returned to Good Life Fitness to resume his regimen, trying to work out a minimum of three times a week. He needed to be strong.

He was becoming acutely aware of people around him, in some cases people he had known for years, who were waging their own private wars with cancer. He had seen his friend Yvonne Silver at a funeral. "Yvonne was in a *wheelchair!*" he reported, obviously distressed. She, too, was fighting cancer, and appeared to be losing. "What is happening to all of us?" he sighed unhappily.

Sara Waxman, the widow of iconic Canadian actor Al Waxman, diligently kept Brian on her cocktail party list and her personal call list. When he told Sara he was looking for a new domicile downtown, she invited him to come to her new condo for drinks. Sara had moved from The Colonnade to a small, chic residence in the heart of Yorkville. It was a dream home, away from prying public eyes but within easy walking distance of everything else he could want, from Hugo Boss and Tiffany's to the Four Seasons and the subway. Furthermore, she had heard that one of the much-coveted two-bedroom condos that opened onto the roof garden and patio was about to become available. Up to that point Brian had been somewhat fixated on a condo near the Windsor Arms hotel, and had actually placed his name on the building's waiting list. But one look at Sara's building and its extraordinary location and he was sold. All he had to do now was figure out how to pay for it.

In the meantime, he was feeling "flirty" again. He liked the feeling, and he wanted to have fun with it, but he was also conflicted about it. He was dying to meet someone, to have a relationship, to have sexual contact. Especially sexual contact. "But," he allowed, "I'm kind of old to be doing this."

Pressed into service as his undercovers agents, Ken Lindsay and Peter Husar invited Brian to dinner in an attempt to set him up with two handsome single gay brothers whom Ken later dubbed "Niles" and "Frankenstein."

"When we were preparing dinner," says Peter, "I remember over-hearing Brian specifically asking them about their gay experience growing up, or coming to terms with it, and things like that, even to the point where he was asking about their sexual history. 'When did you do it? How old were you?' He was very, very interested."

"At the end," Ken recalls, "after the dinner party, Brian told us he wanted to have sex with one of them and live with the other."

"So he invited them both to the night he did the interview for the film festival," adds Peter.

Unofficial Linehan agents Michael Levine and Marcia Martin had also come up with something new for Brian. The working title was "Hollywood, Canada," and the concept was an unabashed homage to the phenomenally successful Heritage Minutes series that revitalizes significant flag-waving moments in Canadian history for Canadian television viewers. What Michael and Marcia were proposing was a series of Canadian-content minutes, each one devoted to a stellar Canadian screen star, written and narrated by Brian.

Brian loved the idea. He also loved the idea of working and getting paid. Marcia and Michael hired producer Mitch Gabourie to make it happen, and Brian started to meet with him.

Around that time, when the spring edition of the Hart House quarterly *HartBeat* was published, alumni learned that the Hart House Record Room "just got a lot more crowded." The headline for the full-page back-cover Coda read:

A music lover's dream collection fills the Hart House
Record Room, owing to the devotion of one man

"An extensive and valuable collection of classical music, which belonged to Dr. Zane Wagman – a dentist and a long-time Hart House member with a lifelong love of music – was donated to the Hart House Music Committee upon his death by his friend and life partner, the broadcaster Brian Linehan."

The article further stated that, according to Mr. Linehan, Dr. Wagman had passed away in Helsinki, attending a music festival. "He died in pursuit of his love of music," said Linehan.

Readers learned that it took fourteen large plastic blue boxes to bring the massive collection to Hart House, that the collection would be housed in a special display case honouring Dr. Wagman, and that Music Committee program adviser Zoe Dille was admittedly "overwhelmed" by the gift. But most of the page was devoted to a striking reproduction of Zane's graduation portrait and some intriguing quotes from Brian.

"I wanted Zane to be remembered for his passion, his knowledge, and his curiosity for music," he told interviewer Nicole Pointon. "The donation of the collection ensures that there will always be another Zane Wagman. That unique young person who will find something in Berlioz or Wagner. Some people are born to listen."

As summer approached, Brian's older sister Connie was about to turn sixty-five on June 4, and she didn't want any fuss made. "No surprise party!" she warned her husband, Danny, and daughter Lesley. Connie wanted to restrict the guest list for her birthday dinner to just the three of them, but Lesley was already in cahoots with her uncle Brian, and together they quietly conspired to make Connie's milestone more memorable. Brian telephoned Aunt Connie, his mother's sister, and invited her to join in a surprise dinner at his big sister's favourite local restaurant, the Black Forest Inn on Hamilton's King Street. Then he booked a limo and asked Norma Rea to be his date. The car arrived at 5:30 p.m., and he and Norma reached Hamilton before 7 p.m., giving them just enough time to hide themselves from sight in a booth at the back of the Black Forest Inn.

The birthday girl arrived with Danny and Lesley a few minutes later. When she suddenly saw Brian beaming back at her, her eyes welled up, and she started to cry. "Oh, don't you start that, you old broad!" said Brian, laughing. "C'mere and give me a hug!"

Connie wiped her tears and joined the laughter. She hadn't seen Brian for months. She was the only family member he ever talked to, and she could only imagine what he'd been going through. He had told her months earlier, of course, that Zane had died in Helsinki. Dropped dead, just like that. Heart attack. What a shock.

"This is one June 4 I'll never forget!" said Connie tearfully, clutching her brother's hand.

It was one June 4 Brian would never forget, either. Earlier that day he was getting his clothes in order, mapping out what he would wear to dinner and the drive to Hamilton, when his telephone rang. It was Yvonne Silver's daughter Karen, calling to tell him that her mother had died that morning. He thanked her for calling, took a moment to compose himself, and dressed for dinner.

"There is so much sadness in this world," he told me quietly one night. "So much pain that people hide from each other. *So* much. I don't think, until now, that I have truly been aware of it."

Later that month, we spent the day and evening together doing the George & Brian show. Like the York cinema and several other Toronto cinemas, the Capitol Fine Arts movie house on Yonge Street had been transformed into event space. The film festival group had rented the new Capitol Event Theatre for the occasion, replete with elegant bar and trayloads of tasty hot and cold hors d'oeuvres. Brian and I spent most of the afternoon hanging out backstage, discussing which stories I should prompt him to tell, and just getting the feel of the place. The reception was well underway by 7 p.m., and we were on stage by 8:15.

Brian told wonderful stories about Shelley Winters refusing to walk onto the set of *City Lights* on camera without a girdle, and delighted the capacity crowd with self-deprecating tales of his salad days at Citytv. At the end of our stint, the assembled audience gave Brian a standing ovation – we were here, after all, to celebrate the gift of his spectacular archives to the film festival reference library – and we were presented with large, matching Birks boxes, which we graciously accepted.

It seemed to me that the evening went off without a hitch. But of course at that time I didn't know about "Niles" and "Frankenstein," neither of whom showed up. "Brian felt really bad," says Ken. "Like he was rejected. 'Why wouldn't they at least be my friends? I've invited them to something kind of neat.' So it was a snub."

After a pleasantly brief meet-and-greet with some of the friends and fans who had showed up, we walked over to Centro, where I had reserved the private dining room for our post-show supper. Our son Joe, our daughter Alex, and our son Marc, all veterans of the Anthony–Linehan Road Show, joined Gail and me, Marc's wife, Linda Eales, and Joan and Dusty Cohl in more light-hearted toasts to the man of the hour.

Brian was having a great evening, and so was I. Neither one of us had had the presence of mind to actually open the Birks boxes we'd received on stage at the end of the show. I simply tucked mine away for safety in the trunk of Gail's car, where I promptly forgot about it. When I rediscovered it a few weeks later, I opened it and discovered a wonderfully candid, silver-framed photograph of the two of us, Brian and me, taken at the film festival in the early 1980s.

I called Brian, who confessed that his Birks box was still sitting unopened in the den. While I waited on the line, he found the box, opened it, and returned to the phone. "Isn't this great!" he said enthusiastically. "How clever of them, to do this!" He paused thoughtfully. "Tell me," he said, "were we *ever* this young?"

"Maybe once," I replied. "A long time ago."

☆

Joe Kertes was the dean of Humber College's burgeoning School of Creative and Performing Arts. An accomplished writer whose novel

Winter Tulips had earned him the Stephen Leacock Award for Humour, Joe was also the producer of *Distinguished Artists*, a series of live interviews with a literary bent, focused primarily on writers. Eleanor Wachtel, whose CBC Radio stints over the years had won her considerable acclaim and respect, acted as host of the series, interviewing her subjects on stage at the Ford Centre in North York. An edited version of these one-on-one sessions would later appear on TVOntario and on one of Moses Znaimer's Citytv spin-offs, *Book Television*.

Watching authors and interpreters of their work be interviewed on television by Eleanor Wachtel, a noted radio personality who was virtually unknown to most television viewers, was just too much for Brian to bear. Consequently, Joe Kertes was somewhat taken aback one day when he picked up the phone.

"Joe," said the voice on the other end of the line, "this is Brian Linehan. Why don't you have *me* hosting your *Distinguished Artists* series instead of Eleanor Wachtel?"

Kertes still marvels at Linehan's internal fortitude. "With Brian," he adds dryly, "there was no beating around the bush *whatsoever.*" There was, however, an opportunity to explore. Would Brian Linehan consider teaching a course in television at Humber College?

Yes, Brian Linehan would consider it.

Joe brought writer-producer Lorne Frohman into the mix. Frohman, an old pro who had successfully worked both sides of the border, coordinated the television courses for Kertes and was just as keen to bring Brian onto the faculty. Negotiations were conducted over dinners at Grano and lunches at Il Posticino, Oregano, and Sammy's. Good food was consumed. Great stories were told. Brian tried not to show it, but he was starting to get excited. Kertes and Frohman realized they might be getting even more in the bargain with Brian than they had originally hoped for. They knew he had great stories to tell, but only when they finally met with him, face to face, did they realize how much he needed to tell them.

They also soon realized that Brian took commitments of any kind very, very seriously. Kertes recalls one occasion when, due to an urgent business matter, they had to postpone a lunch meeting with Brian with only a few hours' notice. "He was *furious,*" Kertes remembers. "He'd rearranged his schedule to accommodate us, and he wasn't shy about letting us know it."

That summer, when Annie and Larry Heisey invited Brian to join Karen Kain and Ross Petty for a weekend at their Georgian Bay cottage, he hesitated. Up to now he'd always gone to the Heiseys' cottage with Zane. But then he thought about it, and realized that if he didn't go anywhere he'd once been with Zane, he would be pretty much housebound. He accepted Anne and Larry's invitation – gratefully and, he hoped, graciously – and enjoyed the summer days away from Little Somalia.

When he returned, he realized it was time to stop postponing the inevitable. It simply had to be done. He called the Rev. Derwyn Shea.

On Thursday, July 24, 2003, while Kevin Hanson and his family were away on a summer holiday, a small group of mourners – Brian, Julie and Derwyn, Michael Levine, Allan and Isaac, Karen and Ross, Maxine Quigley, Pauline Gurden, Carol and Allan, Elizabeth and Michel, Norma Rea, and some of the other neighbours – scattered Zane's ashes in the backyard that he had loved so much in life, almost a year to the day he had died.

He had never really wanted to leave, he'd said. And now Zane was back home, at last, in his beloved garden at 5 Grenadier Heights.

☆

In late August, on a wonderful warm evening, my son Marc and his wife, Linda, hosted a birthday dinner in my honour. Family only: me and Gail, Alex, Joe, and Brian. Brian gave me a wonderful birthday card with a touching personal message inside it, hand-written in his beautiful calligraphy. We sat out on the deck off their kitchen, savouring the sweet summer evening. We had agreed we would not overstay our welcome, but Marc kept opening more bottles of my favourite red wine, and Linda, a wonderful chef, kept bringing out more irresistible treats – artichoke hearts marinated in Spanish spices, succulent shrimps with an addictive aioli, a crisply refreshing salad, beautifully seasoned lamb, and a spectacular dessert, making the evening so festive that we could have stayed all night. And almost did. (Trust me: When your children leave a party before you do because it's "getting late," you should already be home in bed.)

When Gail finally announced that (a) we were leaving and that (b) *she* would be driving, Brian was delightfully tipsy. I was absolutely blotto, and snored most of the way to Islington. (Or so I was told – by two alarmingly reliable sources.) It was a wonderfully silly, giddy, happy evening, and Brian was obviously thrilled to be there with us, even though he had to report to St. Michael's the next morning for another series of tests.

"If they do any blood tests," I teased him, "they'll probably draw pure *vino nobile*."

On Brian's birthday a week later, he was sweetly swamped with calls from friends and well-wishers. That night, still ebullient from the flood of messages he'd received, he joined us for Dusty Cohl's annual pre-film festival dinner at Bistro 990. The guest list, as always, was as eclectic as it was exclusive. Regulars included Barry Avrich, Dianne Schwalm, veteran film programmer Hannah Fisher, and Toronto filmfest veteran Myrna Daniels. This year's "mystery guest" was *National Post* entertainment writer Barrett Hooper, but what made Dusty's dinner even more intriguing that night was that Brian was in one of his Not Speaking to Dianne modes, and Dianne wasn't about to play along.

"Brian was going through one of his spells," she remembers. "And Dusty, the consummate marriage broker, said we're going to do dinner, and it will be great, and you'll come and you'll see Brian.

"I remember coming to the dinner and Brian was very cool to me. I thought, oh, this is going to be a tough night. But, okay, sometimes you've just got to walk in and make it work. And we did. Because I fed the whole evening straight to Brian. Everything was about Brian. *Oh, you should ask Brian about that, he knows more than anyone about that.* And he slowly came around.

"He was curious about something that had come out on video or DVD. And I said, well, I'll see if I can get you one. And he said, 'Dianne, see if you can get me one. Because I have cancer, you know.' He kept saying 'because Dianne, you know, I have cancer.' It was just needle, needle, needle, all through dinner. And I would just say okay, all right. Because this was about making peace and fixing the situation."

Six nights later, he breezed into Spadina Gardens, a Chinese restaurant on Dundas Street, to attend Dusty Cohl's annual Floating Film Festival dinner. Buoyed by the presence of Rex Reed and other chums, he seemed bright and funny and strangely content. A few hours earlier, he had given his first class at Humber, and clearly he had enjoyed almost every minute of it. Lorne Frohman was there to greet him when he arrived, and to introduce him to his class of thirty students. "Good afternoon, ladies and gentlemen," he said, addressing them formally.

But the mischief-maker in him was begging for release, and in no time at all the students were hanging on his every word. They weren't just students to him; they were a brand new audience. And he intended to work very, very hard, just as hard as he had always worked, to please them.

As autumn came, Gemini Awards show producers Steve Sloan and Susan Edwards, both of whom had come to think of Brian as a mentor as well as a friend, hired him once again, this time to host *Countdown to the Geminis*, a one-hour TV special designed to generate audience awareness for the upcoming CBC telecast.

One of his interview subjects, chosen by the Academy and the producers, was Gemini nominee Rick Mercer, whose series *Made In Canada* – the same series that produced the script that Brian had so indignantly rejected years earlier – had dominated the 2002 awards race with a record fourteen nominations. So Brian finally got to work with Rick Mercer, not in the role that Mercer had created for him, but in the role he had created for himself – still the role he loved best – as host and celebrity interviewer Brian Linehan.

"We had a good time," Mercer told me later. "And Brian was very generous. He said he loved *Made In Canada*, and that he now regretted that he had turned us down, and that he hoped we would ask him again some day."

Meanwhile, despite limited opportunities, Brian still loved appearing on television. His publicist pal Rita McKay had come in from Windsor to keep him company in the Islington condo for a few days when Joan Rivers breezed in for a weekend. Rivers had come in earlier than usual, because Brian was supposed to guest with his friend Marilyn Denis on her popular *CityLine* morning show on Citytv, and Brian had invited Joan to come with him. Ken Lindsay gave Rita and Brian a ride to Citytv, where Norma Rea and Peter Husar were awaiting them. Joan Rivers arrived promptly, sparkled brilliantly with Brian on and off camera, and then swept elegantly into a white stretch limo.

For Marilyn Denis, it was a *very* good day at the office.

For Brian, it was a rare chance to show off Joan to his friends and to show off his friends to Joan. For Joan, it was a chance to do something else for Brian. She thought he was making progress, but not enough.

"I tried to make him angry, you know," she told me later. "I said, 'That son of a bitch, what he did to you! To find you have cancer, and then commit suicide!' I mean, the whole thing, the whole checking out, was so *unfair*. But I never felt Brian got that mad at him."

Two weeks later, Brian was back in New York. He stayed with Joan in her wonderful Manhattan palazzo on the East side. On Wednesday, October 29, he went to the Belasco Theatre with Arlene Dahl, Marc Rosen, and Rex Reed for the opening of *Six Dance Lessons in Six Weeks* with Polly Bergen and Mark Hamill. The next day, he rested; he wanted to be in good shape for his evening activities. On Thursday night he went to cheer his dear friend Carole Shelley as she opened in *Wicked* at the Gershwin Theatre. It was a glorious night for both of them. *Wicked* was a big show – a big bona fide Broadway musical – and if audience reaction that night was any indication, *Wicked* clearly had the makings of a hit.

Carole Shelley remembers it fondly. "It was a wonderful night," she says with a happy sigh. "Wonderful, wonderful. And that night, Brian was the giddiest I'd ever known him to be. He was jumping up and down, rushing to get me food, a glass of wine, a glass of water, anything. He was giddy. Because he loved glitzy openings, and because he was so happy for us, for me, for all of us *Wicked* ones!"

The next morning, he wanted to tell Joan Rivers all about it as they drove to her Connecticut retreat. He had her dog on his lap, and Joan was driving. "Tell me when we get out of the city," she instructed him. "If we start talking now, I'll forget where I'm supposed to turn and we'll be driving around for days!"

After they arrived, Joan took him on a tour of the garden.

"Zane would have loved this so much," said Brian, fighting back tears.

"Why don't we plant some rosebushes for Zane?" said Joan, putting her arm in his.

"Zane would love that," he replied.

"Yes," said Joan, "but would *you* like it?"

"Yes," said Brian. "I would love it too."

The next morning, Joan arranged for Brian to meet with the woman who managed the gardens, so he could choose the roses he wanted.

Joan still remembers his first visit to Connecticut. "Brian came to the country, my country house, impeccably dressed. And when I'm in the country, I don't even wear makeup. Which is the scary part," she adds with a throaty chuckle. "He got up the next morning and he came out in the full regalia. And then it was always the turtleneck and the jacket. I mean, there are days when I don't even get dressed. But even in the most countrified of country, in the kitchen, he's got the blazer on."

He was still wearing it when he returned to Manhattan around noon. He had a ticket to see a matinee performance of *Take Me Out*, a new play at the Walter Kerr about a gay baseball player, and that night he was going to the Imperial Theatre to see Hugh Jackman play our friend Peter Allen in *The Boy From Oz*. By the time he boarded the American Airlines jet to Toronto the next morning, he was ready for a few days of peace and quiet. He was surprised at how tired he had gotten, but he didn't regret a minute of it.

Little more than a week later, he guest-hosted a Toronto film festival event, a screening of Billy Wilder's classic *Sunset Boulevard*, which over the years had become a route to immortality for one of Brian's most glamorous fans, the late, great Gloria Swanson. The evening was one of the festival's private Film Club events, held in appreciation of their patrons and donors. On this occasion, the screening was held at the Goethe Institute, and was followed by cocktails, dinner, and conversation back at Toronto International Film Festival Group headquarters. The main dish on the menu was Brian Linehan, who had agreed to comment on the film and share some of his interview clips, and personal memories, of Ms. Swanson.

Brian was in his element, of course, and did not hesitate to use his wicked humour to get laughs. But during the Q&A, sitting in a chair facing festival guests sipping coffee at their tables, he was a touch too wicked for at least one festival patron. After one of his more scandalous responses, she rose to her feet to declare that she had not come to hear him trash celebrated and respected film icons.

Brian was stung by her comments. And, of course, he retaliated. He had been invited here by the TIFFG, he reminded her, to comment on the film and to bring his insights into Hollywood and the industry, and that was precisely what he was doing.

The offended patron stormed out of the room, a TIFFG executive quietly following in her wake. Brian tried to win back the small, intimate gathering, most of whom had clearly been enjoying his candid remarks before this unexpected interruption. He never quite got them back again, and despite his determination to rise above the incident, he felt he had been personally attacked, not so much for what he had said but for who he was – for simply being Brian Linehan.

TIFFG executive David Vella remembers the incident as "unfortunate" but not particularly significant. "We considered the evening a great success," he recalls, "and we had a meeting to discuss making an arrangement with Brian to host, say, four Film Club events each year."

Ken Lindsay and Peter Husar, who had attended the *Sunset Boulevard* event, gave Brian a ride home. "He got angry, of course, and told us what he thought of that woman," says Ken. "In really, really, *really* bad language," adds Peter.

When he woke up the next morning, Brian put the incident behind him. He couldn't spend time worrying about things like that. He was about to start a new future, in a new condo, a wonderful downtown condo in Sara Waxman's building. He was moving out on Zane's birthday, November 28, exactly two years from the day they moved in. Goodbye, Little Somalia. Hello, Yorkville!

Ken and Peter helped him with some of the packing, which was easier than they expected. A lot of stuff was still in the boxes from the move from Grenadier Heights.

It rained on November 28, and not a gentle rain. It was a deluge. Brian thought he was well-prepared, but he hadn't factored in weather. He had also neglected to book the loading dock at 164 Cumberland, because he didn't know you had to pre-book it. Zane would have known that. Brian did not. When the moving van arrived, there was no room for it. The movers drove the van around to Cumberland Street and started walking and wheeling Brian's belongings down the lane, in the rain, to the main entrance of 164.

In no time at all, the police arrived, and insisted that the driver move the van off Cumberland Street. "You can't park here," the cop insisted. "You're obstructing traffic!"

Between pleading his case with Metro's finest, and trying to reach the head of the condo's Board of Directors, *Financial Post* columnist Diane Francis, Brian became hysterical.

Finally, he reached Ms. Francis. "I'm moving in today," he wailed, "and there's no room for the moving van at the loading dock, and the police won't let them park on Cumberland!"

Ms. Francis, he later reported, was less than sympathetic.

It was going to be a long day.

"The whole thing was terribly upsetting for him," says Ken Lindsay. "It rained, it absolutely poured, it never stopped, and all these bad things happened."

When he finally got his clothes and furniture into the condo, he discovered that the previous owner had been somewhat casual about cleaning up the place before he left. "It was just hell," he told Ken and

Peter later that night. "I caught a cold from being outside in the rain so long. And when I got in my apartment, I cried. He left this place so dirty! I've been cleaning out the guest toilet for an hour, and I've been crying the whole time."

He stayed up cleaning until 11 p.m., and then, exhausted, he reached out to turn off the lights. Much to his surprise, the lights stayed on. He switched them on and off again. Nothing.

The previous tenant had apparently done some special electrical wiring that didn't quite meet the condo's construction code. Brian almost burned his hands, even when he wrapped them in a towel, but he finally managed to unscrew the light bulbs and fell into bed.

He woke up the next morning still shell-shocked by the trauma of the move. But the rain had stopped, and he was living in a beautiful condo in Yorkville. And he had plans.

For one thing, he wasn't going to wait so long to get his stuff unpacked and in drawers, in cupboards, up on the walls. For another, he was going to get rid of that godawful glass designer bar in the kitchen. "Brian took such pleasure in removing that glass bar," Peter Husar remembers. "It was a real designer thing, custom-made, worth thousands of dollars. Brian just said 'Garbage!' – and out it went." And he wasn't going to be isolated in the kitchen, either. He was going to knock a hole in the wall and put in a big pass-through window, so he could stay connected with his guests.

Slowly but surely, the condo at 164 Cumberland was coming together. He had a good layout to work with. You walked into a large living room lined with windows overlooking the pergola-strung terrace. The large, bright kitchen was close by, and next to it an attractive guest powder room with a large stall shower. The guest room and the master bedroom both opened onto the terrace, and the ensuite bathroom with walk-in closet was elegantly appointed. He was encouraged by the generous cupboard space, because still to come was the treasure stored in some of the unopened boxes in the guest room, next to Zane's bed and dresser: hundreds of snapshots of Brian with his friends, with his neighbours at Grenadier Heights, with Gail and me in Hawaii; scrapbooks of photos he'd taken on dozens of beach holidays. A photographic record of two young men, one very handsome, one very interesting-looking, leading the kind of Good Life you only read about in magazines.

Much of the correspondence Brian had received over the years had gone into his justifiably famous research files; it was all in his archives now, safely and securely housed in the TIFF reference library. But some correspondence was closer to his heart, and stayed closer to home. A still-unsorted box of letters and cards included Christmas cards from Arianna Huffington and a 1991 invitation from Arlette Brisson, addressed to both Brian and Zane, to a July luncheon in Connecticut to celebrate Joseph Josephson's new book, *Crossing the Rubicon*. Included is a frisky P.S. from Brisson's frisky PR assistant, Frisky Doubleday. "Please note that due to an especially tricky 'placement' for this luncheon – both Gore Vidal and Norman Mailer have said 'yes' – your early reply would be much appreciated. Thanks so much."

Susie and Keir Dullea had written a personal note on a flyer for the play she was directing at the Samuel Beckett Theater on W. 42nd St., sending "much love to you both. All best for '93."

Most of the playbills from the Broadway shows he attended ended up in his research files, but some programs he kept close at hand. One he treasured was from a memorable Manhattan event on May 14, 1979 – *Lerner and Loewe: A Very Special Evening*, at the Winter Garden Theatre. He loved basking in the reflected glory of stage artists with history, and this special evening was steeped in them: Julie Andrews, Kitty Carlisle, Agnes deMille, Alfred Drake, Douglas Fairbanks Jr., Rex Harrison, all company he aspired to.

Almost a decade after that night, Bea Arthur had invited him to escort her to the 1987 Tony Awards, and he still had the brochure for the seating arrangements at the supper ball that followed. The illustrious guest list was a virtual Who's Who of Broadway, and there he was, his name in the same program as George Abbott and James Nederlander and Cameron Mackintosh. The listing for his pal Carole Shelley was under the "S": *Shelley, Carole & guest*. There were quite a few like that. *Fosse, Bob & guest. Rivera, Chita & guest*. His date was listed under "A": *Arthur, Bea*, [table] 54. And he was listed under "L," in the same group as Angela Lansbury and Linda Lavin, between Mayor John Lindsay and John Lithgow: *Linehan, Brian*, [table] 54. He'd kept the menu, too.

Over the years, he had become good friends with two of his theatrical icons, Hume Cronyn and Jessica Tandy. He was thrilled when they personally invited him to attend the 1988 American Academy of Dramatic Arts tribute to them on the roof of the St. Regis hotel. He kept his Stratford Festival ticket stubs for Tandy's perform-ance of *Eve*, which he had attended almost twelve years earlier, tucked away in the same program.

Ah yes. There was still much to do, much to sort, much to organize. And he was up for it. Up for the challenge, up for the sheer Virgo delight of getting his house in order. He was sure his energy would come back. He would will it back, if he had to. He was a man of great self-discipline. He could do it. He could do anything, if he had to.

"Once he got it together he was so proud of that apartment," says Sharon Gless. "When he was having the chemo, he opened up a cupboard and said, 'Look at this! Either people give them to me or I buy them.' And it was loaded with candy bars, because they gave him energy."

So did his teaching stints at Humber College. Every Tuesday afternoon he showed up, without fail, to give his 2 p.m. class at the Lakeshore campus. He loved turning down Tuesday lunch invitations. He had somewhere to go, some place he absolutely had to be: a professional commitment.

"Some of his sessions would go three hours," says Joe Kertes.

And sometimes, just when you weren't expecting it, he would do That Linehan Thing.

"He saw me walking by one day," Kertes remembers, "and he dragged me into the class, and he said to his students, 'Do you know who this man is?' – and then proceeded to rhyme off all my credits, from my early beginnings to my Leacock win. Even *I* was amazed!"

Myrna Daniels believes that teaching at Humber "took a lot of the bitter edge off the last years for Brian. In many cases what Brian substituted for love was the adulation of his audience; it wasn't approval he worked for as much as affection. One of the things that hurt him when he lost his show was the fact that he couldn't get that reassurance. So he loved teaching his students at Humber College because, I think, it was the same kind of thing he was getting back again."

By mid-November, Brian had started showing tapes in class – classic Linehan interviews with Anthony Quinn, Joan Rivers, Rod Steiger. He wanted to do something special for his students before they went home for the holidays, so for his last class in December, he brought books from his personal library and gave them out as gifts. "Most of his students probably never knew how valuable some of those books were," adds Lorne Frohman. "Brian gave away some biographies that had been published *in the fifties!*"

The holidays were fast approaching. Brian decided to repeat his Christmas odyssey of 2002 and spend the festive season in New York. Gail and I thought it was a terrific idea. And this time we wouldn't have to check up on him to make sure he was having a good time. He called Carole Shelley and Arlette Brisson and a handful of other Manhattan chums and booked his flight on Air Canada for December 22.

On Wednesday, December 17, he wasn't feeling all that well. He cancelled his dinner engagement and stayed home instead.

On Thursday, December 18, he feared he was coming down with a cold. Maybe even flu. What a drag! He took a pass on attending a Citytv reception and bundled himself up at home. He was slated to leave for New York in four days and didn't want to fly with a cold. Well, not if he could help it.

On Friday, December 19, he did not feel any better and begged off a dinner date he had made earlier in the week. On Saturday, December 20, he ventured out, but only a block or two, to pick up the papers and some dinner at Pusateri's. Stayed home. Added the dessert that Maxine Quigley had made him.

Maxine's dessert seemed to have miraculous properties, because when he woke up on Sunday morning he felt almost fully recovered. He kept his dinner date with Sara Waxman that night. Not only was she the woman who had brought him to 164 Cumberland, Sara Waxman was also one of Toronto's most quoted restaurant critics, and frequently asked Brian to join her on some of her reviewing expeditions. When he hesitated, she would remind him that she was a widow now, that it was difficult for a woman to go to a restaurant alone, and that he'd really be helping her out if he agreed to be her escort that evening. But he knew she was really just trying to get him out of the house, back in circulation, and he loved her for it. So he went to dinner with Sara, and had a delightful evening.

It wasn't late when he got home, but he unexpectedly found himself too tired to pack, his energy melting away. On Monday morning, December 22, he called Air Canada and cancelled his flight to New York.

He spent the next week home alone, without telling his inner circle of friends – who, of course, were stunned when they finally learned the truth. Ken Lindsay remembers it as "the Christmas where Brian just kind of fell off the face of the earth. Nobody could get hold of him."

Brian thought he would be fine by December 29, the night he was supposed to have dinner with Virginia and David and Ken and Peter, to tell them all about his Christmas in New York. But he wasn't fine, and of course he had nothing to tell them, and he had to cancel.

When he asked Joe Kertes and Lorne Frohman to stop by, they assumed their visit was going to be social. Instead he told them that he couldn't continue teaching, that he was suffering from non-Hodgkins Lymphoma, and that he wasn't well enough to continue the classes. And then he told them about Zane and what had really happened, "and cried, and cried, and cried," says Kertes.

"It was a horrible day," Frohman remembers. "*Horrible.*" They had intended to spend only an hour with him at his new condo. But they felt they couldn't leave him in that state, so they stayed with him all day.

Brian was almost convinced that he would be back on his feet by New Year's Eve. After all, he was simply going to have a quiet dinner with Carol Cowan Levine and her husband, Allan Kaplan. No hats, no horns, no loud music, no physical exertion. But he was still too ill, and had to beg off, and went to bed long before 2004 officially began.

Happy New Year, Mr. Linehan. Let's hope there are better, brighter days just waiting in the wings.

20

"Am I ever going to live this down?"

fter New Year's, I waited for Brian to call, so we could hear all about his adventures in New York. As the days went by, I wondered if he'd decided to extend his stay. I phoned and left a voicemail message welcoming him home. A few days later, I called again. Still no response.

January 2004 was a cruel month. One of my very first mentors, Art Cole, a gruff but gentle giant of a man who had given me my first job at a newspaper, passed away after a ten-year bout with Alzheimer's. Two days later, Doug Creighton, who had founded the *Toronto Sun* and created auspicious new beginnings for me and so many other journalists, also left us. I waited until their funerals were behind me before I left another message for Brian.

On January 14 Maxine Quigley emailed me.

> George, I just wanted you to be aware that Brian L. is in hospital, St. Mike's. I know some of his friends are getting the word out and you may already know. He went for tests Tuesday and his doctor was very concerned about him; his spleen and liver are enlarged and his blood count is down. They've been doing tests today so he's very tired. He had a cold, he thought, all Christmas, and even cancelled out New York, so it turns out it was probably more than just a cold. He doesn't seem to want visitors just yet and has asked that calls be kept down, so perhaps tomorrow might be better to call him. I know he would want you to know if you don't already . . .

He had been admitted the day before. By the time we spoke, the racking cough he had developed over the holidays was subsiding. I was annoyed that he had let us all believe he had gone to New York when in fact he was home, and alone, choosing to wallow in self-pity rather than be with friends who loved him. But I forgot about that as soon as I heard his voice. When I called him in his hospital room, he was just as outrageous and funny as always. Very soon he was holding court again, receiving visitors and enjoying every minute of it.

Sharon Gless was among those who had stopped by to laugh with him. "When he lived uptown," she recalls, "I used to have my assistant deliver what I called 'bread droppings' – he loved the fancy bread from Holt Renfrew's that they have shipped in from Europe." Because the nursing staff didn't want flowers sucking up all the oxygen in Brian's room, friends and visitors were asked not to send him any. So Gless sent him "balloon droppings" – a cluster of helium-filled balloons tied to a small bag of pebbles that provided just enough weight to anchor them.

The phone by his bed seemed to be in overdrive much of the time. My son Marc had phoned him, my son Joseph had come to see him on a lunch break, and he had already had a telephone chat with David Vella, director of development for the Toronto International Film Festival, who had been the point person for our Show-and-Tell interview session six months earlier.

We knew Brian was on the mend, however, when he started reviewing the hospital menu, which was clearly not up to his standards. When Karen Kain and Ross Petty stopped for a bite at The Senator (a renowned Toronto diner) on their way to visit Brian, they alerted Senator owner Bobby Sniderman and his psychiatrist wife, Dr. Marlee Sniderman, that Brian's admiration and affection for the staff at St. Mike's did not necessarily extend to the hospital's "chefs." Upon hearing this, Marlee promptly brought him a care package containing one of his favourite soups, and then brought him culinary treats every day for the next two weeks.

The parade of visitors continued, and he loved all the attention. But he was going through what seemed to be an endless battery of tests, and after twenty minutes or so you could sense the weariness beneath his smiling facade. When Stuart Fink phoned, Brian told him that their telephone conversation would be his "extravagance" for the day.

By January 24, Brian was home again, fortified by a couple of blood transfusions to counteract his low blood count. He expected to get the results of various tests by the end of the month, and planned to resume his weekly teaching stint at Humber College as soon as his strength returned.

"I haven't heard from Joan," he said one morning, matter-of-factly, but I knew he was feeling vulnerable. Joan Rivers had not called him in some time.

"I think she may be working overseas," I said. "In London."

"Perhaps," he said.

"You know how she loves to work," I added. "She loves to be busy."

"It's all right," he said. "You don't have to say any more. It was very generous of her to invite me to stay with her in New York, and she's been very generous with her time. But she's moved on."

"Brian, honestly," I said softly, "I think she's just really, really busy . . ."

"It's all right," he said. "It's fine."

"Brian," I began, "Joan has been wonderful to you –"

"Yes," he agreed, "Joan has been wonderful."

We changed the subject.

On January 29, Brian learned that his test results were so far "better than expected," and his doctor was expressing a "positive" outlook. He was resting up for more tests, and eager to start the new, stronger chemo treatments Dr. Haq had prescribed. When the doctor said she didn't want him to unduly exert himself going back and forth to his condo every day, he checked back into St. Mike's.

This time he found the chemo more exhausting than ever. And this time there were side effects. "My bowels have been bound for days!" he complained to Gail. He told her that his upper body strength had gone, and the muscles in his shoulders, upper arms, and chest seemed to have disappeared.

"He did look smaller to me," she reported after seeing him. She was more concerned about his ongoing physical discomfort. The medications he was taking had resulted in severe constipation. His abdomen was bloated, his belly slightly distended, and he grew increasingly uncomfortable. To give him some relief, Dr. Haq prescribed diuretics, suppositories, stool softeners. But nothing happened.

"Just because you're in the hospital doesn't mean you can't go for a walk," Dr. Haq reminded him.

"I walk around the floor three or four times a day!" he protested.

"No, I mean outside," she explained. "Go for a walk outside. Get some fresh air. It might do you some good!"

The thought of getting some fresh air cheered him considerably. "All right," he agreed, "I will."

He wanted his walk to have a destination. As he was weary of hand washing the few pairs of socks and undershorts he had brought with him to the hospital, he would walk over to The Bay department store at Queen and Yonge to pick up a few more. It was a cold, brilliantly sunny winter day. He put on his wool Hugo Boss slacks, a warm Italian turtleneck, wool socks, and his good Gucci loafers, bundled himself up in his coat, scarf, gloves, and cap, and walked the two city blocks to The Bay.

The store was busy; there was a sale on. When he found the socks and the shorts he wanted, they too were on sale. Bonus. He had gone for a walk. He was getting fresh air. He had just found two items he actually needed, and both of them were on sale. He was genuinely pleased with himself. All in all, he was having a very good day.

He lined up to pay for his socks and shorts; there were only two or three people ahead of him at the cash. He felt a slight rumbling in his abdomen. For a moment he was encouraged, and wondered if he should stop at the men's room on the next floor. But then the rumbling stopped.

Brian was now first in line. The sales clerk took his credit card and was about to ring in the sale when his phone rang. The clerk stopped to answer it. Brian's stomach started to gurgle and rumble audibly, loud enough that people in line behind him could hear it too. He could feel things moving inside him. He thought he had stopped believing in God, but suddenly he was having second thoughts.

Oh God no, not now, not here! he prayed. *Just let me get back to St. Michael's.*

The sales clerk, holding his credit card, continued to talk to the person on the other end of the line. Brian tried to tell him that he was in a hurry, but the clerk kept talking. Brian's rumblings grew louder and louder. He wasn't sure where the men's room was, but he knew something was about to happen.

He felt a twinge, and suddenly felt a hot liquid-like substance inside his Hugo Boss wool slacks, starting to trickle down the back of his legs. He grabbed his credit card out of the clerk's hand and bolted for the exit, pulling his cap down over his eyebrows, desperately hoping no one would recognize him. As he went through the doors he could see that he was leaving a trail behind him, a thin brown line that seemed to be coming from the top of his loafers.

Please, God, please let me get back to my room, please!

His feet were starting to squish in his shoes. Humiliated and terminally embarrassed, he walked as quickly as he could along Queen Street, all the while leaving a trail behind him. He left a trail as he entered the hospital, even though he was still trying valiantly to hold everything in. He ignored the stares of visitors who were busily disinfecting their hands in the lobby. Taking the stairs was unthinkable. He pressed the button for the elevator. He left another trail in the elevator. The trail followed him all the way to his room.

I made it, I made it! he told himself, triumphantly. But when he opened the door to his bathroom, his bowels refused to hold on even one second longer, and he exploded all over the floor.

He spent the next hour cleaning up what he could. His shorts and socks were beyond salvation. He tried to wash out his Hugo Boss slacks and clean up his Gucci loafers, but adding soapy water to the sticky mix didn't help. A nurse tapped lightly on his door and sauntered in to check on him. "How was your walk, Brian?" Then she saw the floor, and gasped.

Brian wiped his hot tears away just long enough to ask her to take his clothes and burn them. She put him to bed and told him she would take care of everything. She wrapped his slacks and shoes in a large plastic bag and told him she would put them in a freezer somewhere until they figured out what to do with them. She called for the cleaning staff. When she learned there were no cleaners available, she rolled up her sleeves and cleaned everything up herself. By now he was more embarrassed than ever.

"You just need to get some rest," she assured him. She raised the back of the bed to the position he liked best. "Are you feeling any better?" she asked.

"Well," he replied, with a sardonic shrug, "I don't feel bloated any more . . ."

☆

Joan Rivers called me to check up on Brian. She was coming to Toronto to do one of her marathon weekend gigs on The Shopping Channel, and wanted to see him. She'd left messages for him at home, but he still hadn't responded. I told her he was back in St. Mike's.

He called me almost as soon as he got off the phone with her, excited and happy. "Joan called!" he reported gleefully. "She's coming to see me!"

On Friday, February 13, Joan Rivers pulled up to St. Michael's in a long white stretch limousine and sailed up to the second floor. The nurses saw her coming from a mile away. "Brian," said the voice on the intercom in his room, "you have a visitor." He was still in bed when Rivers swept into his room. "Oh *this* is nice," she said sarcastically, greeting him with a kiss as she surveyed the scene.

"This is a private room!" he retorted in mock indignation. He was thrilled to see her.

"Of course it's *private!*" She rolled her eyes. "You couldn't get *two people* in here unless they took turns in the bed!" She laughed huskily. "C'mon, get dressed, we're getting out of here."

Brian's jaw dropped. "No, I can't."

"Of course you can."

"Joan, I don't have any clothes!!"

She opened the locker in his room and peered inside. Empty. She turned back to him, eyebrows raised. "How did you get here? Did they send an ambulance for you?"

"No!" He was indignant again. "I'm not *infirm!*"

"So how did you get here?"

"I took a taxi."

"So where are the clothes you wore when you took the taxi here?"

"Gone."

She slipped out of her coat and tossed it over a chair. "Gone where?"

He sighed. "I had a little . . . accident . . ."

She sat on the end of his bed. "Tell me."

He told her the story of his "fresh-air walk" to The Bay, and they both wept with laughter as he did. He was still upset by the incident, but he knew it made a great story.

Joan Rivers walked around his hospital room, taking it all in. She was not impressed. "That hospital was the bleakest place I had ever seen," she recalls. "I hated the room. There were no pictures on the walls. Nothing."

She reached for her coat. Brian's face fell. Was Joan leaving already? It seemed like she had arrived only minutes ago. And now –

"I want to see your new condo," said Joan. "C'mon, get dressed. You can wear your coat and scarf over your dressing gown and pajamas."

Twenty minutes later she had signed him out – "yes, I take full responsibility for him, yes, he will be exclusively in my care" – and suddenly they were ensconced in the white stretch limo that TSC provided for Rivers whenever she worked at the network.

"How often do you get to ride in a Pimp Mobile?" she teased Brian as they pulled up to his Cumberland Street residence. Once inside his condo he gave her the full tour, telling her how he planned to finish each of the rooms. She nodded encouragingly at each notion he proposed, and discussed decorating ideas with him. Brian was extremely appreciative; all of Joan's homes had been featured at one time or another in *Architectural Digest*, a magazine he and Zane absorbed with near-biblical fervour. And when Joan observed that his kitchen far outshone the kitchen in her exquisite New York apartment, he grinned like a kid who had just won first prize at the fair.

"I think one of the things that kept him going at the end," says Joan today, "was just deciding whether he should put the hole in the wall to the kitchen, or do this, or do that. And bringing me over there and looking it over, and figuring it out. It made him think it was a new life."

Before they left the condo Brian put some socks and underwear from his bureau into a gym bag, to bring back to the hospital. "I wonder if I should bring anything else," he mused aloud.

"Given your recent history," said Rivers, deadpan, "you might want to bring an extra pair of pants!"

On the way back to the hospital, Joan insisted they make two more stops. First stop was a bookstore. "I wanted to get him junk," says Rivers. "We went into the bookstore and he picked out a book on Europe right before World War I, and he picked out another book, again something that was so deep. And I said, look, we'll get you the *Enquirer*, I'll get you *Vogue*. Junk, junk, junk. But no. No, he didn't want junk. I said, get anything you want, we are not leaving this store until you get a couple of things to read in the hospital. And he came back with real tomes." Finally, he chose three new non-fiction bestsellers, which Joan quickly had them ring up at the cash register. Then they made their way to a confectioner's, where she bought several boxes of expensive candy and chocolates.

"Joan, that's sweet of you, but I'm not allowed to eat anything like that," said Brian wistfully.

"These are not for you," Joan replied, giving his hand an affectionate pat. "These are for the nurses."

☆

On February 14, Gail and I sailed away with Roger Ebert, Richard Corliss, Hannah Fisher, Barry Avrich, and Joan and Dusty Cohl on the eighth annual Floating Film Festival. It would be our third "floater" sans Linehan, but at least he was with us in high spirits. After sharing all the sordid details of his shopping expedition at The Bay with Gail, he gave her his blessing to tell the story to a handful of people on the cruise, especially Lori McGoran and Joan Cohl, the two women who he believed would fully appreciate the black humour at the core of the story.

On Friday, February 20, Brian was discharged from St. Michael's hospital. When the floating film festival docked in Tampa the next day, Gail flew home, but I remained in Florida for a few more days.

That Sunday, former *Globe and Mail* film critic Betty Lee, an old colleague of mine and an old friend of Brian's, conveyed her concern electronically. "I haven't seen him," she emailed, "but Julia Shea and his friend Norma Rea have reported to me that he has lost considerable weight and is quite weak."

He was scheduled to return to hospital on the Friday but was hoping Dr. Haq would allow him to go home after his treatment this time. He was lying low at his condo, trying to build up his strength, watching television in the evening. He said he was becoming addicted to Rick Mercer's new series, and he was especially enamoured by a risky new CBC drama, *This Is Wonderland*, written and created by one of his favourite playwrights, George F. Walker. His favourite Thursday-night show, he said, was still *Opening Night*, the weekly prime-time commercial-free two-hour arts performance program.

I called him the day I got home.

"You haven't seen me for a while," he said. "I've lost a lot of weight."

"How much?"

"A lot. And also –" he paused dramatically, "my hair is falling out."

He said he had gone back to his old barber, in his old neighbourhood. "And the look on that man's face when he saw me . . ." He let the rest of his sentence trail off. "I just told him," he said with a shrug, "I have cancer, and I'm doing chemotherapy, and my hair is falling out. So I want you to give me a very short cut, very close-shaved to the head, so the hair loss will be less noticeable. And he did."

It was official: Brian Linehan was no longer the Poster Boy for Chemo.

☆

Three days into March, I met Brian for a drink at his condo before we went out to dinner. As usual, CBC Radio was playing softly in the background; he turned it on in the morning as soon as he got up, and only turned it off, if he remembered, when he went to bed. He was wearing a stylishly baggy sweater to mask his weight loss. He proudly showed me the large window-like opening now carved out of the kitchen wall; he had designed it so he would never be out of sight (or earshot) of his guests.

He bundled up and we walked a few steps across the Renaissance Courtyard in front of his lobby for a single malt at Michelle's, an upscale "pub" for simple folk with complex bank accounts. "So this is your local!" I exclaimed. We slipped out of our coats, but Brian kept his scarf wrapped snugly around his neck. Very soon we were both in good spirits, literally and figuratively. His short buzz cut suited him, and he was starting to tolerate the new chemotherapy very well. He was, he said, eating like a horse, trying to gain back some of the weight he'd lost during the last round of chemo. And he was getting a daily injection to boost his blood count and immune system. He was applying his professional discipline to his personal life, conserving his energy, and taking naps in the afternoon. But he was still voraciously reading all four Toronto papers, as well as the *New York Times*, every day.

We left the brasserie and crossed the street to one of our oldest haunts, Il Posto, re-christened Il Posto Nuovo by its new owners. We talked and gossiped. Michael Levine had taken him to dinner at Morton's, the high-end steakhouse franchise from L.A. It was Brian's kind of room – first-class service, fine food, a strong wine list, and absurdly high prices. All in all, the perfect place to dine on someone else's money. "Are the prices really outrageous?" I asked.

"TRULY outrageous," he assured me. "I've told Michael he can take me there once a week," he added mischievously.

He took a sip of his San Pellegrino mineral water. He told me that Joan Rivers had called, and that although he hadn't yet returned to teaching he had asked her if she would do a master class for his students at Humber College. Joan had agreed to do it, and An Evening With Joan Rivers at Humber College was now officially set for April 1.

"April Fool's Day? Perfect!" I said. "Did you pick the date?"

"No," he replied, laughing. "It was the only night Joan could do it."

While we chatted, I was cheered by his appetite. I watched him tuck away a sizeable Caesar salad, a generous serving of butternut squash risotto, and a glass of red wine – all, he assured me, with his doctor's blessings. Finally we got around to talking about Christmas.

Christmas was not a season that Brian cared for, not even remotely, and I didn't know why. Chums had secretly speculated that he didn't want to spend money on gifts, but he received so many gratis books and CDs that he had become a master at re-gifting. I suspected it was something from childhood or adolescence, some experience that had turned him off the Christmas experience. Then again, Zane was Jewish, and Brian might have decided to take a pass on Christmas out of respect for his feelings.

In any case, this past Christmas he had chosen to stay home alone, holed up in his Yorkville condo. I wanted to know why.

"I know I should have called . . ." He took another sip of red wine. "I just gave up. I thought, well, my life has turned to rat shit. I'm living in a beautiful place, but I'm still living in boxes. Zane has abandoned me. And I'm not getting any better. I - GIVE - UP."

He sighed. "I know it was wrong to do that," he said almost apologetically. "I just didn't think that I would have the strength to see it through. But I know that I do. I do have the strength to see it through. All I want to do now," he said, his voice ringing with conviction, "is get better. I want *to live!*"

I raised my wineglass in a toast. "To getting better," I said.

He raised his glass to mine, and smiled. "To getting better."

The next day I told mutual friends that Brian's attitude was very positive and that he seemed to be making some progress.

Stuart Fink was happy to receive the update. In future, he said, he would be more attentive. "I had actually been waiting, silly me, for his promise to get online, so I could share some of the spam I get. Is there any kind of sneaky way we could liberate him a bit from the past and push him, kicking and screaming, into the present? I know he'll love it once he's hooked up. Instant venting, that's Brian."

Brian had resisted technology all his life, often successfully. Years earlier I had coerced him into using a word processor to write his columns for the *Toronto Sun*. Most recently, I had tried to persuade him to get on e-mail, because I knew that just about everyone he wanted to correspond with already had e-mail addresses. Finally, I had resorted to using the research potential of the Internet as the bait, and he had agreed to give it a whirl once he moved into his new condo. He wanted my son Joseph to choose a simple laptop for him, install only those programs he would really need, and then give him simple step-by-step instructions on how to send e-mails and access the Internet.

None of this had happened, of course; nor was it, understandably, a high priority on his current to-do list.

Soon after our dinner, Brian invited Ken Lindsay and Peter Husar for drinks and told them that he'd had some bad news. "He said the cancer was back, and that it was Type 4 Aggressive. It was a horrible thing to hear," says Ken. "But at that point he still felt that it was not hopeless. He had been given some kind of indication from the doctor that it was still something that they could work on. You know, they're going to attack it with whatever process. And you know, it's Team Brian, and we're all rah, rah. But he cried, and it was horrible. We just tried to keep it together."

Most of Brian's chemo sessions that month were only a week apart. Almost every Friday would find him back in the cancer ward, sitting patiently for five hours as more poison was pumped into his bloodstream. If it was true, as he said, that he had long tired of performing at dinner parties, he had apparently stored up enough energy to entertain and amuse his fellow chemo patients with a weekly concert of outrageous comments, scandalous stories, and his trademark wicked wit. Soon patients who were in the process of booking future chemo sessions were asking their doctors if they could reserve a spot "on a day when Brian Linehan will be there."

His chemo sessions were therapeutic for Brian in more ways than he had originally anticipated. He told us of one young woman, the mother of a sunny-faced two-year-old, whose treatments didn't seem to be helping, and how after an hour or two he was finally able to make her laugh out loud. "So many people have so much pain in their lives," he observed, "but they still just go on about their business, getting through each day as best they can. And the rest of us are blissfully ignorant." He was learning some new life lessons. He was learning a new kind of compassion. He was learning that it was not all about him.

Back at the office, I had conveyed Brian's warm sentiments to Rick Mercer and the teams responsible for his other favourite shows. Roger Abbott and Don Ferguson sent him a warm *Air Farce* vest. Mercer and his partner, Gerald Lunz, sent him a knit hip-hop toque to keep his head warm. *Opening Night* delivered one of the special fleece tops it reserved for guest hosts, and *This Is Wonderland* executive producer Bernie

Zukerman sent Brian a show sweatshirt with a note: "Gather you're a fan. So are we. Enjoy the sweatshirt."

Brian was delighted.

Karen Kain had an idea. Toronto businessman and philanthropist Jim Pitblado had chaired the board of the National Ballet of Canada for seven years. He and his wife, Sandra, proud parents of four grown-up children, had become good friends of Karen and Ross. Karen knew that one of their sons, David Pitblado, had been battling non-Hodgkin's Lymphoma for several years, and was now in remission. At one time chair of Toronto Dance Theatre and one of its staunchest supporters, David now lived in London with his wife, who had recently given birth to twin boys. When the couple came home from Britain to spend the holidays with David's family, Karen asked him for a favour: Would he call her friend Brian Linehan and talk to him about his experience with the disease?

"Being the kind of person he was," says Karen, "David Pitblado did more than that. He went over to visit Brian, and they bonded over their mutual battle with the disease. When David went back to London, they faxed each other and phoned each other."

Brian was thrilled, and grateful to Karen for her friendship, her kindness, and her thoughtfulness. He was especially grateful, he told me, "for the privilege – and I use the word 'privilege' advisedly – of meeting someone so intelligent, so compassionate, so generous. He has a wife and twin baby boys and non-Hodgkin's Lymphoma, and I'm complaining?" He checked himself. "We'll have no more of that!"

Karen was pleased and touched by Brian's reaction. "David gave him hope," she says. "David was younger, and he had had it longer."

Other friends were still taking turns making sure Brian had more than enough food on hand at all times. Barbara Murchie, one of a clutch of Citytv alumni who had rallied to his side, was now his chief Guest Chef in Yorkville, and made dinners for him every week. "He was still in good shape and eating very well," she remembers. "He particularly liked Sausage Ragout, a sausage, tomato, red pepper, and pasta dish. I tried giving him just the sauce as he could cook the pasta fresh but he was having none of it. I quickly reverted to preparing the whole thing. He liked hearty peasant dishes mostly. Basque chicken went down well. He liked veal stew, too."

And he still loved going out for dinner, especially when the maitre d' and the waiters made a fuss over him, as they were inclined to do.

Sharon Gless was shooting *Queer As Folk*, wearing paint-brush lipstick and a curly flaming-red "fright wig" for her role as Debby, when she learned that she would be having a longer dinner break than usual. She called Brian. "Are you up for dinner? The only thing is," she warned him, "I'm in full drag. It takes hours to get into this gear, and I don't have time to take it off and put it on again." Brian was definitely up for dinner, especially if she was coming as Debby. He agreed to meet her at the Studio Café at the Four Seasons.

Before she left the set, Sharon called for her driver. "The driver Captain, and these guys are tough, came up to me and said, 'I know you're going to see Brian Linehan tonight. Would you please tell him from all the drivers how much we love him and have for all these years?' I was stunned. The impact that this man had, not just on show business and actors and actresses, but on everyone he met. He really cared, he really did give a shit. It wasn't an act."

Brian was waiting for her, beaming, at the Studio Café. Every head in the restaurant snapped to attention as they sailed in together arm in arm, and he loved every minute of it. "We had far too much fun, as usual," she remembers. "Brian walked me to the car, because he was a gentleman, and I introduced him to my driver, Al Izumi. On the way back to the studio, Al was very quiet, and I said, are you okay? And he said, 'Yeah.' But his mouth was funny, the way some men look when they're trying not to cry. I said, Al, what's wrong? Tell me! . . . He said, 'Meeting Brian Linehan. No one has ever listened to me the way he did. He let me talk without interrupting me. He made me feel like everything I said was so important. I'm not used to that.'"

☆

"Thank you for phoning me back!" Brian exclaimed one day when I returned his call.

"You sounded a bit stressed on the message you left me this morning," I said. "What's up?"

"Susan Edwards and her sister are on their way over to see me!"

I knew how fond Brian was of Susan, and how much he had

enjoyed working with her and Steve Sloan on the Genie Awards. "Brian, you love Susan!" I reminded him. "What's the problem?"

"Her sister," he announced forebodingly, "is a HEALER!!"

"A what?"

"You heard me. Her sister is a healer!!"

"Oh," I said. "Well, that should be interesting . . ."

"Yes, for you and Shirley MacLaine. But NOT for me!"

"Oh for God's sake!" I sighed wearily. "I'm sure it will be just fine."

"Oh sure," he agreed sarcastically. "it will be JUST FINE for you and Shirley, because YOU TWO WON'T BE HERE. Meanwhile, what AM I supposed to do with them?"

"Well," I said, "why don't you make them martinis?"

He paused, thoughtfully. "God, you're good!" he said with begrudging admiration. He paused again. "What if they don't WANT martinis?"

I could see him squirming at the other end of the line. "I don't want to hurt her feelings," he added. "But you know I don't believe in any of that bullshit!"

"Okay," I said. "First, it's not necessary to share that information as they walk in the door."

"You mean I should let them sit down first."

"I mean you should treat them the way you treat all your guests," I told him. "Be charming, be funny, be yourself. Tell them some movie-star stories. It's your condo. You don't have to be 'healed' if you don't want to be!"

"Thank you," said Brian. He was calmer now.

"But, Brian," I added, "be nice. . . . And call me the minute they leave, because I want to know everything!"

"I will," he promised.

Ken Lindsay and Peter Husar phoned Brian a few minutes later, to invite him to dinner.

"I'd love to," he told them, "but I can't, because I have this hocus-pocus thing happening this afternoon, and I don't know how long it will go."

Gillian Edwards had met Brian Linehan when she was the talent co-coordinator on the Genie Awards. She still remembers with great fondness the ovation he received when he walked on stage that night. An ordained spiritualist minister, Gillian had never mentioned that part of her life to him. But she's pretty sure someone did, "because at a rehearsal for one of the award shows, he made a joke, then looked at me and called me Shirley MacLaine," she says with a grin.

On this particular afternoon, Susan Edwards brought Gillian to Brian's condo in Yorkville. "The funny thing is, he talked, I swear, for about two hours, recounting his illness. I never asked. He just started. And he told us the whole story. In the course of that conversation, he talked a lot about the loss of Zane and the pain of the loss. And then he started talking about his illness and just what was going on then and the different series of things that had happened.

"Healing works in funny ways, you know," she says, smiling softly. "After he'd got that out, then we went to his room."

Gillian asked him if he would prefer to lie down or be seated. "I'll go lie down," he said.

After he was lying comfortably on top of the bed, Gillian told him, "Just listen to my voice. What we're going to do now is relax." Susan stood at the foot of his bed, and Gillian stood near the middle. "I said, we're going to lay our hands on you now. And we did just that. He settled down, and I talked him into a relaxed state, and then he drifted off as we worked on him. And I started to do the healing."

She had told him before they started that once he was relaxed, she and Susan would leave him alone. "So we did that. We put a little blankey over him, and we let ourselves out."

I called Brian the next day. "How many martinis did you guys drink?" I teased.

"It was absolutely weird," he reported. "I lay down on my bed, fully dressed, and Gillian and Susan held their hands above me, not even resting them on me, and I started to feel this incredible heat, building, building, surging through me –"

"Until you burst into flames?"

"No," he said quietly. "Until I woke up, four hours later, after a wonderful sleep."

"No kidding!"

I whistled softly. Even I was impressed. And I was already a believer.

"No kidding," he said quietly. "So I got up, locked the front door, had dinner, went back to bed, and had the best sleep I've had in months!"

"Gee," I ventured, as innocently as I could, "good thing Susan brought her sister along!"

He chuckled softly. "Am I ever going to live this down?" he asked. "Especially with you?"

"Probably not," I replied, trying not to laugh.

"I figured as much," he said, with a resigned sigh.

Three days later, Gillian Edwards called Brian at home. "Are you okay?" she asked. "How are you doing?"

"That was the most unique experience," he told her. He tried to articulate the experience, but found he couldn't. "Gillian," he asked, "what exactly did we do?"

"Well, Brian," she replied, "in a way, we just evoked the healing energy that's within all of us. And, really, that's tapping into your essence."

April started with a bang. Joan Rivers flew in from New York and made sure, for Brian's sake, that her master class at Humber College would be a night to remember. Comedy department chief Lorne Frohman personally conducted the interview. The amphitheatre was SRO (Standing Room Only) and Joan was funny, wise, and charming, winning still more fans when she took questions from the students at the end of the session. She received a tidal wave of applause when she arrived, and even more when she took her final bow. But the greatest ovation that night was reserved for visiting professor-on-leave Brian Linehan. When Frohman asked him to stand, so he could be acknowledged, the students from Linehan's class went crazy. Beautifully turned out in a classic Valentino suit that cleverly disguised his shrinking frame, Brian savoured the moment, grinned like a schoolboy, and sat down again, eyes glistening.

At the end of the session, we had a nightcap at a downtown bistro where the regulars seemed delightfully dumbfounded to see Rivers and Linehan in their local. The next morning, Joan, Brian, and I met for lunch at the Four Seasons, giving Studio Café patrons more to talk about. Brian was still flying high from the success of the previous evening.

"Those students obviously think the world of you," Joan told him, "so clearly you've managed to fool them so far!"

Brian beamed. Just seeing his students made him feel stronger.

He felt strong enough, in fact, to go back into the studio. "Hollywood, Canada," the idea hatched by Michael Levine and Marcia Martin to celebrate Canadian film stars, had evolved into a series of fifty one-minute profiles called *Screen Legends*. Brian was signed to write and voice them, and he was excited about it.

"He was ill, but he was sweet, he was generous, he was co-operative, he was having fun," Michael Levine remembers, smiling. "We used to have these incredibly amusing meetings. When we selected the first three subjects – Yvonne De Carlo, Marie Dressler, and Raymond Burr – Brian said, 'Perfect! A slut, a lesbian, and a homosexual, your typical Canadians!' We sat around with Marci, Patrick Watson, and Bruce Yaccato, and we had wonderful times. I have very happy memories of that."

So did Brian. But after he recorded the voice-over narration for the first three *Legends*, he was so drained of energy that he crawled into bed right after dinner. By the end of the month, he was spending most of the day in bed, too weak to do much of anything. The stronger chemo he'd been taking was not working; he now had lesions on his liver. His doctor wanted him to come back to the hospital on two consecutive days, for two more doses of even stronger chemo. Brian was uneasy. He wasn't sure how he'd react to it.

By now he had a regular caregiver who came to the condo every day to give him a much-needed injection. He continued to take anti-reflux pills so he could keep food down, but now there were also pills to counteract nausea in addition to the tranquilizers and anti-depressants – all anathema to him. Brian hated taking pills of any kind. "Ironically," he noted, "if Zane were here, he would have happily popped them all."

He tried to focus on making his condo beautiful, but told me in a quiet moment that he could no longer avoid thinking that where his future and his health were concerned, "it doesn't look good."

Before this latest setback, he had received dozens of solicitous phone calls. He was very touched by these displays of affection and despaired that he couldn't answer them all. But now the sheer volume of calls was overwhelming him. After Zane died, Gail and I brought Brian a new telephone, one with call display, so he could see who was phoning him and decide whether or not he wanted to answer. He loved it. "I only picked up the phone," he would say, "because I saw it was you." Gail shopped for greeting cards to make sure that he would start getting some positive mail on a daily basis, and we started leaving silent messages for him, which he could retrieve whenever he wanted to, without the phone ringing. But some calls he still wanted to take.

Marilyn Lightstone's was one of them. "The last number of years Brian and I talked a lot on the telephone," Marilyn recalls, "but he would rarely be up to seeing me. I got the feeling that he didn't want to get together physically, that he would prefer to talk on the phone. Even though it would be like a two-hour phone call."

He phoned Jane Hawtin, who was surprised to hear from him, and who was obviously concerned about him. "He really called to apologize," says Jane. "And his way of apology was to say, 'I wish that we'd never had cross words.' And I said, I do too. He cried and cried and cried. We talked for a couple of hours, and then we started communicating again."

Meanwhile, he was mad at Dianne Schwalm again. "You never call me and invite me to lunch," he whimpered.

Brian had picked a bad time. Dianne's husband had lost his job, she was trying to hold on to hers, and she was suddenly the breadwinner again. "I thought, I can't play that game," she says. "And if you're going to play that game, I don't have time. Get over yourself. So, I got mad. And . . . well, you know Brian. He shut the door."

He opened it a crack, briefly, when Dianne and Warner Bros. hosted an April 15 farewell send-off for her second-in-command, his friend Mary Sinclair.

"We talked on the phone at great length," Dianne recalls. "I said, I'll come by, pick you up, go have lunch, then we'll go down to Mary's party and I'll bring you home. 'Okay,' he said, 'great, sounds good.'"

The day before the party, he phoned her and said, "I don't think I can make it."

Dianne Schwalm sprang into action, just as she always did. "I said Brian, I'll come and get you myself; we'll just go to the party, we'll come in, we'll see people, you want to see people now, you want to say goodbye, you want to say hello, whatever you want, they need to see you, you need to see them," Dianne remembers. "And he started to cry on the phone. He said, 'I don't think I can do it.'

"I said OK, if you can't do it you can't do it. But don't decide today. Decide the morning of, and I'll have a car on hold. I will personally come and get you."

He even wrote it in his day book: *5 pm – Dianne Schwalm – Limo.*

Dianne arranged for a video shoot at his condo, so he could tape a message to Mary. I happened to stop by for a drink when the cameraman arrived, and Brian insisted that I tape a message for Mary as well. But when the time for the party rolled around, he couldn't handle it. He was finding it harder and harder to put up a front. "Every day he seemed to deteriorate a little bit more," Dianne Schwalm noted, much to her dismay.

Karen Kain was no stranger to cancer, or dying. She had learned most of what she learned about it in her mother's final days, at her bedside. But she was shocked when Brian told her about his unexpected visit with a so-called "angel of death." "Brian said this guy showed up, unannounced and unheralded, in cowboy boots, with a ponytail, and told him he'd come to help him get through it," Karen recalls. "He's apparently used by doctors and hospitals working in palliative care. And Brian was so offended and angry that he threw the guy out of his condo. And while he's doing this he says the guy is taunting him: 'You're going to need me, just you wait and see!'" Brian immediately reported this to Dr. Haq. "And I gather she was very unhappy about it."

Karen felt badly for Brian, but she was also struggling with her own reaction to the incident. "When Brian was telling me all this, I felt so conflicted," she admits. "Not only because I thought it was an awful thing for him to have to go through, but also because I knew he was in complete denial."

Shortly after that, Lorraine Wilson flew in from Vancouver to spend a few days with him at his condo. Brian had just been through two consecutive days of CHOP, a combination of the drugs Cyclophosphamide, Hydroxydaunorubicin, Vincristine, and Prednisolone designed to destroy non-Hodgkin's Lymphoma, and he was feeling weak and weary. Lorraine went out and brought back some dinner for both of them, but he wasn't able to eat all that much. They watched the 2004 Genie Awards together in his bedroom.

"I stayed until the Monday," she recalls, "and I remember that morning I woke up and he was very weak. He had a doctor's appointment at the hospital. They were going to go check his blood work. He was going to go on his own, and I said, no you're not, I'm coming with you! So of course he got dressed and he put on his coat and his scarf like he always did and his paperboy cashmere hat. He put on his dark glasses, and he was so thin at that time, and I said, oh you look so chic, look at you, you look just like a movie star!"

When the cab came, Brian asked the driver for his name. "Of course," adds Lorraine, "so Mr. Linehan could address him properly." At the hospital she sat in the waiting room while Brian was tested. "And after they checked him out, Dr. Haq said, 'You can't go home today, Brian. You're going to have to go through some more tests.' And he just started to cry. I was stunned, because I think he was spent at that time. He was exhausted. He really was. He had nothing left. And we knew at that point that he was terminal. It was only a matter of time."

21

"I hope he knows I loved him."

At his doctor's recommendation, Brian embarked on a marathon four-day chemotherapy session. At first he seemed to be recovering nicely, but it was such a strong dose that he became very hoarse and found it difficult to talk – which for him was a scarier prospect than something as commonplace as cancer. He purposely didn't have the telephone in his room connected, because it seldom stopped ringing, and talking tended to tire him. By the weekend, however, his voice seemed to be on the mend and it looked like he might even be discharged by mid-week.

When left to his own devices, he would read the papers, skim magazines, listen to classical music, and mostly rest, trying to conserve and replenish his strength. He tired quickly and easily, and spoke in a whisper, with great effort. This was mostly a result of the chemo, which had also left him with severe mouth sores that were extremely uncomfortable. Consequently, a ten-minute conversation was enough to exhaust him, which is why he had still not connected his phone. And for some reason he was still getting fevers, which, when added to his current vocal limitations, prevented him from receiving visitors.

Back in Vancouver after her visit with Brian, Lorraine Wilson called Marcia Martin. "You've got to bring him back home," she urged Marci. "You've got to find a way to take him back to his condo."

Ken Lindsay and Marcia Martin started talking – "We really didn't know each other very well," says Ken – and went down to the hospital to meet with a social worker about home care. "Or so we thought." When they arrived at the hospital, they were told that Brian's doctor wanted a word with them. "They took us into this private room, and

Dr. Haq came in and said, 'There's nothing more we can do. Brian's not going to make it.' We just about fell off our chairs."

Joan Rivers's personal assistant Matt Stewart called. Joan had been trying to contact Brian and was worried about him. I returned his call and brought Joan up to speed.

"How is he paying for all this?" she inquired. "It must be costing a fortune!"

"It's Canada," I reminded her. "His hospital stay, the drugs, his meals are all covered by OHIP."

"Including a private room?" Joan was not convinced. "I mean, it's a shitty room, but he probably has to pay extra for it . . ." She hesitated, but only for a second. "Never mind," she said. "Just let me know how much it is."

His windowsill was full of cards from friends and fans. Norma Rea had left a visitors' book at the nurses' station on his floor so that pals who stopped by could leave him a personal note, which his nurses made sure he saw at least twice a day. Myrna Daniels sent him a note and stopped by the nurses' station with an armful of magazines for him. Jane Hawtin, Sara Waxman, and Doug Bassett had left voicemail messages on his home line, asking him to call. We let them know he was back at St. Mike's, and why. Film Reference Library archivist Sylvia Frank, the executive in charge of safe-guarding Brian's gift to the film festival library, and TIFFG development chief David Vella both tried on a number of occasions to see him, but a No Visitors ban was still in effect.

Chaz and Roger Ebert were concerned that Brian didn't seem to be making any progress. "Roger and I will send him messages to be read to him by the nurse," Chaz wrote to me. "Your message confirmed for me what I keep reading in the health journals – that for some people chemotherapy is worse than the disease! And yet some people have chemo and survive it and get better. And I pray that this is just the lull before Brian bounces back. I'm not counting him out yet. If you get to see Brian at all," she added, "please give him a HUG from us. I can't even begin to imagine how debilitating this must be for him."

Bad news travels fast. Sad news travels even faster.

David Pitblado, the young husband and father Brian admired so much, succumbed to non-Hodgkin's Lymphoma, leaving his wife and two eight-month-old sons behind. Karen Kain found herself with a difficult decision to make. "It was so heartbreaking, on so many levels, and Brian was not doing very well," she recalls, "so I decided not to tell him. What I didn't realize was that even on his bad days he was still reading the papers. He read them every day. So he read about David in the newspaper. And he cried. He was very upset with me for not telling him."

The days tumbled down, and so did Brian. In his third week back at St. Michael's, he eased himself out of bed to go to the washroom, took a few steps, and suddenly felt his legs give out from under him. He ended up sprawled on the floor, which shocked him momentarily, then panicked him, again momentarily, until he saw the black humour of his situation. "Help!" he cried, but his voice was so weak that he knew no one could hear him. He lay there, crying and laughing at his fate, until he heard footsteps approaching.

He took a series of deep breaths, conjured up the image of one of the most annoying television commercials of the day, and raised himself up on his now-bruised elbows. "*Help!*" he cried out. "*I've fallen, and I can't get up!*"

This time they heard him. He half expected the nurse who rushed into the room to be laughing. She wasn't. She lifted him gingerly to his feet and helped him back to bed.

He had now lost everything except his sense of humour. "After they got me back in bed," he told me the next day, "I said to myself, you can just forget about your dignity. That's gone. That's a thing of the past. Don't waste your time thinking any more about it."

Another breakthrough. Despite the bruises, he had fallen up. And now he had another great story to tell.

"I don't know how he maintained his sense of humour," Bea Arthur later observed. "But somehow he did. Even when he described the horror of how they pinned him down to take a specimen of bone marrow or something, something that was so terribly painful. But still, the way he presented it . . . he could take moments like that and make them genuinely amusing."

By Sunday, May 23, Brian was entering his fourth consecutive week at St. Michael's hospital and was having a rough time. His most recent bout of chemotherapy had been pretty devastating, and he was still trying to recover from it. He was very thin, very frail, and still wiped out most of the time. "The body," he acknowledged, "can only take so much." Even one as diligently toned and maintained as his had been.

That afternoon, Gail and I had arranged to attend Rex Harrington's final performance of *The Four Seasons*, the stunning showcase that National Ballet of Canada artistic director James Kudelka had created for him, after which we would drive a dozen city blocks to St. Michael's to give Brian a full play-by-play report. I had seen Rex perform the piece several times in several cities, and had championed the exquisite television version produced by prima ballerina Veronica Tennant and directed by Barbara Willis Sweete. The ballet chronicles the four major acts in a man's life – boyhood, manhood, maturity, and death, set to the gloriously passionate music of Vivaldi.

That final Sunday matinee must have been an emotional roller-coaster for Rex. He started on a high note and kept building, building, building. All through the afternoon, I kept wishing Brian could be with us to witness this bravura star turn. He had long been a faithful supporter and devoted admirer of the National Ballet, showcasing all the great dancers on *City Lights*. And he was very partial to Rex, who over the years had proven to be Karen Kain's greatest dance partner.

When we got to the last act, it seemed as if Rex had stopped acting altogether. He had become the role, resisting the inevitable call of death until, spent and exhausted, he was forced to succumb. It was a brilliant, hauntingly memorable performance, and when he emerged to take his final solo bow, the standing-room-only crowd in the Hummingbird Centre leapt to its feet yelling and cheering. Gail and I were on our feet too, our hands sore from clapping. Suddenly, my vision blurred, making it difficult to see the artists on stage. Only then did I realize I was crying. Tears long suppressed started flooding out of me. I tried to speak but could not. A woman in the row ahead of us, clearly moved by Rex's spectacular performance, was also weeping, although not nearly so profusely. Gail reached over and gently stroked my back. In the dark, surrounded by cheering strangers, I had finally found a safe place to let go.

Twenty minutes later, we sat dry-eyed and smiling in Brian's hospital room as he regaled us with a more detailed, delightfully embellished version of his unrehearsed pratfall. "I've been lying in bed so long now," he explained, "that my legs have atrophied!" He moved his feet to the left, and then to the right, showing us an exercise he'd been instructed to do. "I'll have to have physiotherapy when I get out of here," he said, and heaved a little sigh. And then, with a twinkle in his eye: "It's always something!" He knew we knew he was quoting Gilda Radner, and actually managed a grin.

"You don't have to wait 'til you get out of here to start physio," I said.

"I've asked," he replied with a shrug. "All the physiotherapists here are booked solid."

"Get your own therapist!" I suggested. "Someone who can come in and work your legs. Maybe only twice a week. Why not? You can afford it!"

He smiled, genuinely amused by my persistence. "Maybe," he said softly. "We'll see."

I gave his hand a gentle squeeze. He winced. "Sorry!" I exclaimed.

"No no no, you didn't hurt me," he replied reassuringly. And then, with a slight trace of a frown: "Did you use the hand sanitizer on your way in?"

"Yes, I did. Gail and I stop and rinse our hands every time we pass one."

He smiled. "I've been asking people to stop touching me, to not kiss me or touch my hands. My immune system is completely shot. I'm afraid of catching something. I'm so susceptible right now."

"To germs?"

He thought for a minute. "To everything, really."

Months earlier, I had raised the possibility of working with him on a book. Joan Rivers and countless others had urged Brian to write his memoirs, but he had steadfastly refused. "The Book," he called it. When I had proposed the idea of writing "The Book" together, he'd brightened, because that prospect sounded a lot less like work and a lot more like fun.

"I have an idea," I said. "Why don't I take the month of July off? We could do The Book then." I told him I thought I had finally come up with a winning formula. "Remember that book about Bette Davis?"

I turned to Gail, sure Brian already knew where I was going. "This writer," I said, "was doing an unauthorized biography of Bette Davis, and he sent the galleys to her for her comments, in case there were any factual errors, because he was trying to get it right. And she went through it page by page and wrote in the margins, stuff like 'This stuff about the director fighting for me to play the role is bullshit! He never wanted me for this role, not ever, but he had to take me because all the others turned him down!' . . . and sent it back to him. After he read it he called her, and she agreed to let him publish the book with her notes in the margin."

"What's your idea?" asked Brian, his curiosity piqued.

"We'll divide each page into two columns," I said, "and I'll tell these great stories in the first column, and you will contradict me and tell what really happened in the second column."

His eyes were starting to shine. "And I'll say nice things about everybody in the first column," I continued.

"And what will I do?" he asked, leaning forward in bed.

I shrugged. "Why, you'll tell the truth, of course!"

He leaned back on the pillow again, and beamed. "I love it," he said.

"However," I added, "I don't think we can call it 'The Book.' So start thinking of a good title."

"Oh I will!" he promised. "I will."

The next day, I bumped into Air Farceur Roger Abbott in the parking garage under the Broadcast Centre. Roger asked me if we had considered hiring palliative home-care givers so Brian could spend more time in his new condo. As a group we were just beginning to talk about it, albeit reluctantly. We knew Brian wasn't going to get better, but some of us, maybe most of us, didn't want to acknowledge that. Roger recommended a palliative home-care company, and I gratefully took the name and number.

Later that week, on May 28, Marcia Martin and Ken Lindsay arranged to bring Brian home so he could spend a Sunday afternoon in his condo. Marci assembled the Linehan SWAT team. St. Michael's staff had arranged for an ambulance to bring Brian to 164 Cumberland. Norma Rea would be waiting at the condo to greet them. It was not a warm-weather May. I urged Brian to bundle up.

"Don't worry, I will," he promised.

Was there anyone Brian would especially like to see at his condo when he arrived that afternoon? "Yes," he said. "I'd like to see Gillian."

I was booked in meetings most of the day, but the team had no need for more volunteers. "I'm holding all good thoughts for today's excursion," I told Marci.

"Thank you, George," she replied. "I think we're more excited than he is!"

Ken Lindsay called our pal Liloo, the most famous concierge at the Four Seasons hotel, to see if he could borrow a wheelchair for Mr. Linehan. Yes, of course she knew Brian, and yes, of course, she'd have the wheelchair ready. "When he started to get sick," Ken recalls, "Brian used to call her, and she would do stuff for him. She was wonderful to him."

They met him at the ambulance with the wheelchair. They had made up a little kit so he could look like a movie star. "We had sunglasses, and a selection of baseball caps, because movie stars wear baseball caps and sunglasses. But no, he came in that pea hat or whatever you call it, and then he had these great big aviator glasses that were his own. Somehow he had dug those out of somewhere. And he looked just great. He greeted the concierge, the man on duty, by name, and they were all so shocked, because they hadn't seen him."

Gillian Edwards was waiting in the lobby when he arrived. She admits she was shocked – "probably just like you," she adds with a soft smile – that she was the only person Brian asked to see that day. "But, I knew that whatever we were doing was helping him, and I knew that I wanted to be there for him." She smiles again. "It just proves that you never know how you're going to help somebody, in what capacity, when and where."

They wheeled him through the living room into his bedroom, so he could lie down and rest on his own bed. Michael Levine stopped by. Like it or not, Brian had an estate to deal with, and Michael had worked out all the essential details for a charitable foundation that reflected Brian's hopes and dreams for a Canadian star system. Buoyed by Marcia Martin's heartfelt endorsement, Brian signed a new will that would make his foundation a reality.

Gillian was sitting at Brian's bedside when he asked her again to explain the healing process. By now she had seen him on two more occasions, but it was that conversation with Brian that affected her most.

"Gillian," he said, "what is it that we've been doing?"

Gillian had walked him through this before, but was happy to take him there again.

"Well, Brian," she said, "we've been taking you to that part of yourself that we all possess."

He looked away for a moment, into the distance. "Why don't more people know about this?" he asked.

"I'm not sure," she replied. "I think it's because some people are afraid. And I think it's because some people are too busy."

Brian looked back at her, raised one eyebrow, and said, "Well, they *should!*"

☆

Dr. Haq had taken it upon herself to inform Brian's family that he was dying. Brian was not happy about it. Other than his exchanges with Connie, he'd had no contact with his siblings, and aside from catching him on television they hadn't seen him in years. Brian rarely mentioned his brothers and sisters, and when he did it was not in glowing terms.

That weekend, both of his sisters visited him, and during one visit Joan Rivers called. Richard, the nurse who was closest to Brian and consequently closest to all of us, informed Joan that he couldn't put her call through because Brian was visiting with family. "*Family?*" Rivers exclaimed, mystified. "*What* family??"

Connie had known for several months that her famous brother had been diagnosed with cancer. "He sent me a Thanksgiving card," she remembers, "and in the card he told me that he had been diagnosed in March with this non-Hodgkin's Lymphoma, and he was starting chemo and things were going well. 'I'm going to get my health back. I'm going to start a new beginning, a new life.'

"He told me about this class he was teaching at Humber College and how he loved it. And I thought, well, *good!* He seems like he's better; the chemo is working for him. And then I never heard any more about it. Until Norma called to say he was back in hospital."

She knew he wouldn't want her to see him like that. When she went to see him at St. Michael's that weekend, she took a few minutes to compose herself, but she was still not prepared for what she found.

"When I walked in, you know what he said to me? 'Well, it's about time.' And I said, 'I was trying to get myself together.' And I wanted to hug him so bad. And I thought, if I hug him, I'm going to break him in half." She shakes her head. "I was not ready for that."

We visited with him that night, and he told us Connie had come to see him. "As usual," he said, "Connie was crying." He said it with affection, in the same way he had always teased her. "And I told her, Connie, cry if you have to, but please don't feel sorry for me. Because I've had a fabulous life."

Brian's other sister, Carole, and her husband, Bruce Dingwall, drove in from Burlington that weekend. Bruce stopped to get a cold drink, but Carole just walked in, pulled up a chair, and sat down. "Brian looked at me. 'Oh, Carole!' And I said, 'Well, how are you doing, big guy? You don't look so shit hot.' He just smiled, and we started to talk."

At one point, she recalls, he told her he was thirsty. She brought him the juice container he requested. And the straw. And turned the music down for him. And got him some flat ginger ale. And some more juice. And a cool, wet wash cloth for his forehead.

She didn't want to tire him. She said her goodbyes and was about to leave when he called her back to move his tray table closer. And his night stand. And put his *New York Times* on it. And clean his glasses for him. "Now are you sure you have everything close at hand? Because once I go out that door, if I hear my name, I'm not coming back until tomorrow!"

He laughed softly. "Yeah, everything's fine now."

When she got to the door, she turned back and looked at him.

"It's okay, I don't want anything," he said.

"Love you," she said, and walked out.

Patrick Linehan was the first of Brian's brothers to visit. He and his wife, Linda, had just come back from the Bahamas when one of Ronnie's daughters called to tell them about Brian. "When I went into the room, I tried to mask my shock," Patrick says. "Because he was not looking well."

Seeing Brian in his hospital bed made Patrick very sad, he told me. "I said to Brian, 'You know, I don't know what happened. I live in Hamilton, you live in Toronto. I'm married, you have your professional life with entertainment and all that. I work in a steel mill and I'm looking at retiring, and here you are, as sick as you are' – and even at that moment I did not know Brian was dying. . . . I just said to him, 'I don't know what happened, man, but you know I love you.' And he started to cry. I kissed him and I held his hand and I said, 'I'm sorry. I don't know what happened.' He just went, 'Don't worry about it.'"

Patrick Linehan wants to say more, but the words get caught in his throat, and his eyes well up. "I hope he knows I loved him."

☆

When Gail and I stopped by on Sunday afternoon, May 31, two of Brian's younger brothers, Eric and Mico, had been cooling their heels in the second-floor waiting room for several hours. "Brian's brothers are here," one of the nurses murmured as we checked in with them.

"Really!" I didn't know Dr. Haq had notified them. "Does Brian know?"

"Ooooooh yes," she replied, rolling her eyes.

I hesitated. "How long have they been here?"

"A long time," she said pointedly. "They've gone downstairs to get a coffee. I told them he's sleeping and that he may not want to see anybody today. But they just say, 'That's okay, we'll wait.'"

We walked down the hall and knocked gently on the door with the hand-scrawled NO VISITORS sign on it. Brian was clearly anxious, but also clearly relieved to see us. "My brothers are here!" he said incredulously. "And they just won't leave! They've been waiting out there for hours!"

We chatted and gossiped for a good twenty minutes, after which I suggested that Gail and I leave so he would have room to receive his brothers.

"You're not going anywhere!" he insisted. "I'm certainly not going to see them alone. Gail, come and sit in this chair close to me."

"Why don't I go and get them?" I said matter-of-factly.

"All right," he conceded reluctantly. "But you two stay put. And I mean stay. Promise me you won't leave before they do."

We promised.

I walked out to the waiting room and met Eric Linehan and Mico Rodic for the very first time. I gently tried to prepare them for the physical toll that his illness had taken on their brother, because by now the chemotherapy had ravaged him. They nodded.

I brought them to Brian. With Gail's help, using some pillows to prop him forward, he was almost sitting up. He greeted them by their Serbian nicknames and, of course, formally introduced us to "the two youngest members of our dysfunctional family." He called Jovan "Mico," as in Meech-oh, and crooned his name when he said it. "This is the baby of the family." He said it teasingly, but with a note of pride nonetheless.

He told them that they couldn't stay long, that it had been a long day, that he had to rest.

His brothers' faces revealed their deep distress. It was as if they were trying desperately to find the broken link in the family chain, so they could fix it, repair it, and somehow make his pain go away.

Brian looked up at them from his bed. "We were a family once," he said. "But we fucked it up. And it's too late to do anything about it now."

"Don't say that, man," Eric pleaded with him softly.

"I lived with a man for thirty-five years," Brian continued, "and you never even met him!"

"That's all history now, Brian," said Jovan Rodic quietly. "All in the past."

After a few minutes, Brian started closing his eyes. He was very tired, and very weak, and emotionally drained.

"We should go," I murmured to Gail.

"No," said Brian. His eyes opened again.

It was time for the George & Brian Show. Over the months, we had developed an unrehearsed game. I would mention incidents that had happened to us on the road, sometimes as far back as the 1970s. But I would conveniently "forget" certain fairly obvious details, or get them wrong – which, of course, was his cue to remember them. Or correct them.

"Oh, I forgot to tell you," I said, as casually as I could manage. "I saw a show with John Ritter's son on TV. He's very good." I could see the traces of a smile forming on Brian's lips. He already knew where I was going. "Do you remember," I continued, "that time we went to that John Ritter movie? What was it called, *SuperHero*?"

"*Hero At Large*," said Brian weakly.

"Right, now I remember!" I said. "Where was that junket? New York?"

Brian almost grinned. "New Orleans," he said. "We were in New Orleans."

"Right, New Orleans!" I said. "And John Ritter was nervous because that guy from Columbia, the one who had cashed those cheques –"

"David Begelman," said Brian. "And they were Cliff Robertson's cheques."

"Right, David Begelman," I said. "Did he do time for that? But of course this was Hollywood, so now that he had done his time he was running, what was it, United Artists?"

"MGM," said Brian, beaming.

"Right, MGM," I said. I turned to Brian's brothers. "Brian was there for his television show, and I was there for my newspaper column, and John Ritter came to us, because he trusted us, and said, 'Guys, when we get to the theatre for the premiere, what do I say to David Begelman? "Hi, Mr. Begelman, I'm glad you're not a felon any more!?" I mean, I can't exactly say that, can I?'"

"And *I* said," Brian whispered hoarsely, "well, you might as well, because George is going to write that you did!" He smiled, genuinely pleased with himself, and closed his eyes. Once again he had been tested. Once again he had passed the test.

We wished him sweet dreams and left the room with his brothers. Before we left the hospital, Eric pressed me to make a note of his cell phone number. He said he could see that Brian was surrounded by friends. "But please tell the others," he said, "that I am staying here in town, at the Sheraton Centre, and that I would like to be called upon to assist Brian in any way I can."

Jovan – the tall, strapping man who was the "baby" of the family – quietly slipped back into Brian's room after Gail and I had left, and pleaded with him softly. "It's never too late, Brian," Mico told him. "It's only too late if you want it to be. So please don't say it's too late for us."

But, of course, it was.

Marcia Martin went to visit Brian Monday morning and found him quite agitated. He seemed to be a bit mixed up, and his heart was racing. Later that morning, Carole and Eric stopped by for another visit, and Mary Sinclair stopped by in the afternoon. So did Gillian Edwards. "Do you want to go home, Brian?" she asked him.

"Yes. Well . . . I'd like to . . . but I'm not sure . . ."

He seemed to be in rapid decline, slipping away from us a little more each day.

"Tell Brian he should come home," said Sara Waxman, gently urging me to give him her message. "His flowers are starting to bloom!" Sara had wanted to visit him in hospital, and she had taken a taxi to St. Michael's. But she couldn't make herself get out of the cab, and had the driver take her back home. From her windows at the Cumberland Street condo, Sara could monitor the comings and goings in the suites that spilled onto the garden terrace below her. She watched for Brian's return, for any signs of life. If he suddenly needed something, she thought, she could be at his side in minutes.

Barry Avrich stood outside the hospital for an hour, staring at the building, holding a bag of magazines for Brian. Finally, he summoned up the courage to go in.

The nurse who took the magazines into Brian's room came out a minute later.

"He wants you to know that he approves of the selection of magazines," the nurse replied, "but he doesn't want you to see him."

Barry just stood there for a minute, trying to absorb what was happening. "And I just walked the streets after that."

Brian had sent word to Gillian Edwards, asking her to come to St. Mike's to see him. "To be honest," says Gillian, "I don't think I've ever had such a profound experience. . . . We were just sitting in silence, but the silence was so palpable with energy and with kindness. He turned to me at one point and said, 'You know, I enjoy your company.' And I think only people who knew him very well would know what that really meant. And I knew at that moment that it was the utmost gift.

"One time he was talking about the issues he wanted to resolve with Zane, and how was that going to turn out," she remembers. "I said, you know what? He's going to be there to meet you. Just trust it.

"As we were talking, his eyes drifted – now you've got to remember how lucid and clear and precise Brian is – and then all of a sudden he looks off, and he's looking over my shoulder, and he's looking at something. I turned around, and then I knew. I said, 'You see him, don't you.' And he said, 'Yes, I do.' And then we just went on talking, Brian being a very realistic and practical man. But, you know, he just accepted it."

The hardest day for Gillian was the day Dr. Haq told Brian she couldn't save him. Our favourite nurse, Richard, was in the room when Dr. Haq delivered the news. "All those nurses were extremely compassionate," Gillian says. "And then Richard said to me, 'You go in next.' He gave me information to tell Brian about who was going to be there for him, in the ambulance on the ride home, because Brian was still interested in logistics at the time, and he'd been asking to go home prior to this. I think the last two weeks Brian was already slipping in and out of consciousness.

"So I went in after the doctor told him, and he looked at me and said, 'Well, I guess there's no more pretending. It's true.' He had to take that in. I watched him go through some anger, and I offered to leave. And he said, 'No no no, don't go!' He needed to go through that. But what was amazing was, he didn't get stuck. Some people get stuck in that anger."

Gillian sat by his bedside and did more energy work until the nurse came in to change him. As she was leaving, he called out softly after her: "Gillian, come to the condo."

She stopped. "Are you sure?"

"Meet me at the condo," he said.

"Okay," she said. "Okay."

☆

On Tuesday, June 1, I had a commitment to represent CBC Television at a gala dinner cooked up by the founder of the indomitable Famous People Players theatrical troupe, Diane Dupuy. Because of this, I advised members of the inner circle that I would be stopping by Brian's room around noon, in case someone else wanted to take the evening shift.

Marcia Martin was among the first to visit him that morning, and she called me after a brief fifteen-minute stay. "He's having trouble communicating," she reported. "He's confused, and more than a bit exasperated, because he can't make himself understood."

Secretly confident that I would be able to decipher whatever he was trying to say, I strolled into his room a few minutes after noon. "How are you feeling?" I inquired.

He smiled, and tried to shrug his shoulders, but he was so wired up with tubes and cables that even the simple act of shrugging was a challenge for him. He started to speak. I thought I heard one or two noises that sounded like words, but there weren't enough of them to reveal what he might be saying. I asked him to repeat what he had just said. He did so, patiently, trying not to show his frustration. I could understand even less. It was all gibberish.

I got up from my chair. "Brian, I'm sorry, but I can't understand what you're saying. I know how terribly frustrating this is for you. You probably need some rest. Try to get some sleep, if you can. I'll come back later, and we'll talk then."

He nodded his head. And then, while he still had my eye, he raised both his arms in the air and let them fall on his lap in a classic oh-what-the-hell! gesture. I smiled back at him. He closed his eyes, and I left the room.

Brian's baby brother, Mico, came back to see him that afternoon. Brian, he said, slept most of the time. "I was there for a few hours and he slept for most of it," Jovan Rodic told me later. "And when he spoke it was like a whisper."

At 6 p.m., Gail and I attended the Famous People Players dinner gala with CBC producer Robert Sherrin; his celebrated stage designer wife, Astrid Janson; and one of our favourite network publicists, Helicia Glucksman. After I accepted a special award for our network's support of the talented blacklight troupe, we sat down to a roast beef supper.

We were halfway through the main course when I retrieved a voice-mail message from Ken Lindsay. He and Peter Husar had elected to take the evening shift at the hospital. By the time they arrived, Brian was, to all intents and purposes, unintelligible. But now they were calling with information far more dramatic. They had been advised by hospital staff to let Brian's friends and family know that it looked like he might not make it through the night, and if they wanted to say goodbye to him they should do it now.

I informed our tablemates that something had suddenly come up, and Gail and I raced to the hospital. The nurses greeted us softly, sympathetically; they knew why we had come. I had prepared Gail with a description of our noon encounter, when he was using a language unknown to both of us. We braced ourselves and walked in.

He was propped up in bed, eyes wide open, and beamed when he saw us.

"We know it's late," Gail offered somewhat tentatively. "We just wanted to come by."

"I'm so glad!" he said. His voice sounded stronger than it had in weeks. He was back.

He was holding an envelope in his hand, a greeting card someone had dropped off at the nurses' station. He was trying to open it but lacked the physical strength to do so. Gail gently took the card from him, took it out of the envelope, and handed it to him. He smiled gratefully and put it on his tray. He would read it later.

I reminded him of the CBC-TV movie of the week that he had done sometime in the 1970s, and his eyes lit up. He couldn't remember who had directed it, "but Don Francks was in it, and Mavor Moore, and I had to do two stunts."

Stunts? Brian Linehan did his own stunts??

He grinned. "One was falling over a railing. After I got shot, I think." And the other? "I had to drive a car!" Three decades later, he still hadn't learned how to drive.

We moved on to more serious matters.

"They're sending me home tomorrow," he announced. "Dr. Haq came by this morning and told me she can't do anything more for me. She says they've done all they can. I said to her, 'So, Dr. Haq, you're sending me home to die.' And she said, 'Well, Brian, I always told you it was fifty-fifty.'" He shrugged. "So that's that."

"Well!" I said, pretending to be miffed, "I suppose I'll never get you on e-mail now!"

He cocked one eye, and only one, as only he could. "Ya think??" he said, delivering the slang riposte with flawless timing. "One other thing . . ."

"Yes?"

"You'll have to write The Book alone."

"I know," I said. "I know."

"It won't be nearly as much fun," he added, eyes twinkling again.

"No," I said, honestly. "Not nearly."

He knew I was humouring him, that I had no intention of writing The Book.

He said he had met with Michael Levine the previous week and signed all the necessary papers for his estate. We were happy to hear it. Even with Marcia Martin's constant prodding, it had taken Brian months to commit to an exit strategy. And although he was grudgingly grateful to Marci and Michael for making it happen, he didn't want Michael or anyone else giving away the objets d'art and personal possessions he and Zane had treasured. "I want to do it the way Roddy did it," he declared.

Two years earlier, in his ledger, Brian had made a note of Roddy McDowall's last days on earth. McDowall had died of cancer in 1998, in early October. Brian noted that when Roddy was dying, his daily attendants included Elizabeth Taylor, Sybil Burton Christopher, Julie Andrews, Joan Plowright, Doris Roberts, Lauren Bacall, and Tuesday Weld. "*Roddy died surrounded by love, and loving friends*," Brian wrote, in his ornate penmanship. "*Dominick Dunne was also there and wrote movingly about something unique in Hollywood – friendship.*"

Now, almost six years after Roddy McDowall's death, it appeared to be Brian Linehan's turn. And he didn't want to blow it.

"When Roddy knew he was dying," he reminded me, "he would invite friends over for a farewell drink or even a bedside chat, and as they were about to leave he'd say, 'Elizabeth, you've always loved that painting. I want you to have it.' 'Sybil, you've always admired that crystal candelabra. Please take it with you when you go.' That's the way I want to do it." He paused, thinking it through. "Tomorrow after I get home, after I get settled, I may make a list. Unless I'm too tired. Then I'll wait 'til the weekend."

I looked at my watch. "Jesus, it's after eleven o'clock! We'd better leave before they throw us out." Gail kissed Brian on his forehead, which was cool and blissfully fever-free. I stroked his hand and wrapped my fingers around his, and we said our goodnights.

His eyes followed us as we started to leave. "I love you," he said, his voice weaker now.

"And we love you," I said. "More than you know." He could hear my voice starting to go, and he could see my eyes welling up, and a sympathetic smile flickered across his ravaged face.

We closed the door behind us. I never saw him again.

22

"Lorraine, I'm not dead yet."

On Wednesday morning, June 2, before Brian came home, Gail called our friend Judi Schwam in Los Angeles to tell her the news. Judi was devastated. "I feel like someone has just punched a hole in my stomach that will never close again," she responded. "I want so much to be able to talk with him and tell him what a special part of my life he has been but I know I won't ever be able to do that. I can't even write this note to you. Thank you for reaching me. Please let me know what is happening."

Marcia Martin called Lorraine Wilson in Vancouver. "Brian's not doing very well," she told Lorraine. "I think it's going to be soon." Lorraine was torn. She wanted to get on a plane to Toronto, but was afraid she might not get to Brian in time. And after her experience with Mark, she admits, "I really couldn't bear it happening again."

Virginia Morra held Brian's hand in the ambulance when they brought him home. They carried him into the building on a stretcher. Ken Lindsay had left work early so he could be there, waiting for them. "I opened up the apartment and opened up his bed, fluffed his pillows. And then the ambulance guys brought him up on the stretcher and I had to help them. I think Virginia did too. He couldn't sit up, really. But he still came wearing the hat and the sunglasses."

At first things went smoothly enough. After the ambulance attendants departed, however, Ken got a bit anxious. Home-care workers had been booked for round-the-clock duty, but they hadn't yet arrived. "It was just Virginia and me and Brian. And then we realized, oh, we're by ourselves. It's just us. And I was immediately freaked out," Ken says.

Ken called our main man and favourite nurse, Richard. "Richard," said Ken, "did you forget to send something with Brian? Like, a professional?"

Richard told him not to worry, that he and Brian's friends could handle this. But Ken was dubious.

"I would ask Brian, 'Are you comfortable?' Because I was afraid to move him or to cause him pain. We had to put these big sweat socks on his feet, and I remember seeing that his feet were so big. I had to put them on his feet very carefully, because he was having pain."

Peter Husar arrived at the condo an hour or so later. At the beginning, he says, "there were private things that happened to him that home care workers helped with. It was kind of like, 'You have to leave the room.' But after a while it didn't really matter, and I think that's when he must have realized that he was really dying. We were just part of that, and helped with changing him, cleaning him, doing those kind of things."

By late afternoon, Brian's breathing had become laboured. Karen Kain and Ross Petty went to three pharmacies before they could find the morphine drops that had been so helpful to her mother when she was in the last stages of cancer.

I was in Montreal for meetings with producer Matt Zimbel and his creative team, who were attempting to breathe some new life into our annual Canada Day telecast, but Gail made sure that Marc, Alex, and Joe got to see Brian for what would probably be the last time. Seeing him, what was left of him, was a heart-wrenching shock for all three of them. But, like Brian, they rallied. And after Marc quietly pointed out that the male health care worker assigned to Brian was handling him like he was washing a car, the worker was summarily dismissed by Team Brian. A new female health worker was summoned, and Joe was dispatched to purchase adult diapers from a nearby pharmacy.

Joan Rivers had been apprised of the situation. Since Brian was too weak to take phone calls, she decided she would call every day with messages that could be relayed to him. Her Wednesday afternoon message was classic Rivers: "*You think you have problems? I had to have dinner with Barbara Walters twice this week!*" When Marcia Martin relayed the message to Brian, he actually laughed out loud.

Gillian Edwards arrived and visited with Brian in his bedroom. "The energy in the room was palpable," she remembers. "I'm sure everybody felt things in his presence. You didn't need to say things. I think people get scared when people are close to the end, but it also can be very profound. So I did some more healing work, but we didn't talk a lot."

That night, she recalls, "was probably one of the most beautiful nights. A lot of his friends had gathered in his apartment and were having a little cocktail party, talking and sharing. Brian decided he wanted to watch *Will & Grace*. He called his friends in, and they sat down on his bed and they watched *Will & Grace* with him. So he got to hold court. It was beautiful.

"After that, he called me in, and we chatted for a bit. And then he said, 'I'm going to bed now. Would you please tell them to keep the noise down? I need to rest!'"

But by the time Gillian got a chance to deliver his message, there was a new Linehan edict: Brian wanted to see all of them in his bedroom *right now!* So they all trooped in, says Gillian, "and we stood around his bed, and he started to talk to each one of us. And everyone was saying, 'Good night, Brian,' and Alex said something funny, and he was joking with her, and it was really nice . . . and he was so happy to be there."

It was chilly that night in Montreal, and I bundled up to attend post-midnight pre-tapings of performances by Jann Arden, Wilfrid LeBouthillier, Nanette Workman, Ariane Moffat, and Quartetto Gelato in offbeat and unusual outdoor locations. But no matter who was performing I kept thinking about Brian, sleeping peacefully, I hoped, in his condo.

The next morning, I woke up in Montreal and got ready to fly to Halifax to attend a taping of Mary Walsh's smart weekly series *Open Book*. Before I left I sent out an all-points bulletin to Brian's friends.

Brian's two-year struggle with non-Hodgkin's Lymphoma is almost over. After five weeks in St. Michael's hospital, where he received extraordinary care from Donna, Richard and the dedicated, devoted nursing team, he asked his highly esteemed Dr. Haq to let him go home.

She agreed, and yesterday, friends bundled him up and accompanied him, by ambulance, to his wonderful sunny condo at 164 Cumberland, just a martini's throw from the Four Seasons hotel in Yorkville.

It is here that Brian plans to spend his final days. He understands that his life force is waning – he grows weaker day by day – and as long as he is at his condo Brian will receive home care 24/7, which is both much-needed and essential. He will also be surrounded by his closest, oldest friends, from both public and private life.

He very much appreciates all the warm wishes you have sent his way; they have lifted his spirits and brightened his days.

If you'd like to stop by to see him, please call first if you can. Brian has good days, when he's happy to have brief 5-minute visits, and rough days, when he is so exhausted that all he wants to do is sleep. But if you'd like to visit with him, however briefly, don't let that stop you from coming.

Three hours later Lorraine Wilson woke up in Vancouver and called the Yorkville condo to see how Brian was doing. As fate would have it, Peter Husar answered the phone.

"I'd never met Peter," she recalls. "And I told him my experience of Mark dying and I said, I have to tell you, Peter, I can't come if Brian dies before I get there. I just can't handle it."

Peter Husar had uncommon insight into her emotional dilemma. He had gone through a similar experience with his mother, who had passed away before he could reach her bedside.

"Lorraine," said Peter, "I just think you should get on a plane and come."

Lorraine Wilson hung up the phone and called Air Canada.

☆

Joan Rivers left another message that day: *"Hope you're feeling better, but if you're not, remember me in the Will!"* Her message was relayed to Brian, who was thrilled that she had called again. Anne Murray sent her love and good wishes.

Carole Linehan came to visit again. She had come to Brian's condo the day before as well, but none of Brian's friends knew who she was. Carole didn't care. "I got to say my goodbyes." Anne Heisey suddenly showed up unannounced on Thursday afternoon. Her history with Brian had started years earlier with Karen Kain's near-disastrous dinner party and continued through floating film festivals and Brian's visits to the Heisey summer cottage in Ontario and winter home in Florida. But neither Gail nor Karen were present, so no one knew who she was, either.

"I want to see Brian!" she demanded, and marched into his bedroom. She emerged a few minutes later, visibly shaken, and left almost as quickly as she had arrived.

Early that evening, Gillian Edwards visited with him as well. "I sat with him for a little bit," she recalls, "and he woke up, like out of a nightmare, and he looked me right in the eyes and he said, 'Do I have diabetes?' And I said, no, Brian, you do not have diabetes. And he said, 'Oh, thank God!'"

She brought him a cool facecloth for his forehead, "and he drifted off. I knew right then and there that that would be the last time I saw him. His eyes had closed and his breathing was like he had been jogging for hours. It was hard to watch that part. I just remember putting my hand on his forehead, on his third-eye part, and I said goodbye."

The ensuing evening was not without moments of black humour. Ken Lindsay was admittedly still "freaked out" because there was no nurse present. The health workers assigned to Brian, he says, "were basically housekeepers. And they might be able to change a diaper or change the bed or bring him water, but they couldn't give medication."

Lorraine Wilson landed in Toronto at five o'clock, hailed a cab, got to Brian's condo, and knocked on the door. "And bless him, he was still alive." Marci brought Lorraine into Brian's bedroom. "He was lying there, and I just hugged him, and told him I was there for him."

In earlier conversations, Lorraine had urged Brian to consider seeing an energy healer, so she was pleased when she learned he was seeing Gillian Edwards. Now, as she sat on his bed beside Brian, he kept dozing off, but his breathing was becoming increasingly laboured, as if his breath was trapped in his chest. Lorraine had done some energy healing herself, so she put her hand on his chest, "to try to free up his breathing."

Brian opened his eyes, looked down at her hand on his chest, and cocked one eye quizzically.

"Lorraine," he said, "I'm not dead yet."

Lorraine gasped. "I *know* that, Brian!" she retorted indignantly.

"Fine," he said. Pleased with himself, he smiled contentedly and drifted back to sleep.

☆

The weekly series *Mary Walsh: Open Book* was shot over the summer at CBC Halifax and exposed celebrated actress Mary Walsh as the voracious, erudite, and opinionated book reader she was. Mary was scheduled to shoot two episodes on June 3, one in the afternoon, one in the evening, and two more the next day.

"How is Brian doing?" she asked me between tapings.

"Not so great," I admitted.

"I want to send him a message," she said, frowning. "I just don't know what to say."

"Well, he was a big fan of *22 Minutes*," I said. Mary had created the hit TV series *This Hour Has 22 Minutes*, which had just wrapped its eleventh season.

"Yeah yeah yeah," she nodded impatiently. "But what really counts for me is all the support he gave us *before* we were media darlings, *before* we had a hit show. That's what I want to tell him." She pulled a pen out of her purse and scratched his name on a script.

"Give me his home number, darling," she said. "I'll call him tomorrow morning, before I come to the studio."

While Mary Walsh and I were chatting in her dressing room, Peter Husar was embarking on one of the most memorable nights of his life.

"The first part of it," he says, "started off with just Lorraine and me sitting on the bed with Brian. Lorraine and I asked each other what our connection with Brian was, because I had never met Lorraine. And we both shared our stories, in front of Brian. He was smiling at our stories, and he was holding our hands as we were reminiscing. He seemed very happy about all of that, that we had finally made a connection.

"And then he started fidgeting. In those last couple of days, you could tell when he was comfortable. But he'd make this wincing face when he was in pain, when they tried to move him or anything like that. Near the end that just became more of a regular thing. He wouldn't even have to move and he would wince in pain."

Peter reached for the morphine drops that Karen Kain and Ross Petty had secured for Brian. "We put some under his tongue," Lorraine Wilson explains. "It was liquid morphine, and he seemed to relax. Then he started to hallucinate a little bit, and he got very mad at me. He said, 'Lorraine, I can't believe you've betrayed me!' And I said, 'I did? . . . How did I betray you?' And he said, 'You've changed my wall here and put those bookcases there. Who gave you permission to do that?' And I just wanted to cry. Just hearing him say, 'You betrayed me.' So I really had to ground myself and separate myself from my friend and the drugs."

Ken Lindsay remembers a somewhat subdued Lorraine coming from Brian's bedroom into the living room to take a break. "Well, Mr. Linehan just gave me some proper shit!" she told Ken.

"Why?"

"Because I was not authorized to move the walls around!" she exclaimed.

As the night wore on, Lorraine recalls, "Some members of Team Brian were really worried that we were overdosing him." Peter Husar laughs about it now. "We never even gave him the full dosage. But there were several people who were concerned about it. *Don't give him too much!*" And Lorraine said, "Why? What are we going to do, kill him? He's already dying!"

Lorraine and Peter did not wish to be second-guessed. "If you guys are not comfortable with what we're doing," they told Team Brian, "you should call in a specialist."

Team Brian called in a registered nurse. "She checked him," Lorraine recalls, "and she said, 'You need to know that when anybody is doing anything out of love, when you're terminally ill and you're going to die, it's never wrong.' And she actually gave him *more*."

After everybody left that night, Lorraine assumed that aside from Brian and the health care worker, she would be the only one staying overnight at the Yorkville condo. "But Peter wanted to stay," she recalls with a happy smile. And she was glad for his company.

Back in Halifax we wrapped the evening taping and Mary retreated to do homework for the two shows we were scheduled to tape the following day. I assured her I would look after our "guests": CBC icon Hana Gartner, *Maclean's* film critic Brian D. Johnson, Johnson's prize-collecting writer wife Marni Jackson, and transplanted screenwriter John Frizzell, currently based in L.A. I invited them to join me for a nightcap at the pub in the Lord Nelson hotel. Former Citytv and CBC arts broadcaster Laurie Brown was also in Halifax that week, participating in an annual media convention. Brian Johnson told her where we were planning to meet, and she was waiting for us at the Lord Nelson when we arrived.

The Victory Arms Pub was noisy and crowded that night. It was Thursday night, a teasing harbinger of a weekend to come. But it was fine for a nightcap, and none of us were planning to say anything particularly profound over our beers and wine. We were chattering away in all directions, keeping at least two conversations going at all times. I kept glancing at my cell phone, making sure there were no new voicemail messages from Toronto, until John Frizzell caught my eye.

"So," he said, "how is . . . ?"

He placed two fingers under his nostrils, pushing them up, in a little piggy gesture that I recognized instantly as his impression of Brian Linehan. I was immediately taken aback, and suddenly angry. "Who, John?" I inquired, refusing to acknowledge it.

"You know!" he said, and repeated the piggy little gesture.

"No. I don't." I said it coldly, hoping he'd drop the subject and move on.

"Oh you know!" said John, mildly exasperated. "Your friend Linehan. How is he?"

I took a deep breath. "Well," I said, "since you ask . . . he's dying."

Brian Johnson was replying to a question she had asked him when Hana Gartner suddenly stopped him and grabbed my arm. "What?? . . . What did you say about Brian?"

The table was, for the moment, silent. The only quiet table in the Victory Arms Pub on a Thursday night in Halifax.

"I said, he's dying."

I tried to measure my words. "He's been in St. Michael's hospital for the last six weeks, and this week we brought him back to his condo, so he could die at home."

The colour had drained from John Frizzell's cheeks. He was ashen. Clearly shocked, he had the good grace to be genuinely embarrassed. "I'm so sorry," he said softly. "Terribly sorry. I've been in L.A." He stared at me numbly. "I didn't even know he was sick."

The quietest voice at the table belonged to Laurie Brown, who had known Brian for years. She too was an alumnus of Moses Znaimer's Citytv family. "How long has he got, George?" she murmured.

I tried to clear my throat. "He's not expected to last the night." I tried to say it matter-of-factly, but saying it made it real, and making it real made my voice crack.

Laurie saw my eyes starting to well up, and raised her glass of wine in a toast. "To Brian!" she said, almost defiantly.

"To Brian," we echoed, raising our glasses in unison.

It was closing time.

☆

Back in Toronto, Brian fell asleep again. Peter and Lorraine stayed by his side. "We just sat on the bed, one on either side of his bed, and talked. For four hours," Peter recalls.

"Talking about how grateful we were to have him in our lives," says Lorraine. "And remembering stories with him in it."

"And he would fall asleep and wake up, and fall asleep and wake up," says Peter.

After four hours, Peter was weary and went to bed. Lorraine sat with Brian a while longer, then lay down on the living-room couch. She could still hear him breathing – "his breath was quite laboured" – and she dozed off for an hour or so.

On Friday morning, June 4, 2004, Lorraine Wilson got up around five o'clock.

"The caregiver was sitting outside his room. I went in and washed Brian and changed his pajamas. And then I sat there with him, and I got to tell him just how much I loved him. And how grateful I was to have him in my life . . . and that he had made such a difference in everybody's life, and it was time for him to go with Zane, and it was okay to go. I went and woke Peter up and I said, 'I don't think he's going to be here much longer.'"

Peter brushed his teeth and joined her in Brian's bedroom. "We were just saying, you can go. It's okay to go now.

"The laboured breathing from the night before was totally gone, and he was so peaceful. I knew to tell him to go toward the light. I knew to tell him that Zane would be there. And at the same time there was a part of me saying, '*Fuck, what am I doing? I don't know how to help someone die!*'

"I could see his breath changing," Lorraine says. "And then all of a sudden he took this gasp and I knew that was it. There was this incredible grace. That's all I can tell you. We just held him, and it was . . . it was *so beautiful*. He just died in our arms. It was not complicated. It was gentle. And then Peter and I just laid our heads on his chest, and we just couldn't move for about twenty minutes."

They had witnessed the life force leaving him, with their own eyes, their own hearts, and their own minds.

Soon after, Lorraine Wilson called Marcia Martin, and Peter Husar called Ken Lindsay.

Ken was not surprised. "Peter phoned me at 6:30 or 6:45 in the morning," he recalls, "and said, 'He just died.' And Peter was very emotional on the phone. We both were. It was an awful morning.

I remember being in my bedroom and talking out loud to Brian. 'Okay,' I said, 'if it's really true that right after you die you're still around us . . .' and I poured myself some Beefeater gin."

Gail called me in Halifax to assure me that Brian's suffering was over. I cancelled my meetings and called Air Canada.

One by one, the members of Team Brian arrived at his condo.

"Everyone came over. And it was so beautiful," Lorraine recalls. "Virginia and David arrived, and we decorated Brian's bedroom with the most beautiful flowers. We played music that he and Zane used to play. Marci called the funeral parlour, and then Gillian arrived, and we all stood around. I said to everyone, 'Let's just go in and send him off.' So we all stood around the bed and held hands and thanked Brian for his friendship and told him how much we were going to miss him. And that we all loved him."

Gillian was happy that Brian's friends thought to include her, and pleased that they wanted her to be there. They asked her to say a prayer, so she did. "We just all stood around and held hands, with the candles lit and his favourite music on," says Gillian, "and I said a prayer. It sent him on his way, and honoured him."

When the staff from the funeral parlour came in, Team Brian left the room. Lorraine was standing in the kitchen with Gillian when they wheeled him out of the bedroom, in what she and Gillian both remember as a beautiful green velvet shroud.

Exactly one year ago, to the day, Brian's friend Yvonne Silver had died. Exactly one year ago, to the day, Brian and Norma Rea had gone to Hamilton to celebrate the sixty-fifth birthday of Brian's older sister, Connie Linehan Kataric. And in another part of the city, Dianne Schwalm gave her daughter Emily a big hug and wished her a very happy sixteenth birthday.

By the time I landed in Toronto, news of Brian Linehan's death was prominently featured on all the CBC video screens at Pearson International Airport. My driver took me directly to the condo, where I was immediately drafted to help with a barrage of requests for press stories that Marcia Martin and Martha Watson were already juggling.

Citytv was already running a Linehan tribute on its newscasts and its website. When I informed Martha Watson that a very flattering shot of Brian was being flashed on CBC video screens all over the airport, she grinned like a schoolgirl. "Brian will be SO happy!" she exclaimed, laughing.

We took some of the press calls outside, on the garden terrace Brian never lived long enough to enjoy. It was a glorious June day, full of hope, and we warmed ourselves in the sun. A floor above us, Sara Waxman watched the sudden flurry of activity from her apartment windows. Acutely sensitive to our situation, she was too shy to ask if she could join us.

We spent the rest of the day and night in impromptu floods of tears and spontaneous gales of laughter. The grieving had begun.

23

"It was like living with Cole Porter!"

On June 4, 2004, in California, Arlene Ludwig was working on a junket, coordinating television interviews, when Disney publicity chief Georgia O'Connor quietly took her aside. "Arlene, I'm sorry to tell you this, but . . . Brian's gone." Georgia had heard the news from PBS entertainment reporter Patrick Stoner, who had received an email telling him that Brian had died.

In New York, Shirley Lord was shocked. She knew Brian was battling cancer, but from what he'd told her she thought it was treatable. "I wonder," she reflected sadly, "did he know in the end how loved he was?" In Florida, Sharon Gless knew that Brian was terminally ill, but she too was shocked to hear of his passing. "I kept thinking he'd last longer, because he was so willing to get the pain out of him."

Toronto Star columnist Jim Bawden, who had done his first of many interviews with Brian in 1972, reported that one of his editors described Brian as "the Glenn Gould of interviewers, high strung but supremely gifted. I agree." And former CBC Television executive Phyllis Platt, now a successful producer, emailed her personal remembrance: "There's an expression in French – *avoir de l'entregent* – literally to 'know how to behave' that somehow captured Brian for me. He knew how to behave, in any and all situations, putting people at ease, and giving them his best, always. I think we all knew he sent us up behind our backs, in private, but it didn't matter. It was somehow an honour to imagine being spoofed, pilloried, or otherwise noticed, by M. Linehan."

The death of Brian Linehan was noted on all Hamilton newscasts. Some family members were intrigued to learn that their brother was, according to news reports, either fifty-eight or fifty-nine when he died, when he was in fact only three months away from turning sixty-one. But Brian had started "adjusting" his age in the 1970s, dropping a year or two as he did more and more interviews. He had most of us fooled most of the time. Brian's youngest brother, John (Mico) Rodic, believed that at the time of his death Brian was three months away from turning sixty-two; their aunt Connie had him pegged at sixty-three or sixty-four. ("Everybody in the Linehan family lies about their age," Brian's younger brother Eric had once confided. "And if you don't tell anybody, after a while we all forget anyway.")

The morning Brian died, his brothers Patrick and Mico made a personal pilgrimage to Connie's house, to share their grief with their older sister, her husband, Danny, and her daughter, Lesley. After they left, Lesley suggested that her mother pay a visit to Ronnie, the unofficial patriarch of the family. So she did, and Ronnie, who was extremely distressed by the current turn of events, said he would like to meet Zane Wagman – "this man who kept our brother away from the family for thirty-five years."

Connie was incensed. "I thought, either I get up and walk out, and never speak to him again – and I don't want to do that – or I have to fix this up."

She looked directly at Ronnie. "You can't speak to Zane," she said, coldly.

"Why not?" he demanded.

"Because Zane died of a heart attack two years ago!" Ronnie and his wife, Gerri, just sat there, stunned.

Back at the Yorkville condo, preparations were underway for a "family" gathering of a different nature: Michael Levine and Marcia Martin were organizing a Sunday afternoon wake-cum-cocktail party in Brian's honour.

The phone started ringing Saturday morning. What followed was a series of calls from a "Dr. Harris" who claimed to be a close friend of both Brian and Zane. He and his partner wanted to be included in any kind of private gathering that Brian's friends might be planning. Brian's friends, however, had never heard of him, and were understandably reluctant to invite a stranger, who might or might not be a legitimate acquaintance, to the Sunday gathering.

Finally, remembering that he and Isaac had met Gail and me at a garden party at Grenadier Heights some years earlier, "Dr. Harris" gave it one more try. "Is George Anthony there?" he inquired. "If he is, *please* let me speak to him!"

Marcia Martin called me to the phone. "This guy *specifically* asked to speak to you," she said with a helpless shrug. I picked up the phone. "Dr. Harris" told me that we'd met, but that he didn't expect me to remember him. He told me of the years of friendship, the shared birthday dinners, the visits by Brian and Zane to their island cottage. "Brian told us that we were the only gay couple they ever socialized with!" he insisted. As he said it I looked out on the living room, where Ken Lindsay and Peter Husar were chatting with Lorraine Wilson, and wondered if Brian had told them the same thing.

I asked "Dr. Harris" to hold on for a minute, and retrieved Brian's personal phone book. It was all there. Phone numbers for the doctor's office, apartment, and cottage, with pertinent birth date notations. We quickly added Dr. Allan Harris and his partner, Isaac Van Lange, to our Sunday afternoon guest list.

"Again, another part of Brian's life that none of the rest of us knew anything about," observed Karen Kain. "I mean, they weren't making it up! They were obviously close to him." It was the beginning of a series of discoveries we would make after Brian left us.

On Saturday morning, news of Brian's demise hit the papers, and in the next few days we would see stellar pieces by Jim Slotek in the *Toronto Sun* ("City Lights Go Dim"), Jim Bawden in the *Toronto Star* ("The End Of The Interview"), Liam Lacey in the *Globe and Mail* ("The Celebrated Celebrity Hound"), and John McKay, whose affectionate Canadian Press profile was carried in papers from coast to coast to coast. In Los Angeles, Judi Schwam, Ronni Chasen, and Arlene Ludwig joined forces to ensure that the *Los Angeles Times*, *Daily Variety*, and the *Hollywood Reporter* all received the information and photography they needed.

All major media in Canada and the United States included references to Brock Linehan in their obituaries. "Brian Linehan, Canadian celebrity interviewer whose long, complicated questions were spoofed by Martin Short in SCTV 'Brock Linehan' sketches" (*Hollywood Reporter*) . . . "Linehan's habitual long-windedness and obscure questions got the lampoon treatment from fellow Canuck Martin Short" (*Daily Variety*) . . . "Linehan became something of a celebrity himself, so much so that comedian Martin Short parodied him as Brock Linehan on SCTV" (*Los Angeles Times*).

"Brian would have been clipping like crazy," Martha Watson noted dryly. Brian was famous for clipping items of interest and sending them to his friends. It was a practice he had initiated years earlier and continued until he no longer had the strength to do so. When we met for dinner, he would always bring me a bulging manila envelope full of press clippings about Hollywood studio gossip. Karen Kain would receive a selection of dance pieces for her and New York theatre reviews for Ross. (Joan Rivers received bundles of clippings from him too, but at times wished he had been more discriminating. "If someone wrote something nice about you, he sent it to you. If someone wrote something not so nice about you, he sent it to you. It was as if he had turned off his sensors. 'Look, they're writing about you again, isn't that great?' But," she added with a shrug, "sometimes it wasn't.")

On Sunday afternoon, Team Brian gathered at his Yorkville condo: Julia and Derwyn, Ken and Peter, Michael Levine, Maxine Quigley, Pauline Gurden, Norma Rea, Sara Waxman, Marcia Martin and her Manuel, Carol Levine and her husband, Alan Kaplan, Lorraine Wilson, Mary Sinclair, Martha Watson, "newcomers" Allan and Isaac, Gail and me, Joe, Alex, Marc, and his wife, Linda, all of us united by that peculiar mixture of grief and relief. Citytv producer Bob Lawlor mixed some mean martinis in Brian's memory, and after being put through the emotional wringer of the past few weeks, some of us were hit harder than others.

As gracious a politician as a clergyman, Derwyn Shea had prepared his remarks in advance, and was warmly received by our gathering. The Brian we knew and loved, he reminded us, was "a loyal and trusted friend and confidant. Intractable, opinionated, self-confident. Intelligent and witty. The master of the four-minute question. The consummate Canadian interviewer and awards host. Elegant in word, dress, and expectations." That last one drew some quiet murmurs. "Lover of fine food, scintillating conversation, and not above a bit of gossip from time to time" (huge guffaws all around) ". . . galas, limousines, teaching. Sun and surf, and first-class accommodation in hotels, condos, or on Air Canada" (smiles). "A strong sense of order and propriety . . . a friend and a colleague . . . missed by all of us. He has left each of us a blessing of precious memories to cherish. So, my dear friends, the toast is: To Brian – with thanks for the memories and friendship. With Zane at his side, may they both be in peace."

Marcia, Michael, and I followed with our own personal salutes to Brian, and more killer martinis were imbibed.

As per Brian's wishes, there would be no private funeral, no public service. People who inquired were urged to make donations in his name to the Canadian Film Centre and the Toronto Film Festival Group, both non-profit charitable organizations dedicated to the pursuit of excellence in cinema, and both of which Brian had supported. Details of a planned memorial service would be announced later.

I called Shirley MacLaine to give her a play-by-play of Brian's last days. She was happy to hear from me, and greeted news of Brian's fascination with Gillian Edwards with an appreciative chuckle. She knew how doggedly he had resisted spiritual concepts in the past, and was happy that he had made such a strong connection with Gillian.

By Monday morning, various Internet services and blogs were full of feedback and comments, all of it positive. Internet users signed electronic books of condolences and added their own personal comments. Wrote Suzanne Foreman from Brian's hometown of Hamilton: "His wit and passion will echo. In a brief meeting with a younger and deeply-awed me, he was terribly kind and sincerely encouraging." Said Patricia Lawson of Fredericton, New Brunswick: "I always found Brian to be the most informed and thoughtful interviewer bar none, and have missed seeing him on TV the past few years. His presence will certainly be missed. He was a great Canadian." Said Don Anderson of Sydney, Australia: "Mr. Linehan influenced a generation of reporters with his remarkable interviewing style and poise. I probably learned more about entertainment journalism by watching his show on channels 79 and 57 than I did at Ryerson. He was a great journalist and Canadian." Echoed Jason Brookshank of Toronto: "His obvious pride, skill and dedication in his craft made you think you had a responsibility to achieve more in your own endeavours. It is a deep loss to this country."

As Brian's sole executor and the man responsible for his estate, Michael Levine waited only a day or two after Brian's death before informing Marcia Martin and myself that he wanted our input as ex-officio advisors on all major Linehan estate decisions. It seemed to be a foregone conclusion that a memorial to Brian should take place during the upcoming Toronto International Film Festival. All three of us endorsed the timing of a September tribute to Brian. So did filmfest director Piers Handling and his crack TIFF team, who gently reminded us that the twenty-ninth annual Toronto festival was only three short months away. We set to work immediately. Michael Levine hired Rob Richardson, who had staged an elegant Montreal tribute in 2002 to literary icon

Mordecai Richler, to produce the evening for us at the Winter Garden Theatre. Marcia Martin started to explore ways and means by which Citytv, Brian's alma mater and a long-time film festival sponsor, could take an active role in the production. My assignment was casting.

The first person we needed to secure was a strong, erudite host/emcee, one who belonged on stage at the biggest public film festival in the world. Ideally it would be someone who had history with both Brian Linehan and the Toronto film festival. My first and only choice was Roger Ebert.

"George, I'd be honoured," he said. He and Brian, he noted, had been "a little tense and competitive, say, twenty years ago, but thanks to Dusty Cohl's floating film cruises, Brian and I became friends and I was able to enjoy his company, his wit, his passion for showbiz."

Joan Rivers had already told me that she wanted to be at Brian's memorial, no matter when it was held. I called her to let her know it would be in September, and it would take the form of a film festival tribute. "I'll be there," she said, without a moment's hesitation.

My email conversations with Sharon Gless and Martin Short were just as gratifying. Sharon, whom I had never met, volunteered to cut short her September holiday in Italy to fly back to Toronto for the gala evening, And Marty actually had a film in the upcoming festival. He would be coming in from L.A. to publicize it, and he promised to make himself available to join the others on stage at the tribute to Brian.

Making the quartet complete was one of Brian's earliest interview subjects, and one of his most frequent guests over the years, director Norman Jewison, whose Oscar-magnet films had made him as popular with moviegoers as he was with Hollywood studios. In town and on call for the Canadian Film Centre he had founded, Norman also agreed to participate. When TIFF chief Piers Handing confirmed that he would make himself available to open the show, our cast was complete.

I had called Shirley MacLaine, too, and she asked me to send her the date. She was happy to be invited to participate in the tribute, but she was about to start two movies that were shooting back to back, *Bewitched* and *Rumour Has It*. She loved Brian, but given her upcoming schedule she was not overly optimistic about her chances of getting to Toronto on a weeknight in September, and neither was I.

More tributes appeared in the press. *Toronto Life* magazine devoted the last page of its August 2004 issue to a mini-profile of Brian by Adam Sternbergh and an eighteen-photo salute to Linehan interviews on

City Lights. His passing was also noted in *Maclean's*, *Time* magazine, and the fall issue of *InterACTRA*, the glossy newsletter produced by the Canadian performers' union, of which Brian remained a proud member until the day he died. Best of all, for me, was a half-page tribute, personal and from the heart, by *Famous* magazine publisher and Linehan fan Salah Bachir, who recalled being in a restaurant in L.A. when the waiter asked him to carry a handwritten note back to Brian. The note, written on a napkin, turned out to be from Shirley, who was dining in the same restaurant. Bachir also remembered Janet Leigh asking Brian to remind her what Alfred Hitchcock had said about her. Which he did, making her blush. "Brian," Bachir noted, "would say that Janet was too modest to remember when she was being praised."

At the end of July, publisher Kevin Hanson and his family were once again extraordinarily gracious and accommodating. While they were away for the long weekend, a group of Brian's friends gathered in the backyard of 5 Grenadier Heights to scatter his ashes in Zane's treasured garden. Virginia Morra had flown in from Paris, and Lorraine Wilson had flown in from Vancouver, both in time to join the rest of us: chief organizer Marcia Martin, Michael Levine, his ex-wife Carol Cowan Levine, their four children, Carol's husband, Allan Kaplan, Maxine Quigley, Pauline Gurden, Tony Scherman and Margaret Priest, Gillian Edwards, Mary Sinclair, Norma Rea, Ken Lindsay and Peter Husar, and Gail and me.

Michael invited us to say a few words about Brian, and I was planning to say something about how he loved to get laughs, when Marcia Martin gave me an unexpected set-up.

"Brian," she said, "never had to apologize to anyone."

"No," I agreed, "he didn't – because the rest of us spent all of our time apologizing for him!"

The assembled mourners laughed out loud, and I was content. I got a laugh. Brian would be pleased.

I had brought a small Ziploc plastic bag, just big enough to hold a handful of Brian's ashes for Joan Rivers, who had made the request after she realized she was unable to attend. Michael Levine held the urn containing Brian's ashes and we took turns scooping them out and scattering them through Zane's treasured rose bushes. When I approached Michael, he took one look at the Ziploc bag and rolled his eyes. "Apparently Ms. Rivers is not the only one with a sense of humour," he noted dryly. He held out the urn, and I scooped up a handful of Brian for Joan. We scattered some ashes for Rita McKay, who couldn't be there to do it herself, and continued to scatter bits of Brian around the garden, until all the plants and shrubbery were gray with ash.

Ken was trying to comfort Peter, who was awash in tears – a few of us were on the verge of losing it – when I suddenly imagined the Hansons and their children returning home from a sunny holiday weekend to a sombre grey garden. "We can't leave Zane's garden like this," I sniffled. Gail smiled softly and pointed to the silvering sky. The summer rain started seconds later, silky and warm and delicate, and within minutes had washed the garden clean.

Half an hour later, we were gathered at Marcia Martin's house, where a catered light supper awaited us. Wine corks were popped, martinis were mixed, and the reminiscing continued. But so did the sombre mood, until Marci saw Peter and Lorraine consoling each other with a hug. "Ah, I see Dr. and Mrs. Kervorkian have arrived!" she quipped, deadpan. We started laughing again, and the air suddenly seemed lighter, and fresher, and full of hope for better, happier times.

☆

Michael Levine had begun the process of assessing the contents of the Yorkville condo and asked all of us to stop by and choose a personal memento. Michael had chosen to retrieve the prayer rug he had brought Brian from Turkey. Gail and I chose a small mustard bowl that Brian and Zane had used when friends came to dinner, and a wonderful print by one of our favourite artists, Helen Lucas, who years earlier had been part of the charmed Linehan-Wagman circle. I wanted to pick up a keepsake for Joan Rivers, too. On one of the end tables I saw a wrought iron sculpture of a clown precariously walking a tightrope – was there a better visual metaphor for show business than a hard-as-nails balancing act? – and snagged it for her. Today it sits on a table in Joan's country home in Connecticut.

When Sharon Gless returned to the condo at Michael's urging, she noticed a silver cube on an end table. "It was solid and had lots and lots of people all crammed into one spot, and it's very subtle, but if you look very, *very* carefully, you see they're going through sexual moments. And I didn't realize it, so I handed this silver ornament to Michael Levine and I said, well, what about this?"

Michael, she recalls, looked at it and blinked. "Nice," he said sardonically.

Sharon took another look. And blinked. "And I thought 'Oh, Brian! . . . *perfect!*"

She also took home a small antique bell she found by his bedside. "Toward the end of my mother's life, she always kept a bell by the chair she would sit in, so she could summon whomever it was she wanted. So now I have bells of two people that I love. And I figure if I shake it a little, maybe it'll summon Brian.."

Sharon has few regrets about her three-year friendship with Brian. "I asked him one time if he would interview me. I didn't want it for any professional reasons. I wanted it so my family would know me. And he said he would," she added wistfully. "But we ran out of time."

Marci and Michael also invited Brian's sister Connie and her daughter, Lesley, to select keepsakes from the condo. Connie took one of Brian's caps, one of his umbrellas, his sunglasses, and a salt and pepper shaker. At both Michael and Gail's urging, they returned a few weeks later and gathered up some kitchenware for Lesley's new apartment.

☆

The gala was set for the second Friday night of the film festival, September 17. All we had to do now was find a way to finance it. Budgets for the Toronto International Film Festival had been locked long before Brian died; TIFF chief Piers Handling wanted to present the gala as a festival event but had no cash to contribute, so we polled studios, networks, and distributors. Marcia Martin secured her home base, CHUM Television, as lead sponsor. The first call I made was to Cineplex Odeon, and I was disappointed when they declined to participate. But Odeon Theatres, the company that had given Brian his start, was only a distant memory now, and his history with that long-gone establishment was better known by me than by the men currently inhabiting its executive suites. Michael Levine fared much better, reeling in Universal Television, already a major partner in the *Screen Legends* project. After more phone calls, emails, and meetings, we also secured CBC Television and Humber Institute of Technology and Advanced Learning as key sponsors. Additional support came from Corus Entertainment, Famous Players, Warner Bros., and Salah Bachir. Because of these contributions we were able to keep ticket prices low, at thirty-five dollars for general seating for what we hoped would be a clean and uncluttered ninety-minute presentation.

"Linehan Tribute Leads Canuck Fest Initiatives" trumpeted *Playback* magazine in its special pre-filmfest issue. The gala evening also featured prominently in festival programs, especially in the Elgin/Visa Screening Room program. The Elgin Theatre was a TIFF mainstay; during the ten-day run of the festival, thousands of moviegoers wafted through its glass doors day and night. Tucked away seven storeys above the Elgin cinema was the Winter Garden Theatre. Designed by Thomas Lamb as a "double-decker" theatre complex, and built in 1913, the Winter Garden was the top half of a complex that comprised the Canadian flagship of Marcus Loew's legendary theatre chain. The bottom half, the Elgin, was originally known as Loew's Yonge Street Theatre. The Ontario Heritage Trust had purchased the complex in 1981 and, eight years and $30 million later, reopened the Elgin and Winter Garden houses in 1989, restored to their full gold-leaf glory. The Winter Garden, usually reserved for plays and concerts, was now reserved for the Linehan gala, and it seemed to us that there could be no better place to be Celebrating Brian Linehan.

Three days before the gala, Brian's sister Connie told Michael Levine she was still troubled that Brian had had to face his cancer alone, especially after Zane had his heart attack in Finland.

"*Heart attack?*" said Michael, raising his eyebrows.

"Yes," said Connie, wondering why he would question it.

"Okay," said Michael. "No more secrets. You need to know this. Zane didn't have a heart attack. Zane committed suicide."

Connie and Lesley were in shock. Brian had called Connie to give her the news himself: "Zane went to a music festival in Finland," he had told her, "and he died of a heart attack." When Michael Levine told her that Zane had killed himself, she says, "I got a little angry, and I started to cry. Because that was a coward's way out."

On Friday, September 17, some of Brian's siblings rented a stretch limousine to bring them from Hamilton to the gala. Other cousins, nieces and nephews, including some who lived in Toronto, made their own arrangements.

Backstage that night, producer Dan Hughes was shooting interviews for a documentary on Brian for CHUM/City's *Star!* TV. We had a house full of friends and fans, and a strong turnout of undeniably curious media, sparked by coverage that morning heralding the event by

Shelagh Rogers on CBC Radio, Jim Slotek in the *Toronto Sun*, and Bob Thompson in the *National Post*. As ticket holders filed in, they received four-page programs for the evening inspired by the famous *Playbill* programs of Broadway. Michael Levine had made some more phone calls, and the owners of Playbill Inc. in New York, made aware of Brian's passion for theatre, had graciously given us permission to replicate their logo for this once-in-a-lifetime salute.

Shortly after 8 p.m., Piers Handling went on stage at the Winter Garden to welcome the audience, who recognized him immediately and started applauding before he got to the podium. Piers was on a tight schedule; the festival was still in full swing, and he had three films to introduce that evening, at three other venues. When Roger Ebert was introduced, he too received a tumultuous ovation, which he shyly but graciously acknowledged.

He told them we were gathered to salute "a friend, a colleague, an inspiration" and observed that Brian "was lucky enough to come up at a time on television when that kind of professionalism was respected, and given time and attention."

Roger recalled going on the road to promote one of the published collections of his film reviews – 650 of them – and said that being interviewed by Brian "was an eye-opening experience. I believe he read the book." Brian was the only interviewer he met, he added, "who had read *any* of the book. And he'd seen all the films, too!"

He noted that as viewers "we've seen television's attention span shrink and shrink and shrink," but that Brian refused to be part of the quick-hit gossip generation of TV interviewers. Brian, he said, "had too much self-respect, and too much respect for his subjects."

Norman Jewison delighted the crowd with tales of Brian's misadventure with Radie Harris's wooden leg, and told them how pleased Brian was when the film festival awarded him an honorary lifetime pass. When Brian next encountered Norman's wife, Dixie Jewison, he told her he could take her to any movie she wanted to see at the festival.

"But Brian," said Dixie, "I already have a pass."

"Dixie," said Brian, "don't be a bitch!"

Martin Short told of joining Brian in a 1983 Hamilton Homecoming parade "with Joyce Davidson, Eugene Levy, Karen Kain, and the man who played Mr. Whipple 'Please don't squeeze the Charmin' in those toilet paper commercials." Then, as always, said Marty, Brian "was hilarious, he was hysterical, he was *fun*. You always wanted to sit beside him at dinner so you could get all the good gossip. He loved actors, he loved directors. He was *genuinely interested.*"

Roger Ebert agreed. "People who watched Brian," he added, "*learned* something."

"Anyone can do a three-minute interview," said Marty. "It's very hard to make a thirty-minute interview fascinating. That was his gift, and his talent."

Sharon Gless told the audience how she had met Brian at Sara Waxman's cocktail party, how she didn't know he was famous, how they just clicked from their first meeting. "I fell in love and I never recovered."

She told of Brian's impact on her driver, Al Izumi. She said Al was in the audience, and had given her permission to tell that story. She also told of Brian's nightly voicemail messages, which he would leave to amuse her when she finally got home after a long day on the set. "Barbra Streisand turns fifty-eight today – did you send a card?" "Today is William Shatner's sixty-fourth birthday – do we care?"

She admitted she was amazed by how much Brian knew about her, even though she had never been interviewed by him.

"It wasn't just homework," said Roger, nodding. "It was his life."

Gless nodded appreciatively. "Sometimes a love affair is chemistry," she added, "and I sure felt it with him."

Norman Jewison recounted a story Canadian Film Centre director Wayne Clarkson had told him, when Wayne and Brian were participating in a dinner at the Constellation Hotel honouring Janet Leigh. When a power failure delayed the proceedings, Ms. Leigh was desperate to relieve herself before the speeches began, but couldn't find the ladies' room in the dark. Consequently, Wayne and Brian stood guard outside the men's room, stopping all males from entering, so Ms. Leigh could use the facilities. When one male guest demanded to know why he couldn't use the can, Brian barred his way.

"You can't go in there!" Brian hissed. "Janet Leigh is taking a piss!"

Martin Short cracked up. "Now *that's* a friend!" he quipped, still laughing.

Celebrating Brian Linehan was far from all talk. Producer Rob Richardson had assembled some great Linehan vignettes on tape. Highlights included moments from Brian's classic on-camera meetings with everyone from Barbra Streisand ("Can you say that on your show??") to Rompin' Ronnie Hawkins ("The RCMP and James Bond can't get the stuff you get!") to unsolicited testimonials from Oscar winner

Michael Douglas ("Your viewers should know that you are by far the most articulate and intelligent interviewer of the group. You make us feel better about what we do.") to Canadian stage lion Albert Schultz ("It's been one of my lifetime ambitions to sit with you. And I mean that!").

We got to see Brian trying to thank Carol Burnett for agreeing to be interviewed ("Oh, I loved it! . . . I watch you all the time!") and Candice Bergen proclaim to the camera during a Linehan interview: "He is the best talk show person *in the world*."

A nostalgic look at Martin Short's classic SCTV Brock Linehan spoofs was an undisputed highlight. The audience, by now totally captivated, was also treated to a sneak preview of the fifty-episode *Screen Legends* series with a sixty-second portrait of Marie Dressler. Sadly, the male narrator describing Dressler's achievements was not Brian. His voice was so weak on the day he recorded the narration that his soundtrack was unusable, and executive producer Patrick Watson was pressed into service to voice the Dressler *Legend* for Brian's gala.

The showstopper of the evening, served up for dessert, was the glamorous Ms. Rivers, who soon had us laughing and crying. Everyone said Brian was such a great interviewer, she noted, but show business had not been kind to him in his later years. "What upsets me," she told Roger, "is that the last couple of years he had trouble getting work. It's just a *shitty* business!"

"It's even worse," Roger agreed, "when you can't get a job because you're *too good!*"

She told the audience that Brian had shown a lot of grace under fire. As if it wasn't bad enough that he was diagnosed with cancer, he also had to deal with unexpected shock and grief "when Zane, his partner for thirty years, killed himself because he couldn't deal with it."

The intake of breath was audible. Some of it came from the front rows, where most members of the Linehan family were learning of Zane's suicide for the first time. But none of us knew that, of course. Including Joan.

Rivers told them how loyal Brian was, and that whenever she did one of her marathon stints on The Shopping Channel he would keep his television set tuned to TSC, and leave messages for her telling her which pieces he favoured. "He actually *watched* me sell jewellery on the Shopping Channel! . . . I was amazed at the generosity of that."

She relayed how Brian had initially told her he was ill, over morning coffee, in her kitchen in Manhattan. "He said, I have cancer.'" She reached for a Kleenex and dabbed her eyes. "But he said it like Noel Coward."

She reached for another Kleenex. "And," she added, "he *never* picked up a check! . . . he made Barbra Streisand look generous!"

Roger and the rest of the panel fell about guffawing, and the crowd roared its approval. Enough tears had been shed. We were going to leave them laughing after all.

When Roger noted that Brian's estate was set to provide an ongoing endowment for the benefit of young Canadian filmmakers, the film festival audience responded with heartfelt applause.

"How did he leave any money?" teased Jewison, eyes twinkling. "He was always complaining that Moses didn't pay him!"

"I didn't think Brian was that cheap," Marty Short volunteered. Brian, he said, simply had "an impediment in his *reach*."

But leaving his estate to benefit young filmmakers, said Jewison, showed "the quality and the stature of the man." Brian, he concluded, had put his money where his mouth was.

Media response the following morning was gratifying. The *Toronto Sun* headlined Jim Slotek's account "Cryin' For Brian," observing that both laughter and tears flowed at the tribute. In the *National Post* ("Tribute to the Ultimate Film Fan") gossipist Shinan Govani noted, among other things, that (a) there was no sign of Linehan's old boss, Moses Znaimer; (b) some people boycotted the tribute, because they believed it should have been produced while Brian was still alive; and (c) Brian never liked him, and on at least one occasion had made it amply clear "that he didn't care for *moi*." But judging from reaction on the street, Slotek and Govani were both a big hit with their readers that day.

We knew that after he welcomed our audience on Friday night Piers Handling had to leave to introduce a film at another festival venue. What we didn't know was that Piers had sent in a substitute, joined his deputy, Michele Maheux, at the back of the theatre, and stayed through the whole show. "It was *amazing*," he said. Festival publicity chief Gabrielle Free called to report unexpectedly enthusiastic response from the media, who were not always so generously inclined. "And just in case you think I'm just blowing smoke–" said Gaby, and passed the phone in her office to respected *Maclean's* film critic Brian D. Johnson, who echoed her sentiments: "I've never seen anything like this for one of our own."

Brian D. Johnson had just called Brian Linehan "one of our own." At that moment, wherever Brian was, I knew his day had just been made.

Brian's family, on the other hand, had not had such a good day. Brian's niece Lesley remembers that after the gala tribute, "It was the quietest drive back. I think the whole night was very overwhelming for everybody. They had a lot to deal with in a short period of time – to find out he was sick, and then pass away within a week of them seeing him at the hospital. Then not really hearing anything, and then we all get together in September and go to the film festival.

"I think maybe there was the whole issue of looking back and thinking about how things could have been. And then hearing about Zane."

After spending ten minutes in the lobby, listening to reaction to the tribute, Patrick Linehan sensed that "our family is kind of looked down on by Brian's circle." He said someone also referred to the Linehans as a "dysfunctional" family, which disturbed him.

Connie was upset when Joan Rivers told the audience the truth about Zane's death. "Why did she have to do that? Why did she have to come right out and say he killed himself?" But despite her reservations she enjoyed the evening. "I thought it was a beautiful night."

The gala left Mico feeling unsettled. For one thing, he had had to scramble to get tickets for the family, even after tickets were offered to them, because the family couldn't come up with exact numbers as quickly as required. He was also shocked to learn of Zane's suicide from Joan Rivers. And surprised to hear her say that in his final years Brian had trouble finding work. "I was under the impression that he had retired. Was it a forced retirement?"

He too got the distinct impression that Brian's friends "were more than happy to keep us away. If Brian's friends had been really true friends," he told me when we first met, "they would have contacted us much sooner." He paused thoughtfully. "Unless those were his wishes."

Some nieces, nephews, and cousins with whom Brian had had no contact for decades also attended the gala evening. Absent were Brian's younger sister Carole, who had been unsuccessful in her attempts to secure tickets for herself and her husband, Bruce, and Brian's older brother Ronnie, who had taken a pass on attending.

"Ronnie had telephoned Brian a few weeks before he died," his wife, Gerri, told me. "He had made his peace with Brian, and he didn't want to risk getting into another family 'situation,'" she said, choosing her words carefully. "So he decided to keep right out of it."

But Ronnie bristled when his younger brother Patrick told him that some of Brian's friends regarded the Linehan family as "dysfunctional."

"*Dysfunctional??*" he snorted. "*Us??*. . . what a load of crap!"

Ronnie's youngest daughter, Kathleen, rolled her eyes heavenward. "Dad," she said, "the Linehans put the 'fun' in dys*fun*ctional."

Ronnie was not impressed.

He was, however, intrigued to learn that the beautiful tall blonde television actress Sharon Gless was admittedly smitten with Brian. And he was pleased as punch when he heard that Gless had confessed that after meeting Brian she "fell in love and never recovered." Not only that, she had actually told the audience that "sometimes a love affair is chemistry, and I sure felt it with him."

"I'm glad," said Ronnie, beaming. "I'm glad that Brian finally had a relationship with a woman before he died."

Gerri and his daughter looked at each other. "Dad," said Kathleen, "it wasn't like that. Brian and Sharon Gless were *friends*. She didn't mean . . ." But Ronnie wasn't interested in any more details.

"He heard what he wanted to hear," says Gerri. "For him, that was the end of it."

My children were also in the audience that night, and were generous in their comments and in their praise for Roger, Norman, Marty, Sharon and Joan. My son Joe, however, was a bit puzzled. "I didn't get the jokes about Brian being cheap," he told me.

"What didn't you get about them?" I inquired.

"I know Brian didn't pick up a lot of checks," said Joe. "But I don't think he was cheap."

"Okay, not cheap; maybe just 'frugal'," I suggested.

Joe shook his head. Some years earlier, as part of his degree in Fine Arts, he had spent a year studying in Florence. "Before I left for Italy, Brian called me one day and said, 'Joe, Florence is a great city, but you're going to be a long way from home, and you may get into situations where you need some extra cash – situations you might prefer to *not* share with your parents. So if you get into one of those situations, just call me, and I'll send you the money.'"

I was amazed. "Why have you never mentioned this before?" I asked him.

"There was never any reason to mention it," he said with a shrug. "I didn't get into any 'situations,' so Brian didn't have to send me any money. Besides," he added, "he had made it very clear that this was strictly between us. Between Brian and me."

Because I spent all my time at the gala backstage, I never saw any members of the audience that night. It was only later that I learned that Moses Znaimer had arrived at the Winter Garden for the gala but had apparently chosen not to enter the theatre.

On October 4, 2004, exactly four months after Brian died, Michael Levine sent a personal letter to Martin Knelman's home in Toronto.

"Through Brian's months of illness," he wrote, "I thought many times of the article you wrote, so many years ago, and the fact that I had the painful task of delivering it to Brian by hand at the Athenaeum Hotel in London. I am not one who usually comments on journalistic freedom, but I have to say all these years later, that I thought at the time, and I still think, that you actually got it wrong. I think Brian was a fine journalist, and that while his romance with the movies may have struck one as somewhat bizarre, knowing him well, I understand the forces at play in it."

Levine told me he felt compelled to write to Knelman because, as he said at the end of his letter, "I know these issues never get resolved. But I did feel that, after all these years, at the very least, I owed Brian a voice."

More tributes appeared on the Internet, and both IMDb (International Movie Data base) and Wikipedia updated their Linehan bios. I started setting up interviews with some fascinating women who were willing, and in some cases, eager, to talk about Brian.

"Brian maintained our friendship systematically and with care," Karen Kain informed me. "He was the one who made the friendship work."

"Brian wasn't two-faced," said Joan Rivers. "Once you were his friend, he was very, very loyal. He would defend you to the death. Which you don't find at all in our business."

As a friend, said Harriet Blacker, "he was absolutely true blue." And Judi Schwam said Brian made her acutely aware of the demands of friendship. "When he said 'I love you,' you knew he meant it. He had the need to feel necessary, to be appreciated. He needed to be needed. And recognized. Loyal friend that he was, he did need that recognition. And you had a lot to live up to, if you were his friend."

Two celebrated women who played key roles in his life found it more difficult to express their feelings about him.

"When people would say, is Brian a friend of yours," said Jane Hawtin, "I never knew how to answer. I can't think of anybody else in my life that I could say that about. Did he think of me as a friend? I hope so. I'd like to think so. But he was a very complex character. I knew him for twenty years, but I never felt like I really got to know him."

Bea Arthur expressed the same sentiment. "As close as we were, we were never really close. I always enjoyed myself with him, because he was, what is the expression, a 'cornucopia' of shit. He knew *everything*. But I could never get close. It's not that he put up a shield. It was that there was really nothing there." It seemed to her that Brian's fascination with celebrity ruled his life to the extent that, as far as she could see, he had no life of his own. "When he stayed with me, I would stumble out in the morning to make coffee and he would be sitting there in a silk dressing gown, already showered and immaculately groomed, reading the *L.A. Times*. I never saw him *deshabille*. It was like living with Cole Porter!"

When I told her of Brian's desire to emulate Roddy McDowall in his last days, personally giving away prized possessions to friends, she just shook her head. "This fixation, this *obsession* with celebrity!" she said sadly – "right to the end."

Michael Levine knew a different Brian. "It wasn't as if he created something superficial on top of what he was," he says. "This was the real man. It wasn't as if the job had been advertised and Brian stepped in. He created it, like Archie Leach becoming Cary Grant, the working-class kid becoming elegant, soignée."

It wasn't as if any of it had happened by accident, either. Brian's friend Myrna Daniels recalled Brian telling her "how he started at J. Arthur Rank, and how all of a sudden this whole world opened up, and he found he could go all over the world with a blazer and pair of grey pants." Echoed Brian's friend Harriet Blacker: "He was very, very proud of his life."

In the spring of 2003, filmmaker and marketing guru Barry Avrich had invited Brian to co-produce a new documentary with him about a Hollywood untouchable, bonafide empire builder Lew Wasserman of MCA/ Universal renown. Brian was undecided about the project, but liked working with Avrich.

In the spring of 2004, Avrich took out a full-page ad in the Hollywood trades announcing the project – an ad in which Brian

Linehan was listed as one of the producers. Brian whined incessantly about it. "Barry didn't ask my permission!"

"If you don't want to co-produce it," I told him wearily, "tell Barry to take your name off the ad!" But of course he wouldn't, because he loved the thought of everyone in Hollywood seeing his name and Lew Wasserman's on the same project.

In the spring of 2005, almost a year after Brian died, Barry Avrich premiered *The Last Mogul: The Life and Times of Lew Wasserman* at a few U.S. film festivals before opening it in Los Angeles and New York to favourable reviews. Brian Linehan received screen credit – up front, where it counts – as one of the film's producers.

In June, viewers saw the results of almost a year's labour by Citytv producer Dan Hughes and his documentary team. *Brian Linehan: A Life In Lights* premiered on *Star!* TV on Sunday, June 12, followed by a repeat screening on Citytv a few days later. Dan and his team had interviewed many of us, and the special produced some insights and observations that many Linehan fans found fascinating.

"We learned more about ourselves with him than we would have on the couch," Shirley MacLaine told him. And Brian, she said, knew "he was catching lightning in a bottle."

John Travolta recalled that before their first interview Brian had researched his name and discovered that 'travolta' meant 'to take by storm.' "I was just a kid, but I was so taken by that. He's always been so wonderful. He went out of his way to validate me (as an actor) in my first feature film, *Saturday Night Fever*. I was tremendously fond of him."

"I don't think he let too many people in," Joan Rivers noted, "but once he let you in, he was really there for you."

By the time the special was set to air, I had met most of Brian's brothers and sisters and emailed them to let them know when and where it was going to be telecast. Predictably, their reactions were personal and specific. Their aunt Connie was annoyed when Joan Rivers said Brian was not close to his family: "She made me so angry!"

Carole Linehan Dingwall kept her own counsel – "I found it most interesting," she reported dryly – while Mico regarded the sixty-minute special with some suspicion. "If I didn't know better," he told me, "I'd swear they got all their information from one biased source." He acknowledged that the Linehans "were a distant family, not as close as we could have or should have been." But he felt the special suggested that

Brian was rejected by his family – "and that bothers me. But if that was the impression Brian gave his friends, then I understand their reaction to the family when we showed up at the end."

Screen Legends was finally launched in September 2005 at the Toronto film festival. The arrival of the series of short vignettes saluting Canadians in film was heralded by a companion book by McArthur & Company and an official launch at the CHUM Festival Schmooze party. Now narrated by celebrated Canadian stage and screen star Colm Feore, who had graciously stepped in when Brian could not, the series was written by filmmaker Bruce Yaccato and directed by Mitchell Gabourie, tirelessly supported by its executive producers, Michael Levine and Historica Foundation creative director Patrick Watson, and dedicated to Brian, who had only managed to write three of the profiles before his declining health forced him to bow out.

Elegant, informative and fun, the series is a showcase of internationally celebrated Canadians, many of whom headed south because we had no star system of our own to offer them, full of famous faces from Norma Shearer to Genevieve Bujold, from Walter Huston to Donald Sutherland. After premiering at TIFF, the first ten profiles were showcased on *Star!* TV and in the *Toronto Star*, after which all fifty vignettes began airing on CHUM stations and became available for educational use. A year later, *Screen Legends* DVDs were released.

Another series of vignettes dedicated to Brian premiered at the same festival. *Postcards from TIFF* was a series of thirty one-minute interview clips, this time saluting the thirtieth anniversary of the Toronto's annual movie marathon, and featured on-camera anecdotes from such celebrated TIFF travellers as Denys Arcand, Wayne Clarkson, David Cronenberg, Atom Egoyan, Graham Greene, Norman Jewison, Robert Lantos, Sheila McCarthy, Don McKellar, Deepa Mehta, and festival founders Bill Marshall and Dusty Cohl.

One of the *Postcards'* young producers, Micol Marotti, told me she considered Brian a mentor, which is why she dedicated the series to him. "The industry really lost a great friend and a strong promoter," she told the press. "Brian loved the movies and Canadian movie stars and knew how to get the best stories out of them. That is something we hoped to capture with these vignettes."

Michael Levine believes that before Brian there was no real respect for Canadian personalities. "Nobody was there saying, 'These are celebrities, these are our best, we should take pride in them.' The common assumption was, if you're that good, why aren't you in New York or Los Angeles?

"It was Brian who brought out the stage director, the actors, the Norman Jewisons, the Karen Kains and exalted them in their own country."

"I wonder what Brian would think of all these tributes," my wife remarked recently. "Would he be surprised? . . . shocked? . . . thrilled? . . . amused?"

"All of the above," I ventured, "and more."

Brian loved being in the spotlight, but his entire career was based on paying 'tribute,' in one form or another, to other people. In the last weeks of his life he was still doing it, this time by setting up a foundation to help other people become those people.

When Brian and Michael set up Brian's foundation in March 2004, Brian told him, "I really want creative people to have money to live. I really want them to be able to pay their rent, to have time to write the script, or whatever they need to do."

When Brian asked Michael to set the criteria, Michael admittedly "went to my prejudice, which is largely the acting community, because I think it is the cornerstone." And thus the Brian Linehan Charitable Foundation was born.

"I think a lot of Brian's life was shaped by his reading and by his sense of theatre and his sense of film," says Levine. "When you think of Brian's apartment in Yorkville you could see Cary Grant living there, you could see any number of quasi-English gentlemen in that apartment. If somebody met Brian circa 1995 and was asked to draw a profile of where this young man came from, I'm virtually certain that no one would get within 150 miles of the truth."

Levine believes that as a journalist, Brian "somehow seemed to inspire confidence *and* confidentiality." Today, says Roger Ebert, "there are no job openings with that description. Nobody wants an intelligent, well-informed interviewer who can talk to someone for half an hour or an hour."

Shirley MacLaine told *A Life in Lights* producer Dan Hughes that to the end of his life, Brian was "better than any I have ever been interviewed by. Because he *lived* it. He lived and dreamt and *glorified* in it. It was his life." Joan Rivers still believes that "every student in broadcasting school should go and watch his interviews and see what a good interview is all about." And for Ronni Chasen, Brian "wasn't about sound bites. He was about the soul of what was going on – the soul, the heart, the passion."

Film critic Bruce Kirkland agrees. "Brian didn't believe in sound bites. He believed in insight." Today, he says, "a kind of wall has gone up between celebrities and interviewers because, in general, the in-depth thing never happens. Unless you have already have a special relationship with someone, and you can take them aside and have a Brian Linehan moment."

For many of us, Joan Rivers and Michael Levine defined the loss of Brian's private and public persona. For Joan, losing Brian was particularly painful "because I've lost someone I could remember with." For Michael, losing Brian was a blow to the collective consciousness of show business. "Maybe a generation had died by the time Brian got on the scene," he concedes, "but when you think about the fact that he was dealing with people like George Cukor and Gloria Swanson, as well as the Mel Gibsons and the Meryl Streeps, Brian in effect represented a half-century of memory."

Which, thanks to videotape, will continue to live on.

Thanks to Brian's estate and Levine's unflagging dedication to executing his last wishes, Canadian actors and training programs are already reaping the benefits of Linehan's legacy. The first Brian Linehan Scholarship for Outstanding Artistic Promise was awarded at Humber College on October 26, 2005. Limited grants have since been awarded to such active Canadian stage and screen organizations as the National Screen Institute, the brave, young, and ambitious Company Theatre, and Albert Schultz's soaring Soulpepper repertory theatre company. A gift of $1 million to the Toronto International Film Festival Group will result in, among other things, a new research room for the new TIFFG Centre, currently under construction in the Toronto theatre district. The Brian Linehan Research Room will be in the centre's Film Reference Library, which holds original photographs, biographies, scripts, and films, and will be a reference source for film lovers.

The TIFFG also announced that it had received an anonymous gift of $200,000 to create an endowment fund in Brian's name. The fund has already grown beyond the initial $200,000 and will support a program called In Conversation, which features an interview of a high-profile film director or actor, and will take place at least once a year at the new Festival Centre.

☆

On Tuesday, June 1, 2004, the last night I saw Brian, he asked me to write his obituary.

I had teased him, of course. "So *many* people have been waiting for the chance to write your obit! . . . surely you don't want to deprive them of that pleasure?"

He loved it, and even managed a grin.

That was when he reached for my hand. "I want *you* to write my obit," he said, his eyes shining.

"I want me to write your obit too," I said, marvelling at his presence of mind. "But I don't have a column anymore."

He leaned back on the pillows. "I know, I know," he sighed. "But just, you know, *try* . . . ?"

"Okay," I said, "I'll try."

He leaned forward again, and motioned for me to come closer. By now his voice was just a hoarse whisper, but he had something important to say, and he needed to say it.

"I want them to know," he said, "that we had a lot of fun."

And, we did.

Goodnight, Mr. Linehan.

Wherever you are.

Absent Friends

On September 17, 2004, at a gala tribute at the Winter Garden, Sharon Gless kept the crowd entranced with her tale of the close encounter between her friend Brian Linehan and her driver, Al Izumi. Al was in the audience that night, and he had given her his permission to share his story with all of us. Exactly one month later, on October 17, 2004, Al Izumi passed away.

Two weeks later, Team Linehan lost one of its all-star quarterbacks. Norma Rea had been ill for some time, and purposely neglected to mention it. She was a conservative, quiet, refined, bona fide powerhouse who saw Brian through some of his darkest days, and stepped back, into shadows and out of the limelight, whenever she could. She was devoted to him, but her work here was done. She left us on October 30, 2004.

When I first phoned him, Ronnie Linehan was too medicated to speak to me. He was under doctor's care, suffering from an acute depression triggered in part by Brian's death. I told his wife, Gerri, that I would wait a month or two and then call again. "There's no rush," I assured her. "We have lots of time." We didn't. Less than a year after Brian's death, Ronnie Linehan unexpectedly passed away on May 18, 2005.

Smart, sassy, and outspoken, Anne Heisey was a high-living dynamo who adored her husband, Larry, championed the National Ballet and loved sparring verbally with Brian Linehan, who loved her right back. Annie unexpectedly passed away on March 5, 2007.

And finally, as enigmatic as his brothers and sisters, Eric Linehan decided years ago to alleviate the boredom of his shift work at Stelco by writing poetry (yes, on the job). Eric unexpectedly passed away on May 5, 2007, but thanks to the Internet age we live in, you can sample hundreds of his poems at www.poetry.com.

To absent friends. Wherever they may be.

Acknowledgements

I f all the world's a stage, every life is a wide-screen movie. Like characters in *Rashomon*, you see the world from your POV – that's movie talk
for "point of view" – and I see the world from mine. Your perspective
is your perspective. My perspective is my perspective. Everyone who sur-
rounds us is a supporting player. Those who tackle larger, more
significant roles in our lives may earn the rank of co-star. But at both the
beginning and the end of the day, you are the star of your movie and I
am the star of mine.

Brian Linehan produced his life with a stellar ensemble cast, and I
could not have begun to screen his story without the contributions of Bea
Arthur, Barry Avrich, Jim Bawden, Harriet Blacker, Ronni Chasen, Dusty
Cohl, Arlene Dahl, Myrna Daniels, Charles Dennis, Roger Ebert, Gillian
Edwards, Taina Elg, Jane Fairley, Stuart Fink, Vicki Gabereau, Sharon
Gless, Pauline Gurden, Allan Harris, Jane Hawtin, Dan Hughes, Peter
Husar, Norman Jewison, Juliette, Karen Kain, Bruce Kirkland, Slawko
Klymkiw, Martin Knelman, Michael Levine, Marilyn Lightstone, Ken
Lindsay, Shirley Lord, Arlene Ludwig, Melinda Mantel, Marcia Martin,
Rita McKay, Virginia Morra, Maxine Quigley, Joan Rivers, Doris
Roberts, Shelagh Rogers, Marc Rosen, John Sakamoto, Dianne Schwalm,
Judi Schwam, Derwyn Shea, Carole Shelley, Martin Short, Gary Slaight,
Jim Slotek, Maria Topalovich, Stanley Wagman, Martha Watson, Arthur
Weinthal, Lorraine Wilson, David Vella, and Moses Znaimer.

Guest Star billing must be reserved for the Linehan family, who
provided me with such revealing flashbacks, especially Ronnie Linehan's
widow, Gerri, and her daughter Kathleen; Connie Linehan Kataric and
her husband, Danny; Carole Linehan Dingwall and her husband,
Bruce; Patrick Linehan and his wife, Linda; Eric Linehan; John (Jovan)
Rodic, a.k.a. Mico, and his wife, Cathy; and Sadie Linehan's sole surviving sister, their aunt Connie Kotur Buzash. My special thanks to

Mico and Connie for unearthing such wonderful family photographs for me.

Ontario Location Managers who saved my sanity and allowed me to spin words into sentences into paragraphs into chapters include Joan and Dusty Cohl for the use of their country retreat and Jack, Kim, Kevin, and Roberto for the use of their straw-bale oasis. I am also especially indebted to my unsung production manager, Lesley Kataric, who helped me build and cross family bridges to all the Linehans.

Technical Advisers who made major contributions along the way include Mary McMaster, for delivering the transcripts of my interviews with such diligence, accuracy, and enthusiasm; my personal litmus-test readers, Jack Bond, Joan Cohl, and Gail Ganetakos; my secret weapon at the TIFFG Film Reference Library, meticulous archivist Julie Lofthouse; and the publishing team at McClelland & Stewart, especially Chris Bucci, who wondered if I'd ever start writing, and Trena White, who wondered if I'd ever stop.

My personal thanks to Mick Jagger's favourite photographer, Dimo Safari, for his gracious contribution. And I would be remiss if I did not also salute Rosemary Goldhar, Tom Sandler, Paul Schumacher, Rob Wayman, and all the film studio, film festival and network photographers who provided Brian and me, over the years, with an overwhelming collection of happy memories.

Starring Brian Linehan would not exist without the exceptional generosity of Joan Rivers and the extraordinary participation of Michael Levine, who as executor of the Linehan estate opened new doors and gave me hands-on access to the ledgers in which Brian so lovingly recorded the day-to-day events of his life.

Finally, I would like to thank my wife for putting up with me for more than four decades. When we celebrated our silver wedding anniversary, a friend asked her the secret of such a long and successful relationship. "It's true, we've been married for twenty-five years," Gail confirmed with a smile, "but George has only been home for seven of them."

I'm at home a lot more these days, and we're still speaking. Well, mostly.

My mother thanks you, "the Kids" thank you, and Brian thanks you. Me too. Thanks, hon.

George Anthony
September 2007

Index

Abbott, Roger, 266, 280
ABC Television, 105, 183
Academy Awards, 131-32
ACTRA Awards, 87
Adilman, Sid, 116-17
Air Canada, 48-49, 97, 212-13
Alan Hamel Show, 88
Allen, Peter, 58, 143, 247
Allen, Woody, 108-10, 111-13, 121-22
Allicock, Chris, 189
Amarcord (film), 32
American Airlines, 37, 56-58, 69, 97
American Grafitti (film), 32
Amiel, Barbara, 122-23
Anderson, Don, 307
Andrews, Julie, 123
Anka, Paul, 70, 73
Ann-Margret, 73
Anthony, Gail, ix, 44, 59, 77, 100, 151,
  203, 212, 217-18, 220, 243, 245, 258,
  263, 272, 278, 283-85, 289-93, 301,
  304-6, 309, 310, 323
Anthony, George, 220, 242-43, 278;
  access to performers, xi-xiii; Brian
  pulls prank on, 124-26; catered to
  by airlines, 48-49, 56-58, 97, 212;
  catered to by movie studios, xi, 54,
  59; commissions Zane to write
  about classical music, 43-44;
  friendship with Brian, 28-29, 54,
  68-71; "George & Brian Show,"
  54, 242, 285; hires Brian to write
  for *Toronto Sun*, 169-70, 171; intro-
  duces Brian to Joan Rivers, 132-34;

joins CBC Television, 171; last
  contact with Zane, 217-18; last
  visit with Brian, 288-91; pampering
  by movie studios, 37-39, 52, 54;
  recommends Brian for Floating
  Film Festival, 170; returns to
  Toronto Sun, 122-23; at scattering
  of Brian's ashes, 309-10
Arcand, Denys, 236, 322
Arden, Jann, 202
Arkoff, Sam, 78
Arthur, Bea, 80, 96, 149, 152, 226,
  252, 277, 320
Astral Films, 30
Augustyn, Frank, 79
Avrich, Barry, 156, 162-63, 177, 178,
  203-6, 211, 234-35, 237-38, 246,
  263, 286, 320-21

Baby Blue Movie, 27
Bachir, Salah, 309, 311
Badlands (film), 32
Baldwin, James, 19
Ballard, Bill, 202, 203
Ballard, Kaye, 192
Barbra & Brian (Citytv special), 76
Barrie, Andy, 86
Base, Ron, 47-48
Bassett, Doug, 176, 276
Bassett, John W., 46
Bawden, Jim, 76, 115, 155, 185, 303, 305
Baxter, Anne, 76
Bean, Jack, 173
Beatty, Warren, 61, 134-37, 193, 194

shoplifting, 194-99; childhood, 2-13; computer illiteracy, 169-70, 190, 265-66; conducts first TV interview, 29-30; conducts open-ended interviews for Warner Bros., 168-69; confusion over age, 303-4; deals with death of Zane, 222-29, 234-35; diagnosed with non-Hodgkin's Lymphoma, ix, 213-17; dies, 300-302; disconnection from gay culture, 154-56; donates research files to Toronto International Film Festival, 239; donates Zane's music collection to Hart House, 236-37, 241; early interest in movies, 4, 5-6; estrangement from family, 98-99, 101-2, 282-86, 321-22; estrangement from Moses Znaimer, 141-46; expenses covered by studios, 138-40; fascination with celebrity, 21, 37, 77, 79-80, 83-84; fired from CFRB radio, 187-88; first media junkets, 44, 48-50; friendship with George Anthony, 28-29, 68-70, 70-71; friendship with Joan Rivers, x, 133-34, 137, 179-81, 223-24, 258, 260-62; friendships with publicists, 41-42, 50, 80-81, 225-26; friendship with Shirley MacLaine, 74, 159-62; "George and Brian Show," 54; honoured by Toronto International Film Festival, 239, 240, 242-43; hospitalized, 256-62; hosts Genie Awards, 90, 201-2, 209-10; Humber College scholarship created in his name, 324; interviewing style criticized, 83-84, 113, 142-43; jealousy of Roger Ebert, 107-8, 173, 178-79; joins Citytv as movie programmer, 26-28; last days, 288-302; leaves Citytv, 146; legacy, 322-24; love of theatre, 162-63; memorial tribute at Toronto International Film Festival, 307-8, 311-19; moves to Toronto, 15-17; moves to Yorkville, 240, 250-53; need to be accepted, 67, 70-71, 116-17, 131; nose, 106-7; on-camera appearance, 29, 34-35, 76, 106-7; pampered by movie studios, 37-39, 52, 54, 76; parodied by comedians, 84, 111-15, 119-20, 129-30; rapport with subjects, 36, 51-52, 65-66, 73-74, 76, 227; reconciles with Zane, 151-58; relationship with children, 59-60; relationship with other junketeers, 66-68; relationship with staff, 87, 127-28, 189-90; relationship with TV crews, 32-33, 63, 205; relationship with Zane, 92-102, 163, 178-79, 208-9; reputation for research, 35-36, 42-43, 65-66, 73-74, 78, 87-88; resented by competitors, 61-63, 124-26; returns home for last time, 292-300; returns to television full time, 188-91; secrecy around relationship with Zane, xii, 44, 93-94, 96, 224; sense of dignity, 63, 105, 145, 176, 181, 202; sense of humour, xii, 52-54, 62-63, 125-26, 177-78, 249, 277; sensitivity to criticism, 91, 115, 176; separation from siblings, 15; separation from Zane, 147-50; sexual frustration, 147, 154-56, 229-32, 240; specials for CBC Television, 174-75; sued by Woody Allen, 108-13, 121-22; teaches course at Humber College, 243-44, 246-47, 253, 255, 258; as TV guest, 88-89, 201; undergoes chemotherapy, 218, 220, 225, 237-38, 246, 258, 263, 266, 274, 275; weakened by cancer, 253-55, 272-74; wins ACTRA award, 87; works at Janus Films, 19, 21, 22; works at Odeon Theatres, 15-20; writes for *Hamilton Spectator*, 12, 14-15; writes *Toronto Sun* column, 169-71; "yin and yang," 158, 159